lonely planet

Dublin

Fionn Davenport

LONELY PLANET PUBLICATIONS
Melbourne • Oakland • London • Paris

Dublin
4th edition – January 2002
First published – June 1993

Published by
Lonely Planet Publications Pty Ltd ABN 36 005 607 983
90 Maribyrnong St, Footscray, Victoria 3011, Australia

Lonely Planet Offices
Australia Locked Bag 1, Footscray, Victoria 3011
USA 150 Linden St, Oakland, CA 94607
UK 10a Spring Place, London NW5 3BH
France 1 rue du Dahomey, 75011 Paris

Photographs
All of the images in this guide are available for licensing from
Lonely Planet Images.
Web site: www.lonelyplanetimages.com

Front cover photograph
The Ha'penny Bridge over the River Liffey (Richard Cummins)

ISBN 1 86450 345 9

text & maps © Lonely Planet Publications Pty Ltd 2002
photos © photographers as indicated 2002

Printed through Colorcraft Ltd, Hong Kong
Printed in China

**Although the authors
and Lonely Planet try
to make the informa-
tion as accurate as
possible, we accept
no responsibility for
any loss, injury or
inconvenience sus-
tained by anyone
using this book.**

Contents – Text

1

Contents – Maps

3

The Author

Fionn Davenport

Fionn was born and raised in Dublin – an idyllic youth interrupted only by jarring moves to Buenos Aires, Geneva and New York (thanks to his Dad's job) that left him incapable of spending more than a couple of years in any one place without uprooting and moving somewhere else. He stayed in Dublin long enough to complete a degree in French and History at Trinity College (but still took a year off somewhere in the middle) before moving to Paris and then New York. A series of odd jobs and adventures eventually landed him behind an editor's desk, and he spent three years editing other people's travel experiences for a travel publication. These days he splits his time between New York, Dublin and wherever the call of work and travel takes him. He has written about many destinations throughout the world and has previously worked on Lonely Planet's *Spain*, *Dublin*, *Ireland*, *Sicily*, *Britain* and *England* guides.

FROM THE AUTHOR

Writing a book on your home town is never as easy as it sounds. Sure, you know what's what and what is not, you know where's popular and, if you're paying attention, you know where *will* be popular by the time the book comes out.

The problem, however, is that you're not a visitor, nor do you see the city from a tourist's perspective. While researching and writing this guide, I confronted this problem almost daily. How could I give the visitor the benefit of my knowledge without burdening them with a bias that a first-time or short-term visitor to Dublin will not share?

What I have hopefully done is to include the best of what I believe Dublin has to offer. However, in order to write a balanced and inclusive guide, I had to go far beyond my own knowledge of the city and its surroundings. For hard facts and solid basics on tourism, I owe a debt of thanks to Catherine McCluskey at Dublin Tourism, who was very generous with her time and efforts. For map references and other geographical suggestions, I would like to express my gratitude to all those working at the National Map Centre.

No list of thanks, however, would be complete without all of the friends and acquaintances that proved to be invaluable sources of suggestions, pointers and advice. For this, I am deeply indebted to the following people: Helena Conlon, Sinead Dolan, Brendan, Paul and Morgan Ferriter, Feargal Fitzpatrick, Alanna Gallagher, Monnine Griffith, Anto Howard, Lisa McMahon, Fiona Neary, Gareth O'Callaghan, Nicola O'Callaghan, Oda O'Carroll, Peter Soutter, Brian Synnott and Aoife Walsh.

Finally, I want to devote all of my efforts on this book to Sorcha O'-Callaghan, without whose support, help, advice and encouragement (not to mention tolerance and patience) I wouldn't have managed it at all. You're always in my heart and for that, I love you more than you can even imagine.

This Book

This is the fourth edition of LP's *Dublin* city guide. Tony Wheeler wrote the first edition and Tom Smallman and Pat Yale updated the second. The third edition was updated and expanded by Fionn Davenport, who also revised and updated this edition.

From the Publisher

This edition of *Dublin* was produced in Lonely Planet's London office. Abigail Hole was the coordinating editor. Charlotte Beech, Arabella Shepherd, Sam Trafford and Michala Green helped with editing and proofing. Ed Pickard and David Wenk handled the mapping with help from Simon Tillema in the Melbourne office, and Paul Edmunds, James Timmins, Fiona Christie and Rachel Beattie. David also designed and laid out the book. James Timmins drew the climate chart, Annika Roojun designed the cover and Lachlan Ross drew the back-cover map. Lonely Planet Images provided the photographs and the illustrations were drawn by Jane Smith and Nicky Caven. Many thanks to Rachel Suddart and Leonie Mugavin for Getting There & Away information. Thanks also to Tim Ryder, Sara Yorke, Amanda Canning and Fionn Davenport for all their canny assistance.

Thanks

Many thanks to the travellers who used the last edition and contacted us with helpful hints, advice and interesting anecdotes:

Jadwiga Adamczuk, Gordon Adamson, Wilbur S Bailey, Tracy Bays, Richard & Sarah Bennett, John Bourke, Marcella Brown, Nicola Byrne, Sharon Clerkin, Sherla Davies, Kara Davis, Kathy Douglas, Humphrey Evans, Stacy Hague, Tanyia Harrison, KG Hellyen, Maureen Holland, Steven Holland, Field Horne, Patrick James Logue, Sue Johnson, PS Kennedy, Stephen Kinsella, Michael Krischer, Graham & Rosemarie Lenton, Elaine Logan, Tom McCluskey, Michael Middleton, KS Moore, Paul Murphy, Jean O'Sullivan, Tuija Paukkunen, John Perkins, Lisa Pickard, Mary Rice, Jane Robertson, Tom William Skarre, P Skinner, Sandra Standifer, Matthew Starr, Sanford Sternlicht, Marianne Strusinski, Ursula Thummer-Wolf, Kenneth Wardrop, Teresa Webb, Stephanie Wilson, Elad Yom-Tov

Foreword

ABOUT LONELY PLANET GUIDEBOOKS

The story begins with a classic travel adventure: Tony and Maureen Wheeler's 1972 journey across Europe and Asia to Australia. Useful information about the overland trail did not exist at that time, so Tony and Maureen published the first Lonely Planet guidebook to meet a growing need.

From a kitchen table, then from a tiny office in Melbourne (Australia), Lonely Planet has become the largest independent travel publisher in the world, an international company with offices in Melbourne, Oakland (USA), London (UK) and Paris (France).

Today Lonely Planet guidebooks cover the globe. There is an ever-growing list of books and there's information in a variety of forms and media. Some things haven't changed. The main aim is still to help make it possible for adventurous travellers to get out there – to explore and better understand the world.

At Lonely Planet we believe travellers can make a positive contribution to the countries they visit – if they respect their host communities and spend their money wisely. Since 1986 a percentage of the income from each book has been donated to aid projects and human rights campaigns.

Updates Lonely Planet thoroughly updates each guidebook as often as possible. This usually means there are around two years between editions, although for more unusual or more stable destinations the gap can be longer. Check the imprint page (following the colour map at the beginning of the book) for publication dates.

Between editions up-to-date information is available in two free newsletters – the paper *Planet Talk* and email *Comet* (to subscribe, contact any Lonely Planet office) – and on our Web site at www.lonelyplanet.com. The *Upgrades* section of the Web site covers a number of important and volatile destinations and is regularly updated by Lonely Planet authors. *Scoop* covers news and current affairs relevant to travellers. And, lastly, the *Thorn Tree* bulletin board and *Postcards* section of the site carry unverified, but fascinating, reports from travellers.

Correspondence The process of creating new editions begins with the letters, postcards and emails received from travellers. This correspondence often includes suggestions, criticisms and comments about the current editions. Interesting excerpts are immediately passed on via newsletters and the Web site, and everything goes to our authors to be verified when they're researching on the road. We're keen to get more feedback from organisations or individuals who represent communities visited by travellers.

> Lonely Planet gathers information for everyone who's curious about the planet – and especially for those who explore it first-hand. Through guidebooks, phrasebooks, activity guides, maps, literature, newsletters, image library, TV series and Web site we act as an information exchange for a worldwide community of travellers.

Research Authors aim to gather sufficient practical information to enable travellers to make informed choices and to make the mechanics of a journey run smoothly. They also research historical and cultural background to help enrich the travel experience and allow travellers to understand and respond appropriately to cultural and environmental issues.

Authors don't stay in every hotel because that would mean spending a couple of months in each medium-sized city and, no, they don't eat at every restaurant because that would mean stretching belts beyond capacity. They do visit hotels and restaurants to check standards and prices, but feedback based on readers' direct experiences can be very helpful.

Many of our authors work undercover, others aren't so secretive. None of them accept freebies in exchange for positive write-ups. And none of our guidebooks contain any advertising.

Production Authors submit their manuscripts and maps to offices in Australia, USA, UK or France. Editors and cartographers – all experienced travellers themselves – then begin the process of assembling the pieces. When the book finally hits the shops, some things are already out of date, we start getting feedback from readers and the process begins again …

WARNING & REQUEST

Things change – prices go up, schedules change, good places go bad and bad places go bankrupt – nothing stays the same. So, if you find things better or worse, recently opened or long since closed, please tell us and help make the next edition even more accurate and useful. We genuinely value all the feedback we receive. A well-travelled team reads and acknowledges every letter, postcard and email and ensures that every morsel of information finds its way to the appropriate authors, editors and cartographers for verification.

Everyone who writes to us will find their name in the next edition of the appropriate guidebook. They will also receive the latest issue of *Planet Talk*, our quarterly printed newsletter, or *Comet*, our monthly email newsletter. Subscriptions to both newsletters are free. The very best contributions will be rewarded with a free guidebook.

Excerpts from your correspondence may appear in new editions of Lonely Planet guidebooks, the Lonely Planet Web site, *Planet Talk* or *Comet*, so please let us know if you *don't* want your letter published or your name acknowledged.

Send all correspondence to the Lonely Planet office closest to you:

Australia: Locked Bag 1, Footscray, Victoria 3011
USA: 150 Linden St, Oakland, CA 94607
UK: 10A Spring Place, London NW5 3BH
France: 1 rue du Dahomey, 75011 Paris

Or email us at: talk2us@lonelyplanet.com.au

For news, views and updates see our Web site: www.lonelyplanet.com

HOW TO USE A LONELY PLANET GUIDEBOOK

The best way to use a Lonely Planet guidebook is any way you choose. At Lonely Planet we believe the most memorable travel experiences are often those that are unexpected, and the finest discoveries are those you make yourself. Guidebooks are not intended to be used as if they provide a detailed set of infallible instructions!

Contents All Lonely Planet guidebooks follow roughly the same format. The Facts about the Destination chapters or sections give background information ranging from history to weather. Facts for the Visitor gives practical information on issues like visas and health. Getting There & Away gives a brief starting point for researching travel to and from the destination. Getting Around gives an overview of the transport options when you arrive.

The peculiar demands of each destination determine how subsequent chapters are broken up, but some things remain constant. We always start with background, then proceed to sights, places to stay, places to eat, entertainment, getting there and away, and getting around information – in that order.

Heading Hierarchy Lonely Planet headings are used in a strict hierarchical structure that can be visualised as a set of Russian dolls. Each heading (and its following text) is encompassed by any preceding heading that is higher on the hierarchical ladder.

Entry Points We do not assume guidebooks will be read from beginning to end, but that people will dip into them. The traditional entry points are the list of contents and the index. In addition, however, some books have a complete list of maps and an index map illustrating map coverage.

There may also be a colour map that shows highlights. These highlights are dealt with in greater detail in the Facts for the Visitor chapter, along with planning questions and suggested itineraries. Each chapter covering a geographical region usually begins with a locator map and another list of highlights. Once you find something of interest in a list of highlights, turn to the index.

Maps Maps play a crucial role in Lonely Planet guidebooks and include a huge amount of information. A legend is printed on the back page. We seek to have complete consistency between maps and text, and to have every important place in the text captured on a map. Map key numbers usually start in the top left corner.

Although inclusion in a guidebook usually implies a recommendation we cannot list every good place. Exclusion does not necessarily imply criticism. In fact there are a number of reasons why we might exclude a place – sometimes it is simply inappropriate to encourage an influx of travellers.

Introduction

Dublin is one of Europe's most compelling capitals, and an absolute must on any list of top 10 European cities to visit. If you've never visited, make plans to do so; if you have, you won't need us to tell you to return.

Why? Because Dublin is a city with soul, a place that has never lost sight of the fact that people are more fun than museums and that genuine human interaction is not the exclusive preserve of small villages and bored taxi drivers.

Dublin is a vibrant and bustling capital in the throes of the longest period of uninterrupted economic prosperity and growth since the mid-18th century, when it was referred to as the 'second city of the Empire'. British, that is, and it is in its 800-year link with Ireland's neighbour across the Irish Sea that a large part of Dublin's identity was forged. The British hand shaped many corners of the city and during the architectural apogee that was the 18th century, Dublin was redefined on the drawing boards of some of Britain's greatest architects, who added the majestic streetscapes and regal squares that to this day set Dublin apart as the greatest Georgian city in the world.

And then, of course, there's the language. Imposed upon Ireland by its colonial masters, English has long supplanted Irish as the *lingua franca* of the country, but the Irish have gained revenge for this act of cultural piracy by becoming masters of the language; relative to its small size, what other country can boast four Nobel laureates for literature?

Dubliners are intensely proud not just of their celebrated forbears, but also of their city, although at first glance it may be difficult to see why. It is far from the cleanest city in the world, which doesn't do its mottled appearance any favours. Indeed, with the exception of the Georgian aesthetic and a handful of contemporary offerings, there doesn't really seem to be any style to Dublin's architecture, which is a collage of poorly conceived apartment blocks and ugly office buildings. 'So what?' Dubliners will ask you. 'Is an apartment block going to buy you a pint? Is an office building going to tell you a funny story and offer to show you around?' Their advice is simple. 'Relax. Take it easy. Forget about the grimy streets, the eyesores on the skyline and have a good time. You think you have it bad? You're only here for a week, while we have to live with it all the time!' At its best, Dublin is an experience to be savoured, a city where your faith in human nature will be restored. If you don't believe us, just ask any of the thousands of foreigners who came, saw, and stayed.

Underneath Dublin's casual approach to living, however, is a deep-rooted desire not to be left behind. For decades Dublin lived in the shadows of economic deprivation, its best minds and ablest bodies forced to emigrate in order to realise their potential. Not any more. The economic boom of the 1990s has seen a radical reversal in Dublin's fortunes, to the point that the city is a place to *go to* rather than run from. Whether you are a curious tourist, a returning Dubliner or an aspiring immigrant, Dublin has plenty to offer and the means to satisfy your hunger.

Dublin may be the favourite weekend destination of the British, but the city has become home to many others from all parts of the globe. Walk into any cafe and you're as likely to hear an Aussie, American, a Spanish or Italian accent as you are the distinctive sound of a Dubliner. The city's African and Asian communities keep on growing. And while racism *is* an issue, the vast majority of Dubliners are keen to ensure that their city is as welcoming of outsiders as the outside world has traditionally been of Dublin's emigrants.

Facts about Dublin

HISTORY

Dublin may have celebrated its official millennium in 1988, but there were settlements long before AD 988. Before the arrival of the Celts in 500 BC there were some rudimentary farming communities, but it is pretty certain that the Celts were the first to settle in the Dublin area proper. Over the course of the next 2000 years, Dublin's fortunes rose and fell with each wave of foreign settlement. Celts, Vikings, Normans and the English all had a hand in the creation of a city that wouldn't become a fully constituted capital until 1921, with the end of the Anglo-Irish War and the creation of the Irish Free State.

Modern Dublin is then a composite city, a creation of several different cultures, and traces of each can still be found. You might have to look beneath the earth at Wood Quay to find evidence of its Viking past, but you need only look up the hill at the imposing sight of Christ Church Cathedral to witness Dublin's Norman stamp. As for the long period of English rule, it is impossible to visualise what Dublin might have been like without it; from the landscaped elegance of its city gardens to the grandeur of its Georgian architecture, Dublin's modern character is a by-product of English domination. The changes that have occurred since independence have sought to enhance rather than replace what was there before.

Ten Little-Known Facts about Dublin

We guarantee that most Dubliners won't know these facts either...

- The average Dubliner earns €24,125 per annum, giving €15.25 to charity and €205.70 in tips. A quarter of all tips go to taxi drivers even though they earn, on average, four times the average wage in the city, higher than 96% of their clients.
- There are two O'Connell bridges in Dublin. The first, spanning the Liffey, is the only traffic bridge in Europe that is wider than it is long; and the other spans the pond in Stephen's Green.
- Dublin's oldest traffic light is situated in Clontarf. The light, which is still in full working order, was installed in 1893 outside the home of a Mr Fergus Mitchell, who was the owner of the first car in Ireland.
- Dubliners drink a total of 9800 pints per hour between the hours of 5.30pm on Friday and 3am the following Monday.
- Dublin is Europe's most popular destination with travelling stag and hen parties, with around 600 'pre-wedding sessions' arriving every weekend.
- The average 25-year-old Dubliner still lives with his/her parents, preferring to spend their money on cars and clothes rather than a mortgage.
- Dubliners are more likely to buy a stranger a drink than locals from any other area of the country.
- Marlborough St, site of Dublin's only Catholic cathedral, was once the biggest red-light district in Europe with an estimated 1600 prostitutes. It was known locally as the 'Monto' and features in the writings of James Joyce (who lost his virginity to a prostitute).
- The statue of Thomas Davis in College Green replaced a statue of King William of Orange astride a horse. Poor King Billy and his steed met a most ignominious end: blown up six times before being completely destroyed in 1946, the remains were taken to a corporation yard and the horse's huge lead testicles melted down and used to repair a pipe!
- The name Dublin is hardly the sole preserve of Ireland's capital: there are 12 Dublins in the United States and six in Australia.

Early Footprints & Celtic Highways

Although there is evidence of a number of rudimentary settlements dating back to around 6000 BC, the area on which present-day Dublin was built was the preserve of nomadic hunters until the arrival of the Celts in 500 BC. The Celts built the first roads (*slighe* in Gaelic) in Ireland, which converged at a ford over the River Liffey called Áth Cliath in Irish. Legend has it that with the death of the great Ulster warrior Cúchalainn at the hands of southern Gaels, Ulster demanded that a payment of '150 ladies plus 700 white cows with red ears' be offered to avenge the hero's death. In order to get the tribute across the Liffey, a bridge of hurdles was thrown – hence the name. Whatever the truth of the story, the settlement that grew up at this junction was to give Dublin its Irish name, Baile Átha Cliath (Town of the Hurdle Ford).

The Coming of Christianity

Christianity was introduced to Ireland in AD 432 when – according to legend – St Patrick arrived and began converting the locals to the religion of Rome. The spread of the new religion was rapid and thorough (too thorough, according to some). Legend also has it that St Patrick's Cathedral was built on the site of a well where Patrick himself baptised the local chieftains. By the middle of 6th century, Christianity was firmly entrenched and monastic settlements were flourishing around a tidal pool in the estuary of the River Poddle known as Dubh Linn (Black Pool). These monasteries played more than a religious role and served as important centres of learning, attracting not just Irish scholars but students from Saxon Britain as well. In effect, these were Europe's first universities.

The Vikings Are Coming!

While the monasteries were going from strength to strength, the town remained little more than a halting site for traders until the arrival of the Vikings in the 10th century. Raids from the north had become a fact of Irish life, with Norse longboats attacking monasteries and settlements along the coast and rivers and making off with whatever loot

– and local women – they could carry. In AD 837 they built a harbour (or *longphort*) on the banks of the Liffey, but were soon forced out by a Celtic army. In AD 917, however, a massive fleet of Danish and Norse longboats commanded by King Sitric II sailed up the Liffey and established a settlement on the site of present-day Wood Quay, on the northern banks of the River Poddle by the black pool. They built houses of wattle and thatch and laid down strict guidelines on plot sizes and town boundaries – the first planning ordinances of the town they transliterated as 'Dyflinn'.

The town became the most prominent trading centre in the Viking world, with a roaring trade in agricultural exports, slaves, crafts and ship-building. The Vikings, however, didn't have it all their own way. In 1014 an alliance of Irish clans led by Brian Ború soundly defeated a Viking army (which also included some Irish) at the Battle of Clontarf, forever breaking the Scandinavian grip on the eastern seaboard. Rather than abandon Ireland in defeat, however, the Vikings chose to stay, marrying with the native Irish, adopting Christianity and building churches. With the integration of the Vikings, the scene was set for the next wave of invaders, this time from their not-so-friendly neighbour across the sea. By the middle of the 12th century the Normans had completed their conquest of Britain. Now it was Ireland's turn.

The First English Tourists

The arrival of the Anglo-Normans in 1169 was to change the course of Irish history. The first landing, a mixed force of Norman knights and Saxon soldiers led by Richard de Clare (aka Strongbow) – in Ireland's eyes, the first British troops – was in Wexford, but they fought their way up the coast, capturing towns and fortifications before reaching Dyflinn's city gates in 1170. Adopting a tactic that would become all-too-familiar over the coming centuries, they asked to negotiate with the city leaders while a party of knights broke through the walls and captured the city. Dublin was now firmly in Anglo-Norman hands and it remained so for the next 750 years.

Yet the extent of early Anglo-Norman dominance was checked by the presence of fierce Irish warriors. Consequently, the territory under Norman rule was limited to a narrow coastal strip known as the Pale. Beyond it, Ireland remained unbowed and unconquered.

Cathedrals, Castles & Calamities

The Anglo-Normans quickly set about reconstructing and fortifying the city they had captured. The first major project was to replace the old wooden cathedral that stood on the hill above Wood Quay; in 1172 construction began on Christ Church Cathedral, whose hotchpotch of styles – predominantly Romanesque and English Gothic – is still in evidence today. In 1191 a second stone church was built a few hundred yards to the south, again replacing an earlier wooden structure. The church, named after St Patrick, was elevated to cathedral status in 1219. Six years later, the new cathedral was completely redesigned in the style you can see today. In 1204 King John of England commissioned the construction of Dublin Castle, '...for the safe custody of our treasure...and the defence of the city'.

As Dublin grew bigger so did its problems, and over the next few centuries misery seemed to pile upon mishap. In 1317 Ireland's worst famine of the Middle Ages killed off thousands and reduced some to cannibalism. In 1348 Dublin – along with most of Western Europe – suffered the devastation of the Black Death: the bodies were piled into massive lime-covered graves in an area south of the Liberties that is still known today as the Black Pits. The situation was hardly helped by the presence of farm animals, mainly pigs, that roamed the rat-infested streets at will. A series of health regulations, including the banning of beggars during periods of pestilence, went some way towards solving Dublin's hygiene problems – notorious even by the low standards of the Middle Ages.

If bubonic rats and famine weren't trouble enough, Dublin also had its fair share of political problems, hardly surprising considering that it was an overgrown English fortress surrounded by a pretty hostile population. Even its Anglo-Norman keepers had begun to vacillate in their loyalty to the crown: like the Vikings before them, they had become absorbed by Irish culture and, in the words of one disapproving English commentator, 'become more Irish than the Irish themselves'. In 1534, the most powerful of Leinster's Anglo-Normans, Lord (Silken) Thomas Fitzgerald, renounced his allegiance to Henry in the chapter house of St Mary's Abbey (just off present-day Capel St) and launched a rebellion against the crown. In a tragic pattern that would be repeated time again over the coming centuries, the ill-conceived revolt was soon defeated and the young lord hanged, drawn and quartered outside of Tyburn Prison in London. Henry reacted by ordering the surrender of all lands to the English Crown. Three years later, the Irish church was dealt a mortal blow with the order that all monasteries were to be dissolved. Control of all church lands now passed to the newly constituted Anglican Church.

In 1558, Elizabeth I (1533–1603) succeeded to the English throne and her rule was marked by repeated and concerted efforts finally to bring the Irish to heel. In 1598 the Irish, led by the Earl of Tyrone, Hugh O'Neill (1540–1616), inflicted the biggest ever defeat of an English army on Irish soil at the Battle of the Yellow Ford, but the success was reversed three years later at the Battle of Kinsale. O'Neill did achieve a Pyrrhic victory of sorts, as he refused to surrender until 30 March 1603, six days after the death of Elizabeth. His surrender, however, sounded the death knell for Gaelic Ireland and the country was now ready for total Anglicisation. While Ireland languished, Dublin was set to prosper as the bulwark of English domination.

The Protestant Ascendancy

The defeat of Hugh O'Neill put an end to organised rebellion against the Crown, and led to the first Irish 'plantations', where confiscated lands were awarded to loyal English and Scottish subjects of a thoroughly Protestant stock. The most fertile of Irish lands were in Ulster, and the granting of huge swathes of land to loyal subjects of the Crown was to sow the seeds of the trouble afflicting the northern part of the island today. Although most of the Irish were now disenfranchised and reduced to a state of near misery, the aggressive policy of Anglicisation proved beneficial to Dublin's fortunes as the city became a bastion of Protestantism. The chasm between the 'English' city and Irish countryside was so profound that traces of this gulf are still discernible today: in rural areas you might hear some people refer to Dubliners as 'West Brits', a contemptuous dismissal of their Irish credentials.

At the time, however, Dublin's loyalty saved it from the disastrous consequences of Oliver Cromwell's (1599–1658) invasion in 1649, launched as retribution for Ireland's loyalty to Charles I during the English Civil War. In the best tradition of the worst of the marauding Vikings seven centuries earlier, his soldiers murdered, raped, looted and burned their way up and down the eastern coast, but left Dublin alone (except converting St Patrick's Cathedral into a temporary stable for their horses).

The Golden Age

After the restoration of Charles II (1630–85) in 1660, Dublin embarked upon a century of unparalleled growth and development, which mirrored the general decay of the Irish countryside as anti-Catholic measures further disenfranchised the Catholic peasantry. In 1690 the Irish backed the losing side once more, this time taking up arms for the Catholic James II (1633–1701), king of England, Ireland and – as James VII – of Scotland, until he was deposed by the Protestant William of Orange (1650–1702) in 1688. Two years later, James and William met in battle on the banks of the Boyne, north of Dublin, resulting in a final victory for William and the flight of James to France.

William's victory ushered in the punitive Penal Code, which stripped Catholics of most basic rights in a single, sweeping legislative blow – a situation not dissimilar to that faced by South African blacks with the introduction of apartheid some 350 years

later. Ireland's misfortune, however, was to prove Dublin's gain, as the city was flooded with landless refugees willing to work for a pittance. The end of the century also saw an influx into Dublin of Huguenot weavers, who settled in Dublin after fleeing anti-Protestant legislation in France. They established a successful cloth industry that helped fuel the city's growth.

With plenty of cash to go around and eager to live in a city that reflected their newly found wealth, the Protestant nobility embarked on a huge overhaul of Dublin. Speculators bought up swathes of land and commissioned substantial projects of urban renewal, including the creation of new streets, the laying out of city parks and the construction of magnificent new buildings and residences. This golden age of development and construction can roughly be divided into two distinct periods. The first, which lasted from 1660 to 1720, was known as the Anglo-Dutch period: its most magnificent creation was the Royal Hospital at Kilmainham (1680–84), now the Irish Museum of Modern Art (IMMA). The second, which lasted until the end of the 18th century, was named after the line of Georges who sat on the English throne.

It was impossible to build in the heart of the medieval city, so the city's nouveau riche moved north across the river, creating a new Dublin of stately squares surrounded by fine Georgian mansions. Indeed, the new city was so elegant that it was the British Empire's second city, after London, and the fifth-largest city in Europe.

Dublin's teeming, poor, mostly Catholic slums soon spread north in pursuit of the rich, who turned back south to grand new homes around Merrion Square, St Stephen's Green and Fitzwilliam Square.

In 1745, when James Fitzgerald, the earl of Kildare, started construction of Leinster House, his magnificent mansion south of the Liffey, he was mocked for this foolish move away from the centre and into the wilds. 'Where I go society will follow,' he confidently predicted and was soon proved right. Today Leinster House is used as the Irish Parliament and is in modern Dublin's centre.

Modern Disasters

The Georgian boom years were followed by more than a century of trouble and unrest. Greatly influenced by the principles of the French Revolution in 1789 and the general European march towards more inclusive democracies, the Irish – led by a mixed bag of intellectuals, writers, lawyers and other educated types – began to foment revolt against English rule. Even before the 18th century ended the problems had started with the abortive French-backed invasion by Wolfe Tone in 1796 and the equally unsuccessful rebellion led by Lord Edward Fitzgerald, member of the United Irishmen, in 1798. Five years later, in 1803, there was another revolt, but, in what was becoming the Irish fashion, it was idealistic and romantic but badly planned and ill-conceived. Robert Emmet, the ringleader, was executed outside St Catherine's Church in the Liberties and joined what would become an increasingly long list of eloquent Irish martyrs in the struggle against Britain.

The Act of Union, which came into effect on 1 January 1801, created the United Kingdom of Great Britain and Ireland and ended the separate Irish Parliament, whose members moved to the British Parliament at Westminster. This was achieved with more than a little bribery and corruption, but the end of Dublin's governmental role led many of the city's leading citizens to head for England. The dramatic growth that had characterised Dublin in the previous century came to an almost immediate halt and the city fell into a steady decline.

In 1823 the lawyer Daniel O'Connell (1775–1847) launched his campaign to recover basic rights for Ireland's Catholic population. He made real progress for a time, including the passing of the Catholic Emancipation Act of 1829, and he gained the nickname of 'The Liberator'. However, a three-month jail sentence for sedition in 1844 must have frightened him somewhat, for thereafter he chose to agitate only within the law. As Ireland's mettle hardened against British rule following the disastrous effects of the Famine, this decision did not endear him to the population and his efforts and influence faded after he called off one of his 'monster meetings' at Clontarf when the authorities declared it illegal.

Ireland's greatest disaster struck between 1845 and 1849. The food needs of the burgeoning rural population had become overwhelmingly dependent on the easily grown potato, and when potato blight devastated the crop the human cost was truly staggering. The damage was compounded by the British government's shameful adoption of a laissez faire attitude that meant only the most rudimentary relief was offered. Although Dublin escaped the worst effects of the Famine, the streets and squares were still packed with refugees from the impoverished countryside, living in disease-ridden slums. A strict enforcement of a law governing debtors – which resulted in the imprisonment of any person owing more than 10 shillings – packed the city's jails and hardened Irish resentment of British rule. Meanwhile, Dublin's remorseless decline accelerated.

Dublin's wealthier citizens began moving southwards, to the newly built suburbs that were growing up along the coast, which was thanks to the construction of Ireland's first railway line in 1834, linking Kingsport (now Dun Laoghaire) and the city. Over the course of the next 70 years, many of the fine Georgian residences that were once occupied by the now departed Dublin elite became slum dwellings packed with impoverished Dubliners: in 1910 it was reckoned that up to 20,000 Dublin families each occupied a single room. Although Dubliners had never shied away from having a couple of pints to round off the rougher edges of life, alcohol abuse grew incrementally with the hardening of the city's fortunes. A two-week survey of 22 pubs at the turn of the century found that around 46,000 women and 28,000 children were among their customers. Tens of thousands had little possibility of social or economic advancement, destined as they were to be the mule that turned the wheel of the ascendancy.

At the turn of the 20th century Dublin was staunchly divided along sectarian lines, which in turn dictated one's economic and social standing, but there was a substantial

Catholic middle class too. Although their religion precluded them from ever reaching the heights attained by Dublin's Protestant community, they were successful as dentists, barristers, solicitors, merchants, and – in a few cases – directors of large firms. These were derided by the rest of the Catholic community as 'Castle Catholics' (after Dublin Castle, the seat of British power), the lapdogs of the Protestant ascendancy whose manners and accents they aped. Yet paradoxically it was from this Catholic upper middle class that the impetus towards greater independence for Ireland drew its momentum.

In 1870 Isaac Butt (1813–79) founded the Home Government Association, which called for a return to the pre-1801 situation when Ireland had had its own parliament. Butt was essentially a conservative, however, and as Ireland grew more radical in its demands for Home Rule the country turned to the more dashing figure of Charles Stewart Parnell (1846–91). Elected to Westminster in 1875, he campaigned tirelessly for a Dublin parliament and soon was dubbed the 'King of Ireland'. The Liberal British prime minister, William Gladstone, was convinced that Ireland needed some form of self-government and in 1886 introduced the first Home Rule Bill to parliament. It was defeated in the House of Lords. Gladstone introduced it twice more, in 1891 and 1895, but on both occasions the Conservative House of Lords killed it. The Lords' failure to pass the bill eventually resulted in the Parliament Act of 1911, which limited their ability to kill a bill to three times, after which it became law irrespective of their voting.

Parnell's fortunes fared little better. In 1889 a Captain O'Shea filed for divorce from his wife Kitty, naming Parnell as correspondent. Parnell's liaison with a married woman had been known in political circles, but when word got out, public opinion in Britain was so hostile that Parnell's Irish Parliamentary Party (IPP) was forced to ditch their leader in order to maintain their fragile alliance with Gladstone's vote-minded Liberal Party. In Ireland, initial support for Parnell was sabotaged by a pronouncement from the Catholic Church, which declared Parnell to be morally unfit as a leader. This was one of the causes of the often bitter mistrust with which the Church, in its conservative mode, is still held by many Irish, particularly in Dublin. Parnell's fall from grace hastened his premature death in October 1891. He was buried in Dublin's Glasnevin Cemetery and the city's inhabitants, Parnellite to the last, turned out in droves to salute their fallen hero.

The Struggle for Independence

By the turn of the 20th century, Irish efforts to free themselves from British rule had reached an impasse. Irish history was dotted with valiant struggles, but each had been virtually doomed from the start through lack of planning, support and a series of unmitigated disasters that created plenty of heroes but did little to advance the cause of Irish independence. The failure of the IPP to obtain Home Rule at Westminster also convinced many that Britain would never willingly let go of Ireland unless she was forced to. In Dublin, the emergence of unions and other labour organisations introduced a socialist agenda to the struggle for independence, which matched the fight against the British with campaigns for better pay and working conditions for the slum-dwelling working classes.

In 1905 Arthur Griffith (1871–1922) founded a new political movement known as Sinn Féin (meaning 'We Ourselves'), which sought to achieve home rule through passive resistance rather than legislative action. The new party urged the Irish to withhold taxes and its representatives at Westminster to abandon parliament in favour of a national council in Dublin. Meanwhile, the first decade of the new century was marked by labour unrest in Dublin, as trade union leaders Jim Larkin and James Connolly organised strike after strike, culminating in the Great Lockout of 1913, when 20,000 workers defied the might and power of the Employers Federation.

In 1914 Westminster passed a Home Rule bill into law, but suspended its implementation for the duration of WWI. The bill, sensitive to the objections of the Protestant-dominated northern counties of Ulster and the potential threat of the newly

'Big Jim' Larkin & the 1913 Lock-Out

Of all the statues on Dublin's 'monument row', aka O'Connell St, the most impressive is that of James 'Big Jim' Larkin (1876–1947), an imposing figure with arms spread wide in a dramatic pose. It is a fitting tribute to the greatest figure of the Irish labour movement, and the driving force behind the greatest show-down between employers and workers in Dublin's history.

JANE SMITH

Jim Larkin's statue dominates O'Connell St.

It began on 21 August 1913, when 100 employees of the Tramways Company were dismissed for being members of Larkin's Irish Transport & General Workers' Union (ITGWU), which had been a thorn in the side of the Dublin Employers Federation since its foundation in 1909. William Martin Murphy, owner of the Tramways Company and president of the Employers Federation, had declared Larkin and his union a sworn enemy of 'the trade and business of the city' and was eager to crush them once and for all.

The ITGWU did not react until 26 August, when they declared a strike of tram workers to coincide with the opening day of the busiest festival of the social calendar, the Dublin Horse Show. At 10am all trams came to a halt and drivers and conductors literally walked off, leaving passengers stranded and the city in chaos. In a memorable speech from the windows of Liberty Hall, Larkin told his audience that 'this is not a strike, it is a lock-out of the men who have been tyrannically treated by a most unscrupulous scoundrel... We will demonstrate in O'Connell Street. It is our street as well as William Martin Murphy's. We are fighting for bread and butter. We will have our meetings in the street and if any one of our men fall, there must be justice. By the living God, if they want war, they can have it.'

A kind of war did ensue. On one side were the tram workers and other members of the ITGWU, their numbers swelled by thousands of others who had downed tools in protest at the dismissals.

constituted Ulster Volunteer Force (UVF) – whose 140,000 members signed the 'Solemn Oath and Covenant', swearing to resist any efforts to weaken Britain's rule in Ireland – made provisions for the partition of the country in an attempt to assuage the two communities. In the south, nationalists had followed Ulster's lead and established the Irish Volunteer Force (IVF), but with the outbreak of war the more moderate majority enlisted in the British Army, pacified by the promise of Home Rule once the war was over. Although impossible to predict at the time, this act of subservience to the Crown served to harden nationalists' aspirations and eventually led to demands for total independence. First, however, there was a minor matter of another rebellion.

The more radical nationalists – including members of Sinn Féin, radicals within the ranks of the IVF and James Connolly's Irish Citizen Army (ICA; founded in 1913 to protect striking workers) – treated WWI as the perfect opportunity to advance the cause of Irish independence, arguing that 'England's trouble would be Ireland's gain'. Its leaders planned a nationwide revolt for Easter Sunday, 23 April 1916, but in typical form, miscommunication and poor planning, along with the refusal of Arthur Griffith to entertain a violent uprising, meant that the revolt was limited to Dublin. Its chances of success had been further scuppered when the British authorities got wind of the uprising and intercepted an arms shipment destined for the rebellion in County Kerry on 21 April.

Undaunted, the small band of rebels decided to go ahead and on Easter Monday seized Dublin's GPO and a number of other strategic buildings throughout the city. From

'Big Jim' Larkin & the 1913 Lock-Out

On the other side were the employers, lead by Murphy and aided by the police, who broke up meetings and baton-charged the gathered crowds, leaving one man dead. Skirmishes between strikers and 'scabs' – those who had refused to stop working – broke out all over the city.

Larkin promised to address the crowd on O'Connell St on 28 August, but the meeting was banned. Heavily disguised, Larkin spoke anyway, from a window of a hotel owned by... William Martin Murphy. He was arrested and imprisoned.

By the end of September the lockout had intensified. In order to alleviate the misery of the striking workers, food boxes were sent by English trade unions, and the English Labour leader Keir Hardie arrived to lend his support. But Murphy wouldn't budge. Slowly, the striking workers began to starve and as winter approached, the situation became dramatic. In October, it was suggested that the workers' children be sent to England where a number of charitable organisations would take care of them, but the Catholic Archbishop of Dublin, William J Walsh, put a stop to it. He declared, 'I can only put it to them that they can no longer be worthy of the name of Catholic mothers if they so far forget that duty as to send away their little children to be cared for in a strange land, without security of any kind that those to whom the children are to be handed over are Catholics, or indeed are persons of any faith at all.'

On 28 October Larkin was sentenced to seven months in prison and James Connolly took over the strike. He had founded the Irish Citizen Army to defend workers from the actions of the police, but they were fighting a losing battle. After a long winter, the ITGWU announced in February that workers should return to work and the strike was at an end. But while the employers claimed victory, it was the ITGWU that emerged stronger from the strike. Trade unionism became a de facto force in Irish labour relations, and the membership of the ITGWU increased five-fold in the aftermath of the strike.

But what of the two great rivals, Larkin and Murphy? Larkin was released from prison in November after serving only one month of his sentence. Murphy claimed victory, but it was short lived. In 1919 he died, and Larkin went on to become the greatest representative of workers' rights in Irish history.

there they issued a declaration of independence penned by Patrick Pearse (1879–1916), a die-hard nationalist and poet whose stirring speeches and writings have entered the lexicon of Irish history. At the time, however, most Dubliners looked upon the motley band of rebels with a mixture of bemusement and contempt. British troops, convinced that the rebellion wouldn't take place, were initially surprised, but soon rallied and a gunboat was sent down the Liffey to rain shells on the rebels' provisional headquarters.

Pearse and the 14 other leaders – including James Connolly – managed to hold on for about a week, despite the fact that they only had 1500 or so 'soldiers' at their disposal. The British, though, took no chances and bombarded the rebel bases until most of the city centre was a smoking ruin. Finally, the rebels surrendered and its leaders were arrested and marched off to Kilmainham jail. As they were being led away, crowds gathered to mock and jeer them. Then, in hindsight, the British authorities made a terrible mistake. As this was a time of war, the authorities decided to treat the rebels as guilty of high treason and a death sentence was passed on all of them. Fifteen rebels were summarily executed in the yard of Kilmainham jail between 3 May and 8 May, and as news filtered out of their fate, the general consensus was that they had been treated too harshly. When it was discovered that James Connolly had been so badly injured during the fighting that he had to be executed while tied to a chair, and that among those shot was 18-year-old Willie Pearse, executed simply because he was Patrick's brother, passive sympathy for the rebels turned to passionate support.

The following year, the British miscalculated again. They threatened to introduce conscription to Ireland, and the Irish reacted very badly to the news that they would be forced to serve in the killing fields of Europe. When a general election was called in 1918, three-quarters of the Irish seats at Westminster were won by Sinn Féin, leaving the IPP and their promise of Home Rule a redundant anachronism, irrelevant to the radicalised mood that now pervaded the country. Sinn Féin refused to take their seats at Westminster, declared independence and in May 1919 formed the first Dáil Éireann (Irish Assembly, or lower house) in Dublin's Mansion House. It was a declaration of war against Britain.

Except that, as wars went, this wasn't much of one. Mindful that they could never match the British on the battlefield, Sinn Féin's military wing, made up of Irish Volunteers now renamed the Irish Republican Army (IRA), began attacking arms dumps and barracks in hit-and-run strikes. The British countered by strengthening the Royal Irish Constabulary and introducing a tough auxiliary force made up of returning servicemen known as the Black and Tans (because their uniforms combined the dark constabulary colours with soldiers' khaki). Fuelled by anti-Irish prejudice and brutalised by the experiences of trench warfare, the Black and Tans were a violent, unforgiving force that spared no quarter. They met their match, however, in the IRA's commander, a master of undeniably ruthless but effective guerrilla tactics called Michael Collins. Although the British knew his name and had issued a warrant for his arrest, Collins proved a genius at maintaining a low profile, ensuring that no photograph of him ever fell into enemy hands. Throughout the war Collins was able to ride his bicycle all over Dublin, past unsuspecting checkpoints.

By an extraordinary coincidence, Collins' cousin had been inadvertently placed in charge of all secret codes at Dublin Castle, leading Collins to exclaim, 'In the name of God how did these people ever get an empire?' On 10 November 1920, Collins learned that 14 undercover British intelligence officers known as the 'Cairo Gang' had arrived in Dublin that day, and the next morning all were shot as they lay in their beds. That afternoon, the British retaliated by opening fire on a hurling match at Croke Park, killing 11 spectators and one player. Ireland's first 'Bloody Sunday' served to further fortify Irish resolve to free themselves from British rule as well as quash any moral doubts over the often brutal tactics adopted by the IRA.

The fighting was worst in west Cork and other rural areas, where the legendary 'flying columns' – squadrons of guerrilla fighters who attacked as quickly as they dispersed – achieved notable success. In Dublin, however, life continued virtually unchanged for the duration of the war, with the exception of an increased military presence and the occasional shooting.

In May 1921, Irish rebels struck a blow against the British civil service when they burned down the Custom House. Although obviously a military act, it was greeted in Dublin largely as an economic reprieve for tens of thousands of hesitant tax-payers who rejoiced at the burning of the tax records.

The struggle, however, had reached a stalemate, and as foreign pressure was brought to bear on British prime minister Lloyd George to resolve the issue one way or the other, a truce was signed on 11 July 1921.

Independence & More War

The Anglo-Irish Treaty was signed, after months of argument, on 6 December 1921. Unfortunately for both sides, it was far from being a neat agreement. Instead of setting up the Irish Republic for which the IRA had fought, the Treaty merely created the Irish Free State, which was still subservient to Britain on a number of important issues. Worse, from the Irish perspective, it allowed the six Ulster counties that make up Northern Ireland to opt out of the new state. Thus the seeds were planted for a problem that continues to fester.

The Treaty pitted erstwhile comrades against each other in pro-Treaty and anti-Treaty camps. The latter were led by Eamon de Valera, who had escaped execution after the Easter Rising because he was US-born.

Although the Dáil narrowly ratified the Treaty and the general public did the same by a larger margin, civil war broke out in June 1922. Anti-Treaty IRA forces had occupied the Four Courts building on the banks of the Liffey in Dublin and when they refused to surrender, pro-Treaty forces led by Collins shelled them from across the river. The building soon went up in flames, just as the equally beautiful Custom House had a year earlier. In a repeat of the 1916 Easter Rising, O'Connell St followed it into the fire. In one of the more bitter ironies of conflict in Ireland, Dublin suffered far more during the Civil War than it had during the War of Independence a year before. The fighting was particularly vicious as anti-Treaty IRA forces were soon mounting ambushes of Free State forces, just as they had against the Black and Tans. Of the many tragedies that were the hallmark of the war, perhaps none was to have as grave an effect on the history of the new state as the killing of Michael Collins, who was ambushed near Cork on 22 August.

The Dáil then passed a bill making the death sentence mandatory for any IRA member possessing a gun when captured. On 24 November, Robert Erskine Childers, whose yacht, the *Asgard*, had brought arms for the republican cause to Howth in 1914, was executed for possessing a revolver, which had been given to him by Collins. By May 1923, 77 executions had taken place and de Valera, president of Sinn Féin, who had been imprisoned by the Free State authorities for a year, ordered the IRA to drop their arms. The Civil War ground to a halt. This drove a wedge between Sinn Féin as a political force and the IRA as a guerrilla army.

The Irish Republic

Ireland was finally at peace, but many questions were left unanswered. The substantial minority of members of parliament who had been elected on the republican and anti-Treaty platform refused to take their seats, particularly as it would involve an oath of allegiance to the British throne. Without an armed struggle to pursue, the IRA was becoming a marginalised force in independent Ireland and Sinn Féin was

falling apart. In 1926, de Valera created a new party, Fianna Fáil ('Warriors of Ireland'), and in 1927 almost won power, despite the fact that he and his supporters still refused to sit in parliament. After the election he led his party into the Dáil by the simple expedient of not taking the oath but signing in as if he had.

In 1932, de Valera and Fianna Fáil won a general election, repeating this victory, with an increased majority, in 1933, when they called an election to confirm their mandate. They soon jettisoned the Treaty clauses with which they disagreed. The oath to the British Crown went, the British governor general soon followed and, by the outbreak of WWII, Ireland was a republic in all but name, and even that had been changed from the Irish Free State to Éire.

In 1948, Fianna Fáil lost the general election to the direct successor party to the first Free State government, Fine Gael ('Tribe of the Gaels'), in coalition with the new republican Clann na Poblachta led by Sean MacBride, a former IRA officer. The new government declared the Free State to be a republic at last and Ireland left the British Commonwealth in 1949. In 1955 it became a member of the United Nations.

Ireland Today

When Sean Lemass came to power in 1959 as successor to de Valera (Fianna Fáil had won the 1951 election) he sought to stem the high rate of emigration by improving the country's economic prospects. By the mid-1960s his policies had been successful enough to reduce emigration to less than half the level of the mid-1950s, and many who had left began to return. Lemass also introduced universal free secondary education.

In 1973 the Republic became a member of the European Economic Community (EEC). At first, membership brought some measure of prosperity, largely through the Common Agricultural Policy (CAP) and Regional Development Funds, but by the early 1980s Ireland was once more in economic difficulties and emigration rose. In the 1990s, however, Ireland saw a dramatic change in its economic fortunes. Interest rates, which had for many years been prohibitively high, began to tumble, encouraging new business; the Irish punt grew stronger and foreign investment, which had been mollycoddled and underpinned by generous tax incentives, began to reap substantial benefits, such as increased employment and injections of finance. The turnaround in Ireland's economic fortunes has led to the country's economy being dubbed the 'Celtic Tiger'. Ireland is often paraded as an economic role model for the rest of Europe (see Economy later in this chapter). Ireland has been an avid supporter of greater European integration, and has welcomed all efforts towards economic, social and political unity, including the adoption of the common European currency, the euro, which became the only currency of Ireland in February 2002.

Dublin's expansion has continued southwards to Ballsbridge, Dun Laoghaire and beyond and northwards to Howth, but the River Liffey remains a rough dividing line between southern haves and northern havenots. Evidence of EU and private investment adorns the city in the shape of cranes and hoardings, but areas of urban blight and high unemployment linger on. The city is also battling with a rise in drug-related crime.

In 1997 Belfast-born Mary McAleese was elected president, succeeding Mary Robinson, who – despite the limitations of her presidential powers – wielded considerable influence on the government's social policies during her term in office (1990–97), contributing to a marked shift in attitudes away from the traditionally conservative positions on issues such as divorce, abortion and gay rights. It is perhaps a sign of her impact on the world stage that on leaving office she was appointed UN High Commissioner for Human Rights. President McAleese, despite being more conservative than her predecessor, was elected on a promise of following in Robinson's footsteps, and is committed to pursuing a policy of understanding and rapprochement with Northern Ireland's Unionist community.

Fianna Fáil, under the leadership of Bertie Ahern, came to power in a coalition with the Progressive Democrats in 1997. They are a minority government, however, and rely on the support of three independent *Teachta Dála* (TDs; members of the Dáil) to maintain their slim majority.

In 2001 Ireland voted in a referendum on whether to accept the provisions of the Nice Treaty (2000). Although Ireland has always been an enthusiastic supporter of greater European integration and unity, it voted to reject the treaty by a margin of 54% to 46%. Fears that Ireland's jealously guarded neutrality would be compromised by involvement in a new army and that the widening of European Union (EU) membership would greatly reduce Ireland's role in the EU were the mitigating factors in the treaty's rejection. In June 2001, however, the government – reeling from accusations that it had completely mismanaged the referendum campaign – declared that a second referendum would take place in 2002.

The one unresolved problem that remains from 1921 is Northern Ireland, and the road to a permanent peace remains as pot-holed as ever. At the time of writing, the ceasefire brought about by the 1998 Good Friday Agreement had reached a frustrating stalemate. Unionists have dug their heels in on the issue of decommissioning of IRA weapons, while nationalists insist that progress depends on the British government's willingness to go through with a major overhaul of the police service and a substantial downscaling of the military presence. Although a return to full-scale violence is unlikely, the situation remains tense and unpredictable.

GEOGRAPHY

Dublin lies on the east coast of Ireland, about 53° north of the equator, and is divided by the River Liffey. Greater Dublin sprawls around the arc of Dublin Bay, bounded to the north by the hills at Howth and to the south by the Dalkey headland. Greater Dublin is in the administrative region of County Dublin, which is bordered to the north and north-west by County Meath, to the south-west by County Kildare and to the south by County Wicklow.

Postcodes are divided evenly between north and south of the river; all odd numbers are to the north, all even ones to the south. The postcodes for central Dublin are Dublin 1 immediately north of the river and Dublin 2 immediately south. The upmarket Balls-bridge area, which has some of the city's best B&Bs, lies to the south-east of the centre in Dublin 4.

CLIMATE

Dublin enjoys a milder climate than its northerly position might indicate. The sea around Ireland is warm for the latitude because of the influence of the North Atlantic Drift, or Gulf Stream. That merely means it's decidedly chilly rather than downright freezing. The water isn't much warmer at the height of summer (about 15°C) than in the depths of winter (10°C).

Dublin's maximum temperature in July and August ranges from 15° to 20°C, so even then it's wise to have a sweater or light coat. During January and February, the coldest months, daily temperatures range from 4° to 8°C. Major snowfalls are rare. May and June are the sunniest months and generally have between five and 6½ hours of sunshine per day. December has an average of only one or two hours per day. There are about 18 hours of daylight in July and August; it's only truly dark after about 11pm.

It does rain in Ireland (hey, it wouldn't be green if it didn't!); even the drier parts of Ireland – and Dublin is one of the driest – get rain on 150 days in a typical year and it often rains every day for weeks. Dublin receives about 75cm of rainfall annually, so there's much local terminology and humour about the rain – a 'soft day', for instance, is a damp one. Bring an umbrella.

ECOLOGY & ENVIRONMENT

Dublin's worst environmental problem is traffic congestion, which is a major annoyance in much of the city centre. Despite the construction of the M50 bypass, which runs from north-west of the city down towards Dun Laoghaire, city-centre traffic, especially on the quays, is an ugly, frustrating sight. The problem stems from the fact that the vast majority of Dublin's population is suburban and uses cars to get in and out of the city on a

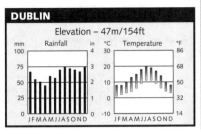

DUBLIN

Elevation – 47m/154ft

Rainfall — Temperature

daily basis. A number of attempts have been made in the last couple of years to alleviate congestion by encouraging commuters to use public transportation. Bus corridors – traffic lanes open to buses only – have been introduced on busy routes; the DART train line has a couple of new stops; suburban rail services have been increased; and the one-way system has been tinkered with and altered to eliminate bottlenecks at major junctions. The first bit of track has also finally been laid for the electrified Luas light rail service that will eventually run a gigantic loop through the city. It will be another 10 years before the loop is complete, but limited service should begin within the next two or three years.

Although recycling is not legally required, the number of recycling bins has increased substantially in recent years. However, there is laziness about the separation of rubbish, despite recycling campaigns.

GOVERNMENT & POLITICS

The Republic of Ireland has a parliamentary system of government. The parliament *(Oireachtas)* has a lower house, or house of representatives, known as the Dáil Éireann, usually shortened to Dáil and pronounced 'dawl'. The prime minister is the *Taoiseach* (pronounced 'teashok'; the plural is *Taosigh*), while the vice-premier is known as the *Tanaiste* (pronounced 'taw-nashta'). The Dáil has 166 elected members and sits in Leinster House on Dublin's Kildare St. Members of the Irish Parliament are known as Teachta Dála (TDs). The upper house (senate) is the *Seanad Éireann*, usually just called the Seanad, and senators are nominated by the Taoiseach or elected by university graduates and councillors around the country.

Ben There, Dunne That, Bought the Taoiseach

A number of Ireland's businesspeople are a truly charitable lot. Or so they would have us believe. After all, if they aren't making secret cash payments to senior politicians in return for political favouritism, then their actions are inspired by a generosity of spirit (and wallet) not seen since a certain Samaritan met a poor man along the road.

Graft in politics is hardly novel, but its wholesale exposure only began in Ireland in February 1997 with the setting up of the McCracken Tribunal (named after its presiding judge). Its brief was to investigate payments made by Ben Dunne, former managing director of the family-owned Dunnes Stores (one of the country's largest retail chains), to the then-Taoiseach, Fianna Fáil's Charles Haughey, and a Fine Gael minister, Michael Lowry.

It all began in February 1992 when Ben Dunne was arrested in a Florida hotel with a bag of cocaine and an employee of a certain agency called Escort in a Flash. Although he got off lightly – he served a month in an English rehab centre – on his return to Ireland he was ousted from the board of directors by his siblings. He sued, and during the ensuing court case it emerged that between 1989 and 1992 he had given 'gifts' totalling €1.65 million to Charles Haughey. The press had a field day with the revelations, and after nearly five years of muddled attempts to kill the story, the government finally gave in to public pressure and set up a tribunal of enquiry.

The McCracken Tribunal never really got a chance to delve too deeply into the allegations, largely thanks to Haughey's refusal to offer full and frank cooperation to the tribunal, but what did emerge was there was a definite pattern of payments made to both Haughey and Lowry, the latter receiving €440,000 to refurbish his house!

In September 1997 a second tribunal was set up to further investigate the Dunne payments. Headed by Justice Michael Moriarty, it sought to establish the extent of the payments and whether they influenced political decisions in Dunne's favour. In typical Irish fashion, the startling revelations of wholesale graft and dodgy payments were treated with a mixture of shock and humour by a largely unflappable nation. During his lengthy testimony, Dunne admitted that he had met the Taoiseach (Haughey) and that he had appeared depressed. In order to 'lift his spirits', Dunne gave him a bank draft of €25,000.

Inevitably, the spotlight was cast on Haughey's personal finances, and it emerged that his house was far from clean. The main revelation was that he and a number of other politicians and business 'friends' held off-shore accounts in the Cayman Islands' Ansbacher Bank, monies which were not subject to tax. During the testimony, it also became clear that Haughey's personal lifestyle was that of a real high flyer, and that during a period when the government had asked the nation to 'tighten its belt' in the face of recession, Haughey was flying to Paris to spend €20,000 on Charvet shirts! Perhaps the most shocking revelation, however, was that Haughey had dipped into a fund set up for the hospitalisation and treatment of Haughey's close colleague in Fianna Fáil, Brian Lenihan, who was suffering from liver cancer (and has subsequently died). At first, Haughey sought to deny the allegations, then announced that he had never taken charge of his financial affairs, leaving them in the hands of his accountant, the late Des Traynor. But both Traynor's son Tony and Haughey's personal secretary, Catherine Butler, testified that Traynor held regular meetings with Haughey.

The constitutional head of state is the president (*An tUachtaran*, pronounced 'awn uk-ta-rawn'), who is elected by popular vote for a seven-year term, but has little real power.

The main political parties are Fianna Fáil, led by Bertie Ahern; Fine Gael, led by Michael Noonan; and the Labour Party (which merged with the small Democratic Left party in January 1999), led by Ruari Quinn. Of the other parties, the one with the biggest support is Sinn Féin – the same party that is at the centre of the political standoff in Northern Ireland – which garners roughly 6% of the electoral vote. They are followed

Ben There, Dunne That, Bought the Taoiseach

The mishandling of money, however, was not limited to Dunne's payments to Haughey and Lowry. In October, the third of the investigative tribunals was set up. The Flood Tribunal was given a brief to investigate the planning history of 726 acres of land in north County Dublin. What appeared at first to be an uninteresting investigation into a localised incident of graft, however, turned out to be the most spectacular of the three tribunals, revealing that the cash-for-political-favours was far more widespread than had previously been assumed.

The early days of the tribunal centred on the testimony of the octogenarian James Gogarty, who revealed that his company had paid the former Minister for Foreign Affairs, Ray Burke, over €100,000 to obtain planning permission. Dismissed by the defense team as an old quack who could hardly be relied upon to give coherent testimony, Gogarty went on to astound the court and thrill the nation with his almost photographic memory of meetings, conversations and events. In June 1998 the tribunal's remit was further widened when it was revealed that Mr Burke had received a further €38,000 from another developer.

The net has widened further since 1998, and it was revealed that a number of senior members of Fianna Fáil had accepted substantial sums of money for planning permission, including former EU Commissioner Pádraig Flynn, who admitted accepting €63,000 from property developer Tom Gilmartin.

The tribunals continue to hear evidence to this day, in what has been termed the 'longest running show in town.' Although Ireland is not alone in dealing with graft scandals, there is a sinister edge to the Irish version, particularly due to the fact that Ireland is a small country and that its political and business elites tend to mix in the same circles. For many observers, the revelations tell of governments that were more concerned with enriching themselves by representing the interests of big business rather than those of the ordinary people.

The practical consequences of the tribunals have been equally sinister. Although there have been several resignations and many reputations have been permanently damaged, charges haven't been brought against any of the major players save one. Charles Haughey went on trial for obstruction of the McCracken Tribunal, but his trial was suspended indefinitely when Mary Harney, the current Tanaiste, made a statement declaring that he should definitely be found guilty, which in the judge's view was deemed to have prejudiced a fair trial. In any case, Haughey is terminally ill, so it is unlikely that he will ever face trial again. More surprising has been the incredible popularity of the current Fianna Fáil-led government, which, despite the burden of allegations aimed at the party and the practices of its former leaders, continues to do well in the polls. Taoiseach Bertie Ahern has done a masterful job of separating the party of today from the party of yesterday, earning him the sobriquet of 'Teflon Taoiseach'.

As for what will happen when the tribunals finally wind up no-one seems to know. Pundits have predicted that charges against one major player will be necessary to justify the long-running and incredibly expensive work of the tribunals, but as to whom that sacrificial lamb will be is anyone's guess. Most recently, the press has targeted the barristers working in the tribunals and the incredible earnings they have made, some earning fees in excess of €1.25 million of taxpayers' money for their work! Perhaps the next tribunal will investigate the tribunals themselves...

by the Progressive Democrats, led by Mary Harney, which split from Fianna Fáil in 1986, and the Socialist Workers' Party, which has one sitting member of the Dáil.

The Republic's electoral system is one of proportional representation, where voters mark the candidates in order of preference. As first-preference votes are counted and candidates are elected, the voters' second and third choices are passed on to the various other candidates.

At the local level, Dublin is governed by three elected bodies. Dublin Corporation supervises the city, a county council looks after

Dublin County and Dun Laoghaire & Rathdown Corporation administers the port town.

At the time of writing, the major political issues of the day were Northern Ireland and the on-going revelations of graft that have emerged out of a series of tribunals of enquiry. The current government, a coalition of Fianna Fáil and the Progressive Democrats, has struggled but has so far maintain its integrity in the face of the evidence that is literally pouring out daily, as it was members of Fianna Fáil that were the main benefactors of graft. (See the boxed text 'Ben There, Dunne That, Bought the Taoiseach' for more on the graft scandals.) A general election will occur sometime before June 2002, but as of writing it appears unlikely that Fianna Fáil will be shifted from power, even though they will probably need an alliance with another party to keep it.

ECONOMY

Ireland, and especially Dublin, is in the midst of the greatest economic boom since independence. The term 'Celtic Tiger' – used to describe the state of the economy – has become somewhat of a tired cliche, but it nevertheless reflects an economy that is healthy in almost every capacity, from record-low interest rates to a negligible rate of inflation. The success has been attributed to a variety of factors. Ireland has been remarkably successful in promoting foreign investment, with many multinational companies opting to set up here thanks to generous tax incentives and a well-educated workforce that nevertheless still earns 28% below the European average. Foreign investment has helped Ireland lead the field in a number of key industries, particularly information technology. As one of the EU's 'poorer' countries, Ireland has also been one of the leading recipients of EU funds, and a policy of wise investment has ensured that Ireland no longer ranks in the lower half of the EU's wealth scale. Add to this the explosion of the tourist industry – which has seen record numbers of visitors in the last decade – and a reversal in the age-old trend of emigration, which since 1995 has seen more people return to Ireland than

leave, and you have the makings of a prosperous economy. Lastly, a new entrepreneurial class has emerged since 1990, mostly of young graduates who have taken advantage of the favourable economic atmosphere to start up businesses.

Yet doubts persist as to the lasting virility of this particular feline. A growing consensus suggests that Ireland is in the middle of a boom-and-bust cycle similar to that in Britain in the 1980s. Some economists have argued that Ireland's dependence on multinational corporations results in a fragile economy at the tender mercy of world trends. The 2001 downturn in the US economy can be seen as a warning shot across Ireland's bow, and as economists argue whether this is merely a slowdown or the beginning of a recession, it is no time for complacency. Problems within the IT industry, an area where Ireland is among the world leaders, has led to substantial job losses in the sector with surely more to come. Although it is premature to talk of an end to the economic miracle, by the time you read this book some of the fantastical optimism that has been such a feature of the last 10 years may have been tempered by a dose of cautious worry.

The single most dramatic economic event since independence – more radical than decimalisation – has been Ireland's adoption of the single European currency, the euro, in January 2002. The punt, Ireland's currency since independence, was phased out in a lightning period of six weeks and replaced by the new currency, which has been value-stabilised at 78.9 old pence to the euro. Since February 2002 the euro has been the only legal tender currency in Ireland. In typical form and despite a consistent campaign aimed at preparing the country for the changeover, most people ignored it until it actually occurred. It will undoubtedly take some getting used to, and you will surely hear grumbling about how great the punt was, even if the vast majority of the Irish voted for the change.

In Dublin, house prices have rocketed since 1994, making it increasingly difficult for those with even a decent income to afford to buy property, and while many have benefited from the economic boom, it has become evident that the gap between rich and poor has broadened substantially rather than narrowed. Although the slums that were the shame of 19th-century Dublin have disappeared, a substantial segment of the population still lives in sub-standard corporation-run housing estates and flats, especially on the north side. Critics argue that the government has used public money to make nice areas in the city nicer and virtually ignored the lower-income areas that need it most.

The government and its supporters have countered that investment in job-creation schemes and the improvement of the city's tourist infrastructure are vital to maintaining economic buoyancy, and have taken steps to show that they do have a social conscience. In early 2001 plans were announced for a €152.4 million renovation of Fatima Mansions, an estate of subsidised blocks of flats on the Grand Canal that have long been plagued by poverty and drug addiction.

POPULATION & PEOPLE

Dublin's population is around 560,000, but over 1½ million people live within commuting distance of the centre. It is by far the most populated part of Ireland, representing approximately 40% of the country's total population of 3.8 million. Northern Ireland's population is about 1.6 million, making a total of 5.4 million for the whole island, the highest figure since 1881, but nowhere near the pre-Famine figure of 8½ million. Deaths and the huge scale of emigration reduced the population to around six million, and emigration continued at a high level for the next 100 years. It wasn't until the 1960s that Ireland's population finally began to increase again. Ireland's population is also remarkably young, with 24% aged under 20 and only 11% over the age of 65.

As Dublin's economic fortunes have increased over the last decade, so the city has become an attractive destination for immigrants, both temporary and long-term, who come in search of work, the chance to learn English and a good time. Aside from the tens of thousands of young EU nationals that have flooded into Dublin over the last five or

so years, the city is also home to around 27,000 non-EU nationals, including a substantial Chinese population. Attracted to the city's English-language institutes, they come on one-year student visas but invariably find illegal work in the city's restaurants and cafes. Responding to pressure to fix the situation, in 2001 the government passed a law that allows non-EU students to work, thereby giving an economic lifeline to many who would otherwise have been reduced to working for less than the basic wage.

EDUCATION

With such a young population it's not at all surprising that over 25% of Ireland's population is in full-time education. Attendance at school is compulsory and free for those up to and including the age of 15, when the majority of students take their Junior Certificate exams.

Nearly 90% of all primary and secondary schools are run by religious denominations and receive state aid. Secondary schools are for children aged 12 and over; those who successfully complete their education at this level receive their Leaving Certificate. On the basis of points scored in these exams they can then apply through a central applications service for admission to tertiary institutions, which are also heavily subsidised by the state. Each university course requires a certain number of points, which depend on the difficulty of the subject – the toughest being medical courses – and the number of places available.

Consequently, competition for university places is very stiff, and students need to attain relatively high standards to score enough to win a place.

Dublin has no shortage of tertiary-level academic institutions. University College Dublin (UCD) has a large campus in the south of the city, at Belfield, and another at Earlsfort Terrace, just off St Stephen's Green. It is Ireland's largest university with over 18,000 students. It is part of the National University of Ireland (NUI), which also has campuses in Cork, Galway and Maynooth, the latter also serving as Ireland's principal seminary school for the priesthood. Other recognised colleges of the NUI are the Royal College of Surgeons, with a campus in the city centre, and the National College of Art & Design, Ireland's foremost art college, near Christ Church Cathedral. Dublin City University (DCU) is a relatively new university, with a campus north of the city centre in Glasnevin. The most prestigious of the lot, however, is Trinity College, Dublin (TCD), the oldest university in Ireland. Since its foundation in 1592, it has set the standard for tertiary-level education in Ireland and has rightfully earned its position as one of Europe's most famous academic institutions, with a list of alumni that would flatter any university save perhaps Cambridge, Oxford and the Sorbonne. Its campus – trod on by 12,000 students and many more tourists – is in the heart of the city centre.

As well as the main universities and colleges, there are a host of other academic institutions, offering a range of diploma courses and – in the case of smaller colleges affiliated with a larger university overseas – degrees. Many of them specialise in business-related courses, including IT, marketing and PR.

There are also a number of technical colleges run by the Dublin Institute of Technology, which provide vocational training. Many courses feature work-placement programs ensuring practical experience for the young graduates. There are also a number of other private colleges throughout the city, which offer a wide variety of courses.

School-leavers who decide not to opt for tertiary education can enrol with Foras Áiseanna Saothair (FÁS), a state-sponsored body that works with registered employers to provide training and work experience for young people. With unemployment at only 8%, FÁS has obviously had remarkable success in creating work for young people who might otherwise have been destined for prolonged unemployment,

ARTS
Architecture

Ask anyone familiar with Dublin to define the city's architecture and they will inevitably refer to it as 'Georgian'. Although the Georgian period lasted less than 100 years, it has

defined the city's style above any other. The intense creativity of the Georgian period contributed to giving Dublin a wonderfully unified feel, despite the fact that in the centuries before and particularly since there were other architectural styles, some more aesthetically pleasing than others.

Pre-Georgian Dublin Dublin's tangled history from its Celtic beginnings to its Viking, Norman and English periods saw fine buildings thrown up, and equally rapidly torn down. As a result, survivors from Dublin's earliest days are either inconsequential (the Protestant St Audoen's Church), fragmentary (bits and pieces of Dublin Castle) or heavily restored (St Patrick's and Christ Church cathedrals).

Viking Dublin has been understandably consigned to the architectural dig (wood-and-mud architecture is hardly durable) and there is surprisingly little left to remind us of the city's Norman past. Imposing Dublin Castle has been so heavily reconstructed over the centuries that it bears little resemblance to the fortress erected by the Anglo-Normans in 1204. Both Christ Church Cathedral (founded in 1038) and St Patrick's Cathedral (finished in 1192) were heavily rebuilt in the 19th century, and while they still have traces of their Anglo-Norman origins – the crypt in Christ Church is the most obvious example – nothing remains of the private houses built around the sides. These were torn down in the 18th century to allow for better views of the cathedrals. St Audoen's Church (Protestant), whose foundations date from 1190, has three magnificent 15th-century bells but little else of note. St Anne's Guild Chapel, the blocked-off south transept of the church, is currently being restored, having been without a roof since 1826. Of the walls that once surrounded the Anglo-Norman city, only St Andrew's Arch on Cooke St remains. So, while the city had some fine buildings, it was hardly Rome. The 18th century, however, made rubble of what came before and replaced it with a new style so elegant that for a time Dublin was one of the finest cities in Europe (see the boxed text 'By George, It's Beautiful' later in this chapter).

Post-Georgian Dublin The dominant style up to 1916 was a form of classicism based on James Gandon's Custom House but, following the destruction of substantial parts of the city during the Easter Rising and the subsequent creation of the Irish Free State, new styles were introduced. Despite some interesting designs such as those of the Department of Finance building on Kildare St – influenced by the Italian futurist movement and Russian constructivism – and the starkly modernist Dublin airport built at the end of the 1930s, it wasn't until the construction of Busáras (Dublin's bus station) after WWII that Dublin began looking like a modern city. This notable International Modernist building, designed by Michael Scott, was to have an influence on architects in Ireland for the next 20 years. Sadly, it was its pioneering use of glass (it used more than any other building in Europe at the time) that was its downfall: huge, unattractive air-conditioning systems had to be installed to cool the building during the summer, thus ruining the aesthetic appeal of the design.

Until the late 1970s, the dominant architectural style in Dublin was the Miesian approach (named after Mies Van Der Rohe, 1886–1969). The Bank of Ireland headquarters building and the Berkeley Library in Trinity, designed by Paul Koralek, are prime examples. By the 1980s, architectural design was at a low ebb, and Sam Stephenson's two offerings, the Central Bank building on Dame St and the Civic Offices at Wood Quay, aroused huge controversy for their ugly, bunker-style design. In fairness to Stephenson, he was not allowed to finish either project: the Central Bank was considered too tall and halfway through the construction of the Civic Offices (which were linked by a glass atrium) Viking remains were found, putting an end to Stephenson's projected design. In the mid-1990s an extension was added to the original building, which proved popular among the public and critics alike.

The slump ended in the 1990s with the re-development of the Temple Bar area, the city's new cultural quarter. The government competition for a plan of how best to develop the area was won by Group 91 Architects, whose projects included the Irish Film Centre, the Ark Children's Centre, the Temple Bar Music Centre, the Gallery of Photography, the Designyard Applied Arts Centre and the Arthouse multimedia centre. Two brand new squares and a curved street (Curved St!) were laid out, and the overall effect has been remarkably successful. Of particular note is Meeting House Square, the highlight of which is the remarkable titanium stage door designed by Spanish architect Santiago Calatrava, who was also responsible for the design of the extraordinary Lyon-Satolas TGV terminal in France and the Alamillo Bridge in Seville.

Other developments worth mentioning outside Temple Bar include the Waterways Visitor Centre (known as 'the box in the docks'), designed in 1994 by Irish architects Ciaran O'Connor and Gerard O'Sullivan, which has a nautical theme, with a metal frame and panelling on the outside and timber throughout the interior. North of the Liffey, HARP (Historic Area Rejuvenation Project) is undertaking a huge program of construction in the Smithfield market area. Popular attractions include the 'new' Old Jameson Distillery, whose ramshackle, abandoned premises were converted into one of Dublin's more interesting museums with a chimney now used as a viewing tower accessed by a glass elevator. The dominant building on the square is the Chief O'Neill's complex, home to the Ceol, the Irish traditional music centre, but the real highlight is the series of imposing gas torches that line the square, recalling the medieval character of Dublin. When lit, the torches are an impressive sight, visible even from the other side of the river.

Today, Dublin's most popular architectural folly is the Gravity Bar, perched atop one of Dublin's highest buildings, the Guinness Storehouse. This floor-to-ceiling glass-panelled circular room, which was originally intended to rotate throughout the day, looks like it has just landed from the far reaches of space, presumably, like all travellers to Dublin, to refuel on Guinness.

By George, It's Beautiful

Dublin's architectural apogee can roughly be placed in the period spanning the rule of the four English Georges, between the accession of George I in 1714 and the death of George IV in 1830. During this time, Dublin's Anglo-Irish Protestant gentry accumulated unprecedented wealth and dedicated themselves towards improving their city.

Roads were widened; gardens and city parks were landscaped; the Liffey was banked with concrete quays; and, most importantly, a number of outstanding architects designed a battery of fine private residences and imposing public buildings. Their inspiration was the work of the Italian architect Andrea Palladio (1508–80), the 16th century's foremost exponent of the theory that architecture should be governed by reason and the principles of classical antiquity. Although the Palladian style was all the rage in England – thanks to Inigo Jones (1573–1652), who returned from Italy in 1614 a converted Palladianist – when it was finally introduced to Ireland in the 1720s it underwent a number of subtle changes. The most obvious was the use of brick on the exterior, but equally important were the contrasts in detail – the use of coloured doors, the delicate tracery of the fanlights and the ironwork of the railings and balconies – which broke an otherwise austere uniformity. Consequently, the Irish version developed its own unique qualities and became known simply as the Georgian style.

The architect credited with its introduction to Dublin's cityscape was Sir Edward Lovett Pearce (1699–1733), who first arrived in Dublin in 1725. He managed to radically change Irish architecture, most notably with his masterpiece, the Parliament House (1728–39). It was the first two-chamber debating house in the world, with the main chamber, the House of Commons, topped by a massive Pantheon-style dome. Surrounding it was a public gallery that could seat up to 700 spectators. Pearce's other great contributions to Dublin architecture were the Lower and Upper Yards in Dublin Castle, although the latter were created according to the designs of Sir William Robinson. Pearce also created two private residences on Henrietta St, still the city's most unified Georgian street.

Pearce's influence on house design was immense and he more or less established the blueprint for all of the Georgian residences that followed. Dublin town houses typically have four storeys, including the basement, with symmetrically arranged windows and an imposing, often brightly painted front door. Granite steps lead up to the door, which, in the best examples, is further embellished with a delicate leaded fanlight.

Inside Dublin's finest Georgian houses, the decoration was usually marked by superbly crafted plasterwork. Some of the finest is the work of Michael Stapleton (1770–1803), which can be seen in Trinity College, Powerscourt House, Ely House near St Stephen's Green and Belvedere House in north Dublin. Also notable is the work of the LaFranchini brothers, Paolo (1693–1770) and Filippo (1702–79), in Newman House on St Stephen's Green and that of Robert West on the building next door and in Newbridge House at Donabate. West's own house is still standing at 20 Dominick St, near King's Inns in north Dublin.

A collaborator of Pearce's on the Parliament House project was the German architect Richard Cassels (1690–1751; aka Richard Castle), who came to Dublin in 1728. His major works include, in County Wicklow, Powerscourt House (1731) and Russborough House (1742–55), which has the largest frontage of any house in Ireland, and Carton House (1739–45) in County Kildare. In Dublin, he designed Nos 85 and 86 St Stephen's Green (1738), which in the 19th century would be joined and renamed Newman House, and Nos 80 and 81, which were bought by Benjamin Guinness in 1862 and altered to create Iveagh House, now the Department of Foreign Affairs. His work on the green was merely a foretaste of his urban masterpiece, Leinster House (1745–51). Commissioned by James Fitzgerald, the Earl of Kildare, Cassels created a country residence in an urban setting, even though at the time its position was ridiculed for being in the far-flung wilds of Dublin.

Dublin's frenzied construction boom attracted such notable architects as Swedish-born Sir William

By George, It's Beautiful

Chambers (1723–96), whose London works included the Pagoda in Kew Gardens (1757–62) and Somerset House (1776–86). Although he never actually visited Dublin, he drew up plans for some of its most impressive Georgian buildings. These included two major projects in Trinity College, the Examination Hall (1779–91) and the Chapel (1798). His most important contributions, however, were Charlemont House (1763), now the Hugh Lane Municipal Gallery of Modern Art, and one of Dublin's most intriguing structures, the Casino at Marino (1755–79).

It was during the last two decades of the 18th century that the city came to match London for grandeur. The Anglo-Irish Ascendancy had unprecedented power over their own affairs, and their confidence seemed boundless. Of all the great architects that worked in Dublin in those years, James Gandon (1743–1823) towered above the rest, and it was his public buildings that did more than most to reflect Dublin's ambitions. His Custom House (1781–91) and Four Courts (1786–1802) remain two of Dublin's most enduring landmarks.

Gandon's great rival in Dublin was Thomas Cooley (1745–84), who was originally entrusted with the commission for the Four Courts but lost out to Gandon when the latter presented more impressive plans. In 1779 Cooley had beaten Gandon into second place in the competition for the design of the Royal Exchange (now City Hall), but upon his death the project was awarded to Gandon, who incorporated Cooley's original design in the far grander scheme visible today. Gandon's last public building was the Law Society at King's Inns (1795–1818), designed to provide housing and study facilities for barristers. Sadly, the project was plagued by delays and in 1808 Gandon handed over the reins to his pupil Henry Aaron Baker.

The Act of Union of 1801, which closed the Irish Parliament and brought Ireland directly under Westminster's rule, was the death knell for the Georgian boom. Francis Johnston (1760–1829) was the last great Georgian architect. When Parliament House was sold in 1803, provisions were made that it could no longer serve as a debating chamber, and Johnston was hired to adapt the building. He radically altered the House of Commons, but he surreptitiously maintained the architectural integrity of the House of Lords. Johnston was also responsible for a number of other Georgian-style buildings, most notably St George's Church (1802), the General Post Office (GPO; 1814) and the addition of an Ionic portico to the Lord Lieutenant's residence in Phoenix Park (1816), now the Irish president's residence, Áras an Uachtaráin.

The collapse of the Irish Parliament and ensuing dip in the city's fortunes put an end to widespread urban development until the 1960s. The result is that large chunks of modern Dublin are still of a piece – of an 18th century piece. The splendid Georgian streets and squares remain Dublin's finest architectural elements.

James Gandon's magnificent Four Courts (1786–1802) were built at the height of the Georgian boom years.

James Joyce & *Ulysses*

Of course, no commentary on Dublin writers is possible without reference to James Joyce, Ireland's most famous author. The man who claimed Dublin could be rebuilt from scratch using his descriptions as a plan spent most of his adult life overseas. He was born in Dublin in 1882 and was the eldest of the 10 Joyce children to survive beyond infancy. His father's roller-coaster financial situation led to a rather varied education, which included a two year spell of self-education at home. He completed his school years at Belvedere College (the building stands on Great Denmark St in north Dublin) and went on to University College, Dublin. He was determined to become a writer when he graduated in 1902, but then considered studying medicine and wandered between Dublin and Paris for the next couple of years.

In 1904 three short stories appeared in an Irish farmers' magazine, written under the pen name Stephen Dedalus; these were later to form part of *Dubliners*. In late 1904, Joyce abandoned Ireland and moved to Pula in what was then Austria-Hungary (now in Croatia) with Nora Barnacle, whom he was not to marry until 27 years later. In 1905 they moved on to Trieste, in Italy, where their two children were born and where he revised *Stephen Hero*, a novel he had started in Dublin, into *A Portrait of the Artist as a Young Man*. He returned to Ireland twice in 1909, but efforts to find a publisher for *Dubliners* failed. It was finally published in 1914, but not until after the first manuscript had been destroyed when the publisher objected to its use of real locations, its language and the stories.

The outbreak of WWI forced the family to move to Zürich, Switzerland, in 1915, where Joyce began work on *Ulysses*. He was always convinced of his own genius but English lessons and grants from literary societies and admirers were his only means of support at the time. His life was further complicated by recurrent eye problems that led to 25 operations for glaucoma, cataracts and other

Literature

Of all the arts it's in literature that Ireland has had the most impact. No other city, Dubliners are proud to boast, can claim three Nobel Prize winners for literature. There's even a Dublin Writers' Museum, which traces Ireland's literary history. Books also take centre stage at Marsh's Library, the Chester Beatty Library and, of course, at the Book of Kells exhibit in the library of Trinity College.

Although writing goes back so far in Ireland – Irish monks were copying Bibles and spreading their learning abroad while England was still in the Dark Ages – it's the Irish mastery of English that is most renowned. One theory to explain this mastery suggests that even though Irish is now a minority language, English is in some respects still a foreign tongue to be played and experimented with in a manner that, say, an English writer would never dare. Using turns of phrase and expressions translated directly from Irish, as well as a perspective unique to Ireland, authors have been able to transform written English to great success. Indeed, Dublin has produced so many writers and has been written about so much that you could easily plan a Dublin literary holiday. *A Literary Guide to Dublin*, by Vivien Igoe, includes detailed route maps, a guide to cemeteries and an eight-page section on literary and historical pubs.

See the boxed texts 'James Joyce & *Ulysses*' and 'Dublin Writers' and 'Deep Thinker, Heavy Drinker' later in this chapter, as well as the Books section in the Facts for the Visitor chapter for more information on books about Dublin.

Dance

The most important form of dance in Ireland is traditional Irish dancing, performed at *céilidhs* (communal dances), often in an impromptu format and always accompanied by an Irish traditional band. In recent years, the phenomenal worldwide success of *Riverdance* and its various spin-offs, including Michael Flatley's *Lord of the Dance*, have done much to revive interest in traditional Irish dancing, making the form sexy, perhaps for the first time ever. However, while these shows have been influenced by Irish dancing

James Joyce & *Ulysses*

difficulties. *A Portrait of the Artist as a Young Man* was finally published in 1916 and in 1918 the US magazine *Little Review* started to publish extracts from *Ulysses*. Notoriety was already pursuing his epic work and the censors prevented further episodes from being published after 1920.

In 1920 Joyce decided to return to Dublin on a visit. He stopped off in Paris where he was persuaded by Ezra Pound to prolong his stay. Joyce once remarked about his decision, 'I came to Paris for a week and stayed 20 years'. It was a good move for the struggling writer. In 1922, Sylvia Beach of the Paris bookshop Shakespeare & Co finally managed to put *Ulysses* into print. Its earlier censorship difficulties ensured it instant success. *Ulysses* follows its characters around Dublin during a single day (16 June 1904, the day Joyce met Nora Barnacle). During this remarkable journey various episodes parallel the voyage of Homer's *Odyssey*, but this literary invention was only a small part of the novel's total achievement. The book ends with Molly Bloom's famous stream of consciousness discourse, a chapter of eight huge and totally unpunctuated paragraphs.

The book's sexually explicit episodes led to the book, 20th-century masterpiece or not, being banned in the USA and the UK. After long delays, *Ulysses* was finally published in the USA in 1933, but not until 1937 in the UK.

Ulysses has been described as one of the 'great unread works of the English language' and may have bent English into totally new and hitherto unthought-of shapes, but Joyce's final work, *Finnegan's Wake* (published in 1939), was even more complex and went part way to inventing a new language, adding further complications through multilingual wordplays. In 1940 WWII drove the Joyce family back to Zürich where the author died in 1941.

---

and feature some extraordinary dancers, they are largely commercial ventures meant for New York's Broadway rather than the dusty halls of rural Ireland. Unfortunately, Dublin is not the best place to engage in, or watch, this form of dancing, its home being in the west and south-west of the country.

Music

Literature may be the field in which Irish artists have had the greatest influence, but their input into the world of music cannot be underestimated. From traditional music right through to the most contemporary pop, tiny Ireland has been disproportionately represented on the world stage. What's more, Irish music has been incredibly influential on a number of genres, not least American country & western, which is a fusion of Irish traditional tunes and the Mississippi Delta blues. And of course everyone has heard of U2, the quintessential Dublin rock band, who have spawned thousands of imitators and in the process joined the ranks of the great dinosaur bands. While in Dublin, you will find that just as pubs are an intrinsic part

of the Dublin lifestyle, music is an intrinsic part of the pub lifestyle, even if for the most part it is modern dance music and rock, rather than traditional tunes, that will be the soundtrack of your visit.

Traditional Music In Ireland, traditional music has survived with greater vigour in Ireland than has comparable music in other European countries, and has influenced Irish musicians working in other musical forms. One of the best examples is a group called the Afro-Celt Foundation, whose style is a great blend of African rhythms and Irish traditional forms.

A wide variety of instruments is used in traditional Irish music, but the most notably Irish include the harp, which is also the country's national emblem; the *bodhrán* (pronounced ''bough-rawn'), a goatskin drum; and the *uillean* pipes, which are played with a bellows squeezed under the elbow (*uillean* in Irish). The fiddle is less purely Irish, but is a mainstay of traditional music, along with the accordion, the banjo and simple tin whistles or spoons. Unaccompanied music fits

Dublin Writers

Jonathan Swift (1667–1745), the master satirist and author of *Gulliver's Travels*, was the greatest Dublin writer of the early Georgian period but he was followed by many others, such as Oliver Goldsmith (1728–74), author of *The Vicar of Wakefield*, and Thomas Moore (1779–1852), whose poems formed the repertoire of generations of Irish tenor singers.

Oscar Wilde (1854–1900) is renowned for his legendary wit, but he was also a writer of immense talent and striking sensitivity. His best-known works are his plays, including *The Importance of Being Earnest* and his delightful children's tale *The Happy Prince*, but critics agree that his most important and mature work is the *Ballad of Reading Gaol*, which he wrote while serving a prison sentence for his homosexuality. Sadly, Wilde paid a heavy toll for the harsh prison conditions and the ignorance of Victorian society, dying not long after his release.

Oscar Wilde

William Butler Yeats (1865–1939) is best remembered as a poet (his collections include *The Tower* and *The Winding Stair*) though he also wrote plays. He helped found the Abbey Theatre, served as senator in the early years of the Irish Free State and in 1938 received one of Dublin's three Nobel Prizes for literature. Playwright and essayist George Bernard Shaw (1856–1950), author of *Pygmalion* and *Saint Joan*, and Samuel Beckett (1906–89), proponent of the theatre of the absurd, who wrote the groundbreaking play *Waiting for Godot*, were the other two prizewinners.

Oliver St John Gogarty (1878–1957) bore a lifelong grudge against James Joyce because of his appearance as Buck Mulligan in Joyce's *Ulysses*. Gogarty presented his own views of Dublin in *As I Was Going Down Sackville Street* (1937) and other volumes of his memoirs. Like Oscar Wilde, he was a renowned wit.

The Informer (1925) by Liam O'Flaherty (1896–1984) is the classic book about the divided sympathies that plagued Ireland during its independence struggle and the ensuing civil war. *The Ginger Man* (1955) by JP Donleavy is a high-energy foray around Dublin from the Trinity College perspective. It received the Catholic Church's 'seal of approval' by being banned in Ireland for many years. From a later era Christy Brown's marvellous *Down All the Days* (1970), set in the '40s and '50s, summed up Dublin's backstreet energy with equal abandon and, together with his first autobiography *My Left Foot*, was the basis for the acclaimed film.

Modern Dublin has continued to produce excellent writers, many of whom have gone on to international recognition. Dublin schoolteacher Roddy Doyle has made a big name for himself with his comic trilogy on north Dublin life – *The Commitments* (1987), *The Snapper* (1990) and *The Van* (1991) – all of which were made into films. His *Paddy Clarke, Ha Ha Ha*, about a Dublin family, won the 1993 Booker Prize. His most recent books, *The Woman Who Walked into Doors* (1997) and *A Star Called Henry* (2000), see Doyle abandon light social comedy in favour of a more mature, observational narrative punctuated with black humour. Patrick McCabe's *Butcher Boy* (1993), was nominated for the Booker Prize and was also turned into a successful film.

NICKY CAVEN

WB Yeats

Dublin Writers

Dermot Bolger's *The Journey Home* (1990) depicts the underside of modern Dublin at its darkest. Political corruption, drugs, violence, unemployment and a pervading sense of hopelessness make this a gloomy book, though it still hurtles along at a fast pace. John McGahern is another modern Irish writer, with titles such as *The Barracks* (1963) and *Amongst Women* (1990) to his credit. Aidan Carl Mathews' work includes the novel *Muesli at Midnight* (1998), which tells of a condemned man's last hours in a prison cell.

Ireland's most important modern writer is John Banville, literary editor of the *Irish Times*. His impressive body of work includes the Booker Prize-winning *Book of Evidence* (1989) and his excellent trilogy *Doctor Copernicus* (1976), *Kepler* (1981) and *The Newton Letter* (1982). *The Untouchable* (1997), is a controversial novel based on the life of Cold War spy Anthony Blunt. His latest novel, *Eclipse* (2000), is about a fictional actor of some renown who simply walks away from his successful life

George Bernard Shaw

and retires to his childhood home. Also worth checking out is novelist Colm Toibin, an excellent writer whose books include *The Heather Blazing* (1994*), The Story of the Night* (1998) and his most recent, *The Blackwater Lightship* (2000).

Ireland has produced its share of women writers. Edna O'Brien enjoyed the accolade of having her *The Country Girls* (1960) banned. Molly Keane wrote several books in the 1920s and 1930s under the pseudonym MJ Farrell, then had a literary second life in her 70s when *Good Behaviour* and *Time after Time* came out under her real name. Maeve Binchy is the writer of blockbusters, which just rise above the sex-and-shopping genre. Her books have lots of Irish settings and *Circle of Friends*, set in Dublin, was made into a film in 1995.

A New Book of Dubliners, edited by Ben Forkner, is a fine collection of Dublin-related short stories written by authors including James Joyce, Oliver St John Gogarty, Liam O'Flaherty, Samuel Beckett, Flann O'Brien, Sean O'Faolain, Benedict Kiely and others. *Finbar's Hotel* (1996), edited by Dermot Bolger, is a collection of short stories by the young lions of the Irish literary scene; all the stories are based in a city-centre hotel, which is certainly the U2-owned Clarence Hotel on Wellington Quay. The

NICKY CAVEN

Samuel Beckett

most recent is the *Penguin Book of Irish Fiction* (2001), edited by Colm Toibin and featuring stories by local talent from Jonathan Swift to Emma Donaghue.

Although Dublin and Ireland played a central part in the work of writers such as Joyce, others became such international names that their Dublin origins are virtually forgotten. As well as Oscar Wilde, George Bernard Shaw and Bram Stoker (1847–1912), the creator of *Dracula*, were both products of the city. In an earlier era it was Dubliner Richard Steele who founded those resolutely English magazines the *Tatler* (1709) and the *Spectator* (1711).

But what about the future? There are plenty of young writers willing and ready to fill the shoes of their illustrious predecessors. A quick scan through the lists of newcomers reveals that the quality of Irish writing is still excellent and that such names as Pat Boran, Philip McCann, Emer Martin and Emma Donoghue will undoubtedly carry the Irish literary torch onwards.

into five main categories (jigs, reels, hornpipes, polkas and slow airs) while there are two main styles of song (*sean nós*, old-style tunes often sung in Irish, either unaccompanied or with the backing of a bodhrán, and more familiar ballads).

As with Irish dancing, Dublin is not the best place to hear traditional sounds, even if there are a number of pubs that put on a 'trad lite' show strictly for tourist consumption (see the Pubs & Bars section in the Entertainment chapter for the best places to hear traditional music). However, it's not even necessary to go to a pub to find music, as buskers are busy in Dublin's streets at all hours of the day, although in this increasingly cosmopolitan city you're as likely to hear Romanian folk tunes or flamenco as traditional Dublin ballads.

Of the groups playing traditional Irish music, perhaps the best known is the Chieftains, and adding the words come bands such as Scullion, the Wolfe Tones and the Fureys. Groups such as Clannad from Donegal, Altan, Dervish and Nomos espouse a quieter, more mystical style of singing best exemplified by the multiple Grammy-winning work of Enya, formerly of Clannad, but now pursuing a successful career in her own right. The enormously popular Dubliners have been around for over 30 years, and while they are more of a folk band than an Irish traditional outfit, they have carried the flag for Irish music since the mid-1960s.

Popular Music Ireland also has a very rich tradition of singer-songwriters, and while many might not be from Dublin, they inevitably end up in the capital as it is the best place for their work to become known. The godfather of them all is Christy Moore, who is enormously popular at home for his ability to capture the essence of ordinary people's concerns in his music. Young up-and-comers include songwriters like Paddy Casey, who is backed by Ireland's most powerful manager, Paul McGuinness (of U2 fame). Singer-songwriter Brian Kennedy has been acclaimed for his mellifluous voice, but his style is on the safe side of easy-listening.

Female singer-songwriters have an equally strong following. For over a decade singers like Mary and Frances Black, Mary Coughlan and Eleanor McEvoy have done well enough, but their coat-tails are being severely tugged by a new crop of young stars whose style is a lot more punchy. The best known of these are Northern Irish sensation Juliet Turner and local star Gemma Hayes.

Ireland's contribution to the rock scene has also been fairly important. In the 1970s and 1980s, bands such as Thin Lizzy, the Boomtown Rats and punk outfits The Undertones and Stiff Little Fingers put Ireland on the world rock map, but none has achieved the untrammelled success of U2. Although now in the twilight of their incredible 21-year career, they still managed to win a Grammy award for Best Single in 2001.

In a class of his own is Belfast-born Van Morrison. Van 'the Man' has been playing his rhythm-and-blues-tinged rock since the 1960s, when he was the front man for the band Them. This cantankerous old genius may have slowed down in recent years, but his worldwide hardcore following remains as strong as ever.

Of the newer Irish bands, the most interesting are The Frames, fronted by former Commitments star Glen Hansard. They've been on the scene for nearly 10 years, but the release of their most recent album, *For the Birds*, has been their most successful by far.

Purists may scoff (and usually do), but Ireland is also fairly well represented in the 'treacle-pop' category. Completely manufactured Boyzone were a runaway phenomenon that more serious pop bands could only dream of. They went their separate ways in 2000, but front man Ronan Keating continues to hit the top of the charts. Boyzone's empty shoes were soon filled by boy wonders Westlife, who recently matched the Beatles' British record of seven number one singles in a row. They were quick to scotch any comparison between them and the Fab Four... even if no-one was making one.

The newest star to emerge is Samantha Mumba, originally from Zaire but raised in Dublin, whose brand of poppy R'n'B was an instant success. The wholesome Corrs from Dundalk have also achieved international success. It seems MOR rock is still as popular as ever.

See the Entertainment chapter for information about music in Dublin and where to find it.

Visual Arts

With the exception of Jack B Yeats (1871–1957), most Irish painters are unknown to all but a dedicated few, and it is commonly assumed that the illustrative arts have never reached the heights they did during the early Christian period, when such masterpieces as the Book of Kells were produced. Yet Ireland has produced other important artists of notable international stature. The National Gallery has an extensive Irish School collection, much of it chronicling the personages and pursuits of the Anglo-Irish aristocracy. Respected portrait painters were Garrett Murphy (1680–1716) and James Latham (1696–1747). In the 19th century, the dominating figure in landscape painting was Nathaniel Hone (1831–1917), who was born in Ireland but worked exclusively in France until 1875, when he returned to his home in north County Dublin. Roderic O'Conor (1861–1940) was the Irish Van Gogh; a painter of great range and distinction who, like the Dutch genius, was attracted to France and never returned. He hated art dealers, rarely sold or exhibited his paintings (though the writer Somerset Maugham got his hands on a few), and became a leading exponent of the Impressionist style.

Irish Modernism is widely recognised to have begun with Jack B Yeats, whose father John was a noted portraitist. Like his brother William, he was a champion of the Celtic Revival Movement, and the characters he painted were usually strong, isolated and solitary. Yeats' range was extraordinary and he was a seemingly effortless master of all of painting's techniques, from watercolour to oils. But most modern Irish artists turned their backs on the nationalism that so defined the work of Yeats. Mainie Jellett (1896–1943) and Evie Hone (1894–1955) were the most important abstract painters of the 1930s and 1940s, and as such are considered two of the most important innovators in modern Irish

painting. In the 1950s, the self-taught Louis LeBrocquy (born 1916) finally gained recognition, even though his critics argue that his work is derivative, over-influenced by the work of such painters as Manet, Degas and – in later years – Francis Bacon (who was born in Dublin). Still, LeBrocquy is perhaps the most important living Irish painter.

Today, Ireland is undergoing another artistic revolution. The New York-based Sean Scully is perhaps the best known of the lot, but he is in fine company, with artists such as Brian Maguire, Dorothy Cross, Mick Mulcahy and Kathy Prendergrast. The Irish-born Michael Craig Martin is another key figure, though he is best known for teaching the new school of British artists, including the bad boy himself, Damien Hirst.

Cinema

Ireland has never had a particularly rich film-making tradition, though hopes were high when James Joyce opened Dublin's first cinema, the Volta, on Mary St in 1909. This absence of a tradition of film-making is largely due to the success of British cinema, which drew the cream of Irish talent across the sea to its own studios, and the general lack of government finance for a domestic film industry. Until the early 1990s, the release of an Irish-made film was greeted with much fanfare, infrequent as it was. This has changed in recent years, however, and as more money is being spent on the promotion of a home-grown film industry (including a very attractive tax incentive package offered by the government), the number of Irish film-makers making their mark on world cinema is slowly increasing.

A number of semi-state bodies have been instrumental in promoting the film industry, including Bord Scannán na hÉireann (Irish Film Board) and the Audiovisual Federation of the Irish Business and Employers Confederation (IBEC), whose membership consists of independent film-makers, TV broadcasters, animators and others. The Film Institute of Ireland/Irish Film Centre also plays an active role in promoting local productions, through the promotion of film culture, the management of the Irish Film Archive and its ownership of the IFC, the only cinema in Dublin that features nonmainstream films.

Ireland, however, has never had a shortage of quality actors and many have achieved international acclaim. We must mention in passing that such notables as Orson Welles and Jimmy Stewart got their first big breaks in Dublin's Gate Theatre, but they were far from Irish – Dubliners are simply content to believe that without their experiences in Ireland they might never have gone as far as they did! Liam Neeson *(Schindler's List)*, Daniel Day-Lewis *(My Left Foot)* and Brenda Fricker *(My Left Foot)* have all won Oscars, while Dublin-born Gabriel Byrne has starred in a series of hits including *The Usual Suspects* and *The Man in the Iron Mask*.

Add to this the success of Dublin director Neil Jordan (whose film credits include *Interview with the Vampire, The Crying Game* and *Michael Collins*) and Dublin producer Noel Pearson (who produced *My Left Foot* and *Dancing at Lughnasa,* based on Brian Friel's play) and the list of local talent is looking pretty good. Treasure Films, a Dublin-based production company run by director Paddy Breathnach and producer Rob Walpole were responsible for Ireland's spin on the Tarantino-esque gangster movie, *I Went Down*. Stuart Townsend is another emerging star, having starred in a number of British-made films, including most recently *All about Adam,* also starring American actress Kate Hudson. Peter McDonald, who starred in *I Went Down* as well, is another emerging talent, as is Karl Geary, the Dublin-born, New York-based actor who has appeared in a number of American films. See Films in the Facts for the Visitor Chapter for details of films set in Dublin.

Theatre

Dublin has a theatrical history as long as its literary one. The city's first theatre was founded in Werburgh St in 1637. Although it was closed by the Puritans only four years later, another theatre named the Smock Alley Playhouse, or Theatre Royal, opened in 1661 and continued for over a century.

The late-19th-century Celtic Revival and

the establishment of the Abbey Theatre by WB Yeats and Lady Gregory may be the first images that spring to mind when Irish theatre is mentioned today, but many plays from an earlier era are still staged. Oliver Goldsmith found fame as a playwright, for *She Stoops to Conquer* (1773), as well as a novelist. Richard Brinsley Sheridan (1751 –1816) introduced the word 'malapropism' to the language via the tongue-twisted Mrs Malaprop from his play *The Rivals* (1775).

The 19th and 20th centuries were rich times for Irish playwrights too. Of course there were Oscar Wilde and George Bernard Shaw (see the boxed text 'Dublin Writers' earlier in this chapter). JM Synge (1871– 1909) transposed the wonderful language of the Irish peasantry – full of bawdy witticisms and eloquent invective – into his plays. His portrayal of the brutality of peasant life in his most famous play, *The Playboy of the Western World* (1907), resulted in near riots when it first opened at the Abbey. Equally controversial was Sean O'Casey (1880–1964), who wrote a powerful trilogy on life in Dublin's slums, *Shadow of a Gunman* (1923), *Juno and the Paycock* (1924) and *The Plough and the Stars* (1926). The lesser-known Lennox Robinson (1886–1958) was also an important contributor to Irish drama; his best works were *Patriots* (1912), a comedy called *The Whiteheaded Boy* (1916) and *The Lost Leader* (1918). In later years he became director of the Abbey. Brendan Behan (1923– 64; see the boxed text, 'Deep Thinker, Heavy Drinker', right) may have drunk himself into an early grave, but he produced a number of important plays in his turbulent life, including *The Quare Fellow* (1954) and *The Hostage* (1958). Although Dublin-born Samuel Beckett (1906–89) spent most of his adult life in Paris and wrote much of his work in French, he is still thought of as an Irish playwright. Many consider his *Waiting for Godot* (1953) to be the modernist theatrical masterpiece. In 1969 his genius was recognised with the Nobel Prize for Literature.

The Abbey today is not nearly as controversial as it was when Synge, Lady Gregory and Yeats had a hand in the playbill. Its role as the national theatre of Ireland ensures

Deep Thinker, Heavy Drinker

JANE SMITH

Brendan Behan

Following a visit to Canada, novelist, playwright and journalist Brendan Behan (1923–64) said 'I arrived at the airport and there was a giant sign which said 'Drink Canada Dry'. So I did'. There are plenty of witty anecdotes about Behan's legendary drinking, each told with the kind of pathos-ridden gusto that is the flavour of so much pub talk. What the anecdotes omit to tell, however, is that Behan's alcoholism scarred his life, made a mockery of his immense talent and eventually killed him.

Behan's relatively short life was not uneventful. From earliest youth he was an ardent republican and acutely sensitive to social injustice; themes that would become central to all of his writings. At 17 he was sentenced to three years' detention in England for sabotage – the fruit of his labours as an IRA volunteer. Deported back to Ireland in 1942, he ran afoul of the law at home and served four years of a 14-year sentence for the attempted murder of a policeman. Upon his release, he decided to become a writer, moved to Paris, but returned in 1950 when he got his first job, writing scripts and short stories for television. Three years later, he landed a job as a columnist for the *Irish Press*, and over the next 10 years he wrote about his beloved Dublin, using wonderful, earthy satire and a keen sense of political commentary that set him apart from other journalists. A collection of his newspaper columns were published in 1963 under the title *Hold Your Hour and Have Another*.

In 1954 he wrote his first play, based on his experience of imprisonment in Dublin's Mountjoy Jail. *The Quare Fellow* was an immediate success, and the play's powerful commentary on the fundamental wrong of capital punishment went down well with audiences in London (1956) and New York (1958). In 1958 he published *Borstal Boy*, an autobiographical account of his earlier imprisonment in England, a tragi-comic classic of prison experience.

That same year, however, he put on his second play, *The Hostage*, considered to be his masterpiece. He uses satire to devastating effect in his portrayal of an English soldier ransomed by the IRA for republican prisoners. The play's delicate subject matter made its resounding London success all the more surprising, leading the now famous Behan to comment, 'the English are wonderful... first they put me in prison, then they made me rich!'

For the rest of his life Behan struggled with the fame that rewarded his talent. His drinking, which began at the early age of eight, became more pronounced, particularly as his drinking jags became the subject of Dublin folklore. He continued writing, producing some extraordinary poetry and a number of books, including *The Scarperer* (1964) and *Confessions of an Irish Rebel* (1964). Despite his genius, however, Behan's last years were a disaster. His drunken antics constantly landed him in prison and hospital, and he managed to have himself barred from dozens of Dublin pubs. His fans, however, forgave him everything and even encouraged him, lapping up his brilliant wit and observations – now delivered in semi-coherent ramblings – as they sought to make a tragic hero out of a man in desperate trouble. Addled by booze, Behan was incapable of reversing his decline and he died of cirrhosis of the liver on 20 March 1964.

that it continues to attract the cream of the acting crop but it hardly pushes the boundaries of theatrical experimentation. However, after several decades in the creative doldrums, Irish theatre is undergoing something of a renaissance thanks to a number of newer companies that stage challenging, thought-provoking contemporary plays as well as new spins on old classics.

Rough Magic, which has achieved notable success through the work of Declan Hughes, specialises in the work of contemporary Irish writers. Pig's Back have earned acclaim for their contemporary take on the classics, such as Molière set in modern times. Cornmarket is a much more experimental group, featuring the work of its co-founder Michael West. His most recent play, *Foley* (2001), is a one-man show exploring the underlying tensions of life in an upper middle-class Irish Protestant family.

Conor McPherson is a talented playwright whose most successful work, *The Weir*, won an Olivier award in 1999. The enormously popular Martin McDonagh was born in London of Irish parents but sets all of his work in the west of Ireland. He had a smash hit on Broadway with *The Beauty Queen of Leenane* (1998), a driving narrative tale that was acclaimed by critics and made its director, Garry Hynes, the first woman ever to win a Tony for direction. The most recent arrival onto the scene is Mark O'Rowe, who thrilled London audiences with *Howie the Rookie* (1999). In 2001, his new play *Made in China* earned him plenty of good reviews.

See the Entertainment chapter for more details about Dublin's theatres.

SOCIETY & CONDUCT

Ireland's economic success, social changes and cultural changes are dispelling old stereotypes of the country as a predominantly poor, rural, agrarian backwater unable to stop the exodus of its children. It has a booming economy that has embraced high technology, and a young population and flourishing arts.

While this holds true for the majority of Ireland, it is especially so in Dublin. The city has a long tradition of liberal cosmopolitanism, and its citizens pride themselves on living in one of the most easy-going capitals in the world. Social stratification exists, but movement between classes is fairly fluid and all to do with personal wealth rather than birth or background. Dubliners have, for the most part, a keen sense of their own history, and the memories of British rule have made them suspicious of any group or class aspiring to establish any kind of permanent foothold on the social ladder. In Dublin, it is an unwritten social rule that no-one is better than anyone else, some just have more money than others.

Yet the growing gap between the 'haves'

and the 'have-nots' has widened at an alarming rate. Many Dubliners are enjoying their share of the Celtic Tiger's success, but it hasn't reached areas such as the Dublin housing estates where drugs and crime are a major problem. Politicians pay constant lip-service to the need to redress the balance, to ensure that wealth is distributed more evenly, but in reality the situation is just getting worse. Property prices in the city have increased by over 150% since 1990 with no signs of levelling off, cutting out a large proportion of the population from the buyers' market. Those living below the poverty line (set at 60% of the average national wage) rose from 31% of the population in 1991 to 38% in 1998. It's paradoxical that there should be a rise in the number of poor at a time of unprecedented national wealth.

The abortion issue, still a bone of contention, has been temporarily resolved in a typically Irish compromise. While abortion is still illegal, it is no longer illegal to provide information on abortion, and women who travel to Britain to terminate their pregnancies can do so without fear of legal sanction. Still, the debate continues, and former president Mary Robinson made a spectacular plea in October 1998 for the legalisation of abortion in Ireland. In 1995 divorce was narrowly accepted in a referendum, making Ireland the last nation in Europe to legalise it.

Dos & Don'ts

Dublin is relaxed and easy-going with few rigid rules and regulations. There is nobody you have to be especially wary of offending, and there are relatively few strict rules of behaviour or dress-code regulations, apart from those dreamed up by ungracious nightclub bouncers. You can jaywalk with impunity and lots of Dublin cyclists even seem to get away with chaining their bikes up to the 'do not park bicycles here' signs in the city.

That said, you should be aware that there is a marked difference in opinion and outlook between the older, more 'traditional' generation and the younger generations of Dubliners. While the former seem to accept that anything to do with such subjects as sex, contraception, divorce and abortion may be part and parcel of modern Ireland, they are still fundamentally suspicious of this social upheaval and are often less than willing to entertain a conversation on those subjects. Religious belief is still quite strong and they might take offence at a foreigner who doesn't respect their strongly held opinions on these matters.

Younger Dubliners couldn't be more different. They have embraced social change as long overdue and are often extremely liberal – and sometimes radical – in their views, almost as though they want to make up for lost time. It seems that the further they get from the old traditions the better! However, as with anywhere else, Dubliners don't like to be reminded of their faults by anybody but other Dubliners, so the best policy is to be relaxed and to accept the good things the people of Dublin have to offer.

RELIGION

Ireland is strongly Catholic, but has a substantial Protestant minority, as well as smaller numbers of adherents to other faiths. The powerful position of the Roman Catholic Church is a subject of considerable controversy and is frequently cited by the Northern Irish as a major barrier to unification. The constitution that was introduced by Eamon de Valera in 1937 noted the church's 'special position' in Ireland as the religion of 'the great majority of its citizens'. However, it didn't make Catholicism the country's official religion and in 1970 even the constitutional 'special position' was rescinded.

Over the last 40 years, the church's enormous influence over Irish life has slowly waned. Church attendance has steadily fallen and while most Irish still claim to be believers, there is a growing sense – especially among younger people – that the church is more and more out of step with modern times. While this growing disillusionment is a Europe-wide phenomenon, in Ireland it has had more tangibly dramatic effects, as small communities once bonded together by the pervasive influence of the local priest have begun to drift apart. Nevertheless, a remarkable statistic showed that in 2001, church attendance in Dublin rose marginally for the first time since 1960, perhaps as a reaction to the hedonistic materialism of the Celtic Tiger, which has seen God replaced with money as the object of many people's worship.

This rise is made all the more remarkable, however, considering the church's own recent scandals. In the last few years it has emerged that sexual impropriety – primarily paedophilia – in church-run schools over the last 40 years was a far more common occurrence than anyone supposed. Despite the widely publicised *mea culpa* of the church for the crimes of the past, its PR machine is struggling in its attempts to exercise some damage control.

The contraceptive pill and condoms are freely available, but in some areas are still taboo subjects not to be discussed. Although abortion is still banned, 25% of all women under 30 have had an abortion, a higher rate than more liberal countries such as the Netherlands – they simply go to Britain for the operation.

LANGUAGE

English is spoken throughout Dublin. Although Irish (a Gaelic language) is spoken in parts of rural Ireland (the north-west, west and south) known as Gaeltacht areas, you'll find that while all Dubliners must learn Irish in school, most of them speak a pidgin version of the language if at all. Still, Irish is considered the official language of Ireland and all official documents, street signs and official titles are either in Irish or bilingual. See the Glossary chapter for some useful Irish words.

Dubliners' command of English – particularly the inventive use of vocabulary – has been lauded throughout the English-speaking world. Furthermore, the various Dublin accents, which range from the quasi-received pronunciation (Oxbridge) of the city's wealthier (read south-side) citizens to the hard north-side and inner-city Dublin twang, are considered by many foreign visitors to have a gentle, mellifluous quality that makes Dubliners easier to understand than their counterparts in other English-speaking countries.

The syntax used by Dubliners – and the

Irish in general – involves a unique word order that is usually related to Irish: for instance, the usual word order in Irish sentences is verb, subject, object. The present participle is also used more frequently in sentences such as 'Would you be wanting a room for the night, then?'. Another linguistic peculiarity is the use of 'after' in such constructions as 'I'm just after my dinner', which is a way of saying 'I have just had my dinner' rather than suggesting that Dubliners chase a dinner that has got away.

Facts for the Visitor

WHEN TO GO

The weather is warmest in July and August and the daylight hours are long, but the crowds will be greatest, the costs the highest and accommodation harder to come by. In the quieter winter months, however, you may get miserable weather, the days are short and some tourist facilities will be shut. Visiting Dublin in June or September has a number of attractions: the weather can be better than at any other time of the year, it's less crowded and everything opens. A visit to Dublin during the weekend nearest St Patrick's Day (17 March) is also recommended. On this day the holiday is celebrated throughout the city centre with a parade, fireworks, street dancing and other special events.

ORIENTATION

The central area of Dublin is neatly divided by the River Liffey into southern and northern halves. The Viking and medieval city of Dublin developed first to the south of the river. The city's Georgian heyday began in the north then moved south again as the northern part prospered then declined.

Nowadays, the River Liffey marks a sharp divide in Dublin's fortunes. The further north you go, the poorer and more run-down Dublin tends to become. Conversely, the further south you go, the more prosperous the streets become.

North of the river, the most important streets for visitors are O'Connell St, the major shopping thoroughfare that leads north to Parnell Square, and Gardiner St, with lots of B&Bs. Many of the hostels are in this area. To the west, the Smithfield area (roughly behind the Four Courts) is emerging as a tourist magnet, although it will be some years before it realises its full potential. Busáras, the main bus station, and Connolly station, one of the two most important train stations, are near the southern end of Gardiner St, which is in the midst of recovering from a lengthy period of dilapidation. Im-

mediately south of the river is the hotspot of Dublin, Temple Bar, where you'll find a concentration of pubs, restaurants, shops and a number of art galleries. Nearby is Trinity College, which lies at the southern end of Grafton St, the city's most exclusive shopping street. On the south side you will also find the best examples of Georgian Dublin, with its stately homes and elegant parks.

Finding Addresses

There are several problems inherent in finding addresses in Dublin and the same problems exist in other Irish towns. One is the tendency for street names to change every few blocks. Another is that streets are subdivided into upper and lower (and even middle) or north and south. On maps, the 'upper' or 'lower' always appears at the end of the street name, and that convention has been followed on the maps in this book. However, in conversation the 'upper', 'lower', 'north' or 'south' is placed at the beginning of the street name, and this is how such names appear in the text of this book. So, on a map you will see Great George's St Lower, but in the text the same street will be referred to as Lower Great George's St. The use of 'south' and 'north' also usually means that the two streets are on opposite sides of the river, rather than running into one another. So, while South Great George's St is to be found off Dame St on the south side, North Great George's St is on the north side of the river, running parallel to Upper O'Connell St. Street numbering sometimes runs up one side of a street and down the other, rather than having odd numbers on one side and even on the other.

MAPS

For most purposes free maps of Dublin are quite adequate. The Dublin Tourism Centre has a basic map of the city centre covering the major sites to see (€0.65), but also has fairly detailed maps for hotels and restaurants. If you need an indexed street directory,

41

the *Dublin Street Guide* (scale 1:15,000, city centre 1:10,000) published by the Ordnance Survey (€10.15) is the best. A handy pocket version of the same (1:10,000) is also available (€4.50), but it does not include the outlying suburbs. The Ordnance Survey also publishes a *Map of Greater Dublin* (scale 1:20,000), which includes a street index and details of bus routes (€6). The Collins Streetfinder Map (scale 1:15,000) is also pretty good, with easy-to-use laminates that won't get damaged in the (inevitable) rain. It costs €6.

You can buy a limited selection of maps in most bookshops and some newsagents, but the *National Map Centre (☎ 476 0471, 34 Grafton Hall, Aungier St)* **(Map 5)** has a comprehensive selection of all OS maps and other geographic sundries.

RESPONSIBLE TOURISM

In a recent poll, German visitors ranked Dublin the dirtiest city in Europe, and it is true that the unseemly sight of litter hardly does the city any favours. While Dubliners are generally proud of their city, they don't really appear to have a visible sense of civic pride. Which, of course, doesn't mean that you shouldn't. Should visitors treat the city the way so many locals do, Dublin would probably drown in a sea of garbage. The oases of cleanliness that are the city's parks are meticulously kept by an ever-watchful team of guardians, and all entrants are expected to clean up after themselves and remove all litter.

If you're doing some walking in the countryside around Dublin, you should also be aware of the pressure on the ecology. Ireland's system of walking trails, called ways, has been established with the co-operation and good will of various bodies, including private landowners, local authorities and voluntary workers. Walkers therefore need to use the ways sensitively by, for instance, minimising disturbance to farm animals and farmland, and by taking home all rubbish, plastics in particular.

For information on conservation issues in and around Dublin check out ENFO's Web site at **W** www.enfo.ie.

TOURIST OFFICES
Local Tourist Offices

The main tourist office is the Dublin Tourism Centre (Map 7; ☎ 605 7700, **e** information@ dublintourism.ie, **W** www.visitdublin.com), in (the now deconsecrated) St Andrew's Church, 2 Suffolk St, Dublin 2. Here you'll find pretty much everything you'll need to kick-start your Dublin visit, including a vast selection of brochures, leaflets and maps as well as a bookshop, cafe, bureau de change and car rental desk. You can also book accommodation and tours, as well as buy tickets for concerts, the theatre and other events. There is a booking fee of €3.80 for all accommodation, €6.35 if it's self-catering. There is also a 10% deposit that is refunded through your hotel bill. The office opens 9am to 5.30pm Monday to Saturday, September to June; 8.30am to 6.30pm Monday to Saturday and 10.30am to 3pm on Sunday, July and August. It can get extremely crowded, with long queues for accommodation and bookings. Luckily, the system works on a take-a-number-and-wait basis, so you can grab a coffee and sit in the cafe while you wait!

If you arrive by sea at Dun Laoghaire, there is a tourist office in the ferryport terminal. It opens 10am to 6pm Monday to Saturday. If you arrive by air, the office is in the main arrivals hall at Dublin Airport. It opens 8am to 10pm daily. The other city-centre branches of Dublin Tourism are at 14 O'Connell St (Map 4), open 9am to 5pm Monday to Saturday; and at Baggot St Bridge (Map 5), in the foyer of the Bord Fáilte office, open 9.30am to noon and 12.30pm to 5pm weekdays. Finally, there is another branch in the Square Shopping Centre in Tallaght, south of the city centre. It opens 9.30am to noon and 12.30pm to 5pm Monday to Saturday.

The head office of Bord Fáilte, the Irish Tourist Board (Map 5; ☎ 1 850 230 330, **e** info@irishtouristboard.ie, **W** www.ireland .travel.ie), is at Baggot St Bridge (entrance on Wilton Terrace). It opens 9am to 5.15pm Monday to Friday.

None of the tourist information offices in Dublin will provide information over the phone. All telephone bookings and reservations are operated by Gulliver Info Res, a computerised information and reservation service that is available at all walk-in offices but, more impressively, from anywhere in the world. It provides up-to-date information on events, attractions and transport, and can also book accommodation. In Ireland, call ☎ 1 800 668 668; from Britain call ☎ 0 800 668 668 66; from the rest of the world call ☎ 00 353 669 792 083.

Tourist Offices Abroad
Offices of Bord Fáilte abroad include:

Australia (☎ 02-9299 6177, e itb@bigpond.com) 5th floor, 36 Carrington St, Sydney, NSW 2000
France (☎ 01 70 20 00 20, e info@irlande-tourisme.fr) 33 rue de Miromesnil, 75008 Paris
Germany (☎ 069-6680 0950, e info@irishtouristboard.de) Untermainanlage 7, 60329 Frankfurt-am-Main
Netherlands (☎ 020-504 0689, e info@irishtouristboard.ne) Spuistraat 104, 1012 VA Amsterdam
New Zealand (☎ 09-379 8720, e patrick.flynn@walshes.co.nz) Dingwall Bldg, 2nd floor, 87 Queen St, Auckland 1
Northern Ireland (☎ 028-9032 7888, e info@irishtouristboard.ie) 53 Castle St, Belfast BT1 1GH
UK (☎ 08000 397 000, e info@irishtouristboard.co.uk) Ireland House, 150 New Bond St, London W1S 2AQ
USA (☎ 212-418 0800 or 1 800 223 6470, e info@irishtouristboard.com) 345 Park Ave, New York, NY 10154

DOCUMENTS
Visas
Citizens of most western countries don't need a visa to visit Ireland. UK nationals born in Great Britain or Northern Ireland don't require a passport, though may be asked for some form of identification. Visas are required from Indians, Pakistanis, non-UK passport Hong Kong citizens and citizens of some African states. See Embassies & Consulates later in this chapter for addresses of where to apply for visa extensions if necessary.

Travel Insurance
A travel insurance policy to cover theft, loss and medical problems is a wise idea. Citizens

of EU countries are eligible for free medical care (with an E111 certificate, which they must obtain from their local health authority before travelling), but other visitors should have medical insurance or be prepared to pay. There is a wide variety of policies and your travel agency will have recommendations. Make sure the policy includes health care and medication in the countries you plan to visit en route to Ireland, covers 'dangerous' activities, such as diving or rock climbing, if they're on your agenda, and includes a flight home for you, and anyone you're travelling with, should your condition warrant it.

Driving Licence & Permits
If you take your own vehicle, you should always carry a Vehicle Registration Document as proof that it's yours. Your normal driving licence is legal for one year from the date you last entered Ireland, unless you have an EU licence, which is treated the same as an Irish licence. If you have a driving licence from outside the EU, it's generally a good idea to obtain an International Driving Permit (IDP). These can be obtained from your automobile association for a small fee.

Hostel Cards
The An Óige (Irish Youth Hostel Association) card, costing €15.25, can be bought at the An Óige offices (Map 4; ☎ 830 4555), 61 Mountjoy St, Dublin 1, or over the phone with a credit card. The An Óige card entitles the holder to a discount of €2 at An Oige/IHH hostels and priority booking, and soon will offer discounts at hostels worldwide. It also gives access to the international youth hostel booking network.

Seniors Cards
Senior citizens usually need only show proof of age to benefit from the many discounts available to them. These include discounts at museums and galleries and free public transport.

Other Documents
Many parks, monuments and gardens in the Republic are operated by Dúchas (see Useful Organisations later in this chapter). From any

of these sites, you can get a great value Heritage Card for €19 (seniors €12.70, students and children €7.60, family €45.70), giving you unlimited access to 70 sites throughout Ireland for one year. Dúchas sites in Dublin that charge an entry fee include the Casino at Marino, Dublin Castle, the Phoenix Park Visitor Centre and Ashtown Castle, St Audoen's Church (Protestant), the Waterways Visitor Centre, St Mary's Abbey and Kilmainham Jail. Dúchas sites within day-trip distance of Dublin are Lusk Heritage Centre, Mellifont Abbey, Knowth and Newgrange in the Boyne Valley to the north; Glendalough to the south charges an admission fee to the visitor centre but not to the site itself.

The Six-Way Combined Ticket is available from Dublin Tourism, covering admission to: Malahide Castle & the Fry Model Railway, Newbridge House, the James Joyce Museum and Tower, the Dublin Writers' Museum, Dublin's Viking Adventure and the George Bernard Shaw House. The ticket costs €24 (under-18s €17.75).

Copies

All important documents (for instance your passport data page and visa page, credit cards, travel insurance policy, travel tickets and driving licence) should be photocopied before you leave home. Leave one copy with someone at home and keep another with you in a safe place, separate from the originals, of course.

There is another option for storing details of your vital travel documents before you leave – Lonely Planet's online Travel Vault. Storing details of your important documents in the vault is safer than carrying photocopies. Your password-protected travel vault is accessible online. You can create your own travel vault for free at **W** www.ekno .lonelyplanet.com.

EMBASSIES & CONSULATES
Your Own Embassy

It's important to realise what your own embassy – the embassy of the country of which you are a citizen – can and can't do to help you if you get into trouble. Generally speaking, it won't be much help in emer-

gencies if the trouble you're in is remotely your own fault. Remember that in Ireland, you are bound by Irish law. Your embassy will not be sympathetic if you end up in jail after committing a crime locally, even if such actions are legal in your own country.

In genuine emergencies you might get some assistance, but only if other channels have been exhausted. For example, if you need to get home urgently, a free ticket home is exceedingly unlikely – the embassy would expect you to have insurance. If you have all your money and documents stolen, it might assist with getting a new passport, but a loan for onward travel is out of the question.

Some embassies used to keep letters for travellers or have a small reading room with home newspapers, but these days the mail-holding service has usually been stopped and even newspapers tend to be out of date.

Irish Embassies & Consulates

Irish diplomatic offices overseas include:

Australia
Embassy: (☎ 02-6273 3022, **e** irishemb@ computech.com.au) 20 Arkana St, Yarralumla, Canberra, ACT 2615
Consulate: (☎ 02-9231 6999, **e** consyd@ ireland.com) Level 30, 400 George St, Sydney, NSW 2000

Canada
Embassy: (☎ 613-233 6281, **e** emb.ireland@ sympatico.ca) 130 Albert St, Ottawa, Ontario K1P 5G4

France
Embassy: (☎ 01 44 17 67 60, **e** irembparis@ wanadoo.fr) 12 ave Foch, 75116 Paris

Germany
Embassy: (☎ 030-220 720) Friedrichstrasse 200, 10117 Berlin
Consulate: (☎ 089-985 723) Mauerkircher-strasse 1A, 81679 Munich

Netherlands
Embassy: (☎ 070-363 0993, **e** postbus@irish .embassy.demon.nl) Dr Kuyperstraat 9, 2514 BA The Hague

UK
Embassy: (☎ 020-7235 2171, **e** ir.embassy@ lineone.net) 17 Grosvenor Place, London SW1X 7HR
Consulates: (☎ 0131-226 7711) 16 Randolph Crescent, Edinburgh EH3 7TT; (☎ 029-2066 2000) 2 Fitzalan Rd, Cardiff CF24 0EB

USA
Embassy: (☎ 202-462 3939, e embirlus@aol
.com, w www.irelandemb.org) 2234 Massa-
chusetts Ave NW, Washington, DC 20008
Consulates: (☎ 212-319 2555, e congenny@
aol.com) Ireland House, 345 Park Ave, New
York, NY 10154; (☎ 617-267 9330,
e irlcons@aol.com) Chase Bldg, 535 Boylston
St, Boston, MA 02116; (☎ 312-337 1868,
e irishconchicago@aol.com) 400 North Michi-
gan Ave, Chicago, IL 60611; (☎ 415-392 0885,
e irishcgsf@aol.com) 44 Montgomery St,
3830, San Francisco, CA 94104

Embassies in Dublin
For citizens of New Zealand, the closest embassy is in London. You'll find the following
foreign embassies in Dublin:

Australia (Map 5; ☎ 676 1517) 2nd floor, Fitz-
wilton House, Wilton Terrace, Dublin 2
Canada (Map 6; ☎ 478 1988) 4th floor, 65-68
St Stephen's Green, Dublin 2
France (☎ 260 1666) 36 Ailesbury Rd, Dublin 4
Germany (☎ 269 3011/3946) 31 Trimleston Ave,
Booterstown, Blackrock, County Dublin
Netherlands (☎ 269 3444) 160 Merrion Rd,
Dublin 4
New Zealand (in London; ☎ 020-7930 8422)
New Zealand House, Haymarket, London SW1
4QT
UK (Map 2; ☎ 205 3700) 29 Merrion Rd, Dublin 4
USA (Map 2; ☎ 668 8777) 42 Elgin Rd, Dublin 4

CUSTOMS
There is a two-tier system for imported
goods: the first tier is for goods bought duty
free, the second for goods bought in an EU
country where taxes and duties have been
paid. Sadly, those travelling to and from
countries within the EU – including Ireland
– can no longer buy goods duty free, as this
was scrapped in 1999. However, this restriction does not apply to those travelling
between Ireland and a non-EU country, although the usual duty free limits still apply.
These are: 200 cigarettes or 100 cigarillos
or 250g of tobacco; 2L of wines (including
sherry and port); 1L of spirits or strong
liqueurs (over 22% alcohol); 60cc of per-
fume; and 250cc of toilet water. The import
and export of currency is not restricted.

Under the EU rules, as long as taxes have
been paid somewhere in the EU there are no
additional taxes if the goods are exported

within the EU – provided they are for
personal consumption. The amounts that
officially constitute personal use are 800
cigarettes (400 cigarillos, 200 cigars or 1kg
of tobacco) and either 10L of spirits, 20L of
fortified wine, 60L of sparkling wine, 90L of
still wine or 110L of beer. If you're arriving
from outside the EU, those aged 16 or over
may bring in goods (for personal use) on
which tax has been paid, only up to the value
of €180. If you're younger than 16, your allowance is €93.

Apart from the usual bans on firearms, ex-
plosives and illegal drugs, it is illegal to bring
into Ireland such things as oral smokeless tobacco, indecent or obscene books and pictures, all meat and meat products, and all
plants and plant products (including seeds).
Dogs and cats from anywhere outside Ireland
and the United Kingdom are subject to strict
quarantine laws. The United Kingdom's Pet
Pilot scheme, whereby animals are fitted with
a microchip, vaccinated against rabies and
blood tested six months *prior* to entry, will
eventually come into force in Ireland. In the
meantime, animals arriving directly into Ireland will be quarantined for six months unless they first pass through the UK and meet
British criteria for entry.

MONEY
Currency
The punt is dead, long live the euro. In February 2002, after a short six-week period of
transition, Ireland bid adieu to the punt and
adopted the euro as its only currency; part of
its ongoing commitment to greater European union. The other EU participants in
European Monetary Union (EMU) are Austria, Belgium, Finland, France, Germany,
Greece, Italy, Luxembourg, the Netherlands,
Portugal and Spain.

The euro (€) is divided into 100 cents (c).
The seven differently sized notes come in denominations of €5, €10, €20, €50, €100,
€200 and €500. There are coins of one, two,
five, 10, 20 and 50 cents, as well as €1 and
€2. Like the other eleven countries that have
also adopted the euro, the reverse side of the
Irish euro coins have a design particular to
Ireland, in this case the Celtic harp. This is

FACTS FOR THE VISITOR

simply to designate it as an Irish euro, but it is still legal tender everywhere else that accepts the euro.

If for some reason you have a wad of Irish punts, don't fret. You can exchange them at any bank or bureau de change for euros, but only until 30 June 2002, after which the only place you can exchange punts is at the Central Bank.

Exchange Rates

country	unit		euro
Australia	A$1	=	€0.58
Canada	C$1	=	€0.73
Japan	¥100	=	€0.92
New Zealand	NZ$1	=	€0.47
UK	UK£1	=	€1.60
USA	US$1	=	€1.12

Exchanging Money

The introduction of the euro has significantly reduced the need for bureaux de change, at least if you're travelling from another European country with the same currency. The UK, which has chosen not to participate in the euro for the time being, still uses the pound sterling, so if you're coming from Britain or Northern Ireland, or anywhere outside the euro zone, you'll need to change money. Most major currencies are readily and easily accepted in banks, bureaux de change and post offices with exchange facilities.

Bureaux de change usually charge more commission than banks, which also offer the best exchange rates. Many post offices have an exchange facility and have the advantage of being open on Saturday morning.

There's a cluster of banks around College Green (Map 6) opposite Trinity College and all have exchange facilities and automated teller machines (ATMs). The Bank of Ireland bureau de change, 34 College Green (Map 6), beside the bank, opens from 9am to 9pm Monday to Saturday (including bank holidays) and from 10am to 7pm on Sunday. American Express (AmEx) and Thomas Cook are across the road from the Bank of Ireland and the Trinity College entrance. American Express (Map 7; ☎ 679 9000), 40 Nassau St, Dublin 2, opens from 9am to 5pm Monday to Friday; on Saturday

the travel agency closes at noon, but the foreign-exchange counter stays open until 5pm. From June to September you can also change money here on Sunday between 11am and 4pm. Thomas Cook (Map 7; ☎ 677 1721), 118 Grafton St, opens from 9am to 5.30pm Monday to Saturday.

Cash There's nothing more convenient than cash, or as risky. We don't recommend that you carry huge wads of cash at any time, but it's a good idea to keep some handy on arrival, at least until you get to an exchange facility. You won't have to go far, however, at least if you arrive by plane. The foreign-exchange counter at Dublin airport is in the baggage-collection area and opens from approximately 7am to 9.30pm in summer (April to September) and from 7.30am to 8.30pm in winter (October to March). There's also an office on the departures level upstairs.

Travellers Cheques & Eurocheques Most major brands of travellers cheques are readily accepted in Ireland. We recommend that you carry them in euros, as you can visit more European countries and avoid costly exchange rates. AmEx and Thomas Cook travellers cheques are widely recognised and branches don't charge commission for cashing their own cheques. Travellers cheques are rarely accepted for everyday transactions so you'll need to cash them beforehand.

Eurocheques can be cashed in Dublin, but special arrangements must be made before you travel if you are thinking of using personal cheques.

ATMs Plastic cards make the perfect travelling companions – they're ideal for major purchases and let you withdraw cash from selected banks and ATMs, the traveller's best friend. Irish ATMs are linked up to international money systems such as Cirrus, Maestro or Plus, so you can get instant cash from your account back home by punching in a personal identification number (PIN). The Allied Irish Bank (AIB) and Bank of Ireland have many conveniently central ATMs. It's a good idea to carry a back-up means of obtaining cash as well though, in case of emergency.

Credit Cards Major credit cards – particularly AmEx, MasterCard and Visa – as well as other credit and charge cards are widely accepted, though some B&Bs will only take cash. You can also use credit cards to withdraw cash, but be sure to obtain a PIN from your bank *before* you leave. You should also ask which ATMs in Ireland accept your credit card. This service usually carries an extra charge, so if you're withdrawing money, take out enough so that you don't have to keep going back.

Lost or Stolen Cards If a card is lost or stolen, inform the police and the issuing company as soon as possible, otherwise you may have to bear the cost of the thief's purchases. Here are some numbers for cancelling your cards. All are 24-hour hotlines:

AmEx	☎ 1 800 282 728
Diner's Club	☎ 1 800 409 204
MasterCard	☎ 1 800 557 378
Visa	☎ 1 800 558 002

Security
Whatever you do with your money or valuables, don't leave them visible. Dublin isn't particularly dangerous, but a good rule of thumb is if it *can* be taken, it *will* be taken. The city's lampposts are adorned with bike locks bereft of their bikes, and if thieves will go to great lengths to rob a bike and leave the lock, they won't think twice about a tasty-looking wallet in your back pocket. The same goes for coats draped on the back of chairs in pubs and cafes, as well as bags sitting at their owners' feet. Muggings also occur, though mostly in run-down parts of the city and late at night.

Your best bet is to split your money into different stashes, preferably keeping the bulk of it in a pouch that you can wear around your neck inside your clothing or in a money belt, which you can wrap firmly around your waist and under your shirt or sweater. To avoid any financial heartache, though, carry as little cash as you can.

Costs
Costs in Dublin have skyrocketed in recent years, and while the average wage earner still earns 28% less than the European mean, the price of virtually everything is comparable to bigger cities such as London or Paris. Dublin is not cheap. Many places to stay, particularly hostels, have different high- and low-season prices. Some places may have not just a high-season but a *peak* high-season price. In this book the highest price levels are quoted. Admission prices to places such as museums and galleries are usually lower for children,

Dublin for Free

Dublin has only recently joined the list of major European tourist destinations and many of the more important places of interest charge fairly high entrance fees. However, all art galleries, including the National Gallery and the Irish Museum of Modern Art, are free, as are all the public gardens and parks, including the National Botanic Gardens in Glasnevin. There are also a number of museums that have resisted cashing in on the tourist boom. They are:

Chester Beatty Library (p97)
Dublin Civic Museum (p106)
Garda Museum (police museum in Dublin Castle; p97)
Natural History Museum (p111)
National Museum (p107)
Pearse Museum (p137)
Royal Irish Academy (p106)

Of Dublin's churches, only Christ Church Cathedral and St Patrick's Cathedral charge an admission fee; all the others are free to visitors, as are all cemeteries, including the notable ones at Glasnevin and Arbour Hill.

There is no charge to enter government buildings. Leinster House, the seat of the Irish legislature, does not charge admission should you wish to sit in on a debate when it is in session; and although arranging tours of the building can be difficult, they too are free.

You can have great fun simply ambling through the streets of Dublin, especially round the markets, the George's St Arcade, Moore St Market and (see the Shopping chapter for details).

students and senior citizens. These child, student and senior prices may sometimes differ.

At the bottom of the scale a hostel dormitory bed will cost from €11.50 to €17.50 per night. A cheap B&B will cost about €23 to €32 per person, and a more luxurious B&B or guesthouse with attached bathroom costs about €45 to €76 per person. Dinner with a glass of wine or a beer in a reasonable restaurant costs from €19 to €32.

Tipping

Although tipping is less prevalent in Ireland than elsewhere in Europe, things are changing fast. Fancy hotels and restaurants usually add a 15% service charge and no additional tip is required, but good service is usually rewarded with a gratuity. Simpler places usually do not add service, and if you decide to tip, it's acceptable to round up the bill or add 15% at most. You don't have to tip taxi drivers, but if you do 10% is fine. For hotel porters €1 per bag is acceptable.

Taxes & Refunds

Value-added tax (VAT) is a sales tax of 20% that applies to most goods and services in Ireland, excluding books and children's footwear. Residents of the EU cannot claim a VAT refund. If you're a resident of a country outside the EU and buy something from a store displaying a Cashback sticker, you'll be given a Cashback voucher with your purchase so that you can reclaim the VAT. This voucher can be refunded in US, Canadian or Australian dollars, British pounds sterling or euros at Dublin or Shannon airport. Alternatively, you can have the voucher stamped at the ferry port and mail it back for a refund.

If you reclaim more than €255 on any of your vouchers you'll need to get the voucher stamped at the customs booth in the arrivals hall at Dublin or Shannon airport before you can get your refund from the Cashback desk.

If you leave the EU from terminal three or terminal four of London's Heathrow airport you must get British customs to stamp your vouchers and then leave them at the Tax Free Shopping Desk. In some circumstances refunds can be posted to you or credited to your credit card.

POST & COMMUNICATIONS
Post

The Irish postal service, An Post, is reliable, efficient and usually on time. Aside from the GPO (General Post Office; Map 4) on O'Connell St, which opens 8am to 8pm Monday to Saturday and 10.30am to 2pm on Sunday, Dublin's main post offices open 9am to 6pm Monday to Saturday. The post office on South Anne St (Map 7), just off Grafton St, and the office on St Andrew's St (Map 7), just opposite Dublin Tourism, are the most convenient in the city centre. There are also smaller sub-offices dotted throughout the city, but they keep shorter hours, from 9.15am to 1pm and 2.15pm to 5.30pm Monday to Friday and 9.15am to 1pm on Saturday. In the branch offices and the GPO, the queues can be very long at lunchtime and on Saturday.

Within Ireland and to Britain, all letters up to 25g cost €0.38; to the rest of the EU, €0.41. For the rest of the world, letters cost €0.57. For letters up to 25g, there is only one class of post. Naturally, anything heavier than 25g is more expensive: a first-class (priority) 50g letter, for instance, will cost €0.44 within Ireland, €0.51 to Great Britain, €0.83 to Europe and €0.95 to the rest of the world. Economy second-class rates are cheaper, but delivery is much slower. Post boxes in Dublin are green and have two slots: one for 'Dublin Only', the other for 'All Other Places'.

Mail can be addressed to poste restante at post offices, but is officially held for two weeks only. If you write 'hold for collection' on the envelope it may be kept for a longer period.

All mail to Britain and Europe goes by air so there is no need to use air-mail envelopes or stickers.

Telephone

To call Dublin from abroad, dial your country's international access code, then ☎ 353 (Ireland's country code), 1 for Dublin (the 0 is dropped for calls from outside Ireland) then the phone number.

Christ Church Cathedral's elegant bridge and lofty vaults; the stark Famine Victims Memorial, Customs House Quay; William Smith O'Brien statue, O'Connell St; and the opulent Bank of Ireland building.

Dublin Castle's Figure of Justice: The scales used to tip in the rain until drainage holes were drilled.

Water Statue, Customs House

Dublin's Coat of Arms

Taking flight in Christ Church

St Patrick's Cathedral's magnificent floor: St Patrick's stands on one of Dublin's earliest Christian sites

Local & National Calls & Rates Local telephone calls from a public phone cost €0.25 for around three minutes, irrespective of when you call. Try to avoid making phone calls in pubs, as they usually cost €0.38 for the same time. If you have access to a private phone, calls are considerably cheaper, around €0.15 for three minutes between 8am and 6pm Monday to Friday. The rest of the time is off-peak, and for the same amount you get about 15 minutes' worth of chat. National or trunk calls are slightly more expensive (depending on where you're calling) but they work out at an average of about €0.63 for three minutes.

Calls to mobile phones are more expensive, around €0.50 per minute at peak time and €0.25 at off-peak times.

The area code for calls to Dublin from outside the city is ☎ 01. You can find other area codes in the front pages of any telephone book.

Directory Enquiries for Ireland and Northern Ireland is ☎ 11811. If you can't put the call through directly, you can call a national operator at ☎ 10.

International Calls & Rates To call someone outside Ireland dial ☎ 00, then the country code, the area code (usually dropping the leading zero if there is one) and then the number. Thus if you wanted to call an ☎ 020 number in London, you would start with ☎ 00 44 20. The one variation is that to call Northern Ireland from Ireland you dial ☎ 048 and then the Northern Irish area code *without* dropping the leading 0. If for whatever reason you can't dial the number directly, you can call ☎ 114 for an international operator, who will put the call through for you. The charge for this is €0.46 on top of the price of the phone call. If you need international directory enquiries, dial ☎ 11818. You will be charged €0.77 for this service.

The cost of a direct-dialled international call from Ireland varies according to the time of day. The good news is that increased competition has brought prices down. Reduced rates apply after 6pm and before 8am. They also apply between midnight and 8am and between 2pm and 8pm on calls to Australia and New Zealand. The cheapest rates are available at weekends, between midnight on Friday and 8am on Monday. Standard charges for one minute are:

Australia	€0.60
France	€0.32
Germany	€0.32
North America	€0.19
New Zealand	€0.63
UK	€0.15

Home Direct Calls Rather than placing reverse-charge calls through the operator in Ireland, you can dial direct to your home country operator and then reverse the charges or charge the call to a local phone credit card. To use the service dial the following codes then the area code and the number you want. Your home country operator will come on the line before the call goes through:

Australia	☎ 1800 5500 61 + number
France	☎ 1800 5500 33 + number
Italy	☎ 1800 5500 39 + number
New Zealand	☎ 1800 5500 64 + number
Spain	☎ 1800 5500 34 + number
UK – BT	☎ 1800 5500 44 + number
USA – AT&T	☎ 1800 5500 00 + number
USA – MCI	☎ 1800 5510 01 + number
USA – Sprint	☎ 1800 5520 01 + number

eKno Communication Service Lonely Planet's eKno global communication service provides low-cost international calls – for local calls you're usually better off with a local phonecard. eKno also offers free messaging services, email, travel information and an online travel vault, where you can securely store all your important documents. You can join online at Ⓦ www.ekno .lonelyplanet.com, or, in Ireland, dial ☎ 1 800 555 180 for the 24-hour customer-service centre. Once you have joined, always check the eKno Web site for the latest access numbers for each country and updates on new features.

Public Phones Most phones, save some old-fashioned ones in pubs, are of the newer glass semi-cubicle variety that accepts coins, phonecards and/or credit cards. All

FACTS FOR THE VISITOR

Emergency Numbers

For emergency assistance phone ☎ 999. This call is free from any phone and the operator will connect you with the type of assistance you specify: fire, police *(gardaí)*, ambulance, boat or coastal rescue. There are gardaí stations at Fitzgibbon St (Map 3; ☎ 836 3113), Harcourt Terrace (Map 2; ☎ 676 3481), Pearse St (Map 5; ☎ 677 8141) and Store St (Map 3; ☎ 874 2761).

Some other emergency services include:

Alcoholics Anonymous (Map 2; ☎ 453 8998, 679 5967 after hours) 109 South Circular Rd, Dublin 8

Drugs Advisory & Treatment Centre (Map 5; ☎ 677 1122) Trinity Court, 30–31 Pearse St, Dublin 2

Poisons Information Centre (☎ 837 9964/6) Beaumont Hospital, Beaumont Rd, Dublin 9

Rape Crisis Centre (Map 5; ☎ 661 4911, freefone 1 800 778 888) 70 Lower Leeson St, Dublin 2

The Samaritans (Map 4; ☎ 1850 60 90 90, 872 7700) 112 Marlborough St, Dublin 1 – for people feeling lonely, depressed or suicidal

come with pretty clear instructions, and you can use them to make International Direct Dialling (IDD) calls as well as all kinds of operator-assisted calls.

We recommend you use a prepaid phonecard (known as a callcard), widely available from newsagents and post offices, amongst others. These come in units of 10 (€2.50), 20 (€4.50) and 50 (€10.20). One unit is the equivalent of a local phone call. A digital display on the telephone indicates how much credit is left on the card. The cheapest place to make international phone calls in Dublin is at the Talk Shop (ℯ info@talkshop .ie, ⱳ www.talkshop.ie), open 9am to 11pm Monday to Saturday and 10am to 11pm on Sunday. It has several branches spread throughout the city centre, including:

(Map 6; ☎ 672 7212) The Granary, 20 Temple Lane, Dublin 2

(Map 3; ☎ 872 0200) 5 O'Connell St Upper, Dublin 1

(Map 2; ☎ 478 1456) Triangular Bldgs, Sth Richmond St, Dublin 2

On average, you will save at least 50% on all international calls, including as high as 80% on calls to faraway places like Australia.

Mobile Phones Virtually everyone in Dublin has a mobile phone. They are the most convenient – and expensive – way to keep in touch. Ireland uses GSM 900/1800, which is compatible with the rest of Europe and Australia but not with the North American GSM 1900 or the totally different system in Japan (though some North American phones have GSM 1900/900 phones that do work here). There are three service providers in Ireland. Eircell (087) is the most popular, followed by ESAT Digifone (086) and the latest arrival, Meteor (085).

All three service providers are linked with most international GSM providers, which will allow you to 'roam' onto a local service once you arrive in Ireland. This will allow you to use your mobile phone in Dublin and make local calls, but you should be aware that you will be charged at the highest possible rate for all calls.

If you receive a call from someone at home, they will also be charged for the price of a local call to a mobile, and you will be charged the difference – in some cases an exorbitant amount.

If you're cost conscious about mobile phone use, we recommend that you leave your mobile phone at home and get a prepaid phone on arrival in Dublin, known as a Ready to Go. For around €50 you will get a phone, your own number and anywhere up to €25-worth of air-time. As you use up your air-time, you simply buy more. Ready-to-Go phones are available at all mobile phone shops in Dublin, while prepaid air-time cards are on sale at nearly all newsagents. Eircell, ESAT Digifone and Meteor have variations on this scheme.

Fax & Telegrams

You can send faxes from post offices or other specialist offices. It can be quite expensive, however: about €1.30 per page locally, between €2.55 and €3.80 to Europe and approximately €5.10 per page to such overseas destinations as Australia or the USA. Phone the operator on ☎ 196 to send international telegrams (known as telemessages).

Email & Internet Access

Travelling with a portable computer is a great way to stay in touch with life back home, but unless you know what you're doing it's fraught with potential problems. If you plan to carry your notebook or palm-top computer with you, remember that the power-supply voltage in the countries you visit may vary from that at home, risking damage to your equipment. The best investment is a universal AC adapter for your appliance, which will enable you to plug it in anywhere without frying the innards. You'll also need a plug adapter for each country you visit – often it's easiest to buy these before you leave home.

Your PC-card modem also may or may not work once you leave your home country – and you won't know for sure until you try. The safest option is to buy a reputable 'global' modem before you leave home, or buy a local PC-card modem if you're spending an extended time in any one country. Keep in mind that the telephone socket in each country you visit will probably be different from the one at home, so ensure that you have at least a US RJ-11 telephone adapter that works with your modem. You can almost always find an adapter that will convert from RJ-11 to the local variety. For more information on travelling with a portable computer, see Ⓦ www.teleadapt.com or Ⓦ www.warrior.com.

Major Internet service providers including AOL (Ⓦ www.aol.com), CompuServe (Ⓦ www.compuserve.com) and AT&T (Ⓦ www.attbusiness.net) have dial-in nodes throughout Europe; it's best to download a list of the dial-in numbers before you leave home. If you access your Internet email account at home through a smaller ISP or your office or school network, your best option is either to open an account with a global ISP, like those mentioned above, or to rely on cybercafes and other public access points to collect your mail.

If you do intend to rely on cybercafes, you'll need to carry three pieces of information with you to enable you to access your Internet mail account: your incoming (POP or IMAP) mail server name, your account name and your password. Your ISP or network supervisor will be able to give you these. Armed with this information, you should be able to access your Internet mail account from any net-connected machine in the world, provided it runs some kind of email software (remember that Netscape and Internet Explorer both have mail modules). It pays to become familiar with the process for doing this before you leave home.

Alternatively, you can collect your email through cybercafes, by opening a free Web-based email account such as those provided by Hotmail (Ⓦ www.hotmail.com) or Yahoo! (Ⓦ mail.yahoo.com). If you want to avoid the junk mail that is a common feature of these accounts, you can open a free eKno Web-based email account online at Ⓦ www.ekno.lonelyplanet.com. You can then access your mail from anywhere in the world from any net-connected machine running a standard Web browser.

Dublin is pretty Internet friendly, and the city centre has literally dozens of cybercafes where you can check and send email or simply surf the Internet. These include:

Central Cyber Café (Map 7; ☎ 677 8298, ⓔ info@centralcafe.ie) 6 Grafton St, Dublin 2. Open 8am to 11pm Monday to Friday, 9am to 11pm on Saturday and 10am to 10pm on Sunday, it charges €6.35 per hour, but students have a 25% discount.

Global Cyber Café (Map 4; ☎ 878 0295, ⓔ info@globalcafe.ie) 8 Lower O'Connell St, Dublin 1. Run by the same folk who run the Central Cyber Café (above); charges and hours are the same.

Internet Exchange (Ⓦ www.internet-exchange.co.uk) has two branches in Dublin: (Map 6; ☎ 670 3000) Cecilia St, Dublin 2; and (Map 7; ☎ 642 2553) Dublin Tourism Centre, St Andrew's Church, 2 Suffolk St, Dublin 2. They open 10am to 11pm daily, and charge €7.60 per hour.

DIGITAL RESOURCES

Ireland has taken to the World Wide Web like a duck to water. There are hundreds of sites to check out, and many hotels, restaurants, transport companies and attractions now have their own Web sites. We have listed them throughout this book if they are of use to travellers.

There's no better place to start your Web explorations than the Lonely Planet Web site (W www.lonelyplanet.com). On this site you'll find succinct summaries on travelling to most destinations on earth, postcards from other travellers and the Thorn Tree bulletin board, where you can ask questions before you go or dispense helpful advice when you get back. You can also find travel news and updates to many of our most popular guidebooks, and the subWWWay section has links taking you to the most useful travel resources elsewhere on the Web. The Irish Web Server Map (W http://slarti.ucd.ie/maps/ireland.html) is a good general guide to most of the Irish Web sites available.

Other interesting and informative links relating specifically to Dublin include the following:

Bord Fáilte The Irish Tourist Board's official site.
W www.ireland.travel.ie

Dublin Corporation The city authority's guide to culture, museums and sights to see.
W www.iol.ie/dublincitylibrary

Dublin Tourism Gives access to most of the services it offers in its city centre office.
W www.visitdublin.com

Entertainment Ireland An excellent guide to what's on in Irish entertainment; includes theatre, music, cinema and exhibition listings, as well as a thumbnail guide to restaurants and museums.
W www.entertainment.ie

Go Ireland This Web site has plenty of information on Ireland, including accommodation, tourist attractions and handy numbers for car rentals, transportation etc.
W www.goireland.com

Indigo The biggest Irish server, with comprehensive services including a full tourist menu, with everything from where to eat to activities for young children.
W www.indigo.ie

Ireland Uncovered Wacky sight with all kinds of bits and bobs, including a guide to cheap drinking in Dublin and an insider's guide to the city's attractions.
W www.irelanduncovered.com

Irish Times Not only can you read the newspaper on the Web, but the links are excellent, offering plenty of information on what to do and see in Dublin.
W www.ireland.com

Local Ireland This is an excellent site, with detailed information and minutiae about Dublin and all other Irish counties.
W www.local.ie

Outhouse Community & Resource Centre The country's premier Web site devoted to Gay & Lesbian affairs.
W www.outhouse.ie

Oxygen A good general information site with plenty of links to listings, reviews and features on all aspects of Irish life.
W www.oxygen.ie

The Real Dublin Pub Guide This is an informative and irreverent guide to Dublin's pubs, with ratings and those all-important bitchy comments that make the best reviews worth reading.
W www.dublinpubs.net

Showbiz Ireland Basically a gossip site for Irish celebrities little and large. Find out what Bono's up to, and what Andrea Corr thinks about marriage, the church, household pets...
W www.showbizireland.com

Wasting Time@Work An irreverent site dedicated to shirking work. Full of jokes and includes the Ballyhoo Examiner, a mock newspaper with some genuinely funny articles (excellent pub-talk material).
W www.p45.net

Whelan's Listings for one of Dublin's premier music venues; essential for anyone looking for great live music in Dublin.
W www.whelanslive.com

Chapters of Dublin History Here you'll find the text of guides to Dublin written during the 19th century. Not only are they beautifully written (rather than 'walks', these guides refer to 'perambulations'), but they are wonderful insights into the city as it used to be when it was still the 'second city of the Empire'.
W http://indigo.ie/~kfinlay/index.htm

BOOKS

A glance in most Dublin bookshops will reveal huge Irish interest sections, whether it's fiction, history and current events, or numerous local and regional guidebooks. See the Literature section in the Facts about Dublin chapter for information on fiction by Irish writers.

Most books are published in different editions by different publishers in different countries. As a result, a book might be a hardcover rarity in one country while it's readily available in paperback in another. Fortunately, bookshops and libraries search by title or author, so they are best placed to advise you on the availability of the following recommendations.

Lonely Planet

Lonely Planet publishes *Ireland* and *Walking in Ireland*, which provide detailed information for people planning to travel around the country, and *Travel with Children*, a guide specifically for those travelling with young children.

Dublin

Dublin – One Thousand Years, by Stephen Conlin, is a fascinating book about the development of Dublin, with a series of illustrations showing how the city looked at various times in its history. The paintings of the area around the black pool *(dubh linn)* in 988 and the same scene again in 1275, with the addition of Dublin Castle, are particularly interesting. *Dublin,* by VS Pritchett, is a little old but gives an evocative and engaging account of an often eccentric city.

For all sorts of minutiae about Dublin buildings and streets check the *Encyclopaedia of Dublin,* by Douglas Bennett. Pat Liddy's *Dublin – A Celebration* is an excellent guide to the city's history, primarily through its architecture. The book is peppered with photos, drawings and illustrations.

CS 'Todd' Andrew's *Dublin Made Me* is a superb account of his early life, growing up around Summerhill (at the top of O'Connell St) and the south Dublin suburb of Terenure. One of the more important figures in the history of modern Ireland, Andrews' book offers a fascinating insight into the city between 1901 and 1930, as well as providing first-hand accounts of the struggle for independence, in which he played a key role.

For a fascinating social history of working-class Dublin check out *44 – A Dublin Memoir,* by Peter Sheridan, a kind of *Angela's Ashes* for the capital. In a similar vein, Phil O'Keefe's *Down Cobbled Streets* tells his story of growing up in the Liberties.

Literary Dublin – a History, by Herbert A Kenny, traces the history of Dublin's rich and diverse literary culture. *A Literary Guide to Dublin,* by Vivien Igoe, includes detailed route maps, a guide to cemeteries and an eight-page section on literary and historical pubs.

Ireland

Two important tomes on Ireland's more recent history are JJ Lee's *Ireland 1912-1985* and the classic *Ireland since the Famine,* by FSL Lyons. Lee's book caused something of a stir when it first came out, as it contends that Ireland's problems were not entirely due to 'perfidious Albion'. Lyons' book is the standard history for all students of modern Ireland; its author was Professor of History at Trinity College.

For books that include a look at contemporary Ireland, we recommend *Ireland & the Irish – Portrait of a Changing Society,* by John Ardagh. It is a well written exploration of the complexities of a nation struggling to make changes without sacrificing the essence of its national character. Mike Cronin's recently published *A History of Ireland* is a thoroughly accessible history of the island from the 12th century to the present day. *Ireland – a History,* by Robert Kee, covers similar ground in a book developed from a BBC/RTE TV series. An excellent book on contemporary Ireland is *She Moves Through the Boom,* by Anne Marie Hourihane, which attempts to see the country through a variety of different eyes, including those of asylum seekers. It is insightful and not short of funny observations.

CS 'Todd' Andrews' *A Man of No Property* is the second volume of his autobiography after *Dublin Made Me* (see under Dublin in this section). In this volume he provides fascinating details and accounts of the key moments of the Irish Republic up to 1980, written by a founder member of Fianna Fáil and a major player in the nation's political history. For an in-depth understanding of Ireland's contemporary history, this is an absolute must.

FACTS FOR THE VISITOR

Women's History Margaret Ward's fascinating biography, *Hannah Sheehy Skeffington – A Life*, is a comprehensive view of the life of perhaps Ireland's most remarkable contributor to the Irish suffragette movement. Margaret Ward is also the editor of *In Their Own Voice: Women and Irish Nationalism*, a collection of first-hand accounts by women who participated in the struggle for Irish independence. Lily Fitzsimons' *Women In Ireland* explores in intricate detail the lives and struggles of ordinary Irish women, set against the backdrop of the independence movement in the early decades of the 20th century.

Northern Ireland Although not quite related to Dublin, the 'Troubles' still dominate the Irish political landscape unlike any other issue. Tim Pat Coogan's *The Troubles* is an excellent history of these complex problems. Peter Taylor's excellent trio of books, *Provos*, *Loyalists* and *Brits* are also worth reading as they offer a compelling insight into the mindset of the three protagonists.

Written by one of Northern Ireland's most respected journalists, David McKittrick's *Nervous Peace* is a collection of all of his articles on Northern Ireland written for the English *Independent* newspaper.

For a more partisan view, Gerry Adams' *An Irish Journal* is the leader of Sinn Féin's account of the period between September 1997 and the end of 2000 – a period when the tenuous ceasefire was severely threatened. Surprisingly, Adams' writing style is often punctuated by humour, shedding greater light on a man for many years vilified by the press as the devil incarnate.

Economy If you're not sick of hearing the words 'Celtic Tiger', we recommend two contrasting titles exploring the roots and results of Ireland's phenomenal economic success. *The Making of the Celtic Tiger*, by Ray MacSharry and Padraic White, eulogises its success, which is hardly surprising considering that Mr MacSharry was Minister of Finance in the 1980s. Kieran Allen's *The Celtic Tiger: The Myth of Social Partnership in Ireland* is more interested in the cracks beneath the surface and argues that the economic 'miracle', though of benefit to many, has benefited far fewer than the government would have us imagine.

FILMS

If you're looking for films set in Dublin or using Dublin as a backdrop, you're in luck. If you're looking for *good* films... well, the list is sadly far too short. All too often film makers, in their desire to win over foreign (American) audiences, descend to presenting the city and its characters in a blithe and cliched way, as though Dublin were populated by odd-sock-wearing barflies who lost their literary genius at the bottom of a pint of beer. OK, Dublin *has* had its fair share of those types, but it's hardly the norm. One critic, appalled by an American film's portrayal of the Irish as a bunch of simpleton ne'er-do-wells, declared that only a pint of Guinness with a potato stuffed into it was more 'oirish' (an interesting word used to define anything that caricatures Ireland and the Irish).

There are, thankfully, some exceptions, none more spectacular than the 1996 biopic, *Michael Collins*, starring Liam Neeson, Julia Roberts and virtually every Dublin-based actor! Dublin audiences were particularly impressed by the full-scale recreation of the 1916 Easter Rising and the bombing of O'Connell St from the Liffey. The film is worth watching for its epic qualities (a first for an Irish film) as well as its (sometimes questionable) insight into the complexities of Collins' character.

The Commitments was a bright and energetic 1991 hit about a north Dublin soul band struggling to make it big. The film, based on Roddy Doyle's book, accurately records north Dublin's scruffy atmosphere, though some Dublin audiences were rather amused by the film's geographical jumps. *The Snapper* (1993) and *The Van* (1996), the other two books in Doyle's Barrytown trilogy, have also been made into films. The latter is perhaps the best of the three, focusing on the troubled relationships within a working-class Dublin family without losing any of the comic brilliance that characterises Doyle's work. More recently, Doyle wrote the screenplay for *When Brendan*

Meets Trudy (2001), a light comedy set in Dublin. He said this served as 'relief' from writing novels, which have become more sombre than his earlier work.

The notorious gangster Martin Cahill, aka The General, is the subject of three films, all released between 1997 and 1999. The first was *The General* (1997), starring Brendan Gleeson as Cahill and Jon Voight as the Cork-born policeman who tries to bring him to justice. Despite a creditable performance by Gleeson and a surprisingly good Cork accent by Voight, the film never quite captures the nasty side of Cahill, preferring instead to portray him as a nice guy born on the wrong side of the law. A far more believable account of Cahill's life is told in the BBC's *Cast A Cold Eye* (1998), starring Ken Stott. If two weren't enough, 1999 saw *Ordinary Decent Criminal*, starring Kevin Spacey. Spacey is a terrific actor, but not even he can save this one, the worst of the three.

Dublin's ganglands also served as the backdrop for *When the Sky Falls* (2000), starring Joan Allen as Sinead Hamilton, the fearless crime-fighting reporter who pays the ultimate price for her endeavours. Hamilton's character is based on the life of journalist Veronica Guerin, who was killed by Dublin gangsters in 1996. The entirely Irish-produced and financed gangster comedy *I Went Down* (1998) tells the story of an unlikely alliance between an ex-con (played by Peter McDonald) and a thug (Brendan Gleeson) who is unhappily estranged from his wife. It is the highest grossing Irish independent film ever and an excellent attempt at the kind of cinematic experiments made so popular by Quentin Tarantino.

Contemporary Dublin serves as the setting for *All About Adam* (2001), a clever film about one man's ability to woo three sisters by affecting an almost chameleon-like ability to appeal to what each woman loves most in a man. It features Dublin actor Stuart Townsend and rising American star Kate Hudson, and is the first mainstream Irish film to avoid the usual stereotypes about Dublin and presents the city in an upbeat, cosmopolitan light.

A quieter, more traditional side of the city was seen in *Circle of Friends*, the 1995 film based on Maeve Binchy's novel of college relationships in Dublin in 1957, starring Colin Firth, Minnie Driver and Chris O'Donnell. An excellent film is *A Man of No Importance* (1994), starring Albert Finney as a gay bus conductor, set in the Dublin of the early 1960s.

Christy Brown's autobiographical novels were the inspiration for the truly wonderful *My Left Foot* (1989), starring Daniel Day-Lewis, Brenda Fricker and Ray McAnally. It makes for a great visual tour of the city – albeit the Dublin of the 1960s – and resulted in Oscars for Daniel Day-Lewis as Best Actor and Brenda Fricker as Best Supporting Actress.

Fans of James Joyce should check out a couple of truly great films based on some of his work. *Ulysses* (1967), starring Milo O'Shea, won an Oscar nomination for Best Adapted Screenplay for its portrayal of a day in the life of Stephen Dedalus. Renowned director John Huston's final film, *The Dead*, released in 1988, was based on a James Joyce story from *Dubliners* and features extremely powerful performances by Angelica Huston and Donal McCann. The often stormy relationship between Joyce and his long-time partner Nora Barnacle is the subject of *Nora* (2000), an average film, but with good performances by Ewan McGregor as the young writer and especially Susan Lynch in the title role.

Dublin has also made many cameo appearances. The number of domestic and international film crews working in the capital at any given time is higher than ever before, with producers and directors eager to use the city as a setting, even when the film is set somewhere else. Alan Parker's 1999 movie of Frank McCourt's international best seller *Angela's Ashes*, though set in Limerick, was actually filmed in Dublin. It is telling of Dublin's rising fortunes that in order to recreate the slum conditions of the story, a special set needed to be built. Kilmainham Gaol provided the set for the 1994 film *In the Name of the Father*, with Daniel Day-Lewis and Emma Thompson, which told the story of the Guildford Four, wrongly convicted of a pub bombing and only released after 14 years in British jails. As well as representing itself, Dublin also served as a substitute for Boston in *Far and Away* (1997), a sentimental yarn about Irish emigrants to America starring Tom Cruise and Nicole Kidman. Older films using Dublin include *Educating Rita* (1983), which featured Trinity College as its quintessentially English university. Dublin Castle and Newman House can be spotted in *Moll Flanders* (1997) starring Julia Roberts.

NEWSPAPERS & MAGAZINES

The main Irish dailies are the *Irish Times*, the *Irish Independent* and the newly constituted *Irish Examiner* (formerly *The Cork Examiner*). The *Irish Times* (€1.25) is Ireland's oldest newspaper and famous for its good journalism, while the *Irish Independent*'s (€1.25) content is a little lighter. The *Irish Examiner* (€1.20) is in its early days as a national newspaper, but it is remarkably good, with in-depth coverage of all Irish-related events and some excellent feature articles. Irish versions of the English tabloid papers (including the *Sun* and the *Mirror*) are also available. The *Evening Herald* (€0.75) is an evening tabloid that frankly provides its best service as a fish-and-chips holder. Sunday papers include the *Sunday Tribune* (€1.40), which has an excellent reputation for good investigative journalism, and the *Sunday Business Post* (€1.40), the best financial newspaper in the country.

For political content, the best magazines are the weekly *Magill* (€2.50) and the satirical fortnightly *Phoenix* (€2.50). Lighter content magazines include the relatively new *Dubliner* (€3.50), which unashamedly embraces Oscar Wilde's dictum that 'history is gossip, and scandal is gossip made boring by morality'.

British papers and magazines are available on the day of issue and are cheaper than their Irish equivalents. Eason's on O'Connell St has a wide selection of foreign and regional Irish newspapers, which are also available in larger newsagents.

You can also read the main Irish dailies on the Web. The *Irish Times* is at **W** www

.ireland.com, the *Irish Examiner* at **W** www .examiner.ie and the *Irish Independent* at **W** www.independent.ie.

RADIO & TV

Radio na Telefís Éireann (RTE) is Ireland's government-sponsored national broadcasting body. There are three state-controlled radio stations. Two of them – RTE Radio 1 and RTE's 2FM – are broadcast in English, and Radio na Gaeltachta is in Irish. There are also various independent radio stations. In Dublin, the popular 98 FM, 104 FM and Today FM (100 FM to 102 FM) play classic rock music; Today FM is especially good on weekdays from 5pm to midnight, when it has an interesting blend of informative talk radio and good alternative music. Also worth checking out are some of the unlicensed 'pirate' stations, including Power FM (97.2 FM), which offers an excellent mix of all kinds of dance music; XFM (107.1 FM), an alternative station; and Trinity FM (96.7 FM), the city's only college radio. For a complete list of Dublin's radio stations and their frequencies look in the *Event Guide*.

Ireland has three state-controlled TV channels, RTE 1, Network 2 and the Irish-language TnaG, as well as an independent station, TV3. British BBC, ITV and Channel 4 programs can also be picked up. An advantage Dublin has over places in Britain is that the two main Sky satellite channels, Sky One and Sky News, are available without a satellite dish.

VIDEO SYSTEMS

Ireland uses the VHF PAL system for video recorders, which is not compatible with NTSC or SECAM.

PHOTOGRAPHY & VIDEO

Dublin is a photogenic but often gloomy city, so photographers should bring high-speed film. The best times of day for taking pictures are early morning and late evening, when the sunlight – if there is any – is low and warm. Remember the rain and bring a plastic bag to keep your camera dry.

Fast-developing services are readily available. Developing and printing a 24-exposure print film typically costs around €10.50 for a one-hour service or from €6.50 to €8 for a slower turnaround. Slide processing costs about €9 per roll and takes a few days, though the Film Bank (Map 5; ☎ 662 4420), 102 Lower Baggot St, has a two-hour service. However, they mainly cater for professionals and have prices to match their high quality – about €5.70 per slide.

TIME
Dublin is on Greenwich Mean Time (GMT) or Universal Time Co-ordinated (UTC), as is London. Without taking daylight-saving time changes into account, when it's noon in Dublin or London, it is 8pm in Singapore, 10pm in Sydney or Melbourne, 3am in Los Angeles or Vancouver and 7am in New York.

As in Britain, clocks are advanced by one hour in mid-March and put back one hour at the end of October.

ELECTRICITY
Electricity is 220V, 50Hz AC. Plugs are of the flat three-pin type, as in Britain.

WEIGHTS & MEASURES
Like Britain, progress towards metrication in Ireland is slow and piecemeal. So as not to confuse you, green roadsigns give distances in kilometres, older white ones measure them in miles and newer white ones give them in kilometres. Speed limits are given in miles, food in shops is priced and weighed in metric, beer in pubs is served in pints and half pints.

LAUNDRY
Most of the hostels offer laundry facilities at lower than commercial rates. Irish self-service laundrettes almost all offer a service-wash facility, where for €6.35 to €9 they'll wash, dry and neatly fold your washing. Many guesthouses and hotels will offer a similar service in conjunction with a local laundry, simply tacking on an extra €2.50 or so delivery charge.

Otherwise, there are several convenient laundries, such as the Laundry Shop (Map 4; ☎ 872 3541) at 191 Parnell St, Dublin 1.

Also in north Dublin is the Launderette at 110 Lower Dorset St (Map 4) near the An Óige Hostel. South of the centre at 40 Great George's St is the lively All-American Launderette Company (Map 7; ☎ 677 2779), which has a handy notice board. Just north of the Grand Canal is Powders Launderette (Map 2; ☎ 478 2655), 42A South Richmond St, Dublin 2. If you're staying north-east of the centre at Clontarf there's the Clothes Line (☎ 833 8480), 53 Clontarf Rd. In Dun Laoghaire there's the Star Laundry (☎ 280 5074), 47 Upper George's St.

TOILETS
The old public toilets once found in the city centre are now gone, leaving Dublin with virtually no public facilities. If you need to go, your best bet is to walk into a bar and use the facilities there; if the bar is empty, it might be a good idea to ask the bartender for permission to use the toilet. Restaurants can be very fussy and often put up signs indicating that toilets are for patrons' use only. The law states that all places open to the public should have facilities for the disabled. Quite a few of the newer bars and restaurants do have these facilities, but many others are slow in upgrading their facilities to comply with the law.

LEFT LUGGAGE
For details of locations and prices of left-luggage facilities, see the Airport, Bus and Train sections in the Getting Around chapter.

HEALTH
Travel health depends on your pre-departure preparations, your daily health care while travelling and how you handle any medical problem that does develop. While the potential dangers can seem quite frightening, in reality few travellers experience anything more than upset stomachs.

There are no serious health problems in Dublin apart from the effects of traffic pollution and the dangers posed by the Irish high-cholesterol breakfast; you might even see mobile cholesterol-testing units around town. Although Ireland is still a largely rural country, there is no risk of rabies infection due to stringent laws that ban the import of any animals or animal products.

Make sure you're healthy before you start travelling. If you wear glasses take a spare pair and your prescription. If you require a particular medication take an adequate supply, as it may not be available locally. Take part of the packaging showing the generic name, rather than the brand, which will make getting replacements easier. It's a good idea to have a legible prescription or letter from your doctor to show that you legally use the medication, to avoid any problems.

Make sure that you have adequate health insurance. See under Travel Insurance in the Documents section earlier in this chapter for details.

Medical Services

The Eastern Regional Health Authority (Map 4; ☎ 679 0700, freefone 1800 520 520, ⓔ erha@erha.ie, ⓦ www.erha.ie), Dr Steevens's Hospital, Dublin 8, has a Choice of Doctor Scheme, which can advise you on a suitable doctor from 9am to 5pm, Monday to Friday. Your hotel or embassy can also suggest a doctor. The ERHA also provides services for those with physical and mental disabilities.

If you experience an immediate health problem, contact the casualty section of the nearest public hospital; in an emergency, call an ambulance ☎ 999. North of the river is the Mater Misericordiae Hospital (Map 4; ☎ 830 1122), Eccles St off Lower Dorset St; south of the river are St James's Hospital (Map 3; ☎ 453 7941) on James's St and Baggot St Hospital (Map 5; ☎ 668 1577), at 18 Upper Baggot St.

The following chemists stay open until 10pm: O'Connell's Late Night Pharmacy, O'Connell St (Map 4) and Dame St Pharmacy, Dame St (Map 6).

Condoms are widely available in Dublin, in both pharmacies and in many bars and clubs. They're also available at the Well Woman Centre (Map 2; ☎ 660 9860), 67 Pembroke Rd, Dublin 4, which can also prescribe the morning-after pill for emergencies. The centre opens from 9am to 8pm on weekdays, and from 10am to 5pm on

Saturday. There's another branch (Map 4; ☎ 661 0083) at 35 Lower Liffey St, which opens from 10am to 12.30pm on Sunday only. These centres can advise on various women's health problems and charge consultation fees on a sliding scale.

The contraceptive pill is available only on prescription, so a visit to a doctor will be necessary.

HIV & AIDS

HIV, the Human Immunodeficiency Virus, develops into AIDS, Acquired Immune Deficiency Syndrome, which is a fatal disease. HIV is a major problem in many countries. Any exposure to blood, blood products or body fluids may put the individual at risk. The disease is often transmitted through sexual contact or dirty needles – acupuncture, tattooing and body piercing can be potentially as dangerous as intravenous drug use.

Fear of HIV infection should never prevent you from having treatment for serious medical conditions.

WOMEN TRAVELLERS

In many ways Ireland is one of the safest and least harassing countries for women. However, outside Dublin, old attitudes often prevail, with women treated more or less as second-class citizens. In Dublin women are treated in the same way as they are in any other westernised, cosmopolitan city. Dublin can even offer some advantages – for example, as pornography has an unusually low profile, women aren't subjected to the daily parade of breasts and bottoms common in British newsagents. They are also not subjected as frequently to the silly comment on the street as they would be in London or Paris, but this has less to do with Dublin males' respect for women and more with the traditional Irish manner of keeping all emotions under wraps! Still, women can find themselves in awkward situations, especially in a pub full of drunken men. Polite but firm refusals of unwanted advances are normally sufficient.

Lone women should exercise care when walking in dodgy parts of town (mainly north of the Liffey). See Dangers & Annoyances later in this chapter for more information.

GAY & LESBIAN TRAVELLERS

Surprisingly for such an overwhelmingly Catholic country, Irish laws on homosexuality are among the most liberal and progressive in Europe. There is a common age of consent of 17, gays and lesbians are not excluded from the armed forces, sexual orientation is included in the Unfair Dismissals Act and in 1990 the adoption of the Prohibition of Incitement to Hatred Act made Ireland only one of four countries in the world to have such a law on its statute books. Despite its dogma on the matter, the Catholic Church has maintained a silent neutrality on the issue.

In Dublin, the gay and lesbian scene is loud, proud and very vibrant. It is not uncommon to see same-sex couples holding hands on the street, and open displays of affection are either ignored or treated with a kind of shy curiosity.

For more information contact Outhouse, the National Lesbian and Gay Federation (Map 4; ☎ 873 4932, e info@outhouse.ie, W www.outhouse.ie), 105 Capel St, Dublin 1. The Gay Switchboard (Map 3; ☎ 872 1055) is in Carmichael House, North Brunswick St, Dublin 7; call between 8pm and 10pm, Sunday to Friday or between 3.30pm and 6pm on Saturday. The Lesbian Line (☎ 872 9911) opens from 7pm to 9pm on Thursday. In the unlikely event that you may require police assistance for harassment or other legal issues, the Garda have a gay & lesbian liaison officer (Map 5; ☎ 677 8141) at Pearse St Garda Station.

In recent years there has also been a flourishing of gay- and lesbian-oriented Web sites, where you can find all kinds of information on accommodation, pubs and clubs as well as chat rooms and forums. These include Gay Ireland (W www.gay-ireland.com) and Irish Queer (W www.channelqueer.com).

Other useful contacts for gays and lesbians include the following:

AIDS Helpline Dublin (☎ 1800 459 459) This advice and counselling service opens 10am to 5pm Monday to Friday.

Dublin AIDS Alliance (☎ 873 3799) Aimed primarily at drug users infected with AIDS and HIV, this helpline opens 2pm to 5pm Monday to Friday.

Gay Men's Health Project (☎ 660 2189) 19 Haddington Rd, Dublin 4. This is a drop-in sexual health clinic for gay men where help and advice is friendly and strictly confidential.

LOT (Lesbians Organising Together; ☎ 872 0460) 5 Capel St, Dublin 1. This is a drop-in resource centre and library for lesbians.

The magazine *In Dublin* has a section on gay and lesbian services, organisations and entertainment. The monthly publication *Gay Community News* (W www.gcn.ie) is available through the Temple Bar Information Centre (Map 6; ☎ 671 5717), 18 Eustace St, Temple Bar, and in a number of cafes around the city centre. On a negative note, in 2001 there was a substantial outbreak of syphilis among gay and bisexual men. Gay organisations have strongly advised that care is taken so as to contain its spread.

DISABLED TRAVELLERS

If you have a physical disability, get in touch with your national support organisation (preferably the travel officer if there is one). They often have complete libraries devoted to travel, and can put you in touch with travel agencies who specialise in tours for the disabled.

Guesthouses, hotels and sights in Ireland are increasingly being adapted for people with disabilities though there is still a long way to go. Public transportation, on the other hand, can be a nightmare: if you're using a wheelchair, forget about getting a bus. Trains are not as big a problem. So long as you call ahead, an employee of Iarnród Éireann (Irish Rail; ☎ 836 6222) will come to meet you and accompany you to the train (although we've heard of several instances where once arrived at the station, no-one was there to help).

Information & Organisations

Bord Fáilte's annual accommodation guide, *Be Our Guest,* indicates which places are accessible by wheelchair. Travel agencies may have access to the most recent details about facilities available for disabled people. The Access Service, with all information on accessibility, is now run by Comhairle (Map 3; ☎ 874 7503), 44 North Great George's St, Dublin 1. They also have a telephone information service at freefone ☎ 1 800 350 150.

Other useful organisations include:

Catholic Institute for the Deaf (☎ 830 0522) 40 Lower Drumcondra Rd, Dublin 9
Cerebral Palsy Ireland (☎ 269 5355) Sandymount Ave, Dublin 4
Cystic Fibrosis Association of Ireland (☎ 496 2433) 24 Lower Rathmines Rd, Dublin 6
Irish Wheelchair Association (Map 5; ☎ 661 6183) 62 Fenian St, Dublin 2

SENIOR TRAVELLERS

Senior citizens are entitled to many discounts in Europe on such things as public transport and museum admission fees, provided they show proof of their age. The minimum qualifying age varies between 60 and 65 for men, and 55 to 65 for women. In Dublin, most attractions offer discounts to seniors; it's worth asking even if you don't see one listed.

In your home country, a lower age may already entitle you to all sorts of interesting travel packages and discounts through organisations and travel agencies catering for senior travellers. Start hunting at your local senior citizens' organisations.

USEFUL ORGANISATIONS

An Óige (Map 4; ☎ 830 4555, fax 830 5808, e mailbox@anoige.ie, w www.irelandyha .org), the Irish Youth Hostel Association, has its office at 61 Mountjoy St, next to the hostel; it's open 9.30am to 5.30pm Monday to Friday.

The Backpackers Centre (Map 4; ☎ 836 4700, e ihh@iol.ie, w www.hostelireland .com), 51 Lower Gardiner St, immediately opposite Busáras, provides information on

---

Dublin for Children

Successful travel with young children requires effort, but it can be done. Try not to overdo things and consider using some sort of self-catering accommodation as a base. This frees you from the limited opening hours of restaurants and hotels and gives more flexibility. Having said that, Dublin is one of the more child-friendly cities in Europe, with provisions made for children in hotels and restaurants.

Include children in the planning process; if they've helped to work out where you're going, they'll be more interested when they get there. Include a range of activities – for example, balance a visit to Trinity College with one to The Ark. Like most big cities, Dublin has plenty to keep children just as entertained as their parents. Some of the sites (the National Wax Museum, Dublin Writers' Museum, the National Museum, The Ark and Hey, Doodle, Doodle) are right in the centre. Others (Dublin Zoo, Kylemore Indoor Karting and Phoenix Park Visitor Centre) are a short bus ride away. A few (Fry Model Railway Exhibition and Newbridge Demesne Traditional Farm) are farther out. But don't forget the city's smaller parks and gardens, which are traffic-free oases where young children can crawl and run to their hearts' content. The Family Bus Travel Wide pass allows up to two adults and four children under 16 years to use all Dublin Bus services for the day for €7; for another €1.25 you can get a pass covering DART and suburban rail services too. Buy passes in advance from the Dublin Bus office in O'Connell St (Map 4) or from ticket agencies around town. For information about the sights mentioned here, see the Things to See & Do chapter and the boxed text 'Kids' Stuff' in the Excursions chapter. The Entertainment chapter includes some children's venues too. For further general information see Lonely Planet's *Travel with Children*.

The Ark (p95)	Fry Model Railway Exhibition (pp212 & 219)
Dublin Writers' Museum (p122)	Newbridge Traditional Farm (pp218 & 219)
Dublin Zoo (p132)	Phoenix Park Visitor Centre (p133)
Fort Lucan Adventureland (p219)	Kylemore Indoor Karting (p140)
Hey, Doodle, Doodle (p95)	National Wax Museum (p124)

---

hostels run by Independent Holiday Hostels (IHH; a tourist board-approved cooperative group), tours and public transport. It's open 10am to 8pm Monday to Friday and noon to 8pm at weekends.

Dúchas, The Heritage Service (Map 5; ☎ 647 3000, e duchas@ealga.ie, w www .heritageireland.ie), is at 6 Upper Ely Place, Dublin 2. For all information concerning the Heritage Card (see Documents earlier in this chapter), call freefone ☎ 1 850 405 000.

The Automobile Association of Ireland or AA (Map 7; ☎ 617 9999, fax 617 9900, e aa@ireland.ie, w www.aaireland.ie) has its headquarters at 23 Suffolk St, Dublin 2.

LIBRARIES
In keeping with Dublin's tradition as a literary capital, the city has plenty of libraries, both private and public. For information on public libraries, contact Dublin Corporation (Map 5; ☎ 661 9000), Cumberland House, Fenian St, Dublin 2. The public library in the ILAC Centre (Map 3; ☎ 873 4333), Henry St, Dublin 1, is well stocked with books and videos on myriad subjects. The Irish Architectural Association archive (Map 5; ☎ 676 3430), 73 Merrion Square, Dublin 2, has books on Dublin's rich architectural heritage, as well as specialised books on, and plans of, significant buildings throughout the city.

CULTURAL CENTRES
Dublin has an international selection of cultural centres including:

Alliance Française (Map 5; ☎ 676 1732) 1 Kildare St, Dublin 2
British Council (Map 5; ☎ 676 4088) Newmount House, 22–24 Lower Mount St, Dublin 2
Goethe Institut (Map 5; ☎ 661 1155) 37 Merrion Square, Dublin 2
Italian Cultural Institute (Map 5; ☎ 676 6662, 662 3268) 11 Fitzwilliam Square, Dublin 2
Spanish Cultural Institute (Map 5; ☎ 668 2024) 58 Northumberland Rd, Dublin 4

DANGERS & ANNOYANCES
Crime
Despite the fact that Dublin is one of Europe's safest capitals, in recent years its good reputation has been somewhat marred by an increase in petty crime, particularly pickpocketing, bag-snatching and car break-ins. So be sure to take the usual precautionary measures and you won't find yourself describing the contents of your bag/wallet/car to a jaded police officer. The most important of these is don't show off your valuables and don't leave anything in your car. The latter is particularly true for rentals and foreign-registered vehicles, seen as an easy target by thieves. You should also bear in mind that insurance policies often don't cover losses from cars. If you're on a bike, be sure to lock it securely. A good tip is to lock your bike on the road side of a pole or bike rack; in this way potential thieves may be dissuaded from picking or breaking your lock by the fact that they'll have to stand on the road in order to do it.

Certain parts of Dublin are unsafe after dark – for example, Gardiner St North, Upper O'Connell St, Dorset St, the area around Connolly Station and the streets west of Christ Church (on the way to Kilmainham). Visitors should avoid run-down, deserted-looking and poorly lit areas. Phoenix Park is not safe at night and you should not camp there. Unfortunately, some of the hostels are also in the rougher parts of north Dublin.

Beggars
Beggars are an increasingly common sight on Dublin streets, and some of them are school-age children, which makes it all the more depressing. If you don't want to give them money, but would like to help in some way, consider buying a copy of the magazine *Big Issues* (€2.55) from a street vendor. It can be a good read, with lots of local insight, and some of the proceeds go to help the homeless and unemployed.

Racism
The influx of nonwhite, English-speaking immigrants and asylum seekers to Dublin has not been without its problems, especially for Africans and, to a lesser extent, Eastern Europeans. The irony is the vast majority of Dubliners deny that they have any racist feelings and that Ireland as a whole is not a racist country. That said, an overwhelming

majority of blacks in Dublin have experienced some kind of racial harassment, especially verbal abuse. Racism *does* exist and *is* a problem. Thankfully, though, the more extreme kind of racism – punctuated by physical intimidation or violence – is infrequent and limited to a mindless minority whose heads are filled with stupid notions about immigrants 'stealing' Irish jobs – a fantasy concocted by reactionary bigots who have jumped onto the 'Ireland for the Irish' bandwagon. Still, there are enough right-minded Dubliners to ensure that in most cases sense and decency will prevail, and it is not unheard of for locals to rally to the side of the victim of racial abuse. If you do experience a problem, be sure to report it to the police.

Violence

Sadly, Dublin has its fair share of drink-induced violence, especially late at night in the city centre. There is no better recipe for a fight than hundreds of drunken youths stumbling out of pubs and clubs at the same time, frustrated by the fact that they can't get more booze and that the trip home involves a two-hour wait at a taxi rank. In nearly all cases, fights start up for reasons that no-one will remember once they've slept off their drunkenness. Trouble, however, is easy to avoid. If you spot any, cross to the other side of the street and keep walking; don't get involved.

Smoking

Smoking has yet to die the social death it seems to have in other western countries. While cinemas are smoke-free, even some quite pricey restaurants still let people light up freely. When you add in the pollution from Dublin's increasingly heavy traffic, you might feel your lungs are due for a bit of fresh air after a few days in the city.

LEGAL MATTERS

If you need legal assistance contact the Legal Aid Board (Map 5; ☎ 240 0900), St Stephen's Green House, Earlsfort Terrace, Dublin 2.

Drugs

The importation of prohibited drugs is illegal and automatically leads to arrest and possible imprisonment. The possession of small quantities of marijuana or hashish attracts a fine and a warning, but most other drugs are treated more seriously. So-called 'party' drugs such as cocaine and ecstasy are considered class 'A' drugs, as is heroin, and possession can result in a prison term.

Public Drunkenness

Although illegal, enormous leeway is granted by the police to displays of public drunkenness. If matters get out of hand, a word in your ear from a police officer is usually enough to send you on your way. Fighting is treated a little more harshly; if you're involved in a fight you may have to spend a night in a cell, to 'cool off'.

The loosening of the licensing laws in 2000, which saw pubs and clubs extend their opening hours (see Business Hours later in this chapter), also has its downside: drinking on the street is now the subject of a €80 fine. Although the practice of drinking on the street outside a crowded pub has continued at some establishments, it is technically illegal and in order to avoid the risk of a fine we suggest that you keep your drinking indoors.

Drinking & Driving

The legal drinking age is 18 (although some pubs and clubs won't serve people under 21 years old) and you may need photographic identification to prove your age. The legal blood-alcohol limit for driving is 80mg of alcohol per 100mL of blood, and although this is the highest in Europe, a crackdown on drunk drivers in the last decade has gone a long way towards eradicating the tolerance shown by the authorities to those caught driving while under the influence. Stiff fines – and sometimes a jail term – can be incurred. Spot checks by the gardaí are increasingly common, especially around holidays such as Christmas.

Traffic offences (such as illegal parking or speeding) incur a fine, for which you're normally allowed 30 days to pay.

BUSINESS HOURS

Offices are open from 9am to 5pm Monday to Friday, but shops stay open a little later.

Thursday is a late shopping day, usually until 8pm. All shops open on Saturday and an increasing number on Sunday, typically from noon to 6pm. In winter, tourist attractions are often open shorter hours, and some may be open fewer days per week or may be shut completely.

After years of pressure, pub hours were finally extended in 2000, but to many still remain too short and too confusing. All pubs are legally allowed to open at 10.30am Monday to Saturday and noon on Sunday, but the majority of Dublin's pubs don't actually open their doors until noon daily. Closing hours differ depending on the day: midnight Monday to Wednesday, 1am Thursday to Saturday and 11.30pm on Sunday. To make matters more complicated, many pubs have obtained legal bar extensions, extending their opening hours to 2.30am. The archaic institution known as 'holy hour' – whereby pubs closed for a couple of hours during the afternoon – has been scrapped, along with the 30-minute difference between summer hours and winter hours. The only days when pubs will definitely be closed are Christmas Day and Good Friday.

Banks are usually open 10am to 4pm Monday to Friday and stay open until 5pm on Thursday. Post offices generally open from 8.30am to 5.30pm or 6pm Monday to Friday and 9am to 1pm on Saturday. Dublin's historically significant GPO (Map 4), on O'Connell St north of the river, has longer opening hours: 8am to 8pm Monday to Saturday, 10am to 6.30pm Sunday and holidays.

PUBLIC HOLIDAYS & SPECIAL EVENTS
Public Holidays
Ireland has the following public holidays:

New Year's Day	1 January
St Patrick's Day	17 March
Good Friday	March/April
Easter Monday	March/April
May Day Holiday	1 May
June Holiday	first Monday in June
August Holiday	first Monday in August
October Holiday	last Monday in October
Christmas Day	25 December
St Stephen's Day	26 December

St Patrick's Day, St Stephen's Day and May Day holidays are taken on the following Monday should they fall on a weekend.

Special Events
St Patrick's Day The most important holiday of the year in Dublin is undoubtedly Christmas, but St Patrick's Day runs a close second. The main Dublin parade, where up to 500,000 spectators watch over 100 marching bands from all over the world, is preceded by a weekend-long street party featuring street theatre, music, a fireworks display and lots of drinking. The single biggest event apart from the parade is the Guinness Temple Bar Fleadh or music festival, with most of the area's pubs celebrating the weekend with music and, again, plenty of drinking. On St Stephen's Green a large *céilidh* attracts thousands of revellers who dance the afternoon away.

Other cultural, musical and sporting highlights of the Dublin year include:

February to April
Six Nations Rugby Ireland plays its home matches at Lansdowne Rd Stadium in Ballsbridge. The highlight of the season is the Ireland-England match, played in Ireland every second year (2003, 2005 and so on).

March to April
Irish Kennel Club Championships The Irish equivalent of Crufts takes place on the 16 and 17 March every year at the National Show Centre (☎ 840 0735) in Cloghran, County Dublin. If dolled-up doggies are your thing, you won't want to miss this one.

Dublin Film Festival Features a usually excellent selection of big- and small-budget films, both domestic and international, at a selected number of cinemas. Call ☎ 679 2937 or check out the Web site at ⓦ www.iol.ie/dff for details.

Easter Bank Holiday
Howth Jazz Festival Takes place in the seaside suburb of Dublin, north of the city. Most gigs are free. Call ☎ 873 3199 for details of who's playing and where.

April to May
Heineken Green Energy Festival One of the

FACTS FOR THE VISITOR

Bloomsday

On 16 June (Bloomsday) Leopold Bloom's journey around Dublin in *Ulysses* is re-enacted; various readings and dramatisations take place around the city. Many of the places visited on that well documented 1904 journey around Dublin can still be found. Some of the interesting reminders of Joyce's Dublin and the chapters of *Ulysses* in which they appear are described here. The names in parentheses refer to the episodes in Homer's *Odyssey* to which Joyce's chapters correspond.

The Martello Tower, Sandycove (right) near Dun Laoghaire, Chapter 1 (Telemachus). After the open-air shave with which the book begins, Buck Mulligan goes for a swim in the nearby Forty Foot Pool. The tower houses the James Joyce Museum, and it's still traditional to swim unclothed in the pool before 9am.

JANE SMITH

St Andrew's Church & Sweny's Chemist Shop (Map 5), south Dublin, Chapter 5 (Lotus Eaters). On his way into the centre, Leopold Bloom stops to observe part of the mass at All Hallows Church. This is now St Andrew's Church on Westland Row, just east of Trinity College and right beside Pearse Station. From there Bloom goes to Sweny's Chemist Shop on Lincoln Place, which is still a chemist shop, still has the name Sweny prominently displayed and still sells lemon soap, though a bar will now cost you €2.55 or €3.80, rather than the fourpence Bloom paid in 1904.

The Oval & Mooney's (Map 4), north Dublin, Chapter 7 (Aeolus). Leopold Bloom and Stephen Dedalus both visit the office of the *Freeman's Journal* and the *Evening Telegraph* on Prince's St North. A branch of BHS now occupies the site. Visits are then made to two pubs. The Oval on Abbey St Middle is still the Oval, but Mooney's on the other side of O'Connell St on Lower Abbey St has changed markedly since Joyce's day and is now the Abbey Mooney. In 1988 a series of 14 pavement plaques were placed in the city to trace Bloom's peregrinations from Middle Abbey St in this chapter to the National Library in Chapter 9.

Thomas Moore statue (Map 6), south Dublin, Chapter 8 (Lestrygonians). Leopold Bloom crosses the River Liffey by the O'Connell St Bridge and walks down Westmoreland St by the Bank of Ireland, ruminating on the amusing position of the statue of poet Thomas Moore on the traffic island where College St meets Westmoreland St. To this day it's a local joke that the author of the poem *The Meeting of the Waters* should have his commemorative statue plonked in front of a public urinal.

Davy Byrne's (Map 7), Duke St, south Dublin, Chapter 8 (Lestrygonians). Having 'crossed under Tommy Moore's roguish finger' Bloom continues by Trinity College, noting the provost's house, where the college provost still resides, and various shops along Grafton St, particularly Brown Thomas. This is still one of Dublin's best-known shops, although it has now moved across the road and its former location is occupied by Marks & Spencer. Finally he turns into Duke St and having glanced into Burton's (no longer there) decides he doesn't like the look of the patrons and turns back to Davy Byrne's. Bloom would hardly recognise Joyce's 'moral pub' today as it was extensively remodelled in the 1940s and then yuppified in the 1980s. If Joyce turned up today he would probably be turned away by the bouncers.

National Library (Map 5), Kildare St, south Dublin, Chapter 9 (Scylla and Charybdis). From Davy Byrne's, Bloom continues down Molesworth St to the National Museum and National Library, both on Kildare St. Stephen Dedalus is also in the library, discussing Shakespeare with a group of famous Dubliners, including the poet and journalist Æ (George Russell; 1867–1935).

Ormond Hotel (Map 5), Ormond Quay, north Dublin, Chapter 11 (Sirens). Although it has been changed considerably over the course of this century, the Ormond Hotel still overlooks the Liffey from Upper Ormond Quay and a plaque outside commemorates its role in *Ulysses*. On the way there from the National Library, Bloom walks along Wellington Quay on the Temple Bar side of the Liffey and contemplates a stop at the Clarence Hotel before crossing the Liffey to the Ormond.

Bella Cohen's & Olhausen's (Map 4), north Dublin, Chapter 15 (Circe). Once near St Mary's Pro-Cathedral, the red-light district of north Dublin (dubbed Nighttown in *Ulysses* and known as Monto to Dubliners in 1904) is no more. The prostitutes left the area when the British army departed in 1922 after Ireland's independence. Bella Cohen was indeed a brothel madam in 1904, though her premises were at 82, not 81, Railway St (then known as Lower Tyrone St). There are still some colourful pubs in the vicinity but this area contains nothing of interest today: it has been totally redeveloped, contains soul-destroying public housing and is definitely not a place to linger at night. In this chapter Bloom also drops into Olhausen's, the pork butcher, at 72 Talbot St to pick up a pig's trotter and a sheep's hoof as a snack. Olhausen's is still in business.

Amiens St (Map 4), north Dublin, Chapter 16 (Eumaeus). Leopold Bloom and Stephen Dedalus, whose paths have crossed several times during the day, finally meet in Nighttown and wander down Amiens St, the main road into the city from Clontarf, which passes Connolly Station and ends by the Busáras. On the way they pass Dan Bergin's Pub (now Lloyd's), Mullett's (still there), the Signal House (now J&M Cleary), the North Star Hotel (still there) and the 1842 Dock Tavern (which, after a spell as the Master Mariner Bar, is now Kenny's Lounge). They then turn into Store St (beside today's Busáras) past the Dublin City Morgue (still there) and the City Bakery (now the Kylemore Bakery).

Gardiner St to Eccles St (Map 4), north Dublin, Chapters 17 and 18 (Ithaca; Penelope). Bloom and Dedalus make the long walk up Gardiner St, now known to travellers as a favourite strip for central B&Bs. At Mountjoy Square they turn left then right to pass by St George's Church and end up at Bloom's home at 7 Eccles St. A private hospital now occupies the site where Molly Bloom's soliloquy ends *Ulysses*, but Georgian houses similar to the original No 7 still stand on the opposite side of the street.

For Joyce fans there are several books that follow the wanderings of *Ulysses'* characters in minute detail. *Joyce's Dublin – a Walking Guide to Ulysses,* by Jack McCarthy, traces the events chapter by chapter with clear maps. *The Ulysses Guide – Tours Through Joyce's Dublin,* by Robert Nicholson, has easy-to-follow maps. It concentrates on certain areas and follows the events of the various related chapters.

city's most important pop and rock festivals, featuring an array of local and international bands at different venues throughout the city, including an open-air gig in Dublin Castle, usually the highlight. Call ☎ 284 1747 for details.

Mardi Gras Held on the last weekend in May, this is Dublin's Gay Pride weekend, which includes a parade and plenty of other festive goings-on. Call ☎ 873 4932 or check W www.webab.ie/dublinmardigras/home.html for details.

June
Irish Open Golf Championship Europe's top pros participate in this annual competition which in recent years has taken place at the Druid's Glen Course in County Wicklow. Call ☎ 676 6650 for information on dates.

Women's Mini-Marathon Sponsored by the *Evening Herald* (second Sunday in June) This popular event is now the largest of its kind in the world, attracting up to 35,000 participants in a 10km run for charity. Call ☎ 670 9461 for entry details.

June to August
Music in the Park Dublin Corporation sponsors a free music festival at different parks throughout the city. Call ☎ 672 3388 or check W www.dublincorp.ie for details.

July
Guinness Blues Festival At venues throughout the city centre, culminating in a live show in front of the Bank of Ireland at College Green. Call ☎ 497 0381 for details.

August
Dublin Horse Show At the Royal Dublin Society Showground, features an international show-jumping competition. Ireland's answer to Wimbledon and Ascot when it comes to showing off one's social status. Call ☎ 668 0866 for further details.

September
All-Ireland Finals The two showcase events of the Gaelic Athletic Association's season are the hurling and Gaelic football finals, which take place on the second and third Sundays in September respectively, at Croke Park, to the north-east of the city centre (Map 2). Call ☎ 836 3222 for details of hard-to-come-by tickets.

October
Dublin Theatre Festival Europe's biggest theatre festival takes place over two weeks beginning on the first Monday of the month. Call ☎ 677 8439 for details or check out the Web site at W www.eircomtheatrefestival.com.

Dublin City Marathon Held on the last Monday of the month. Contact ☎ 677 8439.

November
French Film Festival Organised by the French embassy's cultural department. Contact ☎ 676 2197 for details.

December to January
Funderland Dublin's traditional funfair, featuring all kinds of stomach-turning rides, takes place at the Royal Dublin Society, usually for two weeks starting on December 26.

DOING BUSINESS
A key element of Ireland's economic success over the last decade has been the successful encouragement of foreign business interests to set up in Ireland. Since the early 1980s, successive Irish governments have pursued a policy of using favourable tax incentives to attract foreign investment; in short, if you have a foreign company and are willing to set up in Ireland, you will be exempt from virtually all corporate tax for your first 10 years in Ireland. Furthermore, Ireland is renowned for its highly skilled labour force, which has consistently and expertly adapted itself to the constantly changing requirements of modern industry.

The Industrial Development Authority (IDA) is the state-run organisation responsible for attracting new business to Ireland and encouraging those already here to expand their interests. Traditionally, the IDA has sought to target a fairly diverse range of companies, but has especially concentrated on those industries deemed to be internationally mobile, such as electronics, pharmaceuticals, engineering and financial services providers.

The success of the IDA's campaign is seen in the number of foreign businesses now present in Ireland; for example, in electronics alone there are approximately 200 foreign owned companies using Ireland as a base, employing over 33,000 people on a permanent basis and an additional 5500 people on a temporary or contract basis. In 1997, foreign-owned electronics businesses accounted for over €10 billion-worth of exports from Ireland, 36% of the country's total exports.

At a smaller level, the IDA's sister authority, Forbáirt, is the organisation responsible for the distribution of start-up grants to local businesses. In order to receive a grant, you must apply to the local enterprise board for your area (there is at least one board for each county; the larger, more populated counties, such as Dublin and Cork, have four) who will then consider your application on the basis of viability and potential for growth. It will also investigate similar businesses operating within the area, and if none are deemed to be in direct competition with your venture, you have more than a good chance of receiving a grant. Grants are available to anyone whose business address falls within the jurisdiction of the enterprise board, including all citizens of the EU (as long as they are based in Ireland) and legal residents from outside the EU.

For further information about both the IDA and Forbáirt, check out their respective Web sites at **W** www.idaireland.com and **W** www.forbairt.ie.

WORK

The success of the Celtic Tiger has resulted in unemployment dropping to an all-time low of about 8%. Consequently, opportunities for work have increased, especially in the tourist industry, usually in restaurants and pubs. Today, most of the people working in Dublin's cafes are European, usually Spanish, Italian or French. However, without skills, it is difficult to find a job that pays sufficiently well to enable you to save money. You're almost certainly better off saving in your country of origin. As Ireland is a member of the EU, citizens of any other EU country can work legally in Ireland, as can non-EU citizens who have a student visa, but only for the duration of their visa.

FACTS FOR THE VISITOR

Getting There & Away

AIR

Dublin is Ireland's major international airport and Aer Lingus is the Irish national airline with connections to other countries in Europe and to the USA. Ryanair is the next largest Irish airline, also with routes to Britain and mainland Europe. Aer Lingus has offices throughout Dublin and in virtually every large town in Ireland; Ryanair has streamlined its operations to the extent that you can now only book tickets by phone (☎ 609 7881), at its airport desks (including Dublin airport) or on the Internet (W www.ryanair.com).

Dublin Airport (☎ 814 1111) is 8 miles (13km) north of the city centre. There is an airport departure tax but it is built into the price of the ticket.

Other Parts of Ireland

There are international airports in Cork and Shannon, and regional airports in Donegal, Knock, Kerry and Sligo. All are linked with Dublin. Most journeys within Ireland take between 30 and 40 minutes. The main companies flying domestic routes are Aer Lingus and Aer Arann, who are a part of the former.

For student travel information in Ireland, contact usit Now, run by the Union of Students in Ireland. The usit office (Map 6; ☎ 602 1600, fax 679 2124, W www.usitnow .ie), 19–21 Aston Quay, beside O'Connell Bridge on the south side of the Liffey, is open from 9am to 6pm Monday to Friday (to 8pm on Thursday) and 10am to 5.30pm on Saturday. It has a good notice board for travellers. As well as providing travel information, usit Now also issues International Student Identity Cards (ISICs).

The UK

London to Dublin has taken over from London to New York and London to Paris as the busiest international air route in the world. There are dozens of services on numerous airlines to the Irish capital. Aer Lingus and British Midland fly from Heathrow; Aer Lingus also flies from Gatwick and London Stansted; the franchise partners Cityflyer and British Airways Express fly from Gatwick; Ryanair flies from Gatwick, Luton and Stansted; and KLM uk and Cityjet fly from London City airport. Between London and Dublin, return fares are usually cheaper than one-way fares, as most airlines prefer to sell return tickets. The regular return fare from London to Dublin with Aer Lingus or British Midland starts at UK£79, but can go up to UK£350, depending on availability and when you book. The standard one-way fare from Dublin to Stansted, Luton or Gatwick is €112.50.

Many return fares require a variety of advance-purchase arrangements, minimum stays and so on. Fares also vary depending on which cities, and even which airports, you fly to and from. In London, fares out of Stansted are usually cheaper than those from London City airport, while Heathrow and Gatwick fall somewhere inbetween the two.

The stiff competition between the airlines serving the UK–Ireland routes has seen a proliferation of limited-offer special deals, which appear intermittently. On occasions, there are return fares that come as cheap as UK£15. These should be booked well in advance as seats are limited. A handy Web address for finding the cheapest available flights is at W www.wannabeinireland .com.

UK phone numbers and Web site addresses (where applicable) are:

Aer Lingus
☎ 0845 973 7747
W www.flyaerlingus.ie
British Airways
☎ 0845 7773 3377
W www.british-airways.com
British European
☎ 0870 567 6676
W www.british-european.com

British Midland
☎ 0870 607 0555
W www.flybmi.co.uk
Gill Airways
☎ 0191-214 6666
W www.gill-airways.com
Go Fly
☎ 0870 607 6543
W www.gofly.com
KLM uk
☎ 0870 507 4074
W www.airuk.co.uk
Ryanair
☎ 0870 333 1231
W www.ryanair.ie

In London alone STA (☎ 0870 160 6070, W www.statravel.co.uk), 86 Brompton Rd, London SW7, has 14 branches.

There are many other places in the UK that have direct connections with Dublin. Some of these, with the relevant airlines, are:

Birmingham	Aer Lingus, Ryanair
Bournemouth	Ryanair
Bristol	Aer Lingus, Ryanair
Cardiff	Ryanair
East Midlands	British Midland, Cityjet
Edinburgh	Aer Lingus, Go Fly
Exeter	British European
Glasgow	Aer Lingus, Go Fly, Ryanair
Guernsey	British European
Isle of Man	Manx Airlines
Jersey	British European
Leeds/Bradford	Aer Lingus, Ryanair
Liverpool	Ryanair
Luton	Ryanair, Britannia Airways
Manchester	Aer Lingus, Ryanair
Newcastle	Aer Lingus
Southampton	Cityflyer/ British Airways Express
Teesside	Ryanair

Continental Europe

Dublin is connected to most major centres in Europe. Standard return fares are: Amsterdam €212, Milan €387.50, Paris €140, Düsseldorf €248 and Stockholm €253. Some of the relevant airlines include:

Amsterdam	Aer Lingus, British Airways, British Midlands
Barcelona	Iberia
Bern	Air Engiadina
Brussels	Aer Lingus, Ryanair, Sabena
Copenhagen	Aer Lingus, Scandinavian Airlines (SAS)
Düsseldorf	Aer Lingus
Frankfurt-am-Main	Aer Lingus, Lufthansa
Geneva	Air Engiadina
Helsinki	Aer Lingus, Finnair
Madrid	Iberia
Malaga	Aer Lingus, Cityjet
Milan	Aer Lingus, Alitalia
Paris	Aer Lingus, Air France, Ryanair
Rome	Aer Lingus, Alitalia
Stockholm	Aer Lingus, Finnair
Vienna	Tyrolean Airways
Zürich	Aer Lingus, Crossair

USA & Canada

Direct flights from the USA fly to Dublin as well as Shannon, but because competition on flights is so fierce, it's generally cheaper to fly to London first then pick up a Dublin flight.

Aer Lingus connects Dublin (and Shannon) with Baltimore, Boston, Chicago, Los Angeles, New York and Newark. Its New York office (☎ 800 474 7424) is at 538 Broadhollow Rd, Melville 11747. Continental Airlines links Dublin (and Shannon) with Newark. The other US operator with direct connections to Ireland is Delta Airlines (☎ 800 241 4141), which operates Atlanta–Shannon–Dublin and New York–Dublin, routes linking into its huge US network.

During the summer high season the round trip between New York and Dublin with Aer Lingus costs US$858 midweek or US$918 at the weekend, with an advance purchase of at least 14 days. Tickets bought 45 days prior to departure are cheaper: US$658 midweek and US$718 at the weekend. In the low season (16 October to 16 December and 26 December to 6 April), Dublin–New York costs US$358 midweek and US$418 at the weekend, with only three days' advance purchase required. From Los Angeles to Dublin, high/low-season prices are around US$851/711, and there is no difference between midweek and

GETTING THERE & AWAY

weekend fares. Two weeks' advance purchase is required.

High-season discount return fares from New York to London range from US$500 to US$700; in the low season they range from US$400 to US$500. From the west coast, fares to London cost from around US$150 more.

There are no direct flights that go from Canada to Ireland – visitors have to fly to London and get a connection there. In Canada, Aer Lingus can be contacted by calling ☎ 800 223 6537, although it doesn't actually fly to Canada.

Priceline is a 'name your price' service on the Web (W www.priceline.com). You enter your destination, time of travel and the price you're willing to pay, and if one of the participating airlines has a seat available that it would rather sell at a discount than leave unoccupied, you'll be emailed within an hour.

Check the travel sections of the Sunday editions of such papers as the *New York Times*, *Los Angeles Times*, *San Francisco Chronicle/Examiner* and *Chicago Tribune* for the latest fares.

Offices of Council Travel (☎ 800 226 8624, W www.counciltravel.com) or STA Travel (☎ 800 781 4040, W www.statravel.com) in the USA or Travel CUTS in Canada (☎ 800 667 2887, W www.travelcuts.com) are good sources of reliable discounted tickets.

Australia & New Zealand

Excursion or Apex fares (cheaper tickets with some form of restriction, such as a minimum stay) from Australia or New Zealand to most major European destinations can have a return flight to Dublin tagged on at no extra cost. Return fares from Australia vary from around A$1800 (low season) to A$2500 (high season), but there are often short-term special deals available. STA Travel (☎ 03-9349 2411, W www.statravel.com.au), 224 Faraday St, Carlton, Vic 3053, and Flight Centre (☎ 131 600 Australia-wide, W www.flightcentre.com.au), 82 Elizabeth St, Sydney, are good sources of reliable discounted

tickets. Both have offices throughout Australia.

Some travel agents, particularly smaller ones, advertise cheap air fares in the travel sections of weekend newspapers, such as *The Age* in Melbourne and the *Sydney Morning Herald*. Aer Lingus has an office (☎ 02-9244 2123) in Sydney at 64 York St.

The cheapest fares from New Zealand are available on services travelling via Asia, but the connections on these flights are generally not as good as those on flights via the USA. Round-the-world (RTW) and Circle Pacific fares for travel to or from New Zealand are usually the best value, and are often cheaper than a return ticket. Fares from New Zealand to major European cities usually range from NZ$2099 in the low season to NZ$2499 in the high season.

The *New Zealand Herald* has a travel section in which travel agents advertise fares. Flight Centre (☎ 09-309 6171) has a central office in Auckland at National Bank Towers (on the corner of Queen and Darby Sts) and branches throughout the country. STA Travel (☎ 09-309 0458, W www.statravel.com.nz) has its main office at 10 High St, Auckland, and has other offices in Auckland as well as in Christchurch, Hamilton, Wellington, Dunedin and Palmerston North.

Airline Offices

Airline offices in Dublin include:

Aer Lingus (☎ 886 6705 departures & arrivals, ☎ 886 8888 reservations, e bookings @aerlingus.ie, W www.flyaerlingus.com) 40–41 Upper O'Connell St, Dublin 1; 13 St Stephen's Green, Dublin 2; Jury's Hotel, Ballsbridge, Dublin 4; 12 Upper George's St, Dun Laoghaire

Aeroflot (☎ 844 6166, W www.aeroflot.org) Dublin Airport

Air Canada (☎ 679 3958, W www.aircanada.ca) 7 Herbert St, Dublin 2

Air France (☎ 844 5633, W www.airfrance.co.uk) Dublin Airport

Alitalia (☎ 677 5171, W www.alitalia.co.uk) 4–5 Dawson St, Dublin 2

British Airways (☎ 1814 1111, W www.british-airways.com) Dublin Airport

Air Travel Glossary

Alliances Many of the world's leading airlines are now intimately involved with each other, sharing everything from reservations systems and check-in to aircraft and frequent-flyer schemes. Opponents say that alliances restrict competition. Whatever the arguments, there is no doubt that big alliances are the way of the future.

Courier Fares Businesses often need to send urgent documents or freight securely and quickly. Courier companies hire people to accompany the package through customs and, in return, offer a discount ticket which is sometimes a bargain. However, you may have to surrender all your baggage allowance and take only carry-on luggage.

Fares Airlines traditionally offer 1st class (coded F), business class (coded J) and economy class (coded Y) tickets. These days there are so many promotional and discounted fares available that few passengers pay full fare.

Lost Tickets If you lose your airline ticket, an airline will usually treat it like a travellers cheque and, after inquiries, issue you with another one. Legally, however, an airline is entitled to treat it like cash and if you lose it then it's gone forever. Take very good care of your tickets.

Onward Tickets An entry requirement for many countries is that you have a ticket out of the country. If you're unsure of your next move, the easiest solution is to buy the cheapest onward ticket to a neighbouring country or a ticket from a reliable airline which can later be refunded if you do not use it.

Open-Jaw Tickets These are return tickets where you fly out to one place but return from another. If available, this can save you backtracking to your arrival point.

Overbooking Since every flight has some passengers who fail to show up, airlines often book more passengers than they have seats. Usually excess passengers make up for the no-shows, but occasionally somebody gets 'bumped' onto the next available flight. Guess who it is most likely to be? The passengers who check in late. If you do get 'bumped', you are normally offered some form of compensation.

Reconfirmation Some airlines require you to reconfirm your flight at least 72 hours prior to departure. Check your travel documents to see if this is the case.

Restrictions Discounted tickets often have various restrictions on them – such as needing to be paid for in advance and incurring a penalty to be altered or cancelled. Others are restrictions on the minimum and maximum period you must be away.

Round-the-World Tickets RTW tickets give you a limited period (usually a year) in which to circumnavigate the globe. You can go anywhere the carrying airlines go, as long as you don't backtrack. The number of stopovers or total number of separate flights is decided before you set off and they usually cost a bit more than a basic return flight.

Ticketless Travel Airlines are gradually waking up to the realisation that paper tickets are unnecessary encumbrances. On simple one-way or return trips, reservations details can be held on computer and the passenger merely shows ID to claim their seat.

Transferred Tickets Airline tickets cannot be transferred from one person to another. Travellers sometimes try to sell the return half of their ticket, but officials can ask you to prove that you are the person named on the ticket. On an international flight, tickets are compared with passports.

British Midland (☎ 407 3036, **W** www.flybmi
.com) Dublin Airport
Crossair (☎ 1890 200515, **W** www.crossair.ch)
Dublin Airport
Delta Air Lines (☎ 844 4166, **W** www.delta-air
.com) 3 Dawson St, Dublin 2
Finnair (☎ 844 6565, **W** www.finnair.co.uk)
Dublin Airport
Iberia (☎ 407 3017, **W** www.iberia.com)
54 Dawson St, Dublin 2
Lufthansa Airlines (☎ 844 5544, **W** www
.lufthansa.co.uk) Dublin Airport
Manx Airlines (☎ 260 1588, **W** www.manx
-airlines.com) Dublin Airport
Qantas Airways (☎ 407 3278, **W** www.qantas
.com.au) Dublin Airport
Sabena (☎ 844 5454, **W** www.sabena.com)
Dublin Airport
Scandinavian Airlines (SAS) (☎ 844 5888,
W www.flysas.co.uk) Dublin Airport
Tyrolean Airways (☎ 814 4085, **W** www.aua
.com) 140–142 Pembroke Rd, Dublin 4

BUS

Busáras (Map 4), on Store St, Dublin 1, just
north of the Custom House and the River
Liffey, is Dublin's central bus station.

Other Parts of Ireland

Travelling on buses (referred to as coaches
in Ireland) is substantially cheaper than the
train, albeit a bit slower. Bus Éireann
(☎ 836 6111, **W** www.buseireann.ie), at
Busáras, is the Republic's national bus line,
with services all over the Republic and to
the North. There is also a Bus Éireann
desk in the Dublin Bus office (Map 4) on
O'Connell St. Standard one-way/return
fares to/from Dublin include:

to/from	one-way	return
Cork	€17.15	€26
Galway	€11.45	€15.50
Limerick	€13.25	€20.50
Waterford	€ 8.90	€13.35
Wexford	€10.15	€15.25

Special deals are often available. Irish
Rambler tickets, which can be purchased
from Bus Éireann, give unlimited bus travel
within the Republic of Ireland. They cost
€40.65 (three days), €92.70 (eight days) or
€133.30 (15 days). Children under 16 years
of age pay half fare. Bus Éireann also offers
discounts for return travel in midweek,
available for one week, but you must travel
on either Tuesday, Wednesday or Thursday.
Tickets, valid for one month, cost around
€2 less than an ordinary return.

There are several private bus companies
that run services to various towns and cities
throughout Ireland. Although not nearly as
regular as Bus Éireann's, their services are
usually much cheaper.

Nestor Coaches (☎ 832 0094) has a service three times daily to Galway, leaving
Dublin at 2pm, 6pm and 10pm (single/
return €7.60/10.20, 3½ hours). Departures
are from Tara St DART station, George's
Quay (Map 5). JJ Kavanagh Rapid Express
(☎ 679 1549) offers a service to Waterford,
with nine departures daily Monday to Saturday and eight on Sunday (single/return
€8.90/15.25, three hours). It also runs a
service three times daily to Limerick (sin-
gle/return €7.60/11.45, 3¼ hrs). All JJ Kavanagh buses leave from Custom House
Quay (Map 5).

Bus Éireann runs coaches from Belfast's
Europa station seven times a day, Monday to
Saturday, and six times on Sunday (single/
return €14/19, 3¼ hours). Bus Éireann also
runs five buses daily from Derry (single/
return €14/19, 4½ hours).

TRAIN

The rail network in Ireland is gradually improving, but it is still quite poor compared
to virtually every other European country.
Not only is it expensive, but service is slow
and carriages are often filthy. On the plus
side, distances are short and the longest trip
you can make by train is 4½ hours (from
Tralee in County Kerry). Iarnród Éireann
(Irish Rail; Map 4; ☎ 836 6222), 35 Lower
Abbey St, Dublin 1, operates the Republic's trains on routes that fan out from
Dublin.

Other Parts of Ireland

Connolly station (Map 2; ☎ 836 3333,
W www.irishrail.ie), just north of the Liffey
and the city centre, has trains arriving from

Belfast, Derry, Sligo, Wexford and other points in the north. Heuston station (Map 3; ☎ 836 5421), just south of the Liffey and west of the centre, is the station where services from Cork, Galway, Killarney, Limerick, Waterford and other points in the west, south and south-west arrive.

Examples of regular fares from Dublin are: to Belfast €26.70 (2¼ hours, up to eight per day), to Cork €42.55 (3¼ hours, up to nine daily), to Galway €20.35 (three hours, up to five daily) and to Limerick €33.65 (2¼ hours, up to nine daily). As with buses, special fares are often available. A same-day return from Belfast is the same price as a single fare. First-class tickets cost €7.60 over the standard fare for a single journey. If you're aged under 26 you can get a FairCard for €10.20, which gives you a 50% discount on regular fares. See the next section for information on tickets giving unlimited bus and train travel.

BUS & TRAIN DISCOUNT DEALS

The Emerald Card gives you unlimited travel throughout Ireland on all scheduled services of Iarnród Éireann, Northern Ireland Railways, Bus Éireann, Dublin Bus, Ulsterbus and Citybus. The card costs €157.50 (or around UK£97) for eight days or €272 (around UK£167) for 15 days. Children under 16 years of age pay half fare.

For €11, full-time students can have a Travelsave Stamp affixed to their ISIC card. This gives a 50% discount on Iarnród Éireann trains, and 15% on Bus Éireann services for fares over €1.30. Enquire at a usit Now office for further details (see Other Parts of Ireland under Air earlier in this chapter).

BOAT

Ferry services from Britain and France operate to a variety of ports in Ireland.

The ferry terminal at Dun Laoghaire, the port on the southern side of Dublin Bay, is well equipped and easily accessible by either the DART or bus. Dublin ferry terminal is a 3km walk from the city centre and public transport is linked to its departure

and arrival times. See the Getting Around chapter for details of public transport to and from the terminals. The Internet Ferry Guide (W www.ex.ac.uk/~mspunter/ifg/) has links to ferry and freight services worldwide, including all ferry services to Ireland.

There's no departure tax if you leave Dublin by ferry.

The UK

There are two direct routes to Dublin – one from Holyhead, on the north-western tip of Wales, to Dublin itself, and the other from Holyhead to Dun Laoghaire. The range of prices given below reflects seasonal differences and special offers, which may or may not be available.

Stena Line (☎ 0870 570 7070) operates a passenger and car service between Holyhead and Dun Laoghaire. The high-speed catamaran (High-Speed Service or HSS) takes a little over 1½ hours and costs from UK£24 to UK£26 for a foot passenger (depending on whether you travel midweek or at the weekend) and from UK£169 to UK£209 for a car (prices are for cars with up to four passengers). Stena Line also runs a conventional ferry service from Holyhead to Dublin, but this service does not take foot passengers. The crossing takes 3½ hours and tickets cost from UK£204 to UK£244 for a five-day return and UK£378 for a standard return.

Irish Ferries (☎ 0870 517 1717) also operates ferries between Holyhead and Dublin. Foot-passenger fares range from UK£18 to UK£28 (UK£13.50 to UK£21 for those aged under 26 years), and car fares range from UK£139 to UK£259 for a five-day return, and UK£189 to UK£289 for a midweek return, travelling to/from Ireland on a Tuesday or Wednesday only.

Stena Sealink (☎ 204 7777, W www.stenaline.co.uk) is at Stena Line, The Ferry Terminal, Dun Laoghaire. Irish Ferries (Map 5; ☎ 661 0511, W www.irishferries.ie) is at 2–4 Merrion Row, Dublin 2.

Other ferry services to Ireland from Britain include Swansea to Cork (Swansea Cork Ferries), Fishguard to Rosslare (Stena Sealink), Pembroke to Rosslare (Irish Fer-

GETTING THERE & AWAY

ries) and a variety of services to Northern Ireland (Norse Irish Ferries, P&O and Seacat).

France

From France there are services from Roscoff to Cork, Cherbourg to Cork and Rosslare, and Le Havre to Cork and Rosslare. From Roscoff or Cherbourg to Rosslare (by far the most popular route), single passengers pay from €57 in low season to €107 in high season. A car with up to two passengers costs from €189 to €455, depending on the season. The crossing takes 17½ hours from Cherbourg, 16½ hours from Roscoff. You can also travel to Ireland from France via Britain with the Irish Ferries Landbridge service. These services are operated by Irish Ferries, and offer various promotional rates that are cheaper than regular prices, with no restrictions on the length of your stay. There are only a limited number of Landbridge places on every sailing, and these operate on a first-come, first-served basis. They can also be used by Eurailpass holders. Contact the Association of European Railways for details (☎ 800 356 6711, W www.raileurope.com/us/rail/passes/eurail).

ROAD & SEA

Bus Éireann and National Express operate Eurolines services direct from London and other places in the UK to Dublin. Contact Eurolines in the UK (☎ 020-7730 8235, W www.eurolines.com) or National Express (☎ 0870 580 8080, W www.goby coach.com) for details. Slattery's (☎ 020-7482 1604) of London is an Irish bus company with routes from Bristol, Leeds, London, Liverpool, Manchester and northern Wales to Dublin.

London to Dublin takes about 12 hours, and the price depends on whether you travel overnight (preferable though hardly more comfortable) or during the day. A daytime single/return costs UK£19/28, and an over-night single/return costs UK£36/47. Be warned that the buses are cramped and usually full, and delays are not uncommon.

ORGANISED TOURS

Nearly all organised tours to Ireland devote at least some time to Dublin. For a complete list of reputable tour operators worldwide that offer trips to Dublin, check out the Bord Fáilte Web site (W www.ireland.travel.ie/touroperators).

From the UK

Celtic Links (☎ 01292-511133, W www.celticlinks.co.uk) will also put together an itinerary for any budget, and only sells directly, rather than through travel agencies, thus keeping costs down. CIE Tours International (☎ 020-8667 0011, W www.cietours.ie) organises a wide range of tours, from a basic five-day tour for UK£386 to 10-day tours for around UK£850. Each tour involves at least one day's sightseeing in Dublin. Its season runs from mid-May to October.

From Continental Europe

In France, the Paris-based Gaeland/Ashling tour company (☎ 01 42 71 44 44, W www.gaeland-ashling.com) operates an eight-day 'Dublin and its Celtic Heritage' tour for around €1220, which includes a city tour of Dublin as well as visits to some of Ireland's most popular Celtic sites. Languages & Travel (☎ 04 37 41 12 08, W www.langtra.com), based in Lyons, combines sightseeing tours with language courses in Dublin, for around €220 (1444FF) per week in the low season and €525 (3440FF) in the summer.

The Dutch tour company NBBS Reizen (☎ 020-620 5071, W www.nbbs.nl), based in Amsterdam, does weekend and week-long tours of Ireland, all of which include a Dublin sightseeing program. TEE Travel (☎ 020-471 5781, W www.teetravel.nl), also in Amsterdam, specialises in golfing holidays, including those to Dublin. They do packages that are tailor-made to suit your requirements.

From the USA

Europe Express (☎ 0800 426 3615, W www.europeexpress.com) in Washington can organise customised packages to parts of

Ireland, including biking and walking tours as well as canal barging and regular sightseeing tours. ETM Travel Group (☎ 0800 992 7700, W www.etmtravelgroup.com) of Connecticut runs three-night 'weekend gem' packages to Dublin with accommodation, breakfast and a city tour included from US$289.

Brendan Tours (☎ 818-785 9696, W www.brendantours.com) in Van Nuys, California, is an Irish-American operator that specialises in tours to Ireland, including Dublin. It has a number of 14-day tours primarily aimed at the higher end of the market, with prices ranging from US$2000 to US$3500. Accommodation is in deluxe hotels and the treatment is royal. It also has a Dublin office.

From Australia

In Australia, Adventure World (☎ 02-9956 7766, W www.adventureworld.com.au) of Sydney provides a range of escorted tours to Ireland, some of which take in Dublin.

Warning

The information in this chapter is particularly vulnerable to change: Prices for international travel are volatile, routes are introduced and cancelled, schedules change, special deals come and go, and rules and visa requirements are amended. Airlines and governments seem to take perverse pleasure in making price structures and regulations as complicated as possible. You should check directly with the airline or a travel agent to make sure you understand how a fare (and ticket you may buy) works. In addition, the travel industry is highly competitive and there are many lurks and perks.

The upshot of this is that you should get opinions, quotes and advice from as many airlines and travel agents as possible before you part with your hard-earned cash. The details given in this chapter should be regarded as pointers and are not a substitute for your own careful, up-to-date research.

Getting Around

THE AIRPORT

Dublin airport (☎ 814 1111), 13km north of the city centre, is Dublin's only airport. During 2000–01 the one passenger terminal was almost doubled in size, finally making room for the 15 million passengers that come through it every year. It has a bureau de change in the baggage arrivals area, a branch of the Bank of Ireland on the second level, which keeps regular banking hours and also offers currency exchange, a post office (open 9am to 5pm Monday to Friday), an Aer Rianta (Irish airport authority) desk with information about the airport's facilities, a Dublin Tourism office that books accommodation, a CIE desk with information on trains and buses, plus shops, restaurants, bars, a hairdresser, a nursery, a church and car-hire counters. In the car-park atrium there's the Greencaps Left Luggage and Porterage office (☎ 814 4633), open daily from 6am to 10pm. It charges €3.20/3.80 per item for 24 hours, depending on size.

TO/FROM THE AIRPORT

There are three different bus services between the airport and the city, as well as the ubiquitous, expensive taxi. At the time of writing there was talk of building a rail link between the airport and the centre, but it will remain talk for the foreseeable future.

Airport Bus Services

Airlink Express The Airlink Express Coach, operated by Dublin Bus (☎ 872 0000, 873 4222), runs two services: No 747, between the airport, the central bus station (Busáras, Map 4) and the Dublin Bus offices on O'Connell St (Map 4); and No 748, between the airport and Heuston and Connolly stations (Maps 3 & 4, respectively).

Bus No 747 departs from the airport every 10 minutes between 5.45am and 11.30pm, Monday to Saturday. On Sunday, it departs from the airport every 20 minutes from 7.15am to 11.30pm. From Busáras, buses depart every 10 minutes between 6.30am and 10.45pm Monday to Saturday, and every 20 minutes between 7.30am to 11.10pm on Sunday. All buses to/from the airport and Busáras stop outside the Dublin Bus office on O'Connell St, a five-minute bus journey from Busáras.

Bus No 748 departs the airport every 15 minutes from 6.25am to 9.30pm Monday to Saturday. On Sunday, the first departure is at 7am, the next at 7.45am and then every 25 minutes until 10.05pm. From Heuston Station, buses run every 15 minutes between 7.10am and 10.20pm. On Sunday, the first departure is at 7.50am, the next at 8.40am and then every 25 minutes until 10.50pm. From Connolly Station, buses also run every 15 minutes between 7.20am and 10.30pm Monday to Saturday, and every 25 minutes between 8.55am and 11pm on Sunday (first departure at 8am).

Both services, irrespective of destination, charge a flat rate of €4.55 for adults and €2.55 for children. The trip between the airport and all of the locations in the city centre takes 30–40 minutes, more if there's traffic. Complete timetables are available at the airport or in the city. The demand for seats sometimes exceeds the capacity of the bus, in which case it's worth getting a group together and sharing a taxi (see later in this section).

Aircoach Not to be confused with the Airlink Express, Aircoach (☎ 844 7118, ⓦ www.aircoach.ie) is a privately run service that operates luxury air-conditioned coaches between the airport and 15 locations throughout the city, usually to cater to residents of the city's biggest hotels, but they will pick up anyone. From the airport, coaches run between 5am and 11.30pm daily, and they stop at the following places: the Gresham Hotel on O'Connell St, Trinity College, the American College on North Merrion Square, Jurys Hotel on Pembroke Rd in Ballsbridge, Bewley's Hotel on Simmonscourt Rd, the Ever Ready garage on

Donnybrook Rd, opposite the Burlington Hotel on Upper Leeson St, the Grand Canal on Upper Leeson St, Lucent House on St Stephen's Green, outside the Thomas Pink shop on Dawson St, McCullough Piggot's shop on Suffolk St, Eddie Rocket's fast food on O'Connell St and in front of the Royal Dublin Hotel, also on O'Connell St. At each point there's an Aircoach bus stop with a sign.

Another service departs the airport every 15 minutes between 6.30am and 10.30pm and goes to the Irish Financial Services Centre and Connolly Station on Amiens St before going northward toward Malahide.

Aircoach charges a flat rate of €5.10 per passenger (accompanied children free), irrespective of their destination.

Public Bus With the proliferation of coach services to and from the airport, the slower public bus No 41, 41A or 41C have become the least attractive option. They are the cheapest way to get into the city (€1.40), but are also the slowest and – except for very early in the morning or late at night – the most crowded. The journey to Eden Quay near O'Connell St can take over an hour: It is recommended only to those on the tightest of budgets.

Airport Taxi Services

Taxis may be the most convenient way to travel from the airport, but they're also the most expensive – by a long way. Aside from a minimum charge of €2.30, they are subject to all sorts of additional charges for baggage, extra passengers and 'unsocial hours' – between 8pm and 8am. A taxi between the airport and the centre should cost around €16.50, which makes financial sense between four people. There's a supplementary charge of €1 from the airport to the city, but this charge does not apply from the city to the airport. As elsewhere in the world, it's a good idea to make sure the meter is switched on to avoid any misunderstanding.

TO/FROM FERRY TERMINALS

Buses go to Busáras from the Dublin Ferryport terminal (☎ 855 2222), Alexandra Rd, after all ferry arrivals from Holyhead. Buses

also run from Busáras to meet ferry departures. For the 9.45am ferry departure from Dublin, buses leave Busáras at 8.30am. For the 9.45pm departure, buses depart from Busáras at 8.30pm. For the 1am sailing to Liverpool, the bus departs from Busáras at 11.45pm. All buses cost €2.55.

To travel between Dun Laoghaire's Carlisle terminal (☎ 280 1905) and Dublin, take bus No 46A to St Stephen's Green, or bus Nos 7, 7A or 8 to Burgh Quay, or take the DART (see Train later in this chapter) to Pearse station (for south Dublin) or Connolly station (for north Dublin).

TO/FROM CONNOLLY & HEUSTON STATIONS

The 90 Raillink bus runs between the two stations every 10 to 15 minutes at peak periods and costs €0.85. Connolly station is a short walk north of Busáras; Heuston is by the Liffey, on the eastern side of town.

BUS

Dublin Bus operates an information office (Map 4; ☎ 873 4222 or 872 0000, **W** www .dublinbus.ie) at its head office, 59 Upper O'Connell St. It's open 9am to 5.30pm Monday to Friday and 9am to 2pm on Saturday. Free single-route timetables are available.

You can't miss Dublin's buses. They're usually green double-deckers, although an increasing number are becoming moving billboards for advertisers. There are over 1000 of them in Dublin, moving slowly through the city's traffic like jolly green giants. Bus stops are easily identified by a round plaque atop a long pole, on which you'll find the route number and – in a wonderful display of misguided optimism – the timetable. Although Dublin Bus makes concerted efforts to improve its services, their use can sometimes be a painfully slow and laborious process, and it is not uncommon to wait up to an hour for a bus to come, especially in the far suburbs. The busier routes are more frequent, but you should anticipate at least a 10-minute wait. Smaller buses, known as Imps, are red and yellow, and operate on a hail-and-ride system.

Buses run from around 6am (some start at

5.30am) to 11.30pm daily. Fares are calculated according to stages: one to three stages costs €0.85; four to seven costs €1.10; eight to 12 costs €1.35; and 13 to 23 costs €1.50. The city centre (Citizone) is within a 12-stage radius, so the maximum fare for travelling within the centre is €1.35. Remember that you must tender exact change when boarding; if you give anything more you will be given a receipt for reimbursement, which you can only collect at the Dublin Bus main office. It is commonly assumed by Dubliners that this a fail-safe way for Dublin Bus to make more money: After all, if €2 is tendered on a €1.35 fare, most people wouldn't bother traipsing their way down to O'Connell St for the sake of €0.65.

One-day rambler passes cost €4.50 for the bus, or €6.60 for bus and rail. There are other bus passes that give unlimited bus travel for three days (€8.25) and five days (€12.70). There are no discounts on these passes for students. Weekly bus passes cost €15.90 (€12.70 for students) and a weekly bus and rail pass costs €21.60 (including €2.50 for an ID photo). If you're planning on staying for a month and using a lot of public transport, the monthly bus and rail pass €80 (€55.90 for students) is good value. Bus passes must be bought in advance, at 59 O'Connell St or at any of the bus agencies listed there.

Busáras (Map 4), the central bus station, is just north of the river and the Custom House; it has a left-luggage facility costing €2.50 per item.

Nitelink

Nitelink is a late-night bus service run by Dublin Bus from Monday to Saturday. There are 21 different routes, serving virtually all of the city's suburbs. Buses depart from the triangle formed by College St, Westmoreland St and D'Olier St (Map 5) beginning at 12.30am. From Monday to Wednesday, there are usually only two departures, at 12.30am and 2am. From Thursday to Saturday, departures are at 12.30am, 2am and then every 20 minutes until 4.30am on the more popular routes and until 3.30am on those less frequented. Fares are €3.80 unless you're travelling to the far suburbs (places like Balbriggan in north County Dublin or Ashbourne in County Meath); then the fare is €5.70. Timetables are available at the Dublin Bus office or you can check out its Web site (see the start of this section).

TRAIN

The Dublin Area Rapid Transport (DART; Map 1) provides quick rail access to the coast as far north as Howth and as far south as Bray. Pearse station is convenient for central Dublin south of the Liffey and Connolly station for north of the Liffey. From Monday to Saturday there are services every 10 to 20 minutes, sometimes more frequently, from around 6.30am to midnight. Services are less frequent on Sunday. It takes about 30 minutes from Dublin to Bray at the southern extreme or Howth at the northern extreme. Dublin to Dun Laoghaire only takes about 15 to 20 minutes. There are also suburban rail services north as far as Dundalk, inland to Mullingar and south past Bray to Arklow.

A one-way DART ticket from Dublin to Dun Laoghaire or Howth costs €1.50; to Bray it's €1.70. Within the DART region, a one-day, unlimited travel ticket costs €5.10 for an adult, €2.50 for a child or €8.90 for a family. A one-day ticket combining DART and Dublin Bus services costs €6.60 for an adult and €9.50 for a family (there is no child's rate). A five-day pass allows you unlimited DART and bus travel for €12.70.

All DART and suburban rail stations, as well as the Rail Travel Centre (☎ 836 6222) at Iarnród Éireann (Map 4), 35 Lower Abbey St, Dublin 1, sell weekly and monthly passes for unlimited rail and bus travel on Dublin Bus, DART and suburban rail. A weekly pass costs €21.60 but requires an ID photo (€2.50) and a monthly pass costs €80 (€55.90 for students). Rail-only passes (for use on DART and suburban train services only) cost €16 and €57.50 respectively.

Bicycles can't be taken on DART services, but can be taken on the less-frequent Suburban Rail services, either in the guard's van or in a special carriage at the opposite end of the train from the engine. There is a €2.50 charge for transporting a bicycle.

GETTING AROUND

Heuston station has left-luggage lockers of three sizes, costing €1.90/3.20/5.10 for 24 hours. At Connolly station the facility costs €1.90/3.20.

CAR & MOTORCYCLE

As in most big cities, a car in Dublin is as much a millstone as a convenience, though it can be useful for day trips. If you're going farther afield, a car is a wonderful means of getting around Ireland since there are always interesting diversions down back roads where public transport doesn't venture. The two big disadvantages in central Dublin are traffic, which is a major problem, and parking, which is difficult to find outside of official car parks. The clamping of illegally parked vehicles is rife, and there's absolutely no talking your way out of it once the dreaded yellow clamp is out.

Central Dublin has parking meters and a large selection of open and sheltered car parks. You don't have to go far from the centre to find free roadside parking, especially in north Dublin. However, the police warn visitors that it's safer to park in a supervised car park, since cars are often broken into even in broad daylight close to major tourist attractions. Rental cars and cars with foreign number plates, which may contain valuable personal effects, are a prime target.

When booking accommodation you may want to check on parking facilities. Some B&Bs that claim to offer private parking, especially in the centre, may have a sharing arrangement with a nearby hotel to use its car park – provided it hasn't been filled by the hotel patrons' cars.

As in Britain, driving is on the left and you should only overtake on the outside (to the right) of the vehicle in front of you. Safety belts must be worn by the driver and front-seat passengers. Children aged under 12 are not allowed to sit in the front seats. Motorcyclists and their passengers must wear helmets. Despite frequent apologies from Irish people about the roads there's really little to complain about, although minor roads may sometimes be potholed and are often narrow.

See Driving Licence & Permits under Documents and Drinking & Driving under Legal Matters in Facts for the Visitor for further information on driving rules.

Speed limits are 70mph (112km/h) on motorways, 60mph (96km/h) on other roads and 30mph (48km/h) or as signposted in towns, but are often treated in a somewhat cavalier fashion. Leaded petrol costs about €1 per litre, unleaded costs four or five cents less.

The Automobile Association of Ireland, or AA (Map 6; ☎ 677 9481), is at 23 Suffolk St, Dublin 2, and its breakdown number in the Republic is ☎ 1800 667 788.

Rental

Car rental in Ireland is expensive because of high rates and a 12.5% tax, so you're often better off making arrangements in your home country with some sort of package deal. In high season it's wise to book ahead. There are often special deals, the longer you hire the car for the lower the daily rent, and off season some companies discount all rates by about 25%. Most companies make an extra daily charge if you cross the border into Northern Ireland. The cars are customarily manual; automatics are available but they are more expensive to hire.

Avis, Budget, Hertz, Thrifty and the major local operators, Argus, Dan Dooley and Murrays Europcar are the big rental companies. Murrays Europcar, Budget, Avis and Hertz have desks at the airport, but numerous other operators are based close by and deliver cars for airport collection. Typical high-season rental rates per week with insurance, collision-damage waiver (CDW), VAT and unlimited kilometres are from around €337 for a small car (1.0 or similar), €411 for a medium-sized car (1.4 or similar) and €666 for a larger car (1.6 or similar). There are many smaller local operators with lower prices, but they don't offer the same kind of insurance coverage or unlimited mileage deals as the bigger operators.

People aged under 21 are not allowed to hire a car; for the majority of rental companies you have to be at least 23 years old and to have held a valid driving licence for a minimum of 12 months. Some companies will not rent to those aged over 70 or 75.

GETTING AROUND

Your driving licence is usually enough to hire a car for stays of up to three months.

Motorbikes and mopeds are not available for rent in the Republic of Ireland.

The main car rental companies are:

Avis Rent-a-Car
(Map 5; ☎ 605 7555, W www.avis.com) 1 East Hanover St, Dublin 2
(☎ 844 5204) Dublin Airport
Budget Rent-a-Car
(☎ 837 9802/9611, W www.budgetcarrental.ie) 151 Lower Drumcondra Rd, Dublin 7
(☎ 844 5150) Dublin Airport, Dublin 9
Dan Dooley Car & Van Hire
(Map 5; ☎ 677 2723, W www.dan-dooley.ie) 42–43 Westland Row, Dublin 2
(☎ 844 5156) Dublin Airport
Hertz Rent-a-Car
(Map 2; ☎ 660 2255, W www.hertz.com) 149 Upper Leeson St, Dublin 2
(☎ 844 5466) Dublin Airport
Murrays Europcar
(Map 5; ☎ 614 2800, W www.europcar.com) Baggot St Bridge, Dublin 4
(☎ 844 4179) Dublin Airport
Sixt Rent-a-Car
(☎ 862 2715, W www.icr.ie) Old Airport Rd, Santry, Dublin 9
(☎ 844 4199) Dublin Airport
Windsor Thrifty
(☎ 454 6600, W www.thrifty.ie) Rialto, 125 Herberton Bridge, South Circular Rd, Dublin 8
(☎ 840 0800) Dublin Airport

TAXI

Taxis in Dublin are expensive with a minimum charge of €2.40 and €0.15 for one-ninth of a mile (or 40 seconds) thereafter. In addition there are a number of extra charges – €0.50 for each extra passenger, €0.50 for each piece of luggage, €2.50 for telephone bookings and €0.50 or €1 for unsocial hours (€0.50 from 8pm to midnight, 5am to 8am and all day Sunday; €1 from midnight to 5am and public holidays).

Taxis can be hailed on the street and are found at taxi ranks around the city, including on the corner of Abbey St and O'Connell St in north Dublin, College Green in front of Trinity College and St Stephen's Green at the top of Grafton St. In 2001 there was a deregulation of the taxi industry, which saw

an extra 6000 new permits granted. This was done to alleviate a problematic taxi shortage, especially at the weekend. Although there are more taxis around, it can still be difficult to get one, especially after pubs close between Thursday and Saturday. Long queues at taxi ranks are not at all uncommon during these hours, with waits of one hour or more.

Many companies dispatch taxis by radio, but they too can run out of cars at peak times; be sure to book as early as you can. Try City Cabs (☎ 872 7272) or National Radio Cabs (☎ 677 2222).

Phone the Garda Carriage Office (☎ 666 9850) with any complaints about taxis.

BICYCLE

Despite the shortage of cycle lanes and the heavy traffic, Dublin isn't a bad place to get around by bicycle, as it is small enough and flat enough to make bike travel easy. Many visitors explore farther afield by bicycle, a popular activity in Ireland despite the often less-than-encouraging weather.

Most hostels seem to offer secure bicycle parking areas, but if you're going to have a bike stolen anywhere in Ireland, Dublin is where it'll happen. Lock your bike up well. Considering how popular bicycles are in Dublin, there's a surprising scarcity of suitable bike-parking facilities. Grafton St and Temple Bar are virtually devoid of places to lock a bike. Elsewhere, there are signs on many likely stretches of railing announcing that bikes must not be parked there. Nevertheless, there are some places where you can park your bike, such as the Grafton St corner of St Stephen's Green.

The best cycle shop in town is Cyclelogical (Map 5; ☎ 872 4678), 3 Bachelor's Walk Square. It is the best specialist bike shop for serious enthusiasts, with all the best equipment as well as a good source of information on upcoming cycling events. It does not, however, do repairs. Square Wheel Cycleworks (Map 6; ☎ 679 0838), Temple Lane, Temple Bar, Dublin 2, does do repairs, and will have your bike back to you within a day or so (barring serious damage).

'B Yeats and Oscar Wilde once resided in houses around splendid Merrion Square.

edford Tower, Dublin Castle

It's Guinness o'clock.

Dubh Linn Sculpture Garden

The floor mosaic of the entrance rotunda, City Hall

OLIVER STREWE

OLIVER STREWE

DOUG McKINLAY

OLIVER STREWE

Dubliners: An easy-going, charismatic crowd

Rental

You can either bring your bike with you or rent in Dublin, where you'll have a choice of two kinds of bike. First there's the regular frame bike, either a racer or the all-terrain kind, which you can rent for around €13 per day or €50 per week. The more expensive high-spec aluminium bikes typically cost around €19 per day and €64 per week.

Raleigh Rent-a-Bike agencies can be found all over Ireland. Contact them at Raleigh Ireland (☎ 626 1333), Raleigh House, Kylemore Rd, Dublin 10. Raleigh agencies in Dublin include the following:

Joe Daly
(☎ 298 1485) Lower Main St, Dundrum, Dublin 14
Hollingsworth Bikes
(☎ 296 0255) 1 Drummartin Rd, Stillorgan, Dublin 14
(☎ 490 5094) 54 Templeogue Rd, Templeogue, Dublin 6
Little Sport
(☎ 833 0044) 3 Marville Ave, Fairview, Dublin 3
MacDonald's Cycles
(Map 5; ☎ 475 2586) 38 Wexford St, Dublin 2
(☎ 497 9636) 1 Orwell Rd, Rathgar, Dublin 6
Shankill Cycle Shack
(☎ 282 7577) Barbeque Centre, Old Bray Rd, County Dublin

WALKING

The best way to explore Dublin is by foot. It is a small, compact city, with most sights and areas of interest within easy walking distance of each other. For example, it should take you no more than an hour to walk from the northern tip of O'Connell St down past the Liffey, through the city centre and back out again through the Liberties down to Kilmainham in the west of the city. The suburbs of Ballsbridge and Donnybrook are no more than a 20-minute walk from Grafton St and you could easily reach Phoenix Park in under half an hour.

But Dublin is not really about getting from one place to another in the shortest possible time. It is about taking your time, deviating from your intended route to have a look in a shop window or check out the doorway of a building; it is about stopping to watch a silver-painted mime artist entertain the crowd or listen to a busking duo sing the latest pop hit; it is about having a lie down in St Stephen's Green or Merrion Square because the warm sun is too precious to ignore; it is about having an impromptu drink in a pub. An old Dublin brain-teaser lays down the challenge of walking through the city without passing a pub: Considering that there are over 700 in the city centre alone, it seems an impossible task. But it can be done, Dubliners will tell you: Just go into every one you see!

For walks through the city, see the Dublin Walks chapter and for more information on walks in the Dublin area, see Lonely Planet's *Walking in Ireland.*

ORGANISED TOURS

Many Dublin tours operate only during summer, but at that time you can take bus tours, walking tours and bicycle tours. You can book these directly with the operators, through your hotel, at the various city tourist offices or with a travel agent.

Bus Tours

Bus Éireann You can book Bus Éireann tours directly (Map 4; ☎ 836 6111) at Busáras, or through the Bus Éireann desks at the Dublin Bus office (Map 4) at 59 Upper O'Connell St, or at the Dublin Tourism office (Map 4), which is in St Andrew's Church on Suffolk St.

Bus Éireann has several day tours outside Dublin. There are two separate tours to Wicklow. The first includes a visit to Glendalough as well as a trip through the Wicklow Mountains. It runs from 10.30am, returning at 5.45pm, daily from April to October (adult/child €26/13); from November to March, the tour goes on Wednesday, Friday and Sunday and returns at 4.30pm (adult/child €20.50/10.50). The second tour takes in Powerscourt House, garden and waterfall. It departs at 10am (returning at 5pm) on Tuesday only, and from June to September only (adult/student/child €26/23/13).

North of Dublin, Bus Éireann runs tours to Newgrange and the Boyne Valley. These depart at 10am and return at 5.45pm daily except Friday, from May to September, and

Thursday and Saturday only in April (adult/student/child €26/23/13); and 10am to 4.15pm Thursday and Saturday only, from October to December (adult/student/ child €20.50/18/10.50).

Between June and September there are also day tours to places farther afield such as Kilkenny, the Mountains of Mourne, the River Barrow and the Waterford Crystal factory. Check with Bus Éireann for details or go to its Web site (W www.buseireann.ie).

Dublin Bus Tours with Dublin Bus (☎ 872 0000, 873 4222, W www.dublinbus.ie, 59 Upper O'Connell St) can be booked at its office or at the Bus Éireann counter in the Dublin Tourism office (Map 4) in St Andrew's Church, Suffolk St.

The main tour offered is the Dublin City hop-on, hop-off tour, which operates every 15 minutes between 9.30am and 5pm, and every 30 minutes thereafter until 6.30pm, daily year-round. The whole tour lasts around 1¼ hours, but your ticket allows you to hop on and off as often as you wish at any of the 16 designated stops. You can rejoin the tour at any time throughout the day. The tour covers all of the city centre's major attractions, and while the admission price to the various sights is not included, your ticket does give you a discount at most of the places that charge admission – if you see everything, you'll save something close to €6.50. Tickets cost €10.20 (children half price).

This tour can also be combined with the Ballykissangel tour, which includes a city centre tour before going south to Avoca, the real town behind the fictional TV town of Ballykissangel. The combined price for both tours is €30.50, but be aware that the Ballykissangel tour departs from Connolly Station (the gate for Platform 4) at 1pm daily year-round, so you'll need to do the city tour in the morning to make it in time. If you just want the Ballykissangel tour, the cost is €10.50.

For a taste of Dublin at its weirdest, Dublin Bus runs a Ghost Bus tour, a trip through the city's macabre legends. A storyteller is on hand to relate tales of haunted houses, body snatchings and mummies. At journey's end, everyone is invited to a pub, where an Irish wake is recreated. The 2¼-hour tour runs at 8pm Tuesday to Friday and at 7pm and 9pm at the weekend year-round; it costs €19.

The Coast & Castles tour is a three-hour tour of north county Dublin, taking in the Botanic Gardens in Glasnevin and the Casino at Marino before heading north towards Malahide Castle. The tour then skirts the coast until it gets to the pretty fishing village of Howth before returning to O'Connell St. It departs at 10am daily year-round and costs €15.50 (€8 for children).

The South Coast tour brings you to what is grandly dubbed the Irish Riviera, the stretch of coastline between Dun Laoghaire and Killiney. In between, you visit Sandycove Tower (where Joyce lived for a couple of months) and, further on, the Avoca Handweavers shop in County Wicklow. Departures are at 11am and 2pm daily, year-round. The tour lasts approximately 3¾ hours and costs €15.50 (€8 for children).

Mary Gibbons Tours The trips run by Mary Gibbons Tours (☎ 283 9973, fax 260 1456) include full-day tours of Powerscourt and Glendalough, leaving from the Dublin Tourism office at 10.45am and returning between 5pm and 5.30pm on Thursday, Saturday and Sunday (€28). The real treat, though, is the Boyne Valley tour, which includes a visit to Newgrange, the Boyne Valley and the Hill of Tara, the ancient seat of the Irish high kings. The tour was heralded by Eamonn P Kelly, the Keeper of Irish Antiquities at the National Museum, as 'the authentic tour of Ireland's history'. And, led by expert guides with a profound knowledge of history and archaeology, it does not disappoint. It runs from 10.45am to 5.30pm or 6pm Monday to Wednesday and on Friday. It also leaves from the Dublin Tourism office and costs €28.

Wild Coach Tours The award-winning Wild Coach tours run by *Aran Tours* (☎ 280 1899, W www.wildcoachtours.com) have earned rave reviews from participants and tourism authorities alike. The guides are all uniformly excellent, with plenty of energy and a terrific sense of humour that generates a kind of camaraderie not common in tours. The company runs a full-day tour to Glendalough, which includes a short Dublin City tour before moving south to Avoca, Glendalough, and the scenic Sally Gap in County Wicklow. The tour also includes stops for morning coffee and a pub lunch (not included in the price). Tours depart at 9.30am daily, returning at 5.30pm and cost €28 per adult and €25.50 per student or child.

The Powerscourt afternoon tour is run from 1.30pm to 6pm daily, and costs €19/16.50. The half-day Castle tour to Howth and Malahide, with visits to Malahide Castle and a walk on Howth Head, departs at 9am and returns at 1.15pm daily; it costs €19/16.50. All tours have a variety of pick-up points throughout the city; check the point nearest you when booking.

Other Tour Operators In summer, *Guide Friday/Gray Line* (☎ 670 8822, W *www.hoponhopoff.com*) runs tours around Dublin and farther afield. Reservations can be made through Dublin Tourism (☎ 605 7777) and all tours depart from the Dublin Tourism office on Suffolk St. There are half-day tours to Glendalough (€20.50) departing at 10am and returning at 2pm on Saturday only. Tours to Glendalough, Powerscourt and Russborough House (€36) go from 10.30am to 5.30pm on Sunday. Tours to the Boyne Valley and Newgrange (€21) last from 10am to 2pm on Tuesday and from 2.30pm to 6pm on Saturday.

Old Dublin Tours (☎ 458 0054, W *www.dualwaycoaches.com*) does city sightseeing tours in a double-decker bus that leaves from outside the old tourist office at 14 Upper O'Connell St. From April to October, they run every 10 minutes from 9.30am to 5.30pm daily. From November to March they run every 15 to 20 minutes between 9.30am to 4pm. The cost is €11.50 (€10.50 for concessions) and €4 for children.

Tir na nÓg Tours (☎ 1800 226 242, W *www.tirnanogtours.com*) does all-day tours of Wicklow, including the Sally Gap, Lough Tay, Glendalough, Laragh, Rathdrum and Avoca. A second tour goes north to the Boyne Valley, Monasterboice, Trim Castle and the Hill of Tara. Both tours depart at 9am daily from the Tir na nÓg offices at 57 Lower Gardiner St and at 9.30am from the Dublin Tourism office in Suffolk St. They each cost €26/23/13 per adult/student/child.

Bike Tours
Established in 2000, *Molly Malone Bike Tours* (☎ 086-604 2608, 087-621 2424, W *www.mollybikes.com*) organises four-hour bike tours of the city centre for €21. They run at 11.30am and 4pm daily from May to August, and 12.30pm daily from September to mid-October. Apart from providing bikes, the company also has waterproof gear for anyone silly enough to be in Ireland without adequate protection from the rain. The tours are fairly gentle, with sightseeing stops every 400m and a 45-minute rest.

Walking Tours
During summer there are various walking tours, which are a great way to explore this city. A Trinity College walking tour departs frequently from Front Square just inside the college and costs €8.50, including entry to the Book of Kells exhibition. See the Trinity College section in the Things to See & Do chapter for more details.

Literary Tours Two-hour walks for €6.50 are operated by *Dublin Footsteps Walking Tours* (☎ 496 0641), departing from the James Joyce Room in Bewley's Oriental Café on Grafton St (Map 7) at 10.30am Monday, Wednesday, Friday and Saturday, June to September only. This is a gentle walk through Dublin's Georgian and literary past, bringing you to Merrion Square and back around by St Stephen's Green. The tour is full of historical references and literary anecdotes about Joyce, Wilde and others. At the end of the tour, you can enjoy a chat in Bewley's over a free mug of coffee. Booking is not necessary: just show up.

Ninety-minute walking tours of north Dublin, focusing on sites associated with James Joyce, depart from the James Joyce Cultural Centre (☎ 878 8547) at 35 North Great George's St (Map 4) at 11am and

GETTING AROUND

2.30pm Monday to Saturday; outside the summer months, phone to check departure times. The cost of a tour of the centre and the walk is €5.70.

The **Dublin Literary Pub Crawl** (☎ 454 0228) operates daily, starting at 7.30pm from the Duke pub (Map 7) on Duke St, just off Grafton St. The 2¼-hour tours run daily (with an extra tour at noon on Sunday) between April and October, and from Thursday to Sunday for the rest of the year. The walk is great fun and costs €9/8 for adults /students, though Guinness consumption can quickly add a few pounds to that figure. The two actors who lead the tour put on a theatrical performance appropriate to the various places and pubs along the way; the pubs chosen vary from night to night. This award-winning tour is very popular, so be sure to get to the pub by 7pm to buy tickets.

Historical Tours Run and managed by history graduates of Trinity College, Historical Tours (☎ 845 0241) take two hours and depart from the front gates of Trinity College. The walks take place several times daily from mid-May to September and cost €7/5.

One of our favourite tours is the highly entertaining and interesting **1916 Easter Rising Walk** (☎ 676 2493), which departs from the International Bar on Wicklow St at 11.30am Monday to Saturday and 1pm on Sunday between April and September. The two-hour walk brings you to some of the key sites associated with the Rising, including the GPO, the Four Courts, Trinity College, Liberty Hall and Dublin Castle. The events of that week are brought to life in vivid fashion by the knowledgeable guide, who has also penned a book on the subject (see Books in the Facts for the Visitor chapter). Despite the fact that the subject of the tour is a pitch battle between Irish volunteers and the British forces, the tour is popular with English visitors, who take the light-hearted jesting at England's expense in the jocular spirit that it is intended – the tour even won a 'best of' award in an English magazine. The tour finishes where it starts, and usually ends up with an interesting discussion of Irish history over a

few pints. It costs €9/7 for adults/students. There's a limit of 12 people per tour, so advance booking is recommended.

Macabre Tours In recent years there has been a growth of tours that focus on Dublin's more sinister past, both real and invented.

The Trapeze Theatre Company runs the excellent **Walk Macabre tour** (☎ 087-677 1512, W www.ghostwalk.cjb.com), which is as much a show as a walk through the spooky corners of Georgian Dublin. Invariably, the tour is full of stories about Dublin's king of the horror genre, Bram Stoker, the creator of Dracula, but the real features are the actors' dramatisations, primarily of the darker works of Oscar Wilde and James Joyce. They also recreate some of the city's more brutal murders as well as act out some of their own work. The tours usually run at 7.30pm and by prior arrangement only (maximum 50 people). They depart from St Stephen's Green (Map 5), last 1¼ hours and cost €7.50.

A favourite tour with visitors to Dublin is the 1½-hour **Zozimus Experience** (☎ 661 8646, e info@zozimus.com, W www.zozimus .com), which usually leaves from the gates of Dublin Castle daily at around 9pm between May and October (7pm the rest of the year) on a tour of Dublin's superstitious and seedy medieval past. The costumed guide recounts stories of murders, great escapes and mythical events. The tour finishes with a macabre surprise that is not for the faint-hearted. Tours must be booked in advance and cost €8.

Musical Tours The **Dublin Musical Pub Crawl** (☎ 478 0191, e info@musicalpub crawl.com, W www.musicalpubcrawl.com) leaves from upstairs in Oliver St John Gogarty's pub in Temple Bar at 7.30pm daily, from April to October; Friday and Saturday only in November and from February to March. The focus is on Irish traditional music: Two musicians demonstrate the various styles and explain the music's history in a number of pubs in Temple Bar. The 2½-hour tours usually finish in Isolde's Tower pub, at the west end of Temple Bar. The musicians, drawn from a rotating pool of 25 professionals, are all excellent and the music they play is superb – a far cry from the rubbish that often passes for traditional music in this part of the city. Tours cost €9 for adults and €8 for students and seniors.

In 2002 a five-hour tour was launched by these folks, called the Music & Comedy Coach, a nightly hop-on, hop-off tour of Dublin's pubs, clubs and restaurants. The on-board entertainment consists of local comics and musicians, and the tour brings you to the more off-the-beaten-track destinations, far from the madding tourists. The tours last from 7pm to midnight daily, April to October. Tickets cost €15.50/10.50 for adults/students.

Self-Guided Tours You can also buy various heritage trail leaflets in the tourist office and guide yourself around the city sites. Walks include a Georgian Heritage Trail and a Rock & Stroll Tour of sites associated with Irish music. Around town you'll also spot boards outlining a Malton Trail of sites portrayed by 18th-century artist James Malton in his *A Picturesque & Descriptive View of the City of Dublin*.

Take A Tour/Audio Tours Ireland (☎ 878 7655, 13 Bachelor's Walk) provides guide tapes and audio equipment for city tours

(€8, plus a deposit of €32 or a credit-card number). Tapes, which cover a two- to three-hour walking tour, come in English, French, German, Italian and Japanese – the last being particularly valuable as there are no Japanese-language tours of Dublin. The office is open from 9.30am to 5.30pm Monday to Saturday.

Carriage Tours
At the junction of Grafton St and St Stephen's Green you can pick up a horse and carriage with a driver/commentator. Half-hour tours cost up to €36 and the carriages can take four or five people. Tours of different lengths can be negotiated with the drivers.

Tour Guides
Bord Fáilte-approved guides can be contacted via the *tourist board (☎ 602 4000)*. The recommended fees for a full-day, approved guide in Dublin are from €83 to €102 for an English-speaking guide or €102 to €127 for a guide speaking another language. A reputable firm that hires out guides is *Meridien Tours (☎ 677 6336, 26 South Frederick St)*. English-language guides cost €95 for a full day (€76 for a half day); foreign-language guides cost €121 (€102 for a half-day).

Things to See & Do

Although Dublin's city centre is pretty small (Dubliners prefer 'compact') for a European capital, there's enough to see and do to keep you busy for weeks. Or years, depending on how strong your bond to the pub becomes. The draw of liquid refreshment aside, you can visit all the major attractions comfortably within a matter of days and most of the minor ones as well within a week or more. To travel farther out – and if you plan on anything other than a flying visit we recommend that you do – there are taxis, buses and sightseeing tours and, for the energetic, bicycles are easy to hire. See under Documents in the Facts for the Visitor chapter for information about the Heritage Card for entry to sites administered by Dúchas (The Heritage Service) and the Six-Way Combined Ticket to other sites.

SIGHTSEEING ITINERARIES

Below are two itineraries that can be used as a guide to making your visit to Dublin as complete, informative and fun as possible. See also the Dublin Walks chapter for specific routes through the city. More detailed information on the sites mentioned here can be found either later in this chapter or in the Seaside Suburbs and Excursions chapters.

Weekend

For most visitors who stay for a weekend, museums and galleries don't usually feature high up on their list of priorities. In the past decade or so, Dublin has become famous – or infamous – as one of the great party cities of Europe, even though the pubs and clubs close earlier than any other capital besides London. Still, you can get your fill of merriment and see a couple of sights while you're here. On arrival, we recommend that you get a quick impression of the city centre's geography. A walk from Trinity College to St Stephen's Green along Grafton St is a good starting point: it is the heart of the city and the area where you'll find the biggest concentration of shops, restaurants and pubs.

Devote Saturday morning to visiting Trinity College and the Book of Kells before moving on to the National Gallery and/or the National Museum on Kildare St. Take a walk up O'Connell St, past the GPO and on up to Parnell Square, where you'll find the Hugh Lane Municipal Gallery of Modern Art and the Dublin Writers' Museum. Saturday is also the city's most popular shopping day; the best spots are on or around Grafton St and on the streets around O'Connell St.

Alternatively, you could make the relatively short journey to the Guinness Storehouse and check out the museum devoted to the dark stout, and sample a pint of the best Guinness to be found anywhere in the world. On your way, we recommend that you visit the Chester Beatty Library in Dublin Castle and, just a little farther on, pop your head into St Patrick's Cathedral.

There are plenty of options for Saturday night. You can take in a play at one of the city's theatres or attend a concert – the average Saturday night offers a wide range of choice, from classical to rock and most things in-between, including Irish traditional music. And then there's the pub, the ubiquitous mainstay of all Dublin social life. You can round off your evening over a few pints, and if you want to keep going, you can do so in a nightclub.

Sunday offers less in terms of museum visits, so you might want to take a stroll around the city's landscaped squares, including St Stephen's Green and Merrion Square. If the weather is fine, you can either walk the length of the quays (or take a bus) to Phoenix Park and check out Dubliners at play, either picnicking or engaging in sports. Many shops are also open, so you can indulge in a little souvenir hunting before going home.

One Week

A week affords you plenty of time to see the best of what Dublin has to offer, which you

Dublin: the Best & the Worst

Highlights

- The 'Irish Gold' collection in the National Museum: it's free and it's fabulous

- Chester Beatty Library, our favourite museum in Dublin and one of Europe's most interesting repositories of religious books and other relics

- Trinity College & the *Book of Kells*: one of the world's most beautiful books amid an oasis of Elizabethan tranquillity

- Dublin's Georgian Squares, particularly the supremely elegant St Stephen's Green and Merrion Square

- St Audoen's (Church of Ireland) is Dublin's only surviving medieval parish church

- The Méridian Shelbourne's afternoon tea: you can't get more decadent than this for the price

- A round of golf at Howth's Deer Park course; it's cheap and the views are terrific (keep your head down on those putts, though)

- A pint of Guinness in John Mulligan's of Poolbeg St; a Dublin experience like few others

- Walking around the extraordinary monastic ruins of Glendalough

Lowlights

- Early closing times; recent extensions barely address the problem

- The crass commercialisation of the Temple Bar area

- Late-night Dublin, full of rowdy drunks, vomit and dirt

- Public Transportation: schedules are a loose guideline rather than a rule, buses are slow, and you have to proffer exact change

- You can never get a taxi when you need one

- Dublin's 'rip-off' culture, from bad museums to lousy restaurants

- Racism, particularly against Africans, but also against Eastern Europeans and Irish itinerants

- The Hot Press Irish Rock 'n' Roll Hall of Fame

- Themed uberbars: they're characterless and about as genuine as polystyrene

- Knuckle-headed bouncers acting as a self-appointed fashion police

- Road works: why does the same road have to be dug up four times a month?

will discover does not necessarily include filling your day with museum and gallery visits. Still, a few bona fide attractions are a must: Trinity College, the National Museum, National Gallery, Dublin Castle (especially the Chester Beatty Library) and, on Parnell Square, the Hugh Lane Gallery. These should take no more than two days to visit. Dublin's second-most popular tourist attraction is the Guinness Storehouse, which should take up the better part of half a day: on your way up there, there are a number of attractions worth checking out, including the city's two cathedrals, St Patrick's and Christ Church. The cathedrals are near the area that once formed Viking Dublin and you can check out Dublin's Viking history at Dvblinia, next door to Christ Church. A short walk away is the Liberties, the city's oldest standing neighbourhood, dating back to the Middle Ages.

Over the next couple of days, extend your area of discovery beyond the immediate city centre, taking in such sights as the Casino at Marino – a splendid example of Palladian architecture, the Irish Museum of Modern Art and the gaol at Kilmainham, a short bus ride away from the Guinness Storehouse. Irish whiskey fans will enjoy a visit to the Old Jameson Distillery, on the north side of the Liffey in the Victorian neighbourhood of Smithfield, just a short walk from Father Mathew Bridge. See a play at one of Dublin's famous theatres.

You should still have a couple of days to spare, which you may want to devote to exploring the southern suburbs of Dublin, especially the small seaport towns of Dun Laoghaire, Sandycove and Dalkey, all within easy reach of the centre by DART. In Sandycove you can visit the 18th-century James Joyce Martello Tower, where the writer lived for a short time. If the weather is even mildly pleasant, you might fancy an invigorating stroll along Sandymount Strand, a little closer to the city. Otherwise, you can leave Dublin and devote a day to the monastic ruins of Glendalough in County Wicklow, an hour south of the city and set in a wonderfully picturesque valley of woodland and rushing streams. Nearby is the magnificent Powerscourt House and its equally splendid landscaped gardens.

The River Liffey

It's relatively shallow, not very wide and usually a colour ranging from brown to pea-green, yet the far-from-mighty River Liffey is the city's greatest physical, psychological and social divide. It splits the city in two halves: the southern 'haves' and the northern 'have-nots'. Despite the increased fluidity of the city's newly found economic prosperity, which seems to recognise no boundary in its inexorable march towards the total gentrification of Dublin, the Liffey still serves as the demarcation line between the traditionally prosperous neighbourhoods to the south of it and the working-class enclaves on its northern side. It is spanned by a host of interesting bridges, bounded by a historic array of quays and overlooked by two of Dublin's finest Georgian buildings, the Custom House and the Four Courts. During the 18th century, this watery city-scape was a favourite subject of several great painters, including James Malton (c.1764–1803) and Samuel Brocas (1792–1847); what is remarkable today is how very little the Liffey and its surrounding buildings seem to have changed. The Four Courts and Custom House still overshadow the mass of three- and four-storey buildings that line the narrow quays.

Despite the development and the construction of the widely acclaimed Millennium Bridge, the most interesting bridge remains the pedestrian-only **Ha'Penny Bridge**, one of the city's most enduring symbols and whose crossing is a time-honoured Dublin ritual. In 2001 it was removed for cleaning and restoration, but should be back in place by the time you read this.

South of the Liffey

South Dublin (the south side) is the affluent Dublin where you'll find the fanciest shops, most restaurants of note and the majority of the hotels. You'll also find most reminders of Dublin's early history and the finest Georgian squares and houses. South Dublin is certainly not all there is to Dublin, but it's a good place to start.

TRINITY COLLEGE & THE BOOK OF KELLS (Map 5)

Ireland's premier university was granted its charter by Elizabeth I in 1592 on land confiscated from the Augustinian priory of All Hallows, which was dissolved in 1537. By providing an alternative to education on the Continent, the queen hoped that the college's students would avoid being 'infected with popery'. Archbishop Ussher, whose scientific feats included the precise dating of the act of creation to 4004 BC, was one of the college's founders. Despite the bigotry and questionable scientific ability of its founders, Trinity College is one of the outstanding universities of Europe, with a veritable pantheon of notable graduates and a long-established affiliation with Oxford's Oriel College and St John's in Cambridge.

Originally founded as the College of the Holy and Undivided Trinity, the university's name is officially the University of Dublin, but Trinity College is its sole college. Although it is now in the centre of the city, when it was founded it was described as being 'near Dublin' and was bordered on two sides by the estuary of the Liffey. Nothing now remains of the original Elizabethan college, which was replaced in the Georgian building frenzy of the 18th century.

Until 1793 Trinity College remained completely Protestant apart from one short break. Even when the university relented and began to admit Catholics, until 1970 any Catholic who attended could consider themselves excommunicated. Although hardly the bastion of British Protestantism that it once was – most of its 13,000 students are Catholic – it is still a popular choice for British students –

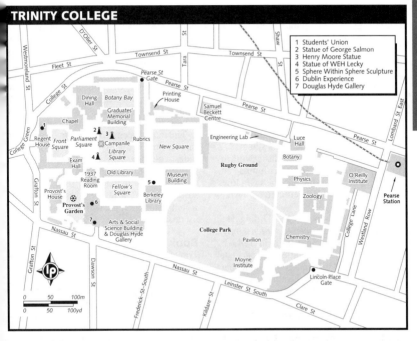

TRINITY COLLEGE

1 Students' Union
2 Statue of George Salmon
3 Henry Moore Statue
4 Statue of WEH Lecky
5 Sphere Within Sphere Sculpture
6 Dublin Experience
7 Douglas Hyde Gallery

especially those who missed out on a place at Cambridge or Oxford. Women were first admitted to the college in 1903, earlier than at most British universities.

The **Trinity College grounds** (☎ 677 2941; admission free; open 8am-10pm daily) cover 16 hectares. For visitors the only restrictions on entry are a ban on dogs, a request not to ride bicycles in the Library Square area and another request not to sunbathe in any part of the grounds except College Park.

Walking tours (☎ 608 1724; €8.50; every 40 minutes, 10.15am-3.40pm Mon-Sat, to 3pm Sun mid-May–Sept) depart from the main gate on College Green (the street in front of the college). The cost is good value since it includes the fee to see the Book of Kells.

Main Entrance

Much of the college today dates from Dublin's 18th-century heyday. The Front Gate or Regent House entrance on College Green

was built between 1752 and 1759 and is guarded by **statues** of the writer Oliver Goldsmith (1730–74) and the orator Edmund Burke (1729–97).

Around the Campanile

The open area reached from Regent House is divided into Front Square, Parliament Square and Library Square. The area is dominated by the 30m-high Campanile, designed by Edward Lanyon and erected from 1852 to 1853 on what was believed to be the centre of the monastery that preceded the college. Earlier there had been a bell tower, designed by the architect Richard Castle, on the same spot. To the north of the Campanile is a **statue of George Salmon**, the college provost from 1886 to 1904, who fought bitterly to keep women out of the college. He carried out his threat to permit them in 'over his dead body' by dropping dead when the worst happened. To the south of the Campanile is a **statue of historian WEH Lecky** (1838–1903). On the grassy expanse of Library Square are a 1969 **sculpture** by British sculptor Henry Moore (1898–1986) and two large **Oregon maples**.

Chapel & Dining Hall

Clockwise around the Front Square from the entrance gate, the first building is the Chapel *(☎ 608 1260, Front Square; admission free; organised tours only)*, completed in 1799 to plans made in 1777 by architect Sir William Chambers (1723–96). It has been open to all denominations since 1972. The Chapel has some fine plasterwork by Michael Stapleton, Ionic columns and painted, rather than stained, glass windows. The main window is dedicated to Archbishop Ussher.

Next to the Chapel is the Dining Hall *(Parliament Square; open to students only)*, originally designed and built in 1743 by Richard Castle but dismantled 15 years later because of problems caused by inadequate foundations. The replacement was completed in 1761 and it's believed to retain elements of the original design. It was extensively restored after a fire in 1984.

Graduates' Memorial Building & the Rubrics

The 1892 Graduates' Memorial Building *(☎ 677 2941, Botany Bay; closed to the public)* forms the north side of Library Square. Behind it are tennis courts in the area known as **Botany Bay**. Legend has it that unruly students housed around the square were considered suitable candidates for the British penal colony at Botany Bay in Australia. On the eastern side of Library Square, the red-brick Rubrics building dates from around 1690, making it the oldest building in the college. It was extensively altered in an 1894 restoration, then underwent serious structural modifications in the 1970s.

Old Library

To the south of the square is the Old Library *(☎ 608 2320, Library Square; admission part of Book of Kells tour)*, built in a rather severe style by Thomas Burgh between 1712 and 1732. The Old Library's 65m-long Long Room contains numerous unique, ancient

texts and the Book of Kells is displayed in the library Colonnades. Despite Ireland's independence, the 1801 Library Act entitles Trinity College Library to a free copy of every book published in the UK. Housing this bounty requires nearly 1km of extra shelving every year and the collection amounts to around five million books. These can't all be kept at the college library, so there are library storage facilities dotted around Dublin.

The magnificent Long Room (see later in this section) is mainly used for the library's oldest volumes. Until 1892 the ground-floor Colonnades formed an open arcade, but this was enclosed at that time to increase the storage area. Earlier, in 1853, the Long Room's storage capacity had been increased by raising its ceiling.

Book of Kells

Trinity College's prime attraction is an illuminated manuscript from around AD 800 – one of the oldest books in the world – the magnificent Book of Kells *(☎ 608 2320, East Pavilion, Library Colonnades; adult/student/children under 12 €5.70/5.10/free, includes admission to the Long Room & temporary exhibitions in the East Pavilion; open 9.30am-5pm Mon-Sat, noon-4.30pm Sun, from 9.30am June-Sept)*. Although the book was brought to the college for safekeeping from the monastery at Kells in County Meath in 1654, it undoubtedly predates the monastery. It was probably produced by monks at St Columba's Monastery on the remote island of Iona, off the coast of Scotland. After repeated Viking raids the monks moved to the temporarily greater safety of Ireland in AD 806, bringing their masterpiece with them to Kells. In 1007 the book was stolen then rediscovered, three months later, buried in the ground. Some time before the dissolution of the monastery, the metal shrine or *cumdach* was lost, possibly taken by looting Vikings who wouldn't have valued the text itself. About 30 of the beginning and ending folios (double-page spreads) are also missing.

The manuscript contains the four New Testament gospels, written in Latin, as well as prefaces, summaries and other text. It's made so wonderful by the superbly decorated opening letters of each chapter and the extensive, complex, smaller illustrations between the lines.

The 680-page (340-folio) book was rebound in four calfskin volumes in 1953. Two volumes are usually on display, one showing an illuminated page, the other showing text. The pages are turned regularly, but if you can't spare the time for the numerous daily visits required to view the entire book, you can purchase a reproduction available via the Trinity College Library for a pittance: US$18,000. Cheaper options are an information brochure and 'documentation kit' for US$98. If that's still too steep, the library bookshop has various cheaper books, including The Book of Kells, which has some attractive colour plates and text, for €17.70.

The Book of Kells is underneath the actual library, alongside the AD 807 **Book of Armagh** and the AD 675 **Book of Durrow**, all part of an exhibition called 'The Book of Kells: Turning Darkness into Light'. Efforts have been made to improve the poor lighting that protects the fragile manuscripts, but another problem remains. Around 500,000 people a year come to see it, leading to queues of at least 30 minutes in June, July and August. If you can, try to visit at some other time of year or arrive early.

The Colonnades also house a busy book and souvenir shop and temporary exhibitions.

Library Long Room

The Long Room (☎ 608 2320, East Pavilion, Library Colonnades; admission part of Book of Kells tour) is lined with shelves containing 200,000 of the library's oldest books and manuscripts, but a continual process of restoring and protecting them means that some, at any given time, may not be there. Also on display is the so-called **Brian Ború's harp**, which wasn't in use when he defeated the Danes at the Battle of Clontarf in AD 1014, as it actually dates from around 1400, making it one of the oldest harps in the country.

Other exhibits in the Long Room include a rare copy of the **Proclamation of the Irish Republic**, read by Patrick Pearse at the be-

ginning of the 1916 Easter Rising. The collection of 18th- and 19th-century **marble busts** around the walls features Jonathan Swift, Edmund Burke and Wolfe Tone, former members of Trinity College.

Reading Room, Exam Hall & Provost's House

Continuing clockwise around the Campanile there's the Reading Room and the Exam Hall or Public Theatre, which dates from 1779 to 1791. Like the Chapel that it faces and closely resembles, it was the work of William Chambers and also has plasterwork by Michael Stapleton. It contains an **oak chandelier** rescued from the Irish Parliament (now the Bank of Ireland) and an organ said to have been salvaged from a Spanish ship in 1702, though evidence indicates otherwise. **Portraits** of Swift, Ussher, Berkeley, Elizabeth I and others connected with the college's history are hung in the Exam Hall.

Behind the Exam Hall is the Provost's House (closed to the public), a fine 1760 Georgian building where the provost, or college head, still resides.

Berkeley Library

To the south-east of the old library is the solid, square, brutalist-style 1967 Berkeley Library (☎ 677 2941, Fellow's Square; closed to the public), designed by Paul Koralek. It has been hailed by the Architectural Association of Ireland as the best example of modern architecture in Ireland. It's fronted by Arnaldo Pomodoro's sculpture **Sphere Within Sphere** (1982–83).

George Berkeley, born in Kilkenny in 1685, studied at Trinity when he was only 15 years old and had a distinguished career in many fields, particularly in philosophy. His influence spread to the new English colonies in North America where he helped to found the University of Pennsylvania. Berkeley in California, and its namesake university, are named after him.

Arts & Social Science Building & Douglas Hyde Gallery

South of the old library, the Arts & Social Science Building (1978) backs on to Nassau St and forms the college's alternative main entrance. Designed by Paul Koralek it houses the Douglas Hyde Gallery of Modern Art (☎ 608 1116; admission free; open 11am-6pm Mon-Wed & Fri, to 7pm Thur, to 4.45pm Sat), which has some extremely good contemporary pieces (see Other Galleries later in this chapter). **Fellows' Square** is bordered on three sides by the two library buildings and the Arts & Social Science Building.

The Dublin Experience

The college's other big tourist attraction is a 45-minute audiovisual introduction to the city, the Dublin Experience (☎ 608 1688, Arts & Social Sciences Building; adult/student €4.20/3.50, €7/5.70 including Book of Kells; hourly 10am-5pm mid-May–Oct). It's well signposted.

Around New Square

Behind the Rubrics building, at the eastern end of Library Square, is New Square. In the highly ornate 1853–57 **Museum Building** (☎ 608 1477, New Square; admission free; open by prior arrangement only) exhibits include skeletons of two enormous giant Irish deer just inside the entrance and geological artefacts in the Geological Museum upstairs. The **Printing House** (1734), designed by Richard Castle to resemble a Doric temple and housing the microelectronics and electrical engineering departments, is at the north-west corner of New Square. One of Dublin's best early architects, Castle was responsible for a number of buildings at Trinity College but, apart from this building, little of his work here has survived.

Towards the eastern end of the college grounds are the **Rugby Ground** and **College Park**, where cricket games are played. There are several science buildings at the eastern end of the grounds. **Lincoln Place Gate** at this end is usually open and provides a good short cut through the college from Leinster St and Westland Row.

BANK OF IRELAND (Map 6)

Directly opposite Trinity College and originally built to house the Irish Parliament, is the imposing Bank of Ireland (☎ 671 1488,

College Green; open 10am-4pm Mon-Wed & Fri, to 5pm Thur). When the parliament voted itself out of existence through the 1801 Act of Union, the building was sold with instructions to alter the interior to prevent it being used as a debating chamber in the future; a spiteful strike at Irish parliamentary aspirations. Subsequently, the central House of Commons was remodelled, but the smaller House of Lords chamber survived. After independence the Irish government installed the new parliament in Leinster House, ignoring the possibility of restoring this fine building to its original use. Architects Robert Park and Francis Johnston converted it after it was sold in 1803.

Despite several architects having worked on the building over time, it avoids looking like a hotchpotch of styles. The original design was the work of Edward Lovett Pearce, who designed the original circular part of the building, constructed between 1729 and 1739. The curving windowless **Ionic portico** has statues of Hibernia (the Roman name for Ireland), Fidelity and Commerce, and the **east front**, designed by James Gandon in 1785, has Corinthian columns and statues of Wisdom (or Fortitude), Justice and Liberty.

Inside, the banking mall occupies what was once the House of Commons, but offers little hint of its former role. The House of Lords is more interesting, with its Irish oak woodwork, mahogany longcase parliament clock and late-18th-century Dublin crystal chandelier. The **tapestries** date from the 1730s and depict the Siege of Derry (1689) and the Battle of the Boyne (1690), the two Protestant victories over Catholic Ireland. In the niches are **busts** of George III, George IV, Lord Nelson and the Duke of Wellington. The 10kg, silver-gilt **mace** on display was made for the House of Commons and retained by the Speaker of the House when the parliament was dissolved. It was later sold by his descendants and bought back from Christies in London by the Bank of Ireland in 1937.

There are tours of the **House of Lords** (admission free; 10.30am, 11.30am & 1.45pm Tues), which include a talk as much about Ireland, and life in general, as the building itself.

AROUND THE BANK OF IRELAND (Map 6)

Close to the bank are several places of interest. In Foster Place, to the west, is the **Bank of Ireland Arts Centre** (☎ 671 1488, Ⓦ www .bankofireland.ie, Foster Place; adult/senior & student €1.90/1.25; open 10am-4pm Tues -Fri). It was refitted and reopened in 1995. It is home to a small museum on the history of banking, with a particular emphasis on the role of the Bank of Ireland in the economic and social development of Ireland since the beginning of the 18th century. The centre also hosts changing exhibits of Irish contemporary art.

The area between the bank and Trinity College, today a constant tangle of traffic and pedestrians, was once a green swathe and is still known as **College Green**. In front of the bank on College Green is a **statue of Henry Grattan** (1746–1820), a distinguished parliamentary orator. Farther up Dame St is a modern **memorial to the patriot Thomas Davis** (1814–45).

On the traffic island, where College Green, Westmoreland St and College St meet, are public toilets (no longer in use) and a **statue of the poet and composer Thomas Moore** (1779–1852), prompting James Joyce's comment in *Ulysses* that standing atop a public urinal wasn't a bad place for the man who penned the poem *The Meeting of the Waters*. At the other end of College St, where it meets Pearse St (Map 6), another traffic island is topped by a 1986 sculpture known as **Steyne**. It's a copy of the *steyne* (the Viking word for stone) erected on the riverbank in the 9th century to stop ships from grounding and removed in 1720.

TEMPLE BAR (Map 6)

Few visitors to Dublin will be unaware of Temple Bar, a maze of streets sandwiched between Dame St and the river between Trinity College and Christ Church Cathedral. One of the oldest areas of the city, its rundown buildings and cobbled streets were revitalised in the 1990s and it is now the most popular part of the city centre. Temple Bar has a number of interesting galleries and small museums, as well as a growing selection of trendy shops, but it is the area's pubs and restaurants that are its biggest draw, attracting tourists in their tens of thousands.

Temple Bar has been ruined by the success it has had since it was first earmarked as the city's 'cultural quarter'. In attempts to recreate a Left Bank atmosphere where artists' studios stood alongside cosy cafes and small boutiques selling ethnic artefacts, developers succumbed to the powerful draw of the mammon and created an overly commercialised quarter full of over-priced restaurants serving indifferent food, tacky souvenir shops and – with one or two exceptions – characterless bars that are more like meat markets than decent Dublin pubs. During the day, however, Temple Bar is pleasant enough; at night (especially at weekends) it overflows with drunken locals and foreigners intent on renaming the area Temple Barf. But if it's no-holds barred hedonism you want... see the Entertainment chapter for more details.

Dame St forms part of the southern boundary of Temple Bar and links new Dublin (centred on Trinity College and Grafton St) and old (stretching from Dublin Castle to encompass Christ Church and St Patrick's cathedrals). Along its route Dame St changes name to Cork Hill, Lord Edward St and Christ Church Place.

Information

The Temple Bar Information Centre (☎ 671 5717) at 18 Eustace St has specific details on the area and publishes a *Temple Bar Guide*.

Temple Bar has various hostels and hotels (see the Places to Stay chapter), which are usually packed to the rafters.

History

This stretch of riverside land was owned by Augustinian friars from 1282 until Henry VIII's dissolution of the monasteries in 1537, after which Sir William Temple (1554–1628) acquired the land that bears his name. The term 'bar' referred to a riverside walkway. Until 1537, Temple Lane was known as Hogges Lane and gave access to the friars' house. During its monastic era the Temple Bar area was marshy land that had only recently been reclaimed from the river. Much of it was outside the city walls and the River Poddle flowed through it, connecting the black pool with the Liffey. In Eustace St is **St Winifred's Well**, built in 1680 on the site of a medieval well.

The narrow lanes and alleys of Temple Bar date from the early 18th century when this was a disreputable area of pubs and prostitution. In the 19th century it developed a commercial character with small craft and trade businesses, but in the first half of the 20th century went into a steady decline, along with most of central Dublin.

In the 1960s the government decided to build a major bus depot in the area bordered by Eustace St to the west and Fownes St to the east. Next to it, a seven-storey shopping centre and office block would complete the picture. However, over the next 20 years the property market hit an all-time low and there seemed neither the money nor the inclination to go through with the project. During the 1980s, many of the condemned buildings were leased out on a short-term basis to local artists and artisans, and the seeds of Temple Bar as Dublin's counter-culture area were sown. By the end of that decade, Temple Bar was still rundown but was now cool: along with artists, the area was now home to the Gay & Lesbian Federation, the Green Party and artistic endeavours such as the Project Arts Centre.

In 1991, the year Dublin was nominated European Cultural Capital, the government set up Temple Bar Properties, whose brief was to develop and manage a cultural quarter alongside a residential and small business area. Despite the lofty ambitions, however, there were telltale signs that the redevelopment was not going to be entirely altruistic, as a number of buildings earmarked by An Taisce for preservation were demolished to make way for new apartment blocks that would net the developer a healthy return. As for the fines that they incurred for destroying protected buildings, they barely made a dent in the profits.

Self-interest aside, the development of Temple Bar has transformed the area. Today, Dublin's most popular quarter boasts two new public squares, a couple of new streets, a host of high-priced residential blocks, a student housing centre, a theatre, a museum, an independent cinema, art galleries, restaurants, hotels and – inevitably – plenty of pubs. Its development continues.

Exploring Temple Bar

The western boundary of Temple Bar is formed by Fishamble St, the oldest street in Dublin, dating back to Viking times – not that you'd know that to see it now. Christ Church Cathedral, beside Fishamble St, dates from 1170, but there was an earlier Viking church on this site. Brass symbols in the pavement direct you towards a mosaic laid out to show the ground plan of the sort of **Viking dwelling** excavated here from 1980 to 1981. The parliamentarian Henry Grattan (whose statue stands outside Trinity College on College Green) and the poet James Clarence Mangan (whose bust can be seen in St Stephen's Green) were both born on Fishamble St.

In 1742 Handel conducted the first performance of his *Messiah* in the Dublin Music Hall, behind Kinlay House (on Lord Edward St), now part of a hotel that bears the composer's name. The chorus was made up of the choirs from the two cathedrals. The Music Hall, opened in 1741, was designed by Richard Cassels, but all that remains of it today is the entrance and the original door, which stand to the left of Kennan's engineering works.

On Parliament St, which runs south from the river to the City Hall and Dublin Castle, the Sunlight Chambers beside the river has a beautiful **frieze** around the facade. Sunlight was a brand of soap manufactured by Lever Brothers, who were responsible for the late-19th-century building. The frieze shows the Lever Brothers' view of the world and soap: men make clothes dirty, women wash them!

Merchant's Arch leads to Ha'penny Bridge. If you cross the bridge to the north side, you'll see the **statue of two Dublin matrons** sitting on a park bench with their shopping bags, dubbed, in typically irreverent Dublin fashion, 'the hags with the bags'.

Back on the south side of the river, the Stock Exchange is on Anglesea St, in a building dating from 1878. The Bank of Ireland occupies Temple Bar's south-eastern corner.

The Ark Aimed at youngsters between the ages of four and 14 is the Ark *(Children's Cultural Centre; ☎ 670 7788, 11A Eustace St; admission free; open 9.30am-4pm Tues-Fri, 10am-4pm Sat)*. Its activities are aimed at promoting an interest in science and the environment as well as the arts. It also provides a good opportunity for visiting youngsters to meet their Dublin counterparts. The centre has an open-air stage for summer events. The sometimes lackadaisical staff need prodding at times, but they're friendly enough.

Hey, Doodle, Doodle Budding young ceramicists get their chance to display their talents at one of the city's more interesting venues for kids, a **studio** *(☎ 672 7382,* W *www.heydoodledoodle.com, 14 Crown Alley; €6.35; 11am-6pm Tues-Sat, 1pm-6pm Sun)*. Kids pick a piece of pottery, paint it whatever way they like, and pick it up a week later after it's been fired and glazed. Although obviously aimed at kids, there's been the odd adult spotted with a paintbrush in hand. Costs range from €4.50 for an egg cup up to €25 for a large platter. A dinner plate costs €19 and a mug €12.70. It gets busy at weekends, and group bookings must be made in advance.

Dublin's Viking Adventure Just off Wood Quay, the old heart of Viking Dublin, is Dublin's Viking Adventure *(☎ 679 6040,* W *www.visitdublin.com/attractions.html, West Essex St; adult/student/family €7/5.40 /19; open 10am-4.30pm Tues-Sat, 11am-4.30pm Sun)*. Besides an extensive collection of artefacts recovered during the excavations at Wood Quay, there is a guided tour of a recreation of Norse Dublin, complete with actors in the costumes of the day.

DUBLIN CASTLE (Map 5)
The centre of British power in Ireland, built on the orders of King John in the early 13th century, Dublin Castle *(☎ 677 7129, Cork Hill, Dame St; adult/student & senior €4/3; open 10am-5pm Mon-Fri, 2pm-5pm Sat &*

Sun) is more correctly described as a palace. Although the castle's construction, on Viking foundations, dates back to the 13th century, the older parts have been built over through the centuries since then. Only the Record Tower remains intact from the original Norman castle.

Under the more recent additions, parts of the castle's Viking foundations remain – known as the Undercroft – and a visit to the subterranean excavations clearly reveal the development of the castle from its original construction. The castle moats, now covered by more modern developments, were filled by the River Poddle on its way to joining the Liffey at Dublin's black pool.

The castle has enjoyed a relatively quiet history despite a siege by Silken Thomas Fitzgerald in 1534, a fire that destroyed much of the castle in 1684 and the events of the 1916 Easter Rising. The building served as the official residence of the British viceroys of Ireland until the Viceregal Lodge was built in Phoenix Park. Earlier it had been used as a prison, though not always with great success, as Red Hugh O'Donnell managed to escape from the Record Tower in 1591 and again in 1592.

The castle's buildings can only be visited as part of a tour. They depart every 20–30 minutes, depending on numbers. The tour includes a visit to the State Apartments, the Undercroft and the Chapel Royal, though State Apartments are used by the government for official functions (such as presidential inaugurations and EU meetings) and so may be closed to visitors. Call ahead to make sure.

Since 2000, the castle has also been home to our favourite museum in Dublin, the fabulous Chester Beatty Library (see later in this section). Although in the castle grounds, the library is separate, is not included in the tour and has separate opening hours.

Castle Tour
The main **Upper Yard** of the castle, with a pedestrian entrance beneath the **Throne Room**, can also be reached directly from Cork Hill or via the **Lower Yard**. From the main (Lower Yard) entrance, the tour takes you round the State Apartments, developed

THINGS TO SEE & DO

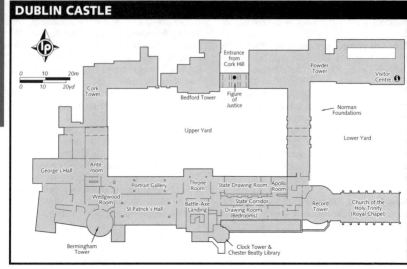

DUBLIN CASTLE

Entrance from Cork Hill

Powder Tower

Visitor Centre

Cork Tower

Bedford Tower

Figure of Justice

Norman Foundations

Upper Yard

Lower Yard

George's Hall

Ante-room

Portrait Gallery

Throne Room

State Drawing Room

Apollo Room

Wedgwood Room

State Corridor

St Patrick's Hall

Battle-Axe Landing

Drawing Rooms (Bedrooms)

Record Tower

Church of the Holy Trinity (Royal Chapel)

Bermingham Tower

Clock Tower & Chester Beatty Library

during Dublin's British heyday, but still used for state occasions. The sequence of rooms visited on the tour may vary.

From the entrance you ascend the stairs to the **Battle-Axe Landing**, where the viceroy's guards once stood, armed with battle-axes. Turning left you pass through a series of **drawing rooms**, formerly used as bedrooms by visitors to the castle. One contains a Van Dyck painting of Elizabeth, second Viscountess of Southampton, aged 17, another a book painted on vellum between 1989 and 1991 as a sort of latter-day Book of Kells. The castle **gardens**, visible from the windows, end in a high wall said to have been built for Queen Victoria's visit to block out the distressing sight of the Stephen St slums. The wounded James Connolly was detained in the first of these rooms following the GPO siege of 1916 before being taken to Kilmainham Gaol to face a firing squad. The ceilings are notable for their beautiful plasterwork, some of which was rescued from Georgian buildings facing demolition elsewhere in the city.

At the end of this series of rooms you cross the **State Corridor** to enter the **Apollo Room** or Music Room, which has a lovely

delicate ceiling dating from 1746, originally in a house on Merrion Row but installed here in the 1960s. You then pass through the long State Corridor and enter the **State Drawing Room**, which suffered serious fire damage in 1941. It has been restored with period furniture and paintings dating from 1740. From there you enter the ornate **Throne Room**, built in 1740. It contains a large throne, said to have been presented to the castle by William of Orange (King William III) after he defeated King James II at the Battle of the Boyne, and a brass 'Act of Union' chandelier that weighs over a tonne and is decorated with roses, thistles and shamrocks.

The long **Portrait Gallery** has portraits of 19th-century British viceroys and ends at an anteroom from where you enter George's Hall, added to the castle in 1911 for George V's visit to Ireland. From these rooms you return through the anteroom to the blue **Wedgwood Room** (yes, the whole room does look like Wedgwood china), which in turn leads to the **Bermingham Tower**, originally dating from 1411 but rebuilt between 1775 and 1777 after the original was damaged by an explosion. The tower was used as a prison on a number of occasions, especially during the independence struggle from 1918 to 1920.

Leaving the tower you pass through the 25m-long **St Patrick's Hall**. The knights of the Order of St Patrick, an order created in 1783, were invested here and their standards are displayed around the walls. Irish presidents are inaugurated here and it is used for receptions. The painting on the ceiling shows St Patrick lighting the fire on Slane Hill, the Irish chieftains ceding power to the Anglo-Normans and the coronation of George III, who created the Order of St Patrick.

St Patrick's Hall ends at the Battle-Axe Landing, but the tour takes you down to the **Undercroft**. Remnants of the earlier Viking fort, the 13th-century Powder Tower and the city wall can be seen in this excavation of the original moat, now below street level.

Bedford Tower

Other points of interest include the Bedford Tower, across the Upper Yard from the main entrance. In 1907 the collection known as the Irish Crown Jewels was stolen from this tower and never recovered.

The entrance to the Upper Yard beside the Bedford Tower is topped by a **figure of justice** that has been a subject of both controversy and mirth. The fact that she faces the castle and has her back to the city was taken as an indicator of how much justice Irish citizens could expect from the British. The scales of justice used to have a tendency to fill with rain and tilt in one direction or the other rather than balancing evenly. Eventually a hole was drilled in the bottom of each pan so the rainwater could drain out.

Royal Chapel

In the Lower Yard is the Church of the Holy Trinity, previously known as the Royal Chapel, which was built in Gothic style by Francis Johnston between 1807 and 1814. Decorating the cold, grey exterior are over 90 heads of various Irish personages and saints carved out of Tullamore limestone. The interior is wildly exuberant, with fan vaulting alongside quadripartite vaulting, wooden galleries, stained glass and lots of lively-looking sculpted angels.

Record Tower

Rising over the chapel is the Record Tower, used as a storage facility for official records from 1579 until their transfer to the Record Office in the Four Courts in the early 19th century. Although the tower was rebuilt in 1813 it retains much of its original appearance, including the massive 5m-thick walls. It now houses the **Garda Museum** (☎ 668 9998; admission free; open 9.15am-5pm Mon-Fri). Its exhibits follow the history of the Irish police force.

Chester Beatty Library

Reached by a separate entrance on Ship St and housed in the Clock Tower is the world-famous Chester Beatty Library (☎ 407 0750, e info@cbl.ie, w www.cbl.ie; admission free; open 10am-5pm Tues-Fri, 11am-5pm Sat, 1pm-5pm Sun; tours available 2.30pm Wed & Sat). Home of the collection of the mining engineer Sir Alfred Chester Beatty (1875–1968), this is our favourite museum in Dublin. Not only are the contents of the museum outstanding, but the layout and design are also excellent; apart from the ubiquitous cafe and gift shop, you can take advantage of the landscaped garden in front of the building and the rooftop garden on the third floor. In fine weather there's nowhere nicer to sit and contemplate – or eat your lunch. These are reasons enough to ensure that the library is near the top of our must-do list while in Dublin.

The outstanding collection includes over 20,000 manuscripts, rare books, miniature paintings, clay tablets, costumes and other objects spread across two floors. On the ground floor you'll find a compact but breathtaking collection of works of art from the Western, Islamic and East Asian worlds, including perhaps the finest collection of Chinese jade books in the world. Also worth examining are the illuminated European texts, which feature exquisite calligraphy, equal to that in the Book of Kells. Audiovisual displays explain the process of book-binding, paper-making and print-making.

The second floor is devoted to the major religions of the world – Judaism, Islam, Christianity, Hinduism and Buddhism. The collection of Qur'ans dating from the 9th to the 19th centuries (the library has over 270 of them) is considered by experts to be the best example of illuminated Islamic texts in the world. And it doesn't stop there. You'll also find some marvellous examples of ancient papyri, including renowned Egyptian love poems from the 12th century, and some of the earliest illuminated gospels in the world, dating to around AD 200. The collection is rounded off with some exquisite scrolls and artwork from China, Japan, Tibet and Southeast Asia, including the two-volume Japanese Chogonka Scroll, painted in the 17th century by Kano Sansetu.

CITY HALL (Map 6)

Fronting Dublin Castle, Dublin's City Hall (☎ 672 2204, W www.dublincorp.ie/cityhall, Cork Hill; adult/student & senior €3.80/ 1.25; open 10am-5.15pm Mon-Sat, 2pm-5pm Sun) was built by Thomas Cooley from 1769 to 1779 as the Royal Exchange and in 1852 became the offices of the Dublin Corporation. The building has a Corinthian portico with six columns, statues of notable Irish citizens and a fine dome. Parliament St (1762), which leads up from the river to the front of City Hall, was the first of Dublin's wide boulevards to be laid out by the Commission for Making Wide & Convenient Streets.

Dublin City Council meets here every first Monday of the month, gathering to discuss the city's business in the Council Chamber, originally the building's coffee room.

A brand-new multi-media exhibition entitled 'The Story of the Capital' traces the history of Dublin from its earliest beginnings up to 2000. It is in the basement of the building.

Across the path that marks the main entrance to Dublin Castle are the **Municipal Buildings** (☎ 672 2171, 16 Castle St; closed to the public), built in 1781 and designed by Thomas Ivory (1720–86). Today they house Dublin Corporation's Rates Office.

ST WERBURGH'S CHURCH (Map 5)

South of Christ Church Cathedral and beside Dublin Castle is St Werburgh's Church (☎ 478 3710, Werburgh St; donations accepted; open 10am-4pm Mon-Fri; phone, or see the caretaker at 8 Castle St to see inside). It stands on ancient foundations, but its early history, however, is unknown. It was rebuilt in 1662, 1715 and again in 1759 (with some elegance) after a fire in 1754. In 1810 the church's tall spire was ordered to be dismantled because authorities feared that rebels would use the vantage point to fire into Dublin Castle, but thankfully the order was not followed through. It is linked with the Fitzgerald family; Lord Edward Fitzgerald, who turned against Britain, joined the United Irishmen and was a leader of the 1798 Rising, is interred in the vault. In what was a frequent theme of Irish uprisings, compatriots gave him away and his death resulted from the wounds he received when captured. Ironically, Major Henry Sirr, his captor, is buried in the graveyard. John Field (1782–1837), the pianist who invented the nocturne, was baptised here – he is buried in Moscow. In the porch you will notice two fire pumps which date from the time when Dublin's fire department was composed of church volunteers.

Despite its long history, fine design and interesting interior, the church is rarely used today.

Werburgh St was the location of Dublin's first theatre and Jonathan Swift was born off the street at 7 Hoey's Court.

CHRIST CHURCH CATHEDRAL (Map 5)

Dublin's most imposing church, just south of the river at the southernmost edge of Dublin's original Viking settlement, is Christ Church Cathedral (Church of the Holy Trinity; ☎ 677 8099, e email@ccdub.ie, Christchurch Place; adult/student €2.50/1.25; open 9.45am-5.30pm). This was also the centre of medieval Dublin, with Dublin Castle nearby and the Tholsel or town hall (demolished in 1809) and the original Four Courts (demolished in 1796) both beside the cathedral. Nearby on Back Lane is the only remaining guildhall in Dublin, the Tailor's Hall (1706), now the offices of An Taisce.

The original church was built in wood in 1038 under the patronage of King Sitric II, the Danish king of Dublin. In 1163 Archbishop Laurence (Lorcan in Irish) O'Toole, later St Laurence, patron saint of Dublin, replaced the secular clergy of Christ Church with Augustinian monks – the ruins of their priory chapter house are still visible outside the cathedral's south wall. Following the Norman invasion of 1169, a group of knights led by Richard Fitzgilbert de Clare, earl of Pembroke (aka Strongbow) funded the construction of a new stone cathedral to replace the wooden Viking structure. Work on the cathedral commenced in 1172, but was not completed until the beginning of the 13th century, by which time both Strongbow and Archbishop had died; the former in 1176 and the latter at Eu in Normandy in 1180.

Nor was their cathedral destined to have a long life: the foundations were essentially a peat bog and the south wall collapsed in 1562, though it was soon rebuilt. Most of what you see from the outside dates from a major restoration (1871–78) by architect George Edmund Street. Above ground the north wall, the transepts and the western part of the choir are almost all that remain from the original. The result is that despite its uniformity, Christ Church is actually a hotchpotch of different styles, ranging from Romanesque to the popular English Gothic of the 19th century.

From its inception, Christ Church was the State Church of Ireland, and when Henry VIII dissolved the monasteries in 1537, the Augustinian priory that managed the church was replaced with a new Anglican clergy. Until the disestablishment of the Church of Ireland in 1869, senior representatives of the crown all swore their allegiance here. Christ Church's fortunes, however, were not guaranteed. By the turn of the 18th century its popularity among the faithful had waned. The upper echelons of Dublin society had migrated to the north side, where they frequented a new favourite, St Mary's Church on Mary St. By the time the street's restoration took place, Christ Church was virtually derelict, to the point that for a time the nave was used as a market and the crypt housed a number of taverns! Today, both Christ Church and the nearby St Patrick's Cathedral

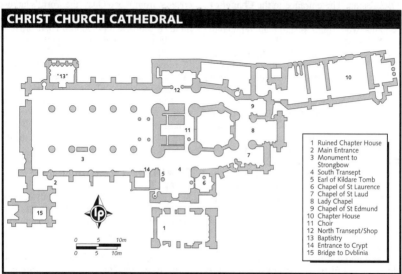

CHRIST CHURCH CATHEDRAL

1 Ruined Chapter House
2 Main Entrance
3 Monument to Strongbow
4 South Transept
5 Earl of Kildare Tomb
6 Chapel of St Laurence
7 Chapel of St Laud
8 Lady Chapel
9 Chapel of St Edmund
10 Chapter House
11 Choir
12 North Transept/Shop
13 Baptistry
14 Entrance to Crypt
15 Bridge to Dvblinia

0   5   10m

are still largely neglected by the mainly Catholic population, and the only way they make ends meet is as tourist attractions.

From the south-eastern entrance to the churchyard you walk past the ruins of the old **chapter house** (1 on map), dating from 1230. The entrance to the cathedral (2) is at the south-western corner and you face the northern wall as you enter. This wall survived the collapse of its southern counterpart, but has also suffered from subsidence, and from its eastern end it leans visibly – at the top it's about 0.5m out of perpendicular.

The southern side aisle has a **monument to Strongbow** (3). The armoured figure on the tomb is unlikely to be Strongbow (it's more probably the earl of Drogheda), but his internal organs may have been buried here. A popular legend relates that the halffigure beside the tomb is of Strongbow's son, who was cut in two by his father when his bravery in battle was suspect.

The **South Transept** (4) is one of the most original parts of the cathedral and contains the superb Baroque tomb of the 19th earl of Kildare (5), who died in 1734. His grandson, Lord Edward Fitzgerald, was a member of the United Irishmen and died in the abortive 1798 Rising. The entrance to the **Chapel of St Laurence** (6) is off the South Transept and contains two effigies, one of them reputed to be of either Strongbow's wife or sister.

On a somewhat macabre note, Laurence O'Toole's embalmed heart is in the **Chapel of St Laud** (7), to which Dubliners quip that 'at least his heart is in the right place'.

At the eastern end of the cathedral is the **Lady Chapel** (8), or Chapel of the Blessed Virgin Mary. Also at the east end is the **Chapel of St Edmund** (9) and the **Chapter House** (10; closed to visitors). Parts of the **Choir** (11), in the centre of the church, and the **North Transept** (12) are original, but the **Baptistry** (13) was added during the 1871–78 restoration. There's a gift shop in the North Transept.

An entrance (14) by the South Transept descends to the unusually large arched **crypt**, which dates back to the original Viking church. Curiosities in the crypt include a glass display-case housing a mum-

mified cat in the act of chasing a mummified mouse, frozen in pursuit inside an organ pipe in the 1860s. Also on display are the stocks of the old 'liberty' of Christ Church, when church authorities meted out civil punishments to wrongdoers. From the main entrance a bridge (15), part of the 1871–78 restoration, leads to Dvblinia.

Dvblinia (Map 5)

Inside what was once the Synod Hall, which was added to Christ Church Cathedral in the restoration of 1871 to 1878, the Medieval Trust has created Dvblinia (☎ 679 4611; adult/student €5/3.80; open 10am-5pm daily Apr-Sept, 11am-4pm Mon-Sat, 10am-4pm Sun Oct-Mar), a medieval heritage centre that tries to bring medieval Dublin to life. It doesn't do too a bad job of it, either, especially for kids. The ground floor is the most tourist-friendly part, with wax models of 10 episodes in Dublin's history, which are explained in a choice of five languages through headsets as you walk around. Here you can also find an answer to that burning question of whether you'd look good in two-coloured hose as you try on medieval garb. Up one floor there's a large selection of objects recovered from Wood Quay, the world's largest Viking archaeological site, as well as a large model of 11th-century Dublin. There are also models of the medieval quayside and of a cobbler's shop. On the top floor is the 'Medieval Fayre', a replica of a fair outside the city gates. Displays include merchants' wares, a medicine stall, an armourer's pavilion, a confessional booth and a bank. You can climb neighbouring St Michael's Tower for panoramic views over the city to the Dublin Hills. There is also a pleasant cafe and the inevitable souvenir shop.

ST AUDOEN'S CHURCHES (Map 3)

St Audoen (aka St Ouen), the 7th-century bishop of Rouen and patron saint of Normandy, has two churches to his name, both just west of Christ Church Cathedral. The more interesting of the two is the **Church of Ireland** (☎ 677 0088, e visits@ealga .ie, Cornmarket, High St; adult/senior/child

€1.20/1.25/0.75; open 9.30am-4.45pm daily June-Sept), the only surviving medieval parish church in the city and one of Dublin's most beautiful places of worship. It was built between 1181 and 1212, though recent excavations unearthing a 9th-century burial slab suggest that it was built on top of an even older church. Its tower and door date from the 12th century, the aisle from the 15th century and various other parts from between the 10th and 12th centuries, but the church today is mainly a product of its 19th-century restoration. A restoration by Dúchas resulted in the addition of a visitor centre in the southern aisle, known as St Anne's Chapel. Here you will find a number of tombstones of leading members of Dublin society from the 16th to the 18th centuries. At the top of the chapel is the tower, which houses the three oldest bells in Ireland, dating from 1423. Further bells were added in 1790, 1864 and 1880; the newer ones were recast in 1983, and the original bells were retuned at the same time. Although the church's exhibits are hardly spectacular, the building itself is very beautiful and a genuine slice of medieval Dublin.

The church is entered from the north through St Andrew's Arch off High St. Part of the old city wall, this arch was built in 1240 and is the only surviving reminder of the city gates.

Joined onto the Protestant church is the newer Catholic **St Audoen's** *(Cornmarket, High St; admission free)*, a large church, where Father 'Flash' Kavanagh used to read Mass at high speed so that his large congregation could head off to more absorbing Sunday pursuits, such as football matches.

ST PATRICK'S CATHEDRAL (Map 5)

Standing on one of Dublin's earliest Christian sites is St Patrick's Cathedral *(☎ 475 4817, e stpcath@iol.ie, w www.stpatricks cathedral.ie, St Patrick's Close; adult/senior, student & child €4.50/3.20; open 9am -5pm Mon-Fri, 9am-6pm Sat, 9am-11am, 12.45pm-3pm, 4.15pm-6pm Sun Mar-Oct, 9am-5pm Mon-Sat, 10am-11am, 12.45pm-3pm Sun Nov-Feb, closed Dec 24-26, Jan 1).*

He's 'Armless

In 1492 a furious argument occurred in St Patrick's Cathedral between the Earl of Kildare and the Earl of Ormonde. Each was supported by his armed retainers, but when strong words were about to lead to blows the Earl of Ormonde retreated to the chapter house. Fortunately, a peaceful settlement was reached and a hole was chopped through the door so the earls could shake hands on the agreement. In extending his arm through the door, thus making it vulnerable to attack from his opponent, the Earl of Kildare added the phrase 'chancing one's arm' to the English language. The hole is still in the door.

The saint is said to have baptised converts at a well within the cathedral grounds. Like Christ Church Cathedral it was built on unstable ground, with the subterranean River Poddle flowing beneath its foundations, and because of the high water table St Patrick's doesn't have a crypt. But again like its rival, it has had frequent restorations, alterations and additions. Take bus No 50, 50A or 56A from Aston Quay or No 54 or 54A from Burgh Quay to get there.

History

Although a church stood on the Patrick St site from as early as the 5th century, the present building dates from 1191, when it was inaugurated by John Comyn, the first Anglo-Norman archbishop of Dublin. It is likely that it was intended to replace Christ Church as the city's cathedral, but the older church's furious resistance to being usurped resulted in the unprecedented existence of two cathedrals virtually a stone's throw from one another, each possessing the rights of cathedral of the diocese. Christ Church lay within the city's walls and St Patrick's outside them; but the main difference between the two was that while the former was a regular cathedral, the latter was termed a secular cathedral. It was dedicated to the twin purposes of worship and learning, testament to Comyn's distaste for monastic orders.

Comyn's successor as archbishop, Henry of London, set about a major restructuring of the new cathedral, which resulted in a sturdier, larger cathedral built in the English Gothic style, completed in 1254 (the Lady Chapel was not added until 1270). It may have been more solid than its predecessor, but apparently it wasn't solid enough. A series of natural disasters plagued the cathedral for the next hundred years, including a storm in 1316 that collapsed the spire. In 1362 a fire destroyed the original tower and part of the west nave, but these were rebuilt in 1370 by Archbishop Minot, hence the tower's name.

St Patrick's troubles, however, were not just structural. Sixteenth-century England's religious turmoil climaxed with Henry VIII's dissolution of the monasteries in 1537, and St Patrick's was ordered to hand over all of its estates, revenues and possessions. The new dean, Edward Bassenet, went so far as to imprison the chapter until they agreed to the hand-over, prompting

Jonathan Swift to write 200 years later of 'one Bassenet...kin to the scoundrel who surrendered the deanery to that beast Henry VIII.' The cathedral's privileges were revoked and it was demoted to the rank of parish church, and was not restored to its previous position until 1560.

When Cromwell invaded Ireland in 1649, he ordered that the nave of the church be used as a stable for his horses, an indignity to which he subjected other Irish churches too. In 1666 the Lady Chapel was given to the newly arrived Huguenots and became known as *L'Eglise Française de St Patrique* (the French Church of St Patrick). It remained in Hugenot hands until 1816. The northern transept was known as the parish church of St Nicholas Without (meaning outside the city), essentially dividing the cathedral into two distinct churches.

Such confusion led to the building falling into disrepair as the influence of the deanery and chapter – previously charged with the

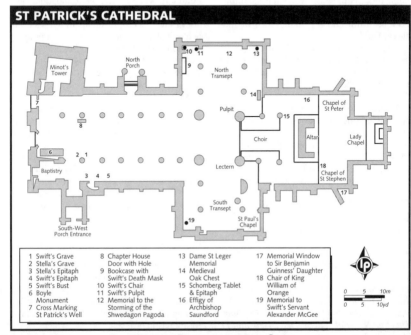

ST PATRICK'S CATHEDRAL

1 Swift's Grave	8 Chapter House	13 Dame St Leger	17 Memorial Window
2 Stella's Grave	Door with Hole	Memorial	to Sir Benjamin
3 Stella's Epitaph	9 Bookcase with	14 Medieval	Guinness' Daughter
4 Swift's Epitaph	Swift's Death Mask	Oak Chest	18 Chair of King
5 Swift's Bust	10 Swift's Chair	15 Schomberg Tablet	William of
6 Boyle	11 Swift's Pulpit	& Epitaph	Orange
Monument	12 Memorial to the	16 Effigy of	19 Memorial to
7 Cross Marking	Storming of the	Archbishop	Swift's Servant
St Patrick's Well	Shwedagon Pagoda	Saundford	Alexander McGee

Map labels: Minot's Tower; North Porch; North Transept; Baptistry; Pulpit; Choir; Lectern; Altar; Lady Chapel; Chapel of St Peter; Chapel of St Stephen; South Transept; St Paul's Chapel; South-West Porch Entrance

0   5   10m
0   5   10yd

church's maintenance – waned. Although the church's most famous dean, Jonathan Swift (who served from 1713–1745; see the boxed text overleaf) did his utmost to protect and preserve the integrity of the building, by the end of the 18th century the building was close to collapse. The first attempts at restoration did not begin until 1843, under the command of Dean Packenham, who served until 1864. Although he managed to restore the Lady Chapel and keep the building from falling down, his efforts were halted by the scarcity of funds provoked by the 1845–49 Famine. The church's real saviour was Benjamin Lee Guinness, who began funding a major restoration in 1864. He was followed by his sons, lords Iveagh and Ardilaun, who finished their father's work.

Church Tour

Entering the cathedral from the south-west porch you come almost immediately to the **graves** of Swift (1 on map) and his long-term companion Esther Johnson (2), better known as Stella. On the wall are the Latin epitaphs of Stella (3) and Swift (4), both written by the latter, and a bust of Swift (5). Also at this end of the cathedral is the huge **Boyle Monument** (6). Erected in 1632 by Richard Boyle, earl of Cork, it was decorated with numerous painted figures of his family members. It briefly stood beside the altar until, in 1633, Dublin's viceroy, Thomas Wentworth, earl of Strafford, had it shifted from its prominent position. Wentworth won this round in his bitter conflict with Boyle, but the latter had the final say when he contrived to have Wentworth impeached and executed. The figure in the centre of the bottom level of the monument is the earl's five-year-old son, Robert Boyle (1627–91), who became a noted scientist. His contributions to physics include Boyle's Law, which sets out the relationship between the pressure and the volume of a gas.

In the church's north-western corner is a cross on a stone slab (7), which once marked the position of St Patrick's original well. The South Transept was formerly a separate chapter house, and an old door (8), which now simply leans against a column at the west end of the cathedral, was once the entry to this. The hole is a result of a 15th-century argument; see the boxed text 'He's Armless'.

The **Swift corner** in the North Transept features a book-filled glass cabinet (9) containing his death mask, his chair (10) and Swift's pulpit (11).

The North Transept also contains various **military memorials** to the Royal Irish Regiments. The first shots in the American War of Independence were fired at one of these Irish military banners. The military monuments also include a depiction of the British forces storming the great Shwedagon Pagoda in Yangon (Rangoon), Myanmar (Burma; 12).

At the other side of the transept is a difficult-to-read memorial (13) to a certain Dame St Leger (1566–1603), who outlived two husbands before dying while giving birth to a child by her third, and a 14th-century oak chest (14).

The **northern choir aisle** has a tablet (15) indicating the grave of the duke of Schomberg, who died during the Battle of the Boyne. Swift provided the duke's epitaph, caustically noting on it that the duke's own relatives couldn't be bothered to provide a suitable memorial. The aisle also has a marble effigy (16) of Archbishop Saundford, who built the Lady Chapel at the eastern end of the building in 1270 before dying a year later.

As a tribute to the Guinness family's role in the cathedral's restoration, the **monument to Sir Benjamin Guinness' daughter** (17) stands beneath a window that bears the words 'I was thirsty and ye gave me drink'! The chapel also has a chair (18) used by William of Orange at a service in the cathedral after his victory at the Boyne.

The **South Transept**, where the clash between the earls of Ormonde and Kildare came to its conclusion (see boxed text 'He's 'Armless'), has various memorials, including one from Swift for his servant, Alexander McGee (19).

An exhibition in the church entitled 'Living Stones' features a comprehensive view of the church's history and symbolism, and also has sections on Jonathan Swift and the important role of music in St Patrick's. Admission is included in the entrance price.

Jonathan Swift

St Patrick's Cathedral is inextricably linked with its famous dean, Jonathan Swift (1667–1745), the noted satirist, author of *Gulliver's Travels* among other writings, and tireless campaigner for fair treatment for the Irish. Swift was born at Hoey's Court, now a derelict little alley beside St Werburgh's Church and a stone's throw from either of Dublin's cathedrals. By the age of three he was said to be a fluent reader and, remarkably, he entered Trinity College when he was just 15 years old.

In 1689 Dublin was in turmoil, following the seizure of the British throne by William of Orange, and Swift moved to England, where he worked as secretary to the wealthy diplomat Sir William Temple. Swift's intelligence and scholarship were much appreciated by Sir William and, despite various trips to Ireland, Swift remained in his employ until the diplo-

Gulliver's Travels, a biting satire, is so simply written that it's a children's favourite.

mat's death in 1699. Swift had been ordained as a priest in 1695 and he returned to Ireland to take up a variety of positions in the Irish Church, first near Belfast, then near Dublin.

The publication of *The Battle of the Books* and *A Tale of a Tub* in 1704, together with a series of political pamphlets, began to cement Swift's reputation not only as a noted satirist and wit but also as an eccentric. He still commuted between Ireland and England, spending three years in England from 1710 to 1713, and yearned for a higher ecclesiastical position (a 'fat deanery or a lean bishopric') in the English Church. His writings, however, had made him enemies and when the Whigs took over from the Tories in 1714 Swift found himself on the wrong side of the political divide. He retreated to Dublin, where he had become dean of St Patrick's Cathedral a year earlier.

Over the next 20 years Swift developed a keen social conscience and a deep concern for Irish impoverishment. He also made the transition from minor to major eccentric. His pen worked overtime righting wrongs, taking tyrants to task and attacking injustice wherever he saw it. His writing often took the form of anonymous tracts, such as his *Proposal for the Universal Use of Irish Manufactures* (1720), which suggested that the Irish take their revenge on England by burning anything from that country except its coal. Swift's *Drapier's Letters* (1724–25), ostensibly written by a humble trader, tore into a corrupt German duchess and her Irish business partner who were planning a

Church Services

St Patrick's Cathedral Choir is perhaps the most famous in Dublin, with a reputation dating back to 1742, when it participated in the first ever performance of Handel's *Messiah*. Today, you can hear the choir perform evensong at 5.35pm Monday to Friday. A real treat are the carols performed around Christmas; call ☎ 453 9472 for details of performances and how to obtain a hard-to-find ticket.

MARSH'S LIBRARY (Map 5)

Marsh's Library (☎ 454 3511, ℮ *marshlib@ iol.ie,* ⓦ *www.kst.dit.ie/marsh, St Patrick's Close; adult/senior & student €2.50/1.25; open 10am-12.45pm, 2pm-5pm Mon & Wed-Fri, 10.30am-12.45pm Sat)* was founded in 1701 by Archbishop Narcissus Marsh (1638–1713) and opened in 1707. It was designed by Sir William Robinson, who was also responsible for the Royal Hospital Kilmainham. The oldest public library in the

Jonathan Swift

crooked financial coup using a permit from the English king to mint coins. Their plan was to gain money by minting coins of copper instead of the standard gold or silver.

In 1729 *A Modest Proposal* modestly suggested that the children of poor Irish parents be eaten by the rich in order to reduce their parents' financial burden. First choice of the children, suggested Swift, should go to landlords who 'have already devoured their parents'. Despite this satirical defence of Irish children, it was said that Swift had absolutely no time for them, so it is a curious twist that he is remembered today primarily for what is often seen as a children's tale, *Gulliver's Travels*, published in 1726.

Swift's private life is full of intriguing mysteries, particularly those relating to Esther Johnson (1681–1728), better known as Stella, who was, depending on the tale, his innocent companion, his lover, his wife from a secretly conducted marriage, his niece or even his sister. He met her in England when she was just eight years old (and he was 22). She was the daughter of Sir William Temple's widowed housekeeper and it has been speculated that both Swift and Stella may have been the illegitimate offspring of Sir William. In 1701 he brought Stella to Ireland, with her chaperone, and lived with or near her until her death. At that time Swift lived in the deanery in the garden beside the cathedral (the present house is a replacement, built in 1781 after its predecessor burned down). On the night when Stella's body lay in the church before her burial, Swift slept in a different bedroom so that he would not see the light in his cathedral. He completed *Journal to Stella* in the darkened cathedral on the nights following her death.

Swift's name is also associated with another Esther, Esther Vanhomrigh or Vanessa. Swift wrote to her with the suggestion that she should come to Dublin, because: 'you will get more for your money in Dublin than in London, and St Stephen's Green has the finest walking gravel in Europe'. Vanessa duly turned up in 1714, but the Irish attraction was more probably the dean than Dublin. The two soon fell out and Vanessa retreated to her town house on Foster Place (at that time known as Turnstile Alley) off College Green where she died, so it is said, of a broken heart. Her grave is said to be somewhere nearby, but now submerged under centuries of urban development.

Jonathan Swift's cantankerous final years were unhappy ones. Hearing loss, terrible headaches and dizzy spells combined to convince him that he was heading towards insanity. It was a possibility his enemies had, no doubt, been suggesting for years. He is remembered not only for his writing and his colourful but secretive personal life, but also for the steps he made towards identifying and promoting a uniquely Irish conscience and spirit. Even in death Swift remained defiant. He composed his own Latin epitaph, because he felt no one else was capable of summing him up. In translation it reads: 'Here is laid the body of Jonathan Swift, Doctor of Divinity, Dean of this Cathedral Church, where fierce indignation can no longer rend the heart. Go, traveller, and imitate if you can this earnest and dedicated champion of liberty. He died on the 19th day of October 1745 AD. Aged 78 years.'

country, it contains 25,000 books dating from the 16th to the early 18th centuries, as well as maps, manuscripts (including one in Latin dating back to 1400) and a collection of incunabula (books printed before 1500). One of the oldest and finest of these is a volume of Cicero's *Letters to His Friends* printed in Milan in 1472.

The heart of the collection was the library of Edward Stillingfleet, bishop of Worcester. This hoard of almost 10,000 books was bought by Marsh in 1705 for UK£2500. Marsh's own extensive collection is also in the library, though he left his collection of Asian manuscripts to the Bodleian Library at Oxford University in England.

The collection also includes various items of Swift's, including his copy of *History of the Great Rebellion*. His margin notes include a number of comments vilifying Scots, of whom he seemed to have a low opinion. Swift also held a low opinion of Archbishop

Marsh, whom he blamed for his not achieving the position in the church he, Swift, felt he deserved. Marsh died in 1713 and was buried in St Patrick's Cathedral. Ironically, when Swift died in 1745, he was buried near his former enemy.

Like the rest of the library, the three **alcoves**, in which scholars were once locked to peruse rare volumes, have remained virtually unchanged for three centuries. The skull in the furthest one doesn't, however, belong to some poor forgotten scholar – it's a cast of Swift's Stella's head. The library's also home to Delmas Conservation Bindery, which repairs and restores rare old books; it makes an appearance in Joyce's *Ulysses*.

Take bus No 50, 50A or 56A from Aston Quay, or No 54 or 54A from Burgh Quay to get there.

DUBLIN CIVIC MUSEUM (Map 7)

In the 18th-century City Assembly House, beside the Powerscourt Townhouse shopping centre, is the Dublin Civic Museum *(☎ 679 4260, 58 South William St; admission free; open 10am-6pm Tues-Sat, 11am-2pm Sun)*. Its displays are related to the city's history, and include an eclectic selection of bric-a-brac, from Viking objects to a model of a tram. In particular look out for the stone head of Lord Nelson toppled from its column in O'Connell St by the IRA in 1966. A showcase houses the small wax artists' models upon which the stone heads representing Ireland's rivers on the Custom House were based. Changing exhibits might include postcards, Dublin coal-hole covers or items relating to local shipwrecks, but it's worth dropping in just to see the architecture.

POWERSCOURT TOWNHOUSE SHOPPING CENTRE (Map 6)

The elegantly converted Powerscourt Townhouse Shopping Centre *(☎ 679 4144, 59 South William St)* was originally designed by Richard Castle. Built between 1771 and 1774, this grand house has a balconied courtyard and, following its conversion in 1981, shelters three levels of modern shops and restaurants. The Powerscourt family's main residence was Powerscourt House in County Wicklow and this city mansion was soon sold for commercial use. The building features plasterwork by Michael Stapleton, who also worked on Belvedere House in north Dublin. Following a lengthy restoration, the building re-opened in 2000 as an elegant shopping centre, with a number of eateries and cafes (see the Shopping chapter for details).

GRAFTON ST (Map 7)

Grafton St is the premier street south of the Liffey. It was the major traffic artery of south Dublin before it became a pedestrian precinct in 1982. It's now Dublin's fanciest, most colourful shopping centre with plenty of street life and the city's most entertaining **buskers**, including poets and mime artists. The street is equally alive after dark as some of Dublin's most interesting pubs are clustered around it (see the Entertainment chapter).

As well as fine shops, such as the Brown Thomas department store (opened in 1848), it features the main branch of ***Bewley's Oriental Café*** *(☎ 677 6761, 78 Grafton St)*, a Dublin institution for anything from a quick cup of coffee or tea to a filling meal. Upstairs in this branch is a small museum (admission free) which relates the history of Bewley's. At the College Green end of the street is the **statue of Molly Malone**.

MANSION HOUSE (Map 7)

The Mansion House *(Dawson St; closed to the public)* was built in 1710 by Joshua Dawson, after whom the street is named. Five years later the house was bought as a residence for the lord mayor of Dublin. The building's original brick Queen Anne style has all but disappeared behind a stucco facade added in the Victorian era. The building was the site for the 1919 Declaration of Independence and the meeting of the first Dáil, or parliament.

ROYAL IRISH ACADEMY (Map 7)

Next door to the Mansion House is the seat of Ireland's pre-eminent society of letters, the Royal Irish Academy *(☎ 676 2570, 19 Dawson St; admission free; open 10.30am-5pm Mon-Fri)*. Its 18th-century library houses many important documents, including an extensive collection of ancient manuscripts such as the Book of Dun Cow. Also held there is the entire library of 18th-century poet Sir Thomas Moore.

NATIONAL MUSEUM (Map 5)

Completed in 1890, the National Museum (☎ 677 7444, e marketing@museum.ie, Kildare St; admission free but donations welcome, guided tours €1.25; open 10am-5pm Tues-Sat, 2pm-5pm Sun) was designed by Sir Thomas Newenham Deane. The star attraction is the Treasury, home to the world's finest collection of Bronze- and Iron-Age gold artefacts and most complete collection of medieval Celtic metalwork.

Ór: Ireland's Gold

During the Bronze and Iron Ages, Ireland's early Celtic artisans produced beautiful gold objects and many of those on display are stunning. Dating from between 2200 BC to after the arrival of the Celts around 500 BC, the collection – begun by the Royal Irish Academy in the late 18th century – ranges from bits of scrap gold to intricately woven jewellery.

In the 500 years from around 2200 BC, gold was often beaten into thin sheets to produce sun discs or crescent-shaped ornaments known as *lunalae*. The sheet gold was decorated with patterns either from the front or by making a raised pattern from behind by the technique known as *repoussé*.

Around 1200 to 1000 BC, larger quantities of gold were used to make earrings, bracelets, necklaces or even waistbands. During this period gold in sheet form was also beaten into armbands. Later still, a wider range of highly decorated gold objects were produced using gold wire or gold foil or by techniques such as casting. Among the items produced were neck rings, dress-fasteners and bracelets.

One fact worth considering is that for the most part, the pieces exhibited here were brought to light not by an archaeologist's trowel but by accident. Most were simply found, often dragged up by a plough or exposed by peat-cutter's saw. More often than

not they would uncover an individual piece, but occasionally a hoard of artefacts would be found, most likely hidden by Celts trying to stop marauding Vikings from laying their hands on their treasures. The sheer quantity of artefacts uncovered are compelling evidence that in prehistoric times Ireland was one the world's leading manufacturers of worked gold, even though very little is known about where exactly the gold came from.

The following are some of the Treasury's finest displays:

Broighter Hoard Discovered in County Derry in 1896, this collection of fine gold objects from the 1st century BC includes a large gold collar of a standard of artisanship unsurpassed anywhere in Europe. Other finds include twisted-gold neck ornaments and a model of a galley complete with oars.

Gleninsheen Gorget This magnificent gold collar dating from around 800 to 700 BC was found in County Clare in 1932.

Mooghaun Hoard The Mooghaun Hoard from County Clare was discovered by railway workers in 1854, and in that year the Royal Irish Academy displayed 146 objects weighing a total of 5kg, including sheet gold collars, gold neck rings and gold bracelets. Unfortunately, only 29 objects have survived; the rest of the find was probably melted down. Replicas are displayed at the museum.

Other Displays The Ballinesker Hoard is a collection of cloak-fasteners, boxes and discs discovered in 1990 in County Wexford. The **Dowris Hoard** of the 8th to 6th centuries BC was a huge find made in 1820. The wonderful Loughnasade bronze war-trumpet dates from the 1st century BC. There are other superb gold collars from the same era as the Gleninsheen Gorget.

Medieval Objects

If the allure of so much prehistoric gold isn't enough, the Treasury is also where you'll find some of the finest examples of medieval metalwork in the world. Ireland's monasteries flourished as centres of learning while the rest of Europe languished in the dark aftermath of the fall of the Roman Empire, and the 2000-year-old tradition of Celtic metalwork was put to perhaps its finest use. Of the treasures included here, two stand out as probably the best of their kind: the Ardagh Chalice and the Tara Brooch, seen at some point by virtually every schoolchild in the country.

Ardagh Chalice In 1868 a farmer digging the ground just outside the village of Ardagh in County Limerick, uncovered a chalice 17.8cm high and 24.2cm in diameter. Made of gold, silver, bronze, brass, copper and lead, the Ardagh Chalice is considered the finest exemplar of Celtic art ever found. Thought to date from the first half of the 8th century, it is made up of 354 individual pieces, including 20 rivets, and features a beautiful band around the outside on which are engraved the names of the 12 Apostles. It is thought that the chalice was originally crafted for the monastery at Clonmacnois, but was stolen by Vikings along with other artefacts in 1125 and transported down the Shannon to the Limerick area, hence its discovery in Ardagh.

Tara Brooch The Tara Brooch was crafted around AD 700 primarily in white bronze, but with traces of gold, silver, glass, copper, enamel and wire beading. It consists of three parts – a ring, a pin and a long chain. The front of the brooch is ornamented with beasts designed in fine traceries of gold wire, fierce looking reptiles that skirt around the outside of the jewels. In addition, there are enamelled studs, amber bands and two amethyst human heads. Decoration on the corner lobes resembles corner ornament in the Book of Durrow. Although the technique and style is comparable to other brooches found in Ireland and England, it is the exquisite detail and delicacy of its construction that make it the most valued of its kind. It is thought that the brooch was crafted for a leading Celt at the court of the Irish high kings at Tara, County Meath, but fell into the hands of marauding Vikings. It was discovered in a box along with other Viking artefacts near the mouth of the River Boyne at Bettystown, County Meath, in 1850.

Other Displays Besides the Ardagh Chalice and the Tara Brooch, there are a number of other pieces that should not be missed. The 12th-century **Cross of Cong** is made of wood, bronze and silver, and enshrined a fragment of wood said to come from the True Cross. This holy relic was presented by Pope Calixtus II to the King of Connaught in 1123 but has since disappeared. The cross remained in Cong, County Mayo, until 1839, when it was bought by the National Museum.

Dating from sometime between the 5th and the 8th centuries, **St Patrick's Bell** is said to have belonged to Ireland's patron saint. Around AD 1100 a shrine of gold wire on a silver backplate was made to house the bell. Originally from Armagh in County Armagh, the bell and shrine were once carried off by a Norman baron and subsequently handed down through generations of the Mulholland family until the late 18th century. Also worth taking time to examine is the Loughnashade Horn, so-named because it was found – along with three others like it – in 1798 at a small natural lake north-east of Navan, County Meath, called Loughnashade. A masterpiece of Celtic metallurgy, it is 1.86m long and made of sheets of bronze riveted together. At the mouth is an intricately designed disc. When played it can produce a very rhythmic noise similar to the Australian didjeridoo, though you'll have to take our word for it. As for the other three found with it, they have since disappeared.

Other Exhibits

If the Treasury hasn't completely exhausted you, you can move on to see the other exhibits in the museum, the most important of which focuses on the 1916 Easter Rising and the independence struggle from 1900 to 1921. Numerous displays relate to this important period of modern Irish history, although sadly the moving prison letters written by leaders of the Easter Rising have been put into storage. Viking Age Dublin upstairs displays exhibits from the excavations at Wood Quay – the area between Christ Church Cathedral and the river, where Dublin Corporation has its headquarters. Recent additions to the Viking display include a full-scale longboat in the square at the front of the museum. There's a good cafe on the ground floor.

Collins Barracks (Map 3)

The National Museum's main annexe is at Collins Barracks (☎ 677 7444, e marketing@museum.ie, Benburb St; admission free), off Ellis Quay on the north side of the Liffey. The former army barracks was completely renovated and opened in 1999 as the National Museum of Decorative Arts & History. Inside, you'll find artefacts ranging from silver, ceramic and glassware pieces, to weaponry, furniture and examples of folk life. While the exhibitions offer a pretty good bird's eye view of Ireland's social, economic and military history over the last 2000 years, it's still a bird's eye view and a little haphazard in its presentation. Not even the use of interactive multimedia displays – a staple of every new Irish museum – helps give a deeper insight into the pieces on show. Many of the pieces, however, are extremely interesting in their own right, and the best are gathered in the **Curator's Choice Exhibition**, which brings together such disparate objects as a 2000-year-old Japanese ceremonial bell and the gauntlets worn by King William of Orange at the Battle of the Boyne in 1690. Museum buffs might also relish the chance to see how curators go about the process of research, restoration and conservation in a section called **The Museum at Work**.

NATIONAL GALLERY (Map 5)

The National Gallery (☎ 661 5133, e artgall@eircom.net, w www.nationalgallery.ie, Merrion Square West; admission free; open 9.30am-5.30pm Mon-Wed, Fri & Sat, to 8.30pm Thur, noon-5.30pm Sun; free guided tours at 3pm Sat, 2pm, 3pm & 4pm Sun) was established by an Act of Parliament in 1854 and opened its doors to the public in 1864. The original collection of 125 paintings has

expanded to include around 2500 paintings and over 10,000 other works in various media such as watercolour, drawing, print and sculpture. Its excellent collection is strong in Irish art, but there are also high-quality collections of every major school of European painting. On the lawn in front of the gallery is a **statue of the Irish railways magnate William Dargan**, who organised the 1853 Dublin Industrial Exhibition at this spot; the profits from the exhibition were used to found the gallery. The building itself was designed by Francis Fowke, whose architectural credits also include London's Victoria & Albert Museum. Nearby is a **statue of George Bernard Shaw**, who was a major benefactor of the gallery. The gallery has three wings: the original Dargan Wing, the Milltown Rooms, which were added between 1899 and 1903, and the Modern Wing added from 1964 to 1968. Take bus No 5, 6, 7, 7A, 8, 10, 44, 47, 47B, 48A or 62 from Trinity College to the gallery.

The **Dargan Wing's** ground floor has the imposing Shaw Room (named after George Bernard Shaw), lined with full-length portraits and illuminated by a series of spectacular Waterford-crystal chandeliers. Upstairs, the rooms are dedicated to the Italian Early and High Renaissance, 16th-century north Italian art and 17th- and 18th-century Italian art. Worth checking out are a series of six canvases by the Spanish master Murillo narrating the story of the The Prodigal Son. During the summer months they are exhibited in Russborough House. The highlight, however, is undoubtedly Caravaggio's The Taking of Christ, which lay undiscovered for over 60 years in a Jesuit house in Leeson St, and was found accidentally by the chief curator of the gallery, Sergio Benedetti, in 1992. Fra Angelico, Titian and Tintoretto are among the other artists represented.

The central **Milltown Rooms** were built to hold Russborough House's art collection, which was presented to the gallery in 1902. The ground floor displays the gallery's fine Irish collection plus a smaller British collection, with works by Reynolds, Hogarth, Gainsborough, Landseer and Turner. One highlight is the room at the back of the gallery displaying works by Jack B Yeats (1871–1957), the younger brother of poet and dramatist William Butler Yeats. Also on display are works by their father, the noted portraitist John B Yeats (1839–1907). Other rooms relate to specific periods and styles of Irish art. Upstairs, the **Milltown Rooms** contain works from Germany, the Netherlands and Spain. There are rooms of works by Rembrandt and his circle and by artists from Seville. The Spanish collection features works by El Greco, Goya and Picasso.

The **Modern Wing** houses modern works and also has French works by Degas, Delacroix, Millet, Monet and Pissarro. The most popular exhibition in this wing occurs only in January, when the gallery hosts its annual display of watercolours by Joseph Turner. The 35 works in the collection are best viewed at this time due to the particular quality of the winter light.

The gallery also has an art reference library, a lecture theatre, a good bookshop and an excellent and deservedly popular restaurant.

LEINSTER HOUSE – IRISH PARLIAMENT (Map 5)

Ireland's parliament, the **Oireachtas na hÉireann** *(☎ 618 3000, 618 3271 for tour information,* **W** *www.irlgov.ie/oireachtas, Kildare St; observation gallery open when parliament is in session, usually 2.30pm-8.30pm Tues, 10.30am-8.30pm Wed, 10.30am-5.30pm Thur Nov-May; pre-arranged free guided tours available weekdays when parliament is in session)* meets in Leinster House. Both the lower house *(Dáil)* and the upper house or senate *(Seanad)* meet here. Parliament sits for 90 days a year, and you get an entry ticket to the observation gallery of the lower or upper house from the Kildare St entrance on production of some identification. The entrance to Leinster House from Kildare St is flanked by the National Library and the National Museum. The house was originally built as Kildare House from 1745 to 1748 for the Earl of Kildare, but its name was changed when he gained the title Duke of Leinster in 1766.

Leinster House was designed by Richard Cassels in the Palladian style and is consid-

ered the forerunner of the Georgian style that became the norm for the city's finer residences. The Kildare St frontage was designed to look like a town house (which inspired Irish architect James Hoban's designs for the American White House), whereas the Merrion Square frontage was made to resemble a country house. Interestingly, the Duke of Leinster was the first of Dublin's genteel class to settle on the south side of the Liffey, away from the then posh north side, thus beginning a trend that continues today.

At the other end of the lawn from the statue of Dargan is a **statue of Prince Albert**, Queen Victoria's consort. Queen Victoria herself was commemorated in massive form on the Kildare St side from 1908 until the statue was removed in 1948. The **obelisk** in front of the building is dedicated to Arthur Griffith, Michael Collins and Kevin O'Higgins, architects of independent Ireland.

The Dublin Society, later renamed the Royal Dublin Society, bought the building in 1814 but moved out in stages between 1922 and 1925, when the first government of the Irish Free State decided to establish its parliament there.

The 60-member Seanad meets in the north-wing saloon, while the 166-member Dáil meets in a less-interesting room that was originally a lecture theatre added to the original building in 1897.

GOVERNMENT BUILDINGS (Map 5)

On the south side of the Natural History Museum, the domed Government Buildings *(☎ 662 4888,* **e** *webmaster@taoiseach .irlgov.ie,* **W** *www.irlgov.ie/taoiseach, Upper Merrion St; free guided tours 10.30am-3.30pm Sat only, tickets from National Gallery ticket office ☎ 661 5133),* designed in a rather heavy-handed Edwardian interpretation of the Georgian style, were opened in 1911. Each 40-minute tour takes about 15 people, so you may have to wait a while for a group to assemble. Tours can't be booked in advance, but on Saturday morning you can put your name down for one later in the day. You get to see the Taoiseach's office, the cabinet room, the ceremonial staircase with a stunning stained-glass window designed by Evie Hone (1894–1955) for the 1939 New York Trade Fair, and innumerable fine examples of modern Irish arts and crafts.

NATIONAL LIBRARY & GENEALOGICAL OFFICE (Map 5)

To the north of the Kildare St entrance to Leinster House is the National Library (☎ 603 0200, W www.nli.ie, Kildare St; admission free; open 10am-9pm Mon, 2pm-5pm Tues & Wed, 10am-5pm Thur & Fri, 10am-1pm Sat), built from 1884 to 1890 at the same time as the National Museum and to a similar design by Sir Thomas Newenham Deane and his son Sir Thomas Manly Deane. Leinster House, the library and museum belonged to the Royal Dublin Society (formed in 1731), which aimed to improve conditions for poor people and to promote the arts and sciences. The library's extensive collection has many valuable early manuscripts, first editions, maps and other items of interest. Temporary displays are often held in the entrance area, and the library's reading room features in Ulysses. There's also an hour-long audiovisual presentation, about the history of Irish books, on the mezzanine floor.

On the second floor is the Genealogical Office (☎ 603 0200, National Library, Kildare St; open 10am-4.45pm Mon-Fri, 10am-12.30pm Sat), where you can obtain information on how best to trace your Irish roots. It once conducted the trace for you (at a fee), but now simply points you in the right direction (for free). See also the boxed text 'Tracing Your Ancestors'.

NATURAL HISTORY MUSEUM (Map 5)

Just as the National Library and the National Museum flank the entrance to Leinster House on the Kildare St side, the National Gallery and Natural History Museum do the same on the Upper Merrion St/Merrion Square side.

The Natural History Museum (☎ 677 7444, e marketing@museum.ie, Merrion St; admission free; open 10am-5pm Tues -Sat, 2pm-5pm Sun) is a rather musty place, scarcely changed since 1857 when Scottish explorer Dr David Livingstone delivered the

---

Tracing Your Ancestors

Tracing your ancestors is a popular activity for visitors to Ireland, and many tourists come to Ireland purely to track down their Irish roots. Success in this activity is more likely if you've conducted some basic research in your home country – in particular, if you've been able to obtain the date and point of arrival of your ancestor(s) – before you come to Ireland.

The Genealogical Office will advise you on how to trace your ancestry, which is a good way to begin your research if you have no other experience. For information on commercial agencies that will do the research for you contact the Association of Professional Genealogists in Ireland (APGI), c/o the Genealogical Office. The **Birth, Deaths & Marriages Register** (☎ 671 1863, Joyce House, West Lombard St; open 9.30am-12.30pm & 2.15pm-4.30pm Mon-Fri), the files of the **National Library** and the **National Archives** (☎ 478 3711, Four Courts) are all potential sources of genealogical information. The National Archives in Dublin Castle are of particular interest to Australians whose ancestors may have arrived in Australia as convicts.

Lots of books are available on the subject. The Irish Roots Guide, by Tony McCarthy, serves as a useful introduction. Other publications include Tracing Your Irish Roots, by Christine Kineally and Tracing Your Irish Ancestors: A Comprehensive Guide, by John Grenham. All these, and other items of genealogical concern, may be obtained from the **Genealogy Bookshop** (3 Nassau St) (Map 7).

---

opening lecture. In the face of the city's newer high-tech museums, its Victorian charm has been beautifully preserved, making it one of Dublin's more interesting museums. Commonly referred to as the 'dead zoo', the museum's huge and well organised collection numbers about 2,000,000, roughly half of which are insects. That moth-eaten look often afflicting neglected stuffed-animal collections has been kept at bay and children are likely to find it fascinating. On the ground floor, the **Irish Room** features a sizeable collection of mammals, birds and butterflies all found in Ireland at some point, including three skeletons of the giant deer, the Irish elk, which became extinct about 10,000 years ago. The World Animals Collection, spread across three levels, has as its centrepiece a remarkable skeleton of a 20m-long fin whale found beached in County Sligo. Other notables include the probably extinct but still much-searched-for Australian marsupial Tasmanian tiger (mislabelled as a Tasmanian wolf), a giant panda from China and several African and Asian rhinoceroses. Also worth checking out is the wonderful **Blaschka Collection**, finely detailed glass models of marine creatures whose zoological accuracy is incomparable.

ST STEPHEN'S GREEN (Map 5)

On warm summer days the nine hectares of St Stephen's Green provide a popular lunchtime escape for city workers. It was originally an expanse of open common land where public whippings, burnings and hangings took place. The green was enclosed by a fence in 1664 when the Dublin Corporation sold off the surrounding land for buildings. A stone wall replaced the fence in 1669 and, within, trees and gravel paths soon followed. By the end of the 17th century restrictions were already in force prohibiting buildings of less than two storeys or those constructed of mud and wattle. At the same time Grafton St, the main route to the green from what was then central Dublin, was upgraded from a 'foule and out of repaire' laneway to a Crown causeway.

The fine Georgian buildings around the square date mainly from Dublin's mid- to late-18th-century Georgian prime. At that time the northern side was known as the Beaux Walk and it is still a centre for some of Dublin society's most esteemed meeting places. Further improvements were made, with seats being put in place in 1753, but in 1814 railings and locked gates were added and an annual fee of one guinea was charged to use the green. This private use continued until 1877 when Sir Arthur Edward Guinness, later Lord Ardilaun, pushed an act through parliament opening the green to the

public once again. He also financed the central park's gardens and ponds, which date from 1880.

A variety of statues and memorials dot the green and, since it was Guinness money that created the park you see today, it's only right that there should be an 1892 statue of Sir Arthur, on the western side of the park. Just north of the **Guinness statue**, but outside the railing, is a **statue of Irish patriot Robert Emmet** (1778–1803), born across the road where Nos 124 and 125 stand; his actual birthplace has been demolished. The statue was placed here in 1966 and is a replica of an Emmet statue in Washington, DC.

Across the road from the western side of the green are the 1863 **Unitarian Church** (☎ 478 0638, St Stephen's Green West; admission free; open 12.30pm-2.30pm Mon-Fri) and the **Royal College of Surgeons** (☎ 402 2100, St Stephen's Green West; closed to the public), which has one of the finest facades on St Stephen's Green. It was built in 1806 and extended from 1825 to 1827 to the design of William Murray. Forty years later Murray's son, William G Murray, designed the Royal College of Physicians building. In the 1916 Easter Rising, the Royal College of Surgeons was occupied by rebel forces led by the colourful Countess Markievicz (1868–1927), an Irish nationalist married to a Polish count. The columns still bear bullet marks from the fighting.

The main entrance to the green was once on this side, but is now reached through the **Fusiliers' Arch** (Map 6) at the north-western corner of the green, which leads from Grafton St. Modelled to look like a smaller version of the Arch of Titus in Rome, the arch commemorates the 212 soldiers of the Royal Dublin Fusiliers who were killed while fighting for the British in the Boer War (1899–1902).

A path from the arch passes by the murky duck pond where you can see bar-headed geese, Canada geese, greylag geese, white-fronted geese, wigeons, tufted ducks, mandarin ducks, moorhens, coots and mallards. Around the fountain in the centre of the green are several **statues**, including a bust of Countess Markievicz. There are a bust of

...ublin Castle's Norman-built Record Tower...

and the Throne Room, dating from 1740

The castle's baroque Bedford Tower

Despite dating from the 13th century, Dublin Castle today is a mixture of more recent styles.

The Book of Kells is kept in Trinity College's Long Room, as are 200,000 other venerable tomes.

Marsh's Library is the oldest in the country.

Writer Oliver Goldsmith strikes a pose at Trinity.

the poet James Clarence Mangan (1803–49) and a curious 1967 **statue of WB Yeats** by Henry Moore nearby. The centre of the park also has a **garden for the blind**, complete with signs in Braille and plants that can be handled.

On the eastern side of the green is a **children's playground** and to the south there's a fine old **bandstand**, erected to celebrate Queen Victoria's jubilee in 1887. Musical performances often take place here in the summer. Near the bandstand is a **bust of James Joyce**, facing Newman House of University College Dublin, where he was once a student.

Just inside the green at the south-eastern corner, near Leeson St, is a **statue of the Three Fates**, presented to Dublin in 1956 by West Germany in gratitude for Irish aid after WWII. The north-western corner, opposite the Shelbourne Hotel and Merrion Row, is marked by the **Wolfe Tone Monument** to the leader of the abortive 1796 invasion. The vertical slabs serving as a backdrop to Wolfe Tone's statue have been dubbed 'Tone-henge'. Just inside the park at this entrance is a **Famine Victims Memorial**.

Unfortunately, some of Dublin's biggest architectural mistakes have been made around St Stephen's Green. Some notable buildings still remain, however, such as the imposing 1867 hotel, now the Méridien Shelbourne (see under Deluxe in the Places to Stay chapter), on the northern side of the green, with statues of Nubian princesses and their ankle-fettered slave girls decorating the front. Just to the east of the Shelbourne is a small Huguenot cemetery (closed) dating from 1693, when many French Huguenots fled here from persecution under Louis XIV.

Some of Dublin's most interesting streets radiate from the green. Grafton St, the main shopping avenue of Dublin, runs from the north-western corner, while Merrion Row, with its popular pubs, runs from the north-eastern. At the south-east is Leeson St, replete with fine Georgian residences.

Harcourt St, from the south-western corner, was laid out in 1775. Well known names associated with the street include Edward

Carson, born at No 4 in 1854; as the architect of Northern Irish Unionism he is perhaps not the most popular figure in Dublin's history, even though he sat in Westminster as the Trinity College candidate (when the university was an electoral district). His reputation in Dublin was further damaged when he served as the prosecuting attorney during Oscar Wilde's trial for homosexuality. Bram Stoker, author of *Dracula*, lived at No 16 and George Bernard Shaw at No 61. From 1859 to 1958 the Dublin–Bray railway line finished at Harcourt St station, then at the bottom of this road, now a huge uberbar, Odeon (see the Entertainment chapter).

Iveagh House
On the southern side of the green is Iveagh House (☎ *478 0822, 80-81 St Stephen's Green)*, named after Lord Iveagh, grandson of Arthur Guinness. Originally designed by Richard Cassels in 1730 as two separate houses, they were bought by Benjamin Guinness in 1862 and altered to create the family's city residence. After independence the house was donated to the Irish State and is now home to the Department of Foreign Affairs.

Newman House
Also on the green's southern side is the recently restored Newman House (☎ *475 7255, 85-86 St Stephen's Green; adult/child €3.80/2.50; open Jun-Aug; guided 40-minute tours only, on the hour, noon-4pm Tues-Fri, 11am-1pm Sat, 2pm-4pm Sun)*, one of Dublin's finest Georgian houses. The Catholic University of Ireland – the former name of University College Dublin – was founded here by John Henry Cardinal Newman in 1865, and while the college's main campus is now out in Belfield in Donnybrook (in the city's southern suburbs), it is still part of the university.

No 85 was built between 1736 and 1738 by Richard Cassels for the parliamentarian Hugh Montgomery, who then sold it to Richard Chapel Whaley MP in 1765. Whaley wanted a grander home so he commissioned another house next door at No 86. Aside from Cassels' wonderful design, the highlight of the design was the **plasterwork**, perhaps the finest in the city. For No 85, the artists were the Italian stuccodores Paulo and Filipo LaFranchini, whose work is best appreciated in the wonderfully detailed Apollo Room on the ground floor. The plasterwork in No 86 was done by Robert West, but it is not quite up to the high standard of next door. When the newly founded, Jesuit-run Catholic University of Ireland took possession of the house in 1865, they made alterations to some of the more graphic plasterwork. On the ceilings of the upstairs salon, for instance, the naked figures were covered with what can best be described as furry swimsuits. One such modesty vest has survived restoration.

During Whaley's residency, the house developed a certain notoriety, largely due to the activities of Whaley's son Buck, a notorious gambler and hell-raiser who once walked all the way to Jerusalem for a bet. He connived to have himself elected to parliament at the tender age of 17 and, fittingly, his name is known today because it adorns one of Leeson St's basement nightclubs. During the university's tenure, however, the residents were a far more temperate lot. The Jesuit priest and wonderful poet Gerard Manley Hopkins lived here during his time as Professor of Classics from 1884 until his death in 1889. Hopkins' bedroom is preserved as it would have been during his residence, as is the classroom where the young James Joyce studied while obtaining his Bachelor of Arts degree between 1899 and 1902. Patrick Pearse, one of the executed leaders of the 1916 Rising and a pretty good writer in his own right, was also a student, as was Eamon de Valera, leader of Sinn Féin, founder of Fianna Fáil and, later, president of Ireland.

In the basement is one of Dublin's most chic restaurants, The Commons (see under Top End in the Places to Eat chapter).

Newman University Church
Next to Newman House is the Catholic Newman University Church (☎ 478 0616, 83 St Stephen's Green; admission free; open 8am-6pm daily), built between 1854 and 1856 with an incongruous neo-Byzantine interior that attracted a lot of criticism at the time. It features much coloured marble and lots of gold leaf. Around the walls are plaques illustrating the Stations of the Cross and there's a bust of Cardinal Newman on the right-hand side. Today this is one of the most fashionable churches in Dublin for weddings.

Iveagh Gardens
Just behind Newman House and visible from Hopkins' room in Newman House are the landscaped Iveagh Gardens (open 8.15am-6pm Mon-Sat, 10am-6pm Sun May-Sept, 8.15am-dusk daily Oct-Apr), accessible from Earlsfort Terrace or Harcourt St. They were designed by Ninian Niven in 1863 and include a rustic grotto, cascade, fountain, maze and rosarium. Until recently, they were one of Dublin's best-kept secrets but no more: on a sunny day you'll have plenty of company.

MERRION SQUARE (Map 5)
Merrion Square, with its well kept central park, dates back to 1762 and has the National Gallery on its western side, while the other three sides are lined with elegant Georgian buildings. Around this square are the hallmarks of the best Georgian Dublin entrances – elegant doors and peacock fanlights, ornate door knockers and often foot-scrapers where gentlemen removed mud from their shoes before venturing indoors. Aside from the Wilde family (see later in this section), Merrion Square residents have included WB Yeats (1865–1939), who lived first at 52 East Merrion Square and later, from 1922 to 1928, at 82 South Merrion Square. George (Æ) Russell (1867–1935), the 'poet, mystic, painter and co-operator', worked at No 84. Daniel O'Connell (1775–1847) was a resident of No 58 in his later years. The Austrian Erwin Schrödinger (1887–1961), co-winner of the 1933 Nobel Prize for physics, lived at No 65 between 1940 and 1956. Dublin seemed to attract authors of horror stories and Joseph Sheridan Le Fanu (1814–73), who penned the vampire classic Carmilla, was a resident of No 70. The UK embassy occupied 39 East Merrion Square until it was burned out in 1972 in protest against events

Derry, Northern Ireland, when 13 civilians were killed by the British army.

Damage to fine Dublin buildings hasn't always been the prerogative of vandals, terrorists or protesters. East Merrion Square once continued into Lower Fitzwilliam St in the longest unbroken series of Georgian houses in Europe. Despite this, in 1961 the Electricity Supply Board knocked down 26 of them to build an office block. The **Royal Institute of the Architects of Ireland** (☎ 676 1703, 8 North Merrion Square; admission free; open 9am-5pm Mon-Fri), however, is fittingly based in a genuine Georgian house a few doors along from the Wilde residence. It hosts different exhibitions throughout the year.

The Leinster Lawn at the western end of the square has the fine **Rutland Fountain** (1791) and an 18m-high obelisk honouring the founders of independent Ireland. On the southern side is a **statue of Michael Collins** (1890–1922), one of the architects of Ireland's independence, who was assassinated during the ensuing Civil War. Merrion Square hasn't always been merely graceful and affluent, however. During the Potato Famine (1845–51), soup kitchens were set up in the gardens, which were crowded with starving rural refugees.

Oscar Wilde House

At 1 North Merrion Square is the first Georgian residence to be constructed on the square, built in 1762. In 1855 the surgeon Sir William Wilde and the poet Lady 'Speranza' Wilde moved here from 21 Westland Row (just north of the square) with their one-year-old son Oscar, and they were to occupy the house until 1876. It is likely that Oscar's literary genius was first stimulated by the creative atmosphere of the house, where Lady Wilde hosted the city's most famous (and best-frequented) literary salon.

In 1994, Oscar Wilde House (☎ 662 0281, e president@amcd.ie, 1 North Merrion Square; donation of €2.50 required; open 10.15am-noon Mon, Wed & Thur) was taken over by the American College Dublin, who set about restoring the ground and first floors to their 19th-century splendour. Following the major restoration, the house is now open

for guided tours only, at 10.15am and 11.15am, and visitors can see Sir William Wilde's study and surgery as well as Lady Wilde's drawing room and dining room.

Just across the street from the house inside Merrion Square is a **statue of Oscar Wilde**, inscribed with some of the witty one-liners for which he was famous.

No 29, Lower Fitzwilliam St

At the south-eastern corner of Merrion Square the Electricity Supply Board, having demolished most of Lower Fitzwilliam St for its new office block, had the decency to preserve one of the fine old Georgian houses. Originally built in 1794, No 29 (☎ 702 6165, e numbertwentynine@mail.esb.ie, w www.esb.ie; adult/student €3.20/1.25; open 10am-5pm Tues-Sat, 2pm-5pm Sun, closed two weeks before Christmas & until after New Year) has been restored by the National Museum to give a good impression of genteel home life in Dublin between 1790 and 1820. Everything is genuine, from the furniture to the paint on the walls. The first occupants were Mrs Olivia Beatty, the widow of a wealthy wine merchant, and her children. Property speculation was obviously a consideration even at that time as she paid UK£320 for it in 1794 but sold it 12 years later for UK£700.

Visitors are shown a short film on the house's history then join a 30-minute tour in groups of nine or less.

UPPER MERRION ST & ELY PLACE (Map 5)

Upper Merrion St runs south from Merrion Square towards St Stephen's Green. Mornington House, 24 Upper Merrion St, is thought to be the birthplace of the Duke of Wellington, who downplayed his Irish origins, although it's possible that his actual birthplace was Trim in County Meath. The building is now part of the The Merrion (see the Places to Stay chapter), one of Dublin's most upmarket hotels.

On the other side of Baggot St, Upper Merrion St becomes Ely (pronounced 'e-lie') Place. Built around 1770 this classic Georgian street features some well preserved houses and has many interesting historical associations.

John Philpot Curran (1750–1817), a great advocate of Irish liberty, once lived at No 4, as did the novelist George Moore (1852–1933). No 6 was the residence of the earl of Clare. Better known as Black Jack Fitzgibbon (1749–1802), he was a bitter opponent of Irish political aspirations and in 1794 a mob attempted to storm the house. **Ely House**, at No 8, is one of the best examples of a Georgian mansion in Dublin. The plasterwork is by Michael Stapleton and the staircase, illustrating the Labours of Hercules, is one of the finest in the city. At one time the surgeon Sir Thornley Stoker (brother of *Dracula* author Bram Stoker) lived here.

Royal Hibernian Academy (RHA) Gallagher Gallery

James Joyce's friend Oliver St John Gogarty (1878–1957) – immortalised as Buck Mulligan in the opening chapter of *Ulysses* – lived for a time at No 25, but it is now the home of the Royal Hibernian Academy (RHA) Gallagher Gallery *(☎ 661 2558, 25 Ely Place; admission free; open 11am-5pm Mon-Wed, Fri & Sat, 11am-9pm Thur, 2pm-5pm Sun)*, a large, well lit gallery that concentrates exclusively on the work of modern Irish and international artists. It is commonly accepted that if your work is shown here, you must be extremely good.

FITZWILLIAM SQUARE (Map 5)

South of Merrion Square and east of St Stephen's Green is Fitzwilliam Square. Built between 1791 and 1825, it was the smallest and the last of Dublin's great Georgian squares. It's also the only one where the central garden is still the private domain of the square's residents. William Dargan (1799–1867), the railway pioneer and founder of the National Gallery, lived at No 2, and the artist Jack B Yeats (1871–1957) lived at No 18. Look out for the attractive 18th- and 19th-century metal coal-hole covers. Today the square is a centre for the Dublin medical profession but at night it is overrun with prostitutes, whose customers are largely drawn from the seedy Lesson St nightclubs.

OTHER MUSEUMS
Shaw Birthplace (Map 2)

About 15 minutes' walk south of St Stephen's Green is the birthplace of playwright George Bernard Shaw, which is now open as a **museum** *(☎ 475 0854, 33 Synge St; adult/concession €5.10/3.80; open 10am-1pm & 2-5pm Mon-Sat, from 11am Sun Easter-Oct)*. The Victorian home has been completely restored and is worth visiting if only to get a look at the domestic life of the 19th century's middle classes. Shaw's mother held musical evenings in the drawing room, and it is likely that her son's store of fabulous characters were inspired by those who attended.

Take bus No 16, 19 or 122 from Trinity College to get there.

Irish-Jewish Museum (Map 2)

In an old synagogue, the Irish-Jewish **Museum** *(☎ 453 1797, 4 Walworth Rd; admission free; open 11am-3.30pm Tues, Thur & Sun May-Sept, 10.30am-2.30pm Sun only Oct-Apr)* was opened in 1985 by the then Israeli president, Chaim Herzog, who was actually born in Belfast. Dublin's small but culturally important Jewish population is remembered through photographs, paintings, certificates, books and other memorabilia. Take bus No 16, 19 or 122 from Trinity College to get here.

OTHER SOUTH DUBLIN CHURCHES
St Stephen's Church (Map 5)

Built in 1825 in Greek Revival style – complete with cupola – and commonly known as the 'pepper-canister church' on account of its appearance, St Stephen's *(☎ 288 0663, Upper Mount St; admission free; open for services only, 11am Sun & 11.30am Wed year-round & 11am Fri July-Aug)* is at the far end of Upper Mount St from Merrion Square and lies in the middle of a traffic island. It is one of the city's most attractive churches, but its proximity to Fitzwilliam Square and its mid-street location has made it a favourite among the city's prostitutes, who stand provocatively in its night-time shadows. It hosts concerts on an ad hoc basis; see the Entertainment chapter for details.

Whitefriars Carmelite Church (Map 7)

This Carmelite Church (☎ 475 8821, 56 Aungier St; admission free; open 8am-6.30pm Mon, Wed-Fri, to 9.30pm Tues, to 7pm Sat, to 7.30pm Sun, 9.30am-1pm holidays) stands on the former site of the Whitefriars Carmelite monastery founded in 1278. The monastery was suppressed by Henry VIII in 1537 and its lands and wealth seized by the Crown. Eventually the Carmelites returned to their former church and re-established it, dedicating the new building in 1827.

In the north-eastern corner is a 16th-century **Flemish oak statue** of the Virgin and Child, believed to be the only wooden statue to escape destruction during the Reformation. The church's altar contains **the remains of St Valentine**, donated to the church by Pope Gregory XVI in 1835.

North of the Liffey

Though south Dublin is noticeably more affluent than north Dublin and has the lion's share of the city's tourist attractions, there are many reasons to head across the Liffey, starting with Dublin's grandest avenue.

O'CONNELL ST (Map 4)

O'Connell St is the major thoroughfare in north Dublin and qualifies as the most important, imposing street in the city. Or at least that was the case until the 1970s, when its glory truly began to fade in favour of the more elegant streets of the south side, particularly Grafton St and environs. Yet the area around O'Connell St, particularly Moore St to the west and Henry St to the east, are where you'll find glimpses of a more traditional Dublin, full of cheap shops, greasy-spoon cafes and street vendors – present-day Molly Malones. It's here, northsiders will argue, the real Dublin still survives, warts and all. But the warts are all too evident, as poor planning, ugly shops and fast-food restaurants – as well as a nasty reputation for being dangerous at night – have reduced Dublin's finest boulevard to a tacky shopping centre.

All this, however, is about to change, as Dublin Corporation has announced a radical overhaul of the street. Over €45 million of public money as well as several hundred million euros of private investment will result in a new plaza in front of the GPO, wider footpaths, a new street linking O'Connell St with Moore St, a major shopping centre and a thorough re-appraisal of the street's building design. The **Monument of Light** (aka the Millennium Spire; originally planned to grace the spot once occupied by Nelson's Pillar; see later in this section) in time for New Year's Eve 1999, was delayed by objections but has finally been approved and should be up by early 2002.

O'Connell St started life in the early 18th century as Drogheda St, named after Viscount Henry Moore, earl of Drogheda.

In the 1740s Luke Gardiner, later Viscount Mountjoy, widened the street to 45m, turning it into an elongated promenade bearing his name.

Gardiner's Mall became Sackville St but was renamed again in 1924 after Daniel O'Connell, the Irish nationalist leader whose **statue** stands at the river end. The 1854 bronze statue features four winged figures that are not, despite their appearance, angels. They're the four Victories and are supposed to illustrate O'Connell's courage, eloquence, fidelity and patriotism. If you inspect them closely you'll notice that two of them are bullet marked, a legacy of the 1916 Easter Rising and the Civil War in 1922.

The central pedestrian area, continuing north from the river, is home to a variety of other statuary, one of which is a **monument to William Smith O'Brien** (1803–64), leader of the Young Ireland Party. The inscription on his monument notes that he was sentenced to death for high treason in 1848, so it either took a long time to carry out the sentence or it was done with remarkable inefficiency. There is also a **statue of Sir John Gray** (1815–75), a newspaper publisher and a pioneer in the provision of mains water in Dublin. Outside the GPO, a **statue of Jim Larkin** (1876–1947), a trade union leader and organiser of the general strike of 1913, represents him in a dramatic pose, throwing his arms in the air.

O'Connell St's most famous monument was a victim of the tendency to 'redevelop' the street in an explosive fashion. In 1815 the street was graced with a Doric pillar topped by a statue of Nelson, the British naval captain who defeated the French navy at Trafalgar in 1805. It predated the famous Nelson's Column in London's Trafalgar Square by 32 years. In 1966, as an unofficial celebration of the 50th anniversary of the 1916 Easter Rising, this symbol of British imperialism was badly damaged by an explosion and subsequently demolished. An aspect of the demolition that never ceases to amuse Dubliners is that while the explosion that originally ruined the statue caused no damage to anything other than poor Nelson, the charges set by the Irish army to demolish the remaining pedestal blew out virtually every window in O'Connell St! Nelson's stone head survives in the Dublin Civic Museum, but the statue's demise put an end to the quip that the main street of the capital city of this most piously Catholic of countries had statues honouring

The Name's the Game

It seems that Dubliners aren't happy with the names given to the various statues, monuments and other assorted sights throughout the city, and in an effort to convey the deeper significance of what these sights represent, they are compelled to make up humorous rhyming names for them. Silly or not, they are often quite funny, a sign of how iconoclastic Dubliners really are.

Just next to the north side of the Ha'penny Bridge is a bronze sculpture of two women sitting on a bench with shopping bags at their feet that is commonly known as 'the hags with the bags'.

At the end of Grafton St is a statue of a woman with a wheelbarrow loaded with cockles and mussels; she is Molly Malone, street vendor extraordinaire and the subject of Dublin's most famous song. But she is in such a serious state of undress that she is known as 'the tart with the cart'.

Not content with giving names to statues, Dubliners express their disapproval of buildings they consider ugly with rhyming names. Consequently, an unappealing apartment complex above The Oak bar on Dame St is 'the yoke on The Oak', and the rather box-like Waterways Visitor Centre in the docklands area is – you guessed it – 'the box on the docks'.

One of the funnier names was given to a well intentioned but ill-advised plan to place a luminous millennium clock in the Liffey underneath the Ha'penny Bridge. It would count down to the end of the century and people would see it from down the river; quite effective, you might think. But the problem was that you couldn't see the luminous numbers due to the dirt in the Liffey, and so 'the time in the slime' was removed.

Dublin's newest monument is the Monument of Light, a 130m-high spire to replace Nelson's Pillar. Dublin's wags have already taken to calling it 'the skewer by the sewer', 'the stiletto in the ghetto' and, in a macabre reference to the area's drug problem, 'the biggest needle in O'Connell St'.

Just across the street from the GPO on O'Connell St is a small statue of James Joyce, his head slightly cocked, his hand leaning on a walking stick. So how do Dubliners choose to remember their greatest writer? As the 'prick with the stick'. Joyce certainly loved his rhyming word play, so we're *almost* sure he would have smiled.

The best names of all are reserved for the Anna Livia statue on O'Connell St. Joyce enthusiasts will know that the author gave the Liffey a woman's personality and name, Anna Livia, and the statue of a woman lying in water was designed and built in tribute. The problem is that it's an ugly statue and the locals don't really like it, so 'the floozy in the Jacuzzi' and 'the hooer in the sewer' were coined. And it doesn't end there. Modern medicine has provided the latest name, which describes the small waterfall at the back of Anna Livia's head that drips water over her suggestively prone body: 'Viagra Falls'.

THINGS TO SEE & DO

three noted adulterers: O'Connell at the bottom of the street, Parnell at the top and Nelson in the middle.

The site of Nelson's demolished pillar is halfway up the street, between Henry and Earl Sts, near the GPO. Close by, a figure of James Joyce stands nonchalantly at the corner of pedestrianised North Earl St. In a **fountain** just beyond the site of the former column is a sculpted figure (1988) of Joyce's spirit of the Liffey, Anna Livia.

Continuing north, the tourist office is to the right, as is the Gresham Hotel, one of Dublin's most genteel. Further on is the **figure of Father Theobald Mathew** (1790–1856), the 'apostle of temperance' – an utterly hopeless role in Ireland. However, this quixotic task resulted in a Liffey bridge bearing his name. The top of the street is completed by the **statue of Charles Stewart Parnell** (1846–91), who was an advocate of Home Rule and became a political victim of Irish intolerance. Despite this it's Parnell who gets the most imposing monument.

General Post Office (GPO; Map 4)

The GPO (see Post & Communications in the Facts for the Visitor chapter) is an important landmark and its focal role in the history of independent Ireland has made it a prime site for everything from official parades to personal protests. The huge building, designed by Francis Johnston and opened in 1818, was the focus of the 1916 Easter Rising when Patrick Pearse, James Connolly and the other five leaders read their proclamation of a republic from its steps. In the subsequent siege the building was completely burned out. The facade, with its Ionic portico, is still pockmarked from the 1916 clash and from further damage wrought at the start of the Civil War in 1922. It was not reopened until 1929.

By an inside window, the *Death of Cuchulainn* statue commemorates Cuchulainn, the greatest of the Knights of the Red Branch, who were loyal to the king of the Ulaids (Ulster). He defended Ulster against the forces of Maeve, queen of Connaught, but is said to have been slain at the age of 27 after being tricked into an unfair fight.

Monument of Light (Millennium Spire; Map 3)

You can't miss it from anywhere in the city: twice the height of Dublin's highest office block, Liberty Hall, this 120m-high stainless steel spire towers over O'Connell St and the surrounding area. Until 1966, the spot on which it stands was occupied by the far less imposing figure of Horatio Nelson – until the statue was blown up by the IRA.

The new monument is an impressive feat of architectural engineering. From a base of only 3m in diameter, it soars over 100m into the sky and tapers into a beam of light, projected through optical glass at its apex. Yet this thoroughly contemporary addition to the city's streetscape and skyline, the brainchild of London-based architect Ian Ritchie, was subject to objections that delayed its construction. Michael Nolan, brother of well known writer Flann O'Brien (Brian Nolan) successfully applied for a court injunction in late 2000, arguing that the proposed monument would significantly alter the cultural, architectural and historic identity of O'Connell St. Dublin Corporation's plans to unveil the monument in time for the millennium were thus scuppered, but the objections were overcome in 2001 and construction began in earnest.

HOT PRESS IRISH MUSIC HALL OF FAME (Map 4)

This **museum** (☎ 878 3345, W *www.mcd .com, 57 Middle Abbey St; adult/student €7.60/5.10; open 10am-6pm daily)* was intended to be a celebration of Ireland's key role in popular music, but in truth it falls far short of that. There's plenty of memorabilia given by Irish stars, from 1960s legend Van Morrison to current phenomenon Westlife. You can see U2 drummer Larry Mullen's first drum kit, the original Live Aid contract received by Bob Geldof, and plenty of other bits and bobs, some more interesting than others. There are also the embarrassingly named Jam restaurant and a 500-seat venue.

Admission is high but includes a headset for the audiovisual tour. If you're a big fan of Irish rock and pop acts, you'll enjoy it. If not, give it a miss.

THINGS TO SEE & DO

CUSTOM HOUSE (Map 4)

James Gandon was 18th-century Dublin's pre-eminent architect. The Custom House is his first great building, and was built between 1781 and 1791 just past Eden Quay, despite opposition from city merchants and dock workers at the original Custom House upriver in Temple Bar. Because of the city's merchants unhappiness about this commercial intrusion Gandon sometimes appeared on site wielding a sword! He was supported by the era's foremost property developer, Luke Gardiner, who saw the new Custom House as a major part of his scheme to shift the axis of the city eastwards from medieval Capel St to what was then Gardiner's Mall (now O'Connell St).

In 1921, during the independence struggle, the Custom House was set alight and completely gutted in a five-day fire, but was later totally rebuilt. The interior, however, was extensively redesigned and another major renovation occurred between 1986 and 1988.

The building stretches for 114m along the Liffey; the best complete view is from across the river, though a close-up inspection of its many fine details is also worthwhile. Arcades, each with seven arches, join the centre to the end pavilions and the columns along the front have harps carved in their capitals. Motifs allude to transportation and trade, including the four **rooftop statues** of Neptune, Mercury, Plenty and Industry, destroyed in the 1921 fire and replaced in 1991. Below the frieze are heads representing the gods of Ireland's 13 principal rivers. The sole female head above the main door represents the River Liffey. The cattle heads honour Dublin's beef trade and the statues behind the building represent Africa, America, Asia and Europe. The building is topped by a copper dome with four clocks and, above that, a 5m-high statue of Hope.

Beneath the dome is the **Custom House Visitor Centre** (☎ 878 7660, Custom House Quay; €1.30; open 10am-12.30pm & 2pm to 5pm mid-Mar–Nov & 10am-12.30pm Wed-Fri & 2pm-5pm Sun Nov–mid-March), which features a small museum on Gandon himself as well as the history of the building.

Just outside the Custom House, on Custom House Quay, is a remarkable set of life-size bronze figures, a memorial to the victims of the Famine (1845–49) made by Rowan Gillespie in 1997. The piece powerfully evokes the drama of Ireland's greatest single tragedy.

ST MARY'S PRO-CATHEDRAL (Map 4)

On the corner of Marlborough and Cathedral Sts, just east of O'Connell St, is Dublin's most important Catholic church, built between 1816 and 1825. The Pro-Cathedral (☎ 874 5441, Marlborough St; admission free; open 8am-6.30pm) was originally intended for what is now called O'Connell St, but fears that such a prominent position would provoke anti-Catholic British attitudes led to its comparatively inconspicuous location. Unfortunately, the cramped Marlborough St location makes it almost impossible to stand back far enough to admire the front with its six Doric columns, modelled on the Temple of Theseus in Athens. Inside, highlights include the altar, carved by Peter Turnerelli, and the alto relief representation of the Ascension, by John Smyth.

Some intriguing questions are connected with the Pro-Cathedral's design and even its name. The competition held in 1814 to find the best design for the church was won by John Sweetman, a former owner of Sweetman's Brewery. But who organised the competition? Why, it was none other than William Sweetman, John Sweetman's brother. And did John Sweetman design the building himself? Possibly not, since he was living in Paris at the time and may have bought the plans from the French architect who designed the similar Notre Dame de Lorette in northern France. The only clue as to the church's architect is in the ledger, which lists the builder as 'Mr P'. And what does 'pro' mean? It's not clear, but Pro-Cathedral seems to imply something like 'unofficial cathedral'...

PARNELL SQUARE (Map 3)

The main squares of north Dublin are poor relations of their great counterparts south of the Liffey, and are generally far less well tended. However, they do have their points of interest.

The northern side of Parnell Square was built on lands acquired in the mid-18th century by Dr Bartholomew Mosse, the founder of the Rotunda Hospital, and was originally named Palace Row. The terrace was laid out in 1755 and Lord Charlemont bought the land for his home at No 22 in 1762. Charlemont's home was designed by Sir William Chambers, who also designed Lord Charlemont's extraordinary Casino at Marino (see later in this chapter). Today the building houses the Hugh Lane Municipal Gallery of Modern Art (see later in this section). The street was completed in 1769 and the gardens were renamed Rutland Square in 1786, before acquiring their current name in 1921.

Next to the gallery is the Dublin Writers' Museum (see later in this section), and overlooking the square from the northern corner is the Abbey Presbyterian Church. In 1966 a section at the north of the square was turned into a **Garden of Remembrance** for the 50th anniversary of the 1916 Easter Rising. Its centrepiece is a 1971 sculpture by Oisín Kelly depicting the children of Lir myth.

There are some fine, though rather run-down, Georgian houses on the eastern side of the square. Oliver St John Gogarty was born at **No 5** in 1878, Dr Bartholomew Mosse was once a resident of **No 9** and the earls of Ormonde used **No 11** as a town house. On the other side of the square is the Sinn Féin Bookshop, at 44 West Parnell Square. The square also contains the Gate Theatre, Ambassador Cinema and Rotunda Hospital.

Rotunda Hospital

Dr Bartholomew Mosse set up the Rotunda Hospital in 1757. This was the first maternity hospital in Ireland or Britain and was built when Dublin's burgeoning urban population was leading to horrific infant-mortality figures. The hospital shares its basic design with Leinster House: Richard Cassels was the

The Children of Lir

The children of Lir were the daughter and four sons of the ancient King Lir. As in most fairy-tales involving ill-treated children, a wicked stepmother (who in this case was also the sister of the children's dead mother) played a key part in the legend. The king's new wife, Aoife, developed an insane jealousy of the children but, lacking the resolve to drown them, she merely enticed them into a lake, Lough Derravaragh (in modern-day Westmeath), to bathe and then cast a spell on them, turning them into swans.

They were forced to spend 900 years on the waters of Ireland – 300 years each on Lough Derravaragh, the Sea of Moyle and the Bay of Erris. Feeling remorseful about what she had done, Aoife allowed them to keep their human voices and to make beautiful music. It wasn't long before the king discovered a group of talking swans and proclaimed that no swan should ever be killed in Ireland. King Dearg, Aoife's father, punished his dastardly daughter by turning her into a demon, but the unfortunate children still had to live out their 900 years as swans.

Christianity had just arrived in Ireland when the time span was up, so the children of Lir, by then old and careworn, were baptised by St Patrick when they finally again took on human form, but they died soon afterwards. Swans remain a protected species in Ireland.

JANE SMITH

Parnell Square's Lir sculpture

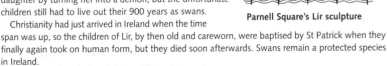

architect of both and re-used the Leinster House floor plan in order to economise.

To his Leinster House design, Cassels added a three-storey tower. To help fund the hospital's operation, Mosse intended to charge visitors to climb the tower, which provided a fine view over the city. The Rotunda Assembly Hall, now occupied by the Ambassador Cinema, was built as an adjunct to the hospital, also to raise funds. Over the main entrance of the hospital is the Rotunda Chapel, built in 1758 with superb coloured plasterwork by Bartholomew Cramillion.

The Rotunda Hospital still functions as a maternity hospital today. The **Patrick Conway** pub (see the Pubs & Bars special section in the Entertainment chapter) opposite dates from 1745 and has been hosting expectant fathers since the day the hospital opened.

Hugh Lane

If wealthy Sir Hugh Lane (1875–1915) became more than a little miffed by the Irish and decided to give his paintings to some other nation, it was scarcely surprising, as he was treated with less respect than he felt he deserved in his own land. Born in County Cork, he began to work in London art galleries from 1893 and five years later set up his own gallery in Dublin. He had a true art dealer's nose for the directions in which art would be heading and built up a superb collection, particularly of impressionist works.

Unfortunately for Ireland, neither his talents nor his collection were much appreciated and in exasperation he turned his attention to opportunities in London and South Africa. Irish rejection led him to rewrite his will and bequeath some of the finest works in his collection to the National Gallery in London. Later he relented and added a rider to his will leaving the collection to Dublin but failed to have it witnessed, thus causing a long legal squabble over which gallery had rightful ownership.

Lane was only 40 years old when he went down with the ill-fated *Lusitania* in 1915 after it was torpedoed off the southern coast of Ireland by a German U-boat.

Hugh Lane Municipal Gallery of Modern Art

The Hugh Lane Gallery (☎ 874 1903, e *ex hibitions@hughlane.ie*, w *www.hughlane.ie, 22 North Parnell Square; admission free, special exhibitions €6.35; open 9.30am-6pm Tues-Thur, 9.30am-5pm Fri & Sat, 11am-5pm Sun Sept-Mar, 11am-8pm Thur Apr-Aug)* has a fine collection of work by the French impressionists and 20th-century Irish artists. The exhibits include sculptures by Rodin and Degas, works by Corot, Courbet, Manet and Monet from the Lane Bequest and numerous works by Irish artists, including Jack B Yeats.

The gallery, founded in 1908, moved to its present location in the splendid 18th-century Charlemont House, formerly the earl of Charlemont's town house, in 1933. The gallery was established by Sir Hugh Lane, the wealthy nephew of Lady Gregory (WB Yeats' patron). Lane died in 1915, a passenger on the *Lusitania*, torpedoed off Ireland's southern coast by a German U-boat. The Lane Bequest pictures, which formed the nucleus of the gallery, were the subject of a dispute over Lane's will between the gallery and the National Gallery in London. A settlement wasn't reached until 1959, and was modified in 1993 allowing 35 of the 39 paintings to be viewed in Dublin over a period of 12 years. Twenty-seven are here for the full duration of the term; the remaining eight alternate in two groups of four between London and Dublin, changing every six years. Since November 1999 the gallery has displayed Manet's *Eva Gonzales*, Pissarro's *Printemps*, Morisot's *Jour d'Été*, and the most important painting of the collection, Renoir's *Les Parapluies*.

The gallery's newest permanent exhibit is the full-scale recreation of the studio of the painter Francis Bacon (1909–92), who was born in Dublin. An extraordinarily successful retrospective of the painter's major works in 2000 was followed by the opening in 2001 of a new permanent exhibition of Bacon's studio and all of its contents.

Dublin Writers' Museum

The Dublin Writers' Museum (☎ 872 2077, *18 North Parnell Square; adult/student/child*

Francis Bacon

It comes as a surprise to many that the foremost British painter of his generation was actually... Irish. Born in Dublin in 1909, Francis Bacon was the son of a racehorse trainer whose education was conducted almost exclusively at home. At 16 his parents were horrified to discover that he was an active homosexual and threw him out. Like so many other great Irish talents, Bacon turned his back on his narrow-minded home and moved abroad, spending time in Berlin and Paris before finally settling in London in 1928. Following a stint as an interior decorator, Bacon turned full-time to painting, and by the end of WWII he emerged as one of the leading artists of his time.

Bacon's style is distinctive: the distorted faces and vivid, violent colours, coupled with his masterful brushstrokes and use of oil, catapulted him to fame and no small amount of notoriety. Critics dismissed him as a warped caricaturist, and it is true that his best-known works are distortions of other painters' creations – Velázquez's *Portrait of Innocent X* became Bacon's series *The Screaming Popes* (1949–55) – but his admirers lauded him for his extraordinary ability to paint isolation, pain and suffering, major themes of post-WWII iconography. In his work, Bacon sought to expose the underbelly of modern society, exploring degradation and horror, perhaps as a reaction to his own very unbalanced life. He was remarkably productive, but destroyed many of his canvases, with the result that only a small percentage of his output remains, mostly in European and American galleries.

Although an affable and jovial man, Bacon's notoriously debauched lifestyle was nearly as well publicised as his genius with a paintbrush. He indulged in virtually everything, and in the 1960s he was the most swinging of swingers. As for his Irish background, when Bacon left Dublin he never looked back. He pointedly denied his roots, which is understandable considering that the Ireland of Bacon's day would have reacted with conservative horror to a man of his appetites.

€5.10/3.80/2.50, includes taped guides in English and other languages; open 10am-5.30pm Mon-Sat, noon-5.30pm Sun) is next to the Municipal Gallery of Modern Art. The building was probably first owned by Lord Farnham, who died in 1800 and bequeathed it to his son. After his death George Jameson, of the whiskey distilling Jameson family, bought the house.

The museum celebrates the city's long and continuing history as a literary centre. Downstairs there's a collection of letters, photographs, first editions and other memorabilia of Ireland's best-known writers. Upstairs, in a wonderful room with plastered ceilings and painted doors, the Gallery of Writers has portraits and busts of some of Ireland's most famous writers, mainly copies of originals on display in the National Gallery. There is, however, a dearth of material about more recent writers, other than the children's authors highlighted on the top floor.

A whole room is devoted to modern children's authors such as Michael Mullen, Carolyn Swift, Vincent Banville and Margrit Cruickshank. As well as having pictures and biographies of the authors, the exhibition features models taken from their books, the best of them being the giant Magus the Lollipop Man, the eponymous hero of Michael Mullen's book, who greets you as you come in. Perhaps best of all, you can sit your brood down and have other (recorded) voices read bedtime stories to them.

In the next room stands Tara's Palace, an outsize doll's house. The original 'Titania's Palace' was built by Major Sir Neville Williamson for his daughter Gwendoline in 1907. In 1967 it was sold to the owners of Wookey Hole in England, and in 1978 to Lego. Tara's Palace is a replica, with 14 of its 23 rooms finished and furnished with fittings from all around the world. The facades are based on Leinster House, Carlton House and Castleton House.

There's also a rooftop Zen Garden, a bookshop and the Chapter One cafe, which is open for the same hours as the museum. Above is the respected Chapter One restaurant (see under Top End in the Places to Eat chapter).

While the museum concerns itself primarily with authors of the deceased variety, next door the **Irish Writers' Centre** (☎ *872 1302, 19 North Parnell Square; admission free*) provides a meeting and working place for their successors.

NATIONAL WAX MUSEUM (Map 4)

Every city worth its tourist traps has a wax museum. Dublin's National Wax Museum (☎ *872 6340, Granby Row; adult/student/child/family €4.50/3.20/2.50/14; open 10am-5.30pm Mon-Sat, noon-5.30pm Sun*), has the usual fantasy and fairy-tale offerings, the inevitable chamber of horrors and a rock music 'megastars' area. An unusual exhibit is a life-size replica of Leonardo da Vinci's *Last Supper.* There are also figures of Irish heroes and politicians such as Wolfe Tone, Robert Emmet, Charles Parnell, the leaders of the 1916 Easter Rising, the *Taosigh* (prime ministers, plural of *Taoiseach*), the presidents, a number of popes and prominent figures from the northern Troubles – John Hume and Ian Paisley, Gerry Adams and David Trimble. Recorded commentaries explain their roles in Irish history. There are also models of Irish cultural figures and numerous Irish TV and sporting personalities.

GREAT DENMARK ST (Map 4)

From the corner of Parnell Square, Great Denmark St runs north-east to Mountjoy Square, passing Belvedere House at No 6. The construction of this house began in 1775 and it has been used as the Jesuit **Belvedere College** (☎ *874 4795, 6 Great Denmark St; closed to the public*) since 1841. James Joyce was a student here between 1893 and 1898 and describes it in *A Portrait of the Artist as a Young Man.* The building is renowned for its magnificent plasterwork by the master stuccodore Michael Stapleton and for its fireplaces by the Venetian artisan Bossi.

MOUNTJOY SQUARE (Map 4)

Built between 1792 and 1818, Mountjoy Square was a fashionable and affluent centre at the height of the Anglo-Irish ascendancy, but today is a run-down example of north Dublin urban decay.

Legend relates that this was the site where Brian Ború pitched his tent at the Battle of Clontarf in 1014. Residents of the square included Sean O'Casey, who set his play *The Shadow of a Gunman* here, though he referred to it as Hilljoy Square. As a child, James Joyce lived just off the square at 14 Fitzgibbon St.

ST GEORGE'S CHURCH (Map 3)

St George's Church (*Hardwicke Place; closed to the public*), off Temple St, was built by Francis Johnston from 1802 in Greek Ionic style and has a 60m-high steeple, which was modelled on that of St Martin-in-the-Fields in London. The church's bells were added in 1836. Although this was one of Johnston's finest works and the Duke of Wellington was married here, it's now used as a dance club and is called the Temple Theatre (see the Entertainment chapter).

ST MARY'S CHURCH (Map 3)

Between Wolfe Tone and Jervis Sts, St Mary's (*Mary St; closed to the public*) was designed in 1697 by Sir William Robinson, architect of the Royal Hospital Kilmainham. It was completed in 1702 and is the most important church to survive from that period. The church was a popular one among 18th-century Dublin's social elite: many famous Dubliners were baptised there and Arthur Guinness was married there in 1793. In 1747 John Wesley, the founder of Methodism, preached for the first time in Ireland in St Mary's. Today, however, like so many other fine old Dublin churches, it's no longer in use.

ST MARY'S ABBEY (Map 4)

All that remains open of this Cistercian abbey, near the junction of Capel St and Mary's Abbey, is the **chapter house** (☎ *872 1490, Meeting House Lane; adult/student €1.25/0.60; open 10am-5pm Wed & Sun mid-June–mid-Sept*), which hardly does justice to what was once the most powerful and wealthy monastery in Ireland. Built in 1180, the abbey played a dominant role in Irish church politics until Henry VIII ordered the dissolution of the monasteries in 1537. Only three years earlier Silken Thomas Fitzgerald, the most important of Leinster's Anglo-Norman lords, had renounced his allegiance to Henry in the chapter house, which had been a popular meeting place for rebels conspiring against the English monarch.

JAMES JOYCE CULTURAL CENTRE (Map 4)
North Great George's St was a fashionable address in 18th-century Dublin, but like so much of the north side of the city, fell on hard times when the Act of Union turned the city into a backwater. James Joyce's family lived in north Dublin for a time and he would have been familiar with the street. The dancing instructor, Denis Maginni, who taught in the front room of No 35, appears several times in *Ulysses*. In CS Andrews' *Dublin Made Me* (see Books in the Facts about Dublin chapter), Maginni is described as 'egregious and ludicrous. Every afternoon he strolled up O'Connell St in silk hat, morning coat, lavender waistcoat, striped trousers, silver-topped malacca cane and gold watch-chain'. Sadly, after Maginni's departure the house, like most of the others along the street, fell into disrepair.

In 1982, the house was taken over by another dapper gentleman, Senator David Norris, a charismatic Joycean scholar and gay-rights activist. It has now been restored and converted into the James Joyce Cultural Centre (*☎ 878 8547*, *e joycean@iol .ie*, *w www.jamesjoyce.ie*, *35 North Great George's St; adult/student & senior €4.50/ 3.50; open 9.30am-5pm Mon-Sat, 12.30pm-5pm Sun; one-hour tours of north Dublin, adult/student & senior €9/6.50, 2.15pm Mon-Sat).*

Visitors see the room where Maginni taught and a collection of pictures of the 17 different Dublin homes occupied by Joyce's family and the real individuals fictionalised in his books. Some of the building's fine plaster ceilings are restored originals, others careful reproductions of Michael Stapleton's designs.

Norris' efforts have resulted in the entire street getting a much-needed facelift. It now boasts some of the city's finest Georgian doorways and fanlights.

ST MICHAN'S CHURCH (Map 4)
Named after a Danish saint, St Michan's Church (*☎ 872 4154, Lower Church St; adult/student/senior €2.50/1.90/0.65; open 10am-12.45pm, 2pm-4.45pm Mon-Fri, 10am-12.45pm Sat*) was founded by Danes in 1096, though there's little trace of the original. The battlement tower dates from the 15th century, but the church was rebuilt in 1686, considerably restored in 1828 and again in the 20th century after the Civil War, during which it had been damaged.

The church contains an organ from 1724, which Handel may have played for the first-ever performance of his *Messiah*. The organ case is distinguished by the fine oak carving of 17 entwined musical instruments on its front. A skull on the floor on one side of the altar is said to represent Oliver Cromwell. On the opposite side is the Stool of Repentance, where 'open and notoriously naughty livers' did public penance. The church's main attraction, however, is a little more gruesome. In the underground vault are bodies that have been preserved to varying degrees by the magnesium limestone of the room, rather than by mummification. They are, naturally, a popular tourist attraction.

CROKE PARK & GAA MUSEUM (Map 4)
About 800m northwest of Mountjoy Square is the home of the Gaelic Athletic Association (GAA; the governing body of Ireland's national sports, Gaelic football and hurling) and the country's largest stadium, Croke Park, where the All-Ireland finals are played in September. In the 1870s, the site was developed as the 'City & Suburban Racecourse', but was bought by the GAA in 1913 and immediately renamed Croke Park in honour of the association's first patron, Archbishop Croke of Cashel. Over the next 40 years the stadium was slowly rebuilt in an ad hoc manner, but in 1998 plans were unveiled to rebuild virtually the entire grounds and turn it into a state-of-the-art

65,000-all-seater venue. By the time you read this book the stadium should be near completion.

On 10 November 1920, during a hurling match between Dublin and Tipperary, Croke Park was the setting for the greatest atrocity of the War of Independence. In retaliation for the killing of 14 members of the secret service, the British Army opened fire on the crowded stadium, killing 10 spectators and a Tipperary player, Michael Hogan. When a new stand was constructed in 1924, it was named after the unfortunate hurler.

The stadium's history is part of the exhibit at the new GAA Museum (☎ 855 8176, New Stand, Croke Park, Clonliffe Rd; adult/student/child €3.80/2.55/1.90; open 9.30am-5pm daily May-Sept, 10am-5pm Tues-Sat, noon-4pm Sun Oct-Apr), a must for sporting enthusiasts. The history of these most Irish of games is explored in fascinating, interactive detail. You can also test your skills at both Gaelic football and hurling; the former is a hard-fought game similar to Australian Rules Football (only with a round ball), while the latter, played with a flat bat (called a hurley) and a small leather-bound ball (called a slíotair) is considered the fastest team sport in the world.

Take bus No 3, 11, 11A, 16, 16A or 123 from O'Connell St to get to Croke Park.

SMITHFIELD (Map 4)

Dublin's newest hotspot is the area in and around Smithfield Square, bordered to the east by Church St, to the west by Blackhall Place, to the north by North King St and to the south by Arran Quay. At the centre of this major development is the old hay, straw, cattle and horse Smithfield Market, which has now been replaced by a magnificent new civic space. The flagship of the Historic Area Rejuvenation Project (HARP) whose brief is to restore the north-west inner city, it features a pedestrianised piazza bordered on one side by 26m-high gas lighting masts, each with a 2m-high flame. The old cobblestones were removed, cleaned up and put back along with new granite slabs that give the whole square a thoroughly modern feel without sacrificing its traditional beauty.

The whole concept is the work of two Irish architects, Michael McGarry and Siobhán Ní Éanaigh, who won out against stiff international competition. As part of the inauguration in 1999, U2 were granted the keys to the city on the square.

Bordering the eastern side of the square are two of the city's best new museums, Ceol, and a little farther off, the Old Jameson Distillery. In keeping with its traditional past, the old **Fruit & Vegetable Market** still plies a healthy wholesale trade on the square's western side. Although far from complete, Smithfield is expected to challenge the tourist attentions so far commanded by Temple Bar, though developers are keen to avoid the kind of crass commercialism that has plagued the area south of the Liffey. But commercial interests have not entirely been ignored, and in 2001 the first of many open-air concerts was held in Smithfield Square, featuring an impressive array of Irish and international artists headlined by the now-legendary Buena Vista Social Club.

Old Jameson Distillery

Where does Irish whiskey get its particular colour and smooth bouquet from? While most people have heard the term 'single malt', how many actually know what this means? These are just some of the secrets you can learn at the Old Jameson Distillery (☎ 807 2355, Bow St; adult/student €6.30/3.80; tours every 30 minutes 10am-5.30pm daily) an enormous museum devoted to Irish whiskey. It opened in 1997 after a €8.9 million renovation of the old Jameson distillery, where Ireland's best-loved whiskey was produced from 1791 until its closure in 1966, when Jameson, along with the other main Irish producers, united to form Irish Distillers, with an ultra-modern distillery in Middleton, County Cork. The museum can only be visited by guided tour, but it's well worth it. A short film kicks off the tour, after which visitors are led through a recreation of the old factory, where the guide explains the entire process of whiskey distilling from grain to bottle. Visitors are then invited into the Jameson Bar where they are offered a complimentary glass of the 'hard stuff' (as it is referred to in Dublin vernacular). The tour finishes with a surprise competition, but you'll have to visit to find out what it is! There is also a restaurant on the premises.

Ceol

This **museum** (☎ 817 3820, **e** info@ceol.ie, **w** www.ceol.ie, Smithfield Village; adult/student €6.35/5.10; open 10am-6pm Mon-Sat, 11am-6pm Sun), in the Chief O'Neill's complex, is devoted entirely to ceol – of the Irish traditional kind. If you have notions of a musical quartet keeping time by tapping their feet on a sawdust floor with half-drunk pints at arm's length, this ultra-modern, interactive museum will dispel them. The sleek finish of the place may seem like an unlikely setting for a journey through the history of traditional music, but it is an excellent and informative introduction to the complexities of the genre.

The museum's interactive displays cover virtually every aspect of the entire tradition of Irish music both sung and instrumental from the Middle Ages, through the early attempts to catalogue the thousands of jigs, reels and hornpipes in the 18th century, and on to the explosion of the distinctly Irish sound on the international stage after WWII.

The wonderful audiovisuals detail the music's unique characteristics and sounds, with particular emphasis on the four main instruments: uilleann (elbow) pipes, fiddle, flute and button accordion. Of particular interest is the room devoted to song, especially the sean nós style, an ancient form that involves the telling of a story through song punctuated by plenty of grace notes. There are plenty of video performances by some of Ireland's best players. Kids will enjoy the game of musical twister, in which floor pads light up as a tune is played and the listener is invited to re-create the tune by standing on the pads.

The complex also includes a bar and a hotel (see the Entertainment and Places to Stay chapters).

The Chimney

As part of the ongoing development of the Smithfield area, an old distillery chimney (nicknamed 'the flue with the view'), built by Jameson's in 1895, has been converted into Dublin's first and only 360-degree **observation tower** (☎ 817 3820, Smithfield Village; adult/student €6.35/5.10). A glass lift shuttles visitors to the top, where behind the safety of glass they can see the entire city, the sea and the mountains to the south. On a clear day, it makes for some nice photo opportunities, but Dublin's lack of panoramic beauty (the city looks like a gigantic building site punctuated by green copper domes) makes the admission fee seem rather excessive. You're better off seeing the city from the Gravity Bar at the top of the Guinness Storehouse (see later in this chapter): it's more expensive, but at least you get to see the exhibits and enjoy a lovely pint while you stare out the window.

ARBOUR HILL CEMETERY (Map 2)

West of the Jameson distillery is a small cemetery (Arbour Hill; admission free; open 9am-4.30pm Mon-Sat, 9.30am-noon Sun) that is the final resting place of all 14 of the executed leaders of the 1916 Easter Rising, including Patrick Pearse and James Connolly. The burial ground is plain, with the 14 names inscribed in stone. Beside the graves is a cenotaph bearing the Easter Proclamation. Government leaders come every Easter Monday to pay their respects to the fallen heroes of Ireland, and it is also a popular gathering place for Irish republicans of all shades. During anniversary celebrations of the 1916 Rising, republican leaders and some politicians make speeches and pay their respects to the fallen here.

KING'S INNS & HENRIETTA ST (Map 4)

Accessible from Constitution Hill and Henrietta St, King's Inns (☎ 874 4840, **w** www.kingsinns.ie, Henrietta St; open only to members & their guests) is home to the Dublin legal profession. This classical building by James Gandon suffered many delays between its design in 1795, the start of construction in 1802 and its completion in 1817. Along the way several other architects were recruited, including Francis Johnston, who added the cupola late in the day.

The city's original law courts stood just to the west of Christ Church Cathedral, south of the Liffey. Collett's Inn, the first gathering place for lawyers, was later established in Exchequer St and was in turn followed by Preston Inn, which stood on Cork Hill where the City Hall stands today. In 1541, when Henry VIII staked his claim to be King of Ireland as well as England, the lawyers' society took the title of King's Inns. The society moved to a new site on land that had been confiscated from the Dominican Convent of St Saviour, but when that site by the Liffey was taken over to become the Four Courts the King's Inns moved to their present home.

Henrietta St, running south-east from the building, was Dublin's first Georgian street and has buildings dating from 1720. Sadly, this is another of north Dublin's run-down areas and the street is now in a state of disrepair. These early Georgian mansions were both larger and more varied in style than their later counterparts.

FOUR COURTS (Map 3)

The Four Courts (☎ 872 5555, Inn's Quay; admission free), with its 130m-long facade, was designed by James Gandon and built between 1786 and 1802, engulfing and incorporating the Public Records Office built a short time earlier. The more recent building includes a Corinthian-columned central block connected to flanking wings with enclosed quadrangles. The ensemble is topped by diverse statuary.

There are fine views over the city from the upper rotunda of the central building. The original four courts – Exchequer, Common Pleas, King's Bench and Chancery – branched off this circular central building. The Dominican Convent of St Saviour (1224) formerly stood here, but was replaced first by an early version of the King's Inns and then by the present building. The last parliament of James II was held on the site in 1689.

The Four Courts played a brief role in the 1916 Easter Rising without suffering any damage, but in 1922 anti-Treaty republicans seized the building and couldn't be per-

suaded to leave. Michael Collins shelled the building from across the river. As the republican forces retreated, the building was set on fire and many irreplaceable early records were destroyed. This event sparked off the Civil War and the building wasn't restored until 1932. Visitors can attend sessions of the court, but only in the public gallery.

West of the City Centre

Although there's plenty to see in and around Dublin's city centre, both north and south of the Liffey, a couple of real highlights lie to the west of the centre. There you'll find the world-famous St James's Gate Brewery, the home of Guinness, and its brand-new visitor centre, the Guinness Storehouse – already Dublin's most popular attraction. A little farther on is the Irish Museum of Modern Art, housed in a wonderful 17th-century building, and, nearby, Kilmainham Gaol, once Dublin's most notorious prison. North of the Liffey is Phoenix Park, Europe's largest enclosed city park and location of the Irish president's residence.

ST JAMES'S GATE GUINNESS BREWERY & GUINNESS STOREHOUSE (Map 3)

Heading westwards from central south Dublin, past St Audoen's churches, Thomas St metamorphoses into James's St in the area of Dublin known as the Liberties. Along James's St stretches the historic St James's Gate Guinness Brewery (closed to the public), whose world-famous black beer is virtually synonymous with Dublin and Ireland. From its foundation by Arthur Guinness in 1759, on the site of the earlier Rainsford Brewery, the Guinness operation has expanded down to the Liffey and across both sides of the street. In all, it covers 26 hectares and for a time was the largest brewery in the world. The oldest parts of the site are south of James's St; at one time there was a gate spanning the entire street.

In its early years Guinness was only one of

dozens of Dublin breweries but it outgrew and outlasted them all. At one time a Grand Canal tributary was cut into the brewery to enable special Guinness barges to carry consignments out onto the Irish canal system or to the Dublin port. When the brewery extensions reached the Liffey in 1872, the fleet of Guinness barges became a familiar sight. There was also a Guinness railway on the brewery site, complete with a corkscrew tunnel. Guinness still operates its own ships to convey the vital fluid to the British market. Over 50% of all the beer consumed in Ireland is brewed here, four million pints of it a day.

As an employer, the company reached its apogee in the 1930s, when there were over 5000 people working here, making it the largest employer in the city. For nearly two centuries it was also one of the best places to work, paying 20% more than the market rate and offering a comprehensive package of subsidised housing, health benefits, pension plans, longer holidays and life insurance. In the 19th century, young women of marrying age in Dublin were advised by their mothers to get their hands on a Guinness man as he'd be worth more than most alive or dead! Today, however, the brewery is no longer the prominent employer it once was; a gradual shift to greater automatisation has reduced the workforce to around 600.

The brewery is far more than just a place where beer is manufactured. It is an intrinsic part of Dublin's history and a key element of the city's identity. Accordingly, the quasi-mythical stature of Guinness is the central theme of the brewery's brand-new museum, the **Guinness Storehouse** (☎ 408 4800, Ⓦ www.guinness.com, St James's Gate; adult/student €11.50/7.60; open 9.30am-7pm Mon-Sat, 11am-4.30pm Sun Apr-Sept, 9.30am-5pm Mon-Sat, 11am-5pm Sun Oct-Mar). It opened in December 2000 in place of the old – and much smaller – Guinness Hop Store around the corner on Crane St, which no longer did justice to the ever-expanding ambitions of one of the world's most renowned brewers. It is the only part of the brewery that is open to visitors. Take bus No 21A, 78 or 78A from Fleet St to get here.

The **Hop Store** was the city's second-most visited attraction (after the Book of Kells), and this overpriced, over-hyped and over-the-top paean to the black gold was designed and built to cash in on Guinness' popularity – and it has done so with remarkable success. Judging from the look of the place, you'll see why this extraordinary beer is deemed to have auric qualities. It's a massive building, with nearly four acres of floor space spread about seven storeys, at the centre of which is a stunning atrium that rises to the top of the building, 60m up. Even the official opening was impressive, with (now former) US president Bill Clinton as guest of honour.

Less of a museum and more a modern 'experience', the Storehouse features a dazzling array of audiovisual, interactive exhibits that cover most aspects of the brewery's story and explain the brewing process in overwhelming detail. From the ground floor, where a copy of Arthur Guinness' original lease lies embedded beneath a pane of glass in the floor, up through the various exhibits, you can't escape the feeling that the company has pulled out all the stops in its efforts to mythologise their product. Consequently, each exhibit is littered with overly prosaic eulogies to the beer and the 'magic' performed to create it. Some of the statements are plain silly, such as the one that declares that 'the equipment you see around you, like the building you're standing in, comes from another time, when machines were works of art'. Hardly, but all part of the aggressive marketing strategy that underpins the company's success.

Cynics (and beer lovers) will argue that there is really only one reason to come here: to enjoy the pint of Guinness that comes with the end of the tour. Most agree that the pint served here is the best in the world – even though the company maintains that it is no different to that served anywhere else. All agree, however, that the *Gravity Bar* where it is served is truly magnificent. At the very top of the building, with a 360-degree panoramic view of Dublin, it is a spectacular place to enjoy this excellent beer. It was designed to rotate slowly on its own axis, but safety considerations have kept it still, although by the time you read this they might have sorted the problem out.

IRISH MUSEUM OF MODERN ART & ROYAL HOSPITAL KILMAINHAM (Map 3)

The Irish Museum of Modern Art *(IMMA; ☎ 612 9900, Military Rd; admission free; open 10am-5.30pm Tues-Sat, noon-5.30pm Sun)* is the country's foremost gallery for contemporary Irish art. It is housed in the former Royal Hospital at Kilmainham, built between 1680–84 as a retirement home for veteran soldiers, a role it fulfilled until 1928. After languishing until 1980, it was extensively restored and reopened as an art gallery in 1991. Take bus No 24, 79 or 90 from Aston Quay to get here.

There is a particular focus on the work of contemporary Irish artists, such as Louis Le Brocquy, Sean Scully, Richard Deacon, Richard Gorman and Dorothy Cross. Regular temporary exhibitions top up the permanent collection, which also includes a painting each by such heavy hitters as Picasso and Miró. The work is well laid out, with plenty of white space.

While the collections are undoubtedly fascinating, it is the building itself that earns most of the plaudits. The inspiration for the design came from James Butler, duke of Ormonde and Charles II's viceroy in Ireland, who had visited Paris and was greatly taken by Les Invalides. Upon his return to Ireland, he commissioned Sir William Robinson – whose other work included Marsh's Library – to design something akin to Les Invalides for Dublin. What he created was Dublin's finest 17th-century building, the highpoint of the Anglo-Dutch style that was all the rage at the time. Furthermore, it was the first truly classical building in Dublin and marked the beginning of the frenzied architectural creativity that would climax in the Georgian boom. It preceded the well known Chelsea Royal Hospital in London, which had a similar role. Royal Hospital residents were often referred to as 'Chelsea Pensioners' although there was no connection.

After it finally closed in 1928, the building fell into serious disrepair, but thankfully Robinson's plans and designs were intact so when restoration finally began in 1980, the architects were able to recapture the building's former elegance. Fittingly, the restoration was completed in 1984, on the 200th anniversary of its construction. A year later, it was granted the prestigious Europa Nostra award for 'its distinguished contribution to the conservation of Europe's architectural heritage'.

In 2001, a new heritage **itinerary** *(adult/student €3.20/1.25)*, run in conjunction with Dúchas, was launched to make the most of the building's treasures. Highlights of the tours, which are run Tuesday to Sunday from June to September only, include the Banqueting Hall, complete with the 22 portraits commissioned specially for the room, and the stunning baroque chapel, which has papiermache ceilings and a set of exquisite Queen Anne gates. Also worth seeing are the fully restored formal gardens. Free guided tours of the museum's exhibits – which include a new exhibition space in the restored Deputy Master's House at the north-eastern corner of the gardens – are held on Wednesday and Friday at 2.30pm and on Sunday at 12.15pm. Tours for groups are held Tuesday to Friday (10am and 11.45am, 2.30am and 4pm) but bookings must be made two weeks in advance. There's a good cafe and bookshop on the grounds.

KILMAINHAM GAOL (Map 3)

Built between 1792 and 1795, Kilmainham Gaol *(☎ 453 5984, Inchicore Rd; adult/child & student €4.50/1.90; open 9.30am-6pm Apr-Sept, 9.30am-5pm Mon-Fri, 10am-6pm Sun Oct-Mar)*, to the west of IMMA, is a solid, grey, threatening, old building. During each act of Ireland's long, painful path to independence from Britain at least one part of the performance took place at the prison.

The uprisings of 1799, 1803, 1848, 1867 and 1916 all ended with the leaders' confinement in Kilmainham. Robert Emmet, Thomas Francis Meagher, Charles Stewart Parnell and the 1916 Easter Rising leaders were all visitors, but it was the executions in 1916 that most deeply etched the gaol's name into the Irish consciousness. Of the 15 executions that took place between 3 and 12 May after the Easter Rising, 14 were conducted here, including that of James Connolly, who was so badly injured during the fighting that he had to be strapped to a chair to face the firing squad. As a finale, prisoners from the Civil War struggles were held here from 1922, but that chapter is played down when you visit the jail. Even the passing comment that the final prisoner released from Kilmainham was Ireland's future president, Eamon de Valera, doesn't reveal that he had been imprisoned by his fellow Irish citizens. The building was finally closed for good as a jail in 1924.

An excellent audiovisual introduction to the old building is followed by a lively, thought-provoking guided tour. Incongruously sitting outside in the yard is the ship *Asgard*, which successfully broke the British blockade and delivered arms to nationalist forces in 1914. The tour finishes in the gloomy yard where the 1916 executions took place.

Take bus No 23, 51, 51A, 78 or 79 from the city centre to reach the gaol.

Kilmainham Gate

The Kilmainham Gate was designed by Francis Johnston (1760–1829) in 1812 and originally stood, as the Richmond Tower, at the Watling St junction with Victoria Quay, near the Guinness Brewery. It was moved to its current position opposite the prison in 1846 as it obstructed the increasingly heavy traffic to the new Kingsbridge station (now Heuston station), which opened in 1844. The railway company paid for the gate's dismantling and reassembly.

PHOENIX PARK (Map 2)

Comprising 709 hectares, Phoenix Park is one of the world's largest city parks, dwarfing Central Park (337 hectares) in New York and larger than all of the major London parks put together. The park has gardens and lakes, a host of sporting facilities (including a motor-racing track), the second-oldest public zoo in Europe, a castle and visitor centre, various government offices, the Garda Síochána (police) Headquarters, the residences of the Irish president and the US ambassador, and even a herd of 300 deer.

From the Anglo-Norman invasion up to 1537, the park was part of the lands owned by the Knights of Jerusalem, keepers of an important priory on what is now the site of the Royal Hospital, Kilmainham. After the dissolution of the monasteries by Henry VIII the lands passed into the hands of the king's viceroys. In 1671 the Duke of Ormonde, James Butler, introduced a herd of fallow deer, 1000 pheasants and some partridge and turned it into a royal deer park. Nine years later a wall was constructed around the park and it remained the preserve of the British Crown and its Irish court until 1745, when the viceroy, Lord Chesterfield, threw it open to the public.

The first of the park's great mansions was Newtown House, built in 1668 as the home of the Phoenix Park Ranger. In 1751, however, the house was demolished and a new residence constructed, now the central section of Áras an Uachtaráin.

The name Phoenix is probably a corruption of the Irish phrase for clear water, *fionn uisce*. The park played a crucial role in Irish history, as Lord Cavendish, the British chief secretary for Ireland, and his assistant were murdered here, outside what is now the Irish president's residence, in 1882 by members of an Irish nationalist group called The Invincibles. Lord Cavendish's home is now called Deerfield, and is used as the US ambassador's residence.

Near the Parkgate St entrance to the park is the 63m-high **Wellington Monument** obelisk. This took from 1817 to 1861 to build, mainly because the Duke of Wellington fell from public favour during its construction. At this south-eastern corner of the park are the **People's Garden**, dating from 1864, and the Victorian bandstand in the **Hollow**. Just north of the Hollow is **Dublin Zoo**. Chesterfield Ave separates the Hollow and the zoo from the Phoenix Park Cricket Club of 1830 and from **Citadel Pond**, usually referred to as the Dog Pond. Behind the zoo, on the edge of the park, is the Garda Síochána (police) Headquarters.

Going north-west along Chesterfield Ave, which runs right through the park, you pass the **Áras an Uachtaráin**, the Irish president's residence on the right. On the left the **Papal Cross** marks the site where Pope John Paul

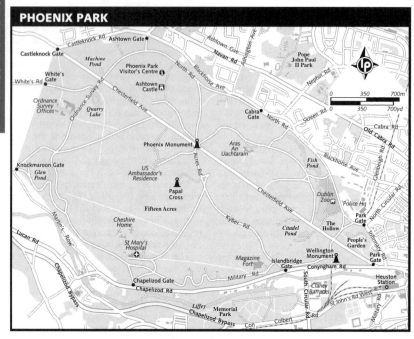

PHOENIX PARK

II preached to 1¼ million people in 1979. In the centre of the park the **Phoenix Monument**, erected by Lord Chesterfield in 1747, looks so unphoenix-like that it's often referred to as the Eagle Monument. To the north-west of the monument stand the **Phoenix Park Visitor Centre** and **Ashtown Castle**. The southern part of the park has many football and hurling pitches; although they occupy about 80 hectares (200 acres), the area is known as the Fifteen Acres.

At the north-western end of the park near the White's Gate entrance are the offices of **Ordnance Survey Ireland** *(☎ 802 5300; admission free; open 9am-12.30pm & 1.15pm-4.45pm Mon-Thur, to 4.15pm Fri)*, the government mapping department. This building was originally built in 1728 by Luke Gardiner, who was responsible for the architecture in O'Connell St and Mountjoy Square in north Dublin. In the building's *map shop (☎ 802 5349; open 9am-4.45pm Mon-Fri)* you can buy all of the Ordnance Survey

maps for any of the 26 counties of Ireland. South of this building is the attractive rural-looking **Furry Glen** and **Glen Pond** corner of the park.

Back towards the Parkgate St entrance is the **Magazine Fort** *(closed to the public)* on Thomas's Hill. Like the nearby Wellington Monument, the fort was no quick construction, the process taking from 1734 to 1801. It was also a target in the 1916 Easter Rising. The building is currently unsafe, but there is talk of restoring it at some point in the future.

Dublin Zoo

Designed by Decimus Burton in 1830, the 12-hectare Dublin Zoo *(☎ 677 1425, **e** info @dublinzoo.ie, **w** www.dublinzoo.ie; adult/ child/family €8.90/5.30/27; open 9.30am-6pm Mon-Sat, 10.30am-6pm Sun May-Sept, 9.30am-4pm Mon-Fri, 9.30am-5pm Sat, 10.30am-5pm Sun Oct-Apr)*, in the south-eastern corner of Phoenix Park, used to be a rundown zoo where depressed animals used to depress visitors, but a substantial facelift has ensured that while hardly a wildlife park, it's a much more pleasant place to stroll around in. It is home to over 700 animals, including tamarins, rhinos, tapirs and the usual complement of felines. The zoo is well known for its lion-breeding program, which dates back to 1857 and includes among its offspring the lion that roars at the start of MGM films. Those tough felines are part of a new exhibit called 'African Plains', part of the zoo's restructuring program, which has seen all of the apes gathered in a 'World of Primates' section and penguins, polar bears and other frozen-climate creatures in 'Fringes of the Arctic'. The one thing they haven't managed to fix, however, is the depression that seemingly afflicts the polar bears, who seem rightly incapable of coming to terms with the narrow confines of their world, a far cry from the northern tundras. Still, the zoo has gone to great lengths to make it visitor-friendly, and the presence of new babies or animals on breeding loans from other zoos will surely generate a couple of 'oohs' and 'aahs', if only from the kids. There are also plenty of children's activities including a Meet the Keeper program, where they can help feed the animals. There's a Pet's Corner, a zoo train and a nursery for infants.

Take bus No 10 from O'Connell St or bus No 25 or 26 from Middle Abbey St to reach the zoo.

Áras an Uachtaráin

The **residence of the Irish president** (☎ 617 1000, Phoenix Park; admission by special tour only) was built in 1751 and enlarged in 1782, and then again in 1816, on the latter occasion by the noted Irish architect Francis Johnston, who added the Ionic portico. From 1782 to 1922 it was the residence of the British viceroys or Lords Lieutenant. After independence it became the home of Ireland's governor general until Ireland cut its ties with the British Crown and set up the office of president in 1937.

The Phoenix Park Visitor Centre (see the following section) runs free one-hour tours

of the house every Saturday between 10.30am and 4pm. Tickets can be collected at the visitor centre, and after a 10-minute introductory video to the house's history there's a free bus transfer to the Áras itself. You get to see five state rooms and the tour finishes in the president's study. On the way, you visit the small visitor centre in the basement, set up during Mary Robinson's tenure as president. The bus then takes you back to the Phoenix Park Visitor Centre.

Phoenix Park Visitor Centre & Ashtown Castle

The Phoenix Park Visitor Centre (☎ 677 0095; adult/student €2.50/1.25; open 9.30am-5pm Mar & Oct-Nov, to 6pm Apr-Sept, to 4.30pm Sat & Sun Nov-Mar) is in what were the stables of the papal nunciate. A 20-minute video outlines the history of the park, and two floors of exhibits include a reconstruction of the Knockmaree Cist, a tomb containing two skeletons dating back to about 3500 BC discovered in the Fifteen Acres in 1838. Visitors are taken on a tour of the adjacent four-storey Ashtown Castle, a 17th-century tower-house that had been concealed inside the later building of the papal nunciate until the latter was demolished in 1986; box hedges surrounding the tower trace the ground-plan of the lost building.

Children keen on all things furry should enjoy the Great Slumber Party exhibition upstairs. A walk-through tunnel looks at animals' sleeping habits, letting youngsters peep in on a mock-up badger's sett, fox's earth, and so on. The remarkably cheap family ticket, covering two adults and up to eight (!) children, costs €6.35. Kids under six are free. To get here, take the No 37 or 29 bus from Middle Abbey St in the city centre.

North of the City Centre

If you haven't completely exhausted yourself doing the rounds of all of the city's visitor attractions already included, there are a few more left, only a little further afield. North of the city are Glasnevin Cemetery, Dublin's version of Paris' Père Lachaise and, nearby, the Botanic Gardens. To the north-east is the wonderful architectural folly that is the Casino at Marino and the suburb of Clontarf.

THE ROYAL CANAL

Two canals encircle central Dublin: the older Grand Canal to the south (see South of the City Centre later in this chapter), and the newer Royal Canal to the north. Constructed from 1790, by which time the Grand Canal was already past its prime, the Royal Canal was a commercial failure, but its story is a colourful one. It was founded by Long John Binns, a sometime director of the Grand Canal Company who quit the board because of a supposed insult over his being a shoemaker. He established the Royal Canal for revenge but since it duplicated the purpose of the earlier canal it never made money. The Duke of Leinster became a major backer for the canal on condition that it was routed past his mansion near Maynooth. In 1840 it was sold to a railway company that considered the canal's route convenient for a railway line. Tracks still run alongside much of the disused canal through the city.

The Royal Canal towpath provides a relaxing walk to the north of the city centre. You can join it beside Newcomen Bridge at North Strand Rd, just north of Connolly station, and follow it to the suburb of Clonsilla over 10km away, and beyond. The walk is particularly pleasant past Binns Bridge in Drumcondra. At the top of Blessington St, near the Dublin International Youth Hostel, is a large pond that was used as a filter bed when the canal also supplied drinking water to the city. It now attracts swans and other water birds.

NATIONAL BOTANIC GARDENS

Founded in 1795 the National Botanic Gardens (☎ 837 7596, Botanic Rd, Glasnevin; admission free; open 9am-6pm Mon-Sat, 11am-6pm Sun Apr-Oct, 10am-4.30pm Mon-Sat, 11am-4.30pm Sun Nov-Mar), directly north of the centre in Glasnevin, function both as a scientific resource and as a popular

public park. The area was used as a garden long before 1795 but only Yew Walk, also known as Addison's Walk, has trees dating back to the first half of the 18th century.

The 19.5-hectare gardens, flanked to the north by the River Tolka, contain a series of curvilinear **glasshouses** dating from 1843 to 1869. The creator of the glasshouses, Dubliner Richard Turner, was also responsible for the glasshouse at the Belfast Botanic Gardens and the Palm House at London's Kew Gardens. Within these Victorian masterpieces you will find the latest in botanical technology, including a series of computer-controlled climates reproducing environments in different parts of the world. The gardens also have a **palm house**, built in 1884. Among the pioneering botanical work conducted here was the first attempt to raise orchids from seed, back in 1844. Pampas grass and the giant lily were first grown in Europe in these gardens.

To reach the gardens, take bus No 13, 13A or 19 from O'Connell St or bus No 34 or 34A from Middle Abbey St.

GLASNEVIN CEMETERY

Beside the National Botanic Gardens (though not accessible from them) is **Prospect Cemetery** (☎ 830 1133, Finglas Rd; admission free), the largest in Ireland. More commonly known as Glasnevin Cemetery, it was established in 1832 for Roman Catholics, who faced opposition when they conducted burials in the city's Protestant cemeteries. Many of the monuments and memorials have overtly patriotic overtones with numerous high crosses, harps, shamrocks and other Irish symbols. The most imposing memorial is the enormous monument to Cardinal Mc-Cabe (1837–1921), archbishop of Dublin and primate of Ireland.

A round tower is a handy landmark for locating the tomb of Daniel O'Connell, who died in 1847 but was reinterred here in 1869 when the tower was completed. Charles Stewart Parnell's tomb (1891) is topped with a huge granite rock. Other notable people buried here include Sir Roger Casement, executed for treason by the British in 1916, whose remains were not returned until 1964;

Michael Collins (1890–1922), a leading figure in Ireland's final struggle for independence; Jim Larkin (1876–1947), a prime force in the 1913 general strike and Gerard Manley Hopkins (1844–89), the poet. There's also a poignant memorial to the men who have starved themselves to death for the cause of Irish freedom over the century.

The most interesting parts of the cemetery are at the south-eastern end, near Prospect Square. The cemetery wall still has watchtowers, from which lookouts watched for body snatchers. Part of *Ulysses* is set in the cemetery and there are several clues for Joyce enthusiasts to follow among the tombstones.

Take bus No 40, 40A or 40B from Parnell St to get to the cemetery.

CASINO AT MARINO

The casino (*☎ 833 1618,* **W** *www.heritage ireland.ie, off Malahide Rd, Marino; adult/ child & student €2.50/1.25; guided tours only, 10am-5pm daily May & Oct, 9.30am-6pm daily June-Sept, noon-4pm Wed & Sun Feb-Mar & Nov, noon-5pm Thur & Sun Apr)* is just off Malahide Rd, north of the junction with Howth Rd in Marino, north-east of central Dublin. In Italian, the word *casino* means a house of pleasure (as in gambling) or a summer home, and this 18th-century folly is one of Ireland's finest examples of the latter. It was built for the somewhat eccentric James Caulfield (1728–99), later earl of Charlemont, who had returned from a grand European tour with a huge art collection and a burning passion for Italian architectural – Palladian – style.

On his return, he appointed the architect Sir William Chambers to build the casino, a process that started in the late 1750s and continued through the 1760s and much of the 1770s. The project never really came to a conclusion, in part because the earl's extravagances had frittered away his fortune.

Externally, the building's 12 Tuscan columns, forming a temple-like facade, and huge entrance doorway suggest that it encloses a simple single open space. Only when you go inside do you realise what a wonderful extravagance it is. The interior is a convoluted maze planned as a bachelor's retreat but eventually put to a quite different use. Flights of fancy include carved draperies, ornate fireplaces, chimneys for central heating disguised as roof urns, downpipes hidden in columns, beautiful parquet floors built of rare woods and a spacious wine cellar. All sorts of statuary adorn the outside, the amusing fakes being the most enjoyable. The towering front door is a sham, and a much smaller panel opens to reveal the interior. The windows have blacked-out panels to disguise the fact that the interior is a complex of rooms rather than a single chamber.

When the earl married, the casino became a garden retreat rather than a bachelor's quarters. The casino was designed to accompany another building where he intended to house the art and antiquities he had acquired during his European tour, so it's perhaps fitting that his town house on Parnell Square, also designed by Sir William Chambers, is now the Municipal Gallery of Modern Art.

Despite his wealth, Charlemont was a comparatively liberal and free-thinking aristocrat. He never enclosed his demesne and allowed the public to use it as an open park. Nor was he the only eccentric in the area at that time. In 1792 a painter named Folliot took a dislike to the earl and built Marino Crescent at the bottom of Malahide Rd purely to block his view of the sea. Bram Stoker (1847–1912), author of *Dracula*, was born at 15 Marino Crescent.

After Charlemont's death his estate, crippled by his debts, quickly collapsed. The art collection was dispersed and in 1870 the town house was sold to the government. The Marino estate followed in 1881 and the casino in 1930, though it was in a decrepit condition when the government acquired it. Not until the mid-1970s did serious restoration begin, and it still continues. Although the current casino grounds are a tiny fragment of the original Marino estate, trees around the building help to hide that it's now surrounded by a housing estate.

Take bus No 20A, 20B, 27, 27B, 42, 42C or 123 from the city centre, DART to Clontarf Rd to reach the Casino.

THINGS TO SEE & DO

CLONTARF & NORTH BULL ISLAND

Clontarf, a bayside suburb about 5km north-east of the centre, takes its name from *cluain tarbh*, the bull's meadow. On Good Friday in 1014, Brian Ború defeated the Danes at the Battle of Clontarf, though in the struggle the Irish hero was killed, along with his son and grandson. The Normans later erected a castle here that was handed on to the Knights Templar in 1179, rebuilt in 1835 and later converted into a hotel.

The **North Bull Wall**, extending from Clontarf about 1km into Dublin Bay, was built in 1820 at the suggestion of Captain William Bligh of HMS *Bounty* fame, in order to stop Dublin Harbour from silting up. The marshes and dunes of North Bull Island, which formed behind the wall, are a popular nature reserve. Many birds migrate here from the Arctic in winter, and at times the bird population can reach 40,000; watch for shelducks, curlews, and oystercatchers on the mud flats and listen for larks in the dunes. You reach the **interpretative centre** (☎ *833 8341, North Bull Island, County Dublin; admission free; open 10am-6pm daily*) on the island by walking across the 1.5km-long northern causeway. Bus Nos 30 and 32X run to the start of the causeway on James Larkin Rd. The Royal Dublin golf course and St Anne's golf course are also on the island (see under Golf in Activities later in this chapter).

South of the City Centre

To the south of the city centre is the elegant suburb of Ballsbridge and the Royal Dublin Showground. There are also additional galleries and museums, and the Grand Canal makes for some pleasant walks.

THE GRAND CANAL (Map 2)

Built to connect Dublin with the River Shannon in the centre of Ireland, the Grand Canal makes a 6km loop around south Dublin. At its eastern end the canal forms a harbour connected with the Liffey at Ringsend. The Royal Canal performs a similar loop through north Dublin. True Dubliners, it is said, are born within the confines of the canals. The canal hasn't been used commercially since 1960 but some stretches are attractive and enjoyable to stroll or cycle along. It's about 2km from Mount St Bridge west to Richmond St along a particularly beautiful part of the canal, with a cluster of pubs providing refreshment at the Richmond St end.

Grand Canal Dock & Ringsend

At Ringsend the Grand Canal enters the Liffey, through locks opened in 1796. The large Grand Canal Docks, flanked by Hanover and Charlotte quays, have been in the throes of a huge program of urban development, with new office buildings going up all around it. The docks themselves are also used by windsurfers (see Activities later in this chapter).

At the north-western corner of the dock is **Misery Hill**, once the site of public executions. Even more macabre was the practice of bringing the corpses of those already hanged at Gallows Hill, near Upper Baggot St, to be strung up here for public display for between six and 12 months.

Waterways Visitor Centre

Upstream from the Grand Canal Docks is the Waterways Visitor Centre (☎ *677 7510,* e *waterwaysireland@ealga.ie, Grand Canal Quay; adult/child & student €2.50/1.25; open 9.30am-5.30pm June-Sept, 12.30pm-5.30pm Wed-Sun May & Oct*), built by Dúchas as an exhibition and interpretative centre covering the construction and operation of Irish canals and waterways. The centre is the most visible example of the new development that's in progress for the area, a stark contrast to the dereliction that once pervaded the area. A 10-minute video outlines the role of the canals, while display boards and an interactive video give more detailed information. Particularly impressive is a model of a barge slowly working its way through a pair of locks.

Mount St to Leeson St

On Mount St Bridge is a **memorial to the Easter Rising of 1916**. A little farther along, Baggot St crosses the canal on the **Macartney Bridge**, built in 1791. The head office of Bord Fáilte (the Irish Tourist Board) is on the northern side of the canal.

This lovely stretch of the canal, with its grassy, tree-lined banks, was a favourite haunt of the poet Patrick Kavanagh. One of his poems requested that he be commemorated by 'a canal bank seat for passers-by' and his friends obliged with a seat beside the lock. A little farther along on the north side you can sit beside a **bronze replica of Kavanagh** himself, comfortably lounging on a bench watching his beloved canal.

Farther west the **Circular Line** isn't quite as interesting and is better appreciated on a bicycle than on foot.

BALLSBRIDGE (Map 2)

South-east of central Dublin, the suburb of Ballsbridge was mainly laid out between 1830 and 1860 and many of the streets have British names with a distinctly military bearing. Many embassies, including the flashy circular US embassy, are in Ballsbridge. It also has some mid-range B&Bs and several top-end hotels. The main attractions in Ballsbridge are the Royal Dublin Society Showground and the Lansdowne Rd rugby and football (soccer) stadium (see the Football & Rugby section in the Entertainment chapter).

Royal Dublin Society Showground

Founded in 1731, the Royal Dublin Society horse show was involved in the establishment of the National Museum, Library, Gallery and Botanic Gardens. The showground, on Merrion Rd in Ballsbridge, is used for exhibitions throughout the year, but the main event, the **Dublin Horse Show** (☎ 668 0866 for tickets, postal address: Ticket Office, PO Box 121, Ballsbridge, Dublin 4; general admission €7.60, seating €8.90-15.25), reflects the society's agricultural background. The show takes place in the first week of August and includes an international showjumping contest among other events. Tickets can be booked in advance by contacting the Ticket Office. Ask at the tourist office or consult a listings magazine for details of other events held at the showground.

PEARSE MUSEUM

Patrick (or Padráig in the Irish he worked hard to promote) Pearse was a leader of the 1916 Easter Rising and one of the first to be executed at Kilmainham Gaol. St Enda's, the school he established with his brother Willie to further his ideas of Irish language and culture, is now a museum (☎ 493 4208, e visits@ealga.ie, St Enda's Park; admission free; open 10am-1pm, 2pm-5.30pm May-Aug, to 5pm Feb-Apr & Sept-Oct, to 4pm Nov-Jan) and memorial to the brothers. St Enda's Park (sometimes known as Pearse Brothers Park) is at the junction of Grange Rd and Taylor's Lane in Rathfarnham, about 4 km south-west of the city centre. Take bus No 16 from the city centre to get there.

OTHER GALLERIES

Apart from the major galleries mentioned earlier in this chapter, Dublin boasts many private galleries, arts centres and corporate exhibition areas.

Douglas Hyde Gallery (Map 7) (☎ 608 1116, Arts Building, Trinity College, entrance on Nassau St; admission free; open 11am-6pm Mon-Wed & Fri, to 7pm Thur, to 4.45pm Sat) is one of the city's more interesting galleries, with a rotating showcase of top-class Irish and international work across two levels.

Gallery of Photography (Map 6) (☎ 671 4653, Meeting House Square, Temple Bar; admission free; open 11am-6pm Mon-Sat) is the country's best photographic gallery, with changing exhibitions in its two galleries.

Kerlin Gallery (Map 7) (☎ 670 9093, Anne's Lane, South Anne St; admission free; open 10am-5.45pm Mon-Fri, 11am-4.30pm Sat) is, along with the RHA Gallagher Gallery, the Shangri-la for Irish artists, conclusive proof that one's reached the big leagues.

Other Dublin galleries include the following:

Designyard (Map 6) *(☎ 677 8453, Applied Arts Centre, 12 East Essex St; admission free)* This gallery is home to constantly changing exhibitions of sculpture, jewellery and other handicrafts, all for sale.

Graphic Studio Gallery (Map 6) *(☎ 679 8021, Through the Arch, Cope St, Temple Bar; admission free)* Only work by new Irish artists gets exhibited at this place.

Original Print Gallery (Map 6) *(☎ 677 3657, Black Church Studio, 4 Temple Bar; admission free)* This gallery does exactly what it says on the door, with work mostly by Irish artists.

Rubicon Gallery (Map 5) *(☎ 670 8055, 10 St Stephen's Green; admission free)* This is one of the city's more prestigious galleries and has constantly changing exhibitions by local and international talent.

Solomon Gallery (Map 7) *(☎ 679 4237, Top Floor, Powerscourt Townhouse Shopping Centre, 59 South William St; admission free)* Strictly contemporary work is shown in this bright, airy gallery.

Taylor Galleries (Map 5) *(☎ 676 6055, 16 Kildare St, Dublin 2; admission free)* Spread across three floors of a fine Georgian building, the big guns of the Irish contemporary art world are shown in permanent exhibition, while rotating exhibits feature the work of those who'd love to join them.

Temple Bar Gallery & Studios (Map 6) *(☎ 671 0073, 679 9259, 5 Temple Bar; admission free)* An exciting gallery that features the work of up-and-coming international artists, with work in all media.

Activities

A perennial criticism of Dublin is the lack of accessible, good quality facilities for all manner of sporting activities, at least compared to other European capitals. That said, there is still plenty to do in Dublin.

BOWLING

There are two kinds of bowling available in Dublin. Indoor ten-pin bowling is very popular. You are usually charged per hour for a lane, which can accommodate up to six people. Rates vary depending on the time and day you want to bowl: before 6pm Monday to Thursday it costs about €24,

after 6pm it costs around €30, and around €32 at all times Friday to Sunday. Venues open round the clock include **Leisureplex Coolock** *(☎ 848 5722, Malahide Road; bus No 42 or 43 from the city centre)*, **Village Green Centre** *(☎ 459 9411, Tallaght; bus No 49, 65, 65B or 77A from the city centre)* and **Stillorgan Bowl** *(☎ 288 1656, Stillorgan; bus No 46A, 46B, 63, 84 or 86 from the city centre)*.

The more genteel outdoor game is played at **Herbert Park (Map 2)** *(☎ 665 1875, Ballsbridge)* and at **Kenilworth Bowling Club** *(☎ 497 2305, Grosvenor Square)* in Rathmines.

CYCLING

Ireland has produced its fair share of cycling champions (such as former world champion Sean Kelly and 1988 Tour de France winner and world champion Stephen Roche), but competitive cycling is not nearly as popular as it is in continental Europe.

For full information about competitive cycling events, including the Tour of Ireland, contact the Federation of Irish Cyclists (☎ 855 1522) at 619 North Circular Rd, Dublin 9.

The outdoor cycling track at **Eamon Ceannt Park (Map 2)** *(☎ 454 0799, Crumlin)*, to the south, is a good venue for anyone looking to avoid the traffic, as is a good cycle around Phoenix Park. Alternatively, those of sound leg and lung might want to venture farther afield, as far as North Bull Island to the north of the city or down to the Wicklow Mountains.

Bicycles can be rented for about €65 per week plus deposit. There are two dozen firms around the city that rent them; see Bicycle in the Getting Around chapter for details of rental outlets.

GOLF

Golf is enormously popular in Ireland, and with only a few exceptions is largely free of the snobbery that afflicts the game on the continent. There are more than 20 private and public nine-hole and 18-hole club courses in and around Dublin and typical fees range from around €13 to as much as €95 per day (more at weekends), depending on the course. There are a couple of excellent championship courses that allow non-members to play, but only on production of a handicap certificate and by prior reservation. Not quite as challenging and not nearly as beautiful, public courses have no such requirements, and you can hack away to your heart's content, while still respecting course rules.

The best private courses in and around Dublin include:

Portmarnock Golf Links (☎ 846 0611, e reservations@portmarnock.com, w www.portmarnock.com, Strand Rd, Portmarnock; green fees €51 with no restrictions on visitor playing time) Take bus No 32, 32A, 102 or 230 from the city centre; it's about 17km to the north-east.

Royal Dublin (☎ 833 6346, Dollymount, Dublin 3; green fees €76-88; open to nonmembers Mon-Tues, Thur-Fri, to 4pm Sat, after noon Sun) This course is about 15km to the north-east; take bus No 30 from the city centre.

St Anne's Golf Club (☎ 833 6471, Bull Island Nature Reserve, Dollymount, Dublin 3; green fees €25-36; nonmembers welcome Mon-Sat only) Take bus No 30, 103 or 130 from the city centre; it's 6.5km to the north-east.

All public courses charge €13 on weekdays and €24 at weekends, and are open from 8am to dusk. These include:

Corballis Golf Links (☎ 843 6583, Donabate, Co Dublin) Take bus No 33B from the city centre; it's 5km to the north.

Deer Park (☎ 832 2624, e sales@deerpark.iol.ie, Howth, County Dublin) Take bus No 31 or 31A from the city centre; it's about 10km north-east.

Elm Green (☎ 820 0797, Castleknock, Dublin 15) Take bus No 38, 39, 70, 76A or 250 from the city centre; it's about 10km north-west.

For more information about golf, Dublin Tourism publishes the free *Golfing Around Dublin*, available at the main tourist office in Suffolk St. You can also check out w www.golfdublin.com for information about the city's public courses.

In 2001, **Golf D2 (Map 6)** (☎ 672 6181, Cow's Lane; open noon-10pm Mon-Fri, 10am-8pm Sat), the city's first – and only – virtual golf centre, opened. In Temple Bar, this is a state-of-the-art centre, where you

hit real balls with real clubs into a large screen onto which is projected the computer-generated course. You can play a variety of matches on over 30 of the world's most famous courses, including St Andrew's, Valderrama and Pebble Beach. The place is also good for practising, as the computer program features a driving range. The price is €26 per hour for one person, €19 each for two and €15.50 each for three. Advance bookings are advisable.

TENNIS

Most tennis courts in the city are privately owned and are open only to members, there are a couple of public courts which must be booked in advance. You can play at **Albert College Park** (☎ 837 3891, Glasnevin, Dublin 9; bus No 13 or 34 from the city centre); **Bushy Park** (☎ 490 0320, Terenure, Dublin 6; bus No 15, 15A, 15B, 16, 16A, 17 or 49 from the city centre) and **Herbert Park** (☎ 668 4364, Ballsbridge, Dublin 4; bus No 5, 7, 7A, 8, 18 or 45 from the city centre). Public courts are usually free, except maybe around Wimbledon time when they charge a nominal fee, not more than €2.50.

WATER SPORTS
Beaches & Swimming

Even a hot summer's day is unlikely to raise the water temperature much above freezing but there are some pleasant beaches and many Joyce fans feel compelled to take a dip in the **Forty Foot Pool** at Dun Laoghaire as Buck Mulligan did in *Ulysses*. Sandy beaches near the centre include **Sutton** (7km), **Portmarnock** (10km), **Malahide** (10km; this beach holds a very popular Christmas Day swim for the very brave), **Claremont** (12km) and **Donabate** (15km). Although the beach at **Sandymount** is nothing special, it's only 5km south-east of central Dublin.

Most swimming pools in Dublin are small, crowded and not quite hygienic. On the plus side, they don't charge very much for a 40-minute session, usually around €3.20 for adults and €2.20 for children. The best of the lot, at least in terms of convenience to the city centre, is the recently reopened **Markievicz Leisure Centre (Map 5)**

(☎ 672 9121, Townsend St; admission €4.50; open 7am-10pm Mon-Fri, 9am-6pm Sat, 10am-4pm Sun).

Sailing & Windsurfing

The coastline north and south of Dublin is popular for sailing. Howth, Malahide and Dun Laoghaire are the most popular sailing centres, but you can also go sailing at Clontarf, Kilbarrack, Rush, Skerries, Sutton and Swords. See Activities under Dun Laoghaire in the Seaside Suburbs chapter for details of sailing clubs there.

In Malahide, **Fingall Sailing School** *(☎ 845 1979, Upper Strand Rd, Broadmeadow Estuary)* offers dinghy sailing courses.

Windsurfing enthusiasts should head for Ringsend's **Surfdock Centre** *(☎ 668 3945, Grand Canal Dock, South Dock Rd)*, which operates from a barge. The centre runs windsurfing courses costing from €38 for a three-hour 'taster' session to €140 for a 12-hour course. You can also rent sailboards for €15.50 per hour.

GO-KARTING

Children as young as three are strapped into karts and let loose on the 350m course of **Kylemore Indoor Karting** *(☎ 626 1444, Unit 1A, Kylemore Industrial Estate, Killeen Road; 15-minute practice session €15.25, full race €35.50; 11am-midnight Mon-Fri, from 10am Sat & Sun).* This place is great, offering thrills (but thankfully no spills) for children and adults alike. There are all kinds of racing here, including a Grand Prix championship race (for the bigger kids), which comes complete with a voice-over from Formula One TV commentator Murray Walker. If you win a race, you get a trophy.

To get to the course, take the No 18 or 79 bus from D'Olier St in the city centre.

COURSES
Language

Dublin is an extremely popular centre for learning English, particularly among people from other largely Catholic countries (mainly Spain, Italy, France and Portugal). Students come here in huge numbers every summer and are a colourful part of the city scene.

Bord Fáilte publishes a list of schools recognised by the Department of Education for the teaching of English as a foreign language. Some schools run summer courses or provide various specialised programs – for businesspeople, for example.

Private language schools all run a selection of part- or full-time courses. Part-time courses usually cost between €152 for six hours per week and €360 for 12 hours per week. Full-time courses, which often include social activities as well as up to 20 hours' tuition per week, cost around €380 per week. Schools can often arrange accommodation.

Some approved schools in Dublin are:

Academy of English Studies Ireland (☎ 679 6494, fax 279 6465, ⓔ *acadublin@eircom.net, 33 Dawson St, Dublin 2)* **Map 6**

Applied Language Centre (☎ 706 8520, fax 269 4409, ⓔ *alc@ucd.ie, University College Dublin, Belfield, Dublin 4)*

Dublin School of English (☎ 677 3322, fax 626 4692, ⓔ *admin@dse.ie, 10-12 Westmoreland St, Dublin 2)* **Map 6**

English Language Institute (☎ 475 2965, fax 475 2967, ⓔ *elin@iol.ie, 99 St Stephen's Green, Dublin 2)* **Map 5**

Dublin Walks

WALK 1: MOUNTJOY SQUARE TO ST STEPHEN'S GREEN

Walking between Mountjoy Square and St Stephen's Green takes you from one part of the city's Georgian heritage to another. You start at one of Dublin's great Georgian squares, in the run-down northern part of the city, proceed down O'Connell St, the city's major thoroughfare, cross the Liffey and finish at another of the great Georgian squares, this time in the city's wealthiest area. The walk will take around two hours. Many of the attractions en route are described in greater detail in the Things to See & Do chapter of this book.

Mountjoy Square (1 on map) is one of Dublin's magnificent squares but it has fallen on hard times. The fine buildings are still there, just waiting for a north Dublin renaissance. From the north-western corner of the square walk up Upper Gardiner St and turn left along Lower Dorset St to No 7 Eccles St (2), the fictional home of Joyce's Leopold and Molly Bloom in *Ulysses*. Apart from a plaque and a relief of Joyce's face, there's nothing to see because the house was demolished to build a nursing home in 1982. Real-life residents of Eccles St included the architect Francis Johnston, whose home at No 64 (3) has survived, though in a rather shabby state. At one time Johnston had his own private bell tower in the back garden until neighbours complained about the noise.

Turn around and cross Lower Dorset St on to North Temple St. On Hardwicke Place by Temple St is the fine St George's Church (4) designed by Francis Johnston, whose house we just left. And where did the church's bells come from? Why, from Johnston's back garden bell tower of course! We wonder how Johnston would have reacted to know that the real noise coming from the church these days is the thumping beat of dance music rather than the sound of his bells.

Turn right on to Denmark St and pass the Jesuit-run Belvedere College (5). James Joyce attended the school between 1893 and

1898 and went on to become its most famous graduate. The tall spire of the Abbey Presbyterian Church (6) on the corner of North Parnell Square and Frederick St looms in front of you. Built in 1864, it is often referred to as Findlater's Church after the grocery magnate who financed the building's construction.

The northern slice of Parnell Square is the Garden of Remembrance (7), opened in 1966 to commemorate the 50th anniversary of the Easter Rising. The sculpture (8) here illustrates the legend of the Children of Lir, who were transformed into swans by their wicked stepmother. Outside the garden is a small monument (9) to the victims of a Loyalist paramilitary terrorist bomb campaign in Dublin on 17 May 1974. The writer Oliver St John Gogarty (1878–1957) was born at 5 East Parnell Square (10).

On the northern side of the square, facing the park, are the Dublin Writers' Museum (11) and the Hugh Lane Municipal Gallery of Modern Art (12). Walk around the square, noting more fine but dilapidated Georgian buildings on the western side of the square, one of them housing the Sinn Féin offices and bookshop (13). The southern part of Parnell Square is occupied by the Rotunda Hospital (14), built in 1757. As you walk along the southern side of the square look for the Patrick Conway pub (15), which opened in 1745. In the south-eastern corner of the square is the Gate Theatre (16) in part of the old Rotunda complex.

O'Connell St, Dublin's major boulevard, begins at this corner of the square and sweeps south to O'Connell Bridge and the Liffey. Unfortunately, the street has had a hard time of it this century. One side was burnt out in the 1916 Easter Rising, the other during the Civil War, and whatever remained was ripped out by short-sighted property developers in the 1960s and '70s.

Despite this, O'Connell St has numerous points of interest, including a varied collection of statues down the centre, the first of which is a grandiose statue of Charles Stew-

DUBLIN WALKS

WALK 1: MOUNTJOY SQUARE TO ST STEPHEN'S GREEN

1 Mountjoy Square
2 Leopold & Molly Bloom's House
3 Francis Johnston's House
4 St George's Church
5 Belvedere College
6 Abbey Presbyterian Church
7 Garden of Remembrance
8 Children of Lir Monument
9 Bombing Monument
10 Oliver St John Gogarty House
11 Dublin Writers' Museum
12 Hugh Lane Municipal Gallery of Modern Art
13 Sinn Féin Bookshop
14 Rotunda Hospital
15 Patrick Conway
16 Gate Theatre
17 Charles Stewart Parnell Statue
18 Anna Livia Statue
19 Monument of Light
20 James Joyce Statue
21 General Post Office (GPO)
22 Daniel O'Connell Statue
23 O'Connell Bridge
24 Ha'penny Bridge
25 Bewley's Oriental Café
26 Thomas Moore Statue
27 Bank of Ireland
28 Trinity College Entrance
29 Thomas Cook
30 Molly Malone Statue
31 Davy Byrne's
32 Huguenot-Style Houses
33 National Library
34 Leinster House (Irish Parliament)
35 National Museum
36 Bram Stoker's House
37 Méridian Shelbourne
38 Huguenot Cemetery
39 Wolfe Tone Monument; Famine Victims Memorial

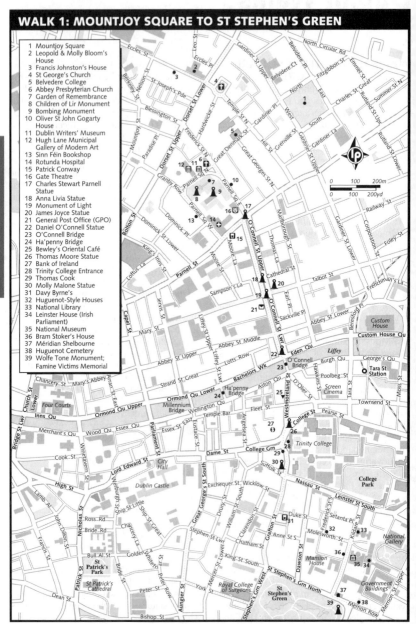

art Parnell (17). Continue down O'Connell St, passing the fountain statue of Anna Livia (based on the Irish name for the Liffey), referred to by locals as 'the floozy in the Jacuzzi' among other names (18). The Henry St-Earl St crossing was the former position of Nelson's Pillar, blown up by the IRA in 1966. It's now been replaced by the 120m-high Monument of Light (19), which was originally intended to be put up in time for the millennium, but safety concerns and objections delayed its erection until early 2002. There's a notable statue of James Joyce (20) at the O'Connell St end of pedestrianised Earl St. His bemused look perhaps reflects the irony that a writer whose masterpiece was banned in his own country throughout his life should be so honoured. However, we'd like to think that is more a reaction to the nickname with which ordinary Dubliners refer to it, as 'the prick with the stick'.

On the other side of O'Connell St, the GPO (21) towers over the street. Its role as the starting point for the 1916 Easter Rising makes this an important site in Ireland's recent history. At the river end of the street the statue of Daniel O'Connell (22) looks squarely up the street that bears his name.

Cross the Liffey on O'Connell Bridge (23), the most important bridge in the city. If you look to the right you can see the pedestrian Ha'penny Bridge (24). Across the bridge you join Westmoreland St and pass Dublin's famous Bewley's Oriental Café (25). At the bottom of Westmoreland St, on the left, is a statue of the poet Thomas Moore (26), eloquently plonked by a public toilet.

To the right is the long, curving, windowless facade of the Bank of Ireland (27), which started life as the Irish Houses of Parliament. When the Act of Union subsumed the Irish Parliament into the British one, the building became a bank. Perhaps surprisingly it did not become the parliament building for independent Ireland. On the left is the main entrance to Trinity College (28), flanked by statues of Edmund Burke and Oliver Goldsmith looking out over College Green, once a real green but now filled with buildings, including Thomas Cook (29).

Your steps now take you into Grafton St,

A statue of the much-serenaded
Molly Malone stands on Grafton St.

passing the statue of the fictional Molly Malone (30). In the song named after her, she 'wheeled her wheelbarrow, through streets broad and narrow', which is what she's doing here, although Dubliners will tell you that she belongs on the less fashionable north side, on or near Moore St. In typical Dublin fashion the notably well endowed statue has been dubbed 'the tart with the cart'. In summer, pavement artists are often busy producing chalk pictures here.

Road traffic has to turn into Nassau St but you can enter the pedestrianised area of Grafton St, Dublin's fanciest shopping street. At the next corner, turn left off Grafton St into Duke St, where the famous pub, Davy Byrne's (31), is situated. At the bottom of Duke St turn right on to Dawson St and left into Molesworth St, looking for the gabled Huguenot-style houses (32) built between 1736 and 1755.

Molesworth St brings you out on to Kildare St, facing the back of Leinster House (34), the Irish parliament. It is flanked on either side by the similarly designed National Library (33) and National Museum (35). Turn right down Kildare St, looking for the sign at No 30 (36) announcing that Bram Stoker, the author of *Dracula*, used to live there. At the bottom of the road the Méridian Shelbourne

DUBLIN WALKS

(37) sits on the corner, facing St Stephen's Green. The Shelbourne, Dublin's premier hotel, opened for business in 1824, though the present building only dates back to 1867. At the front of the hotel, note the statues of Nubian princesses and their slave girls with fettered ankles. Past the hotel is a Huguenot Cemetery (38), a reminder of the French Huguenots who came to Ireland from the late 17th century. Opposite the hotel, on the northwestern corner of St Stephen's Green, is the Wolfe Tone Monument (39) dedicated to the leader of the failed 1796 invasion. You'll also find a monument to the victims of the mid-19th-century Potato Famine (40).

Back on the other side of the road, the Méridian Shelbourne is a good place to end this stroll, because if you've timed it right you can drop in for afternoon tea.

WALK 2: VIKING & MEDIEVAL DUBLIN

This walk is an exploration of the Viking and medieval city built between the 9th and 12th centuries. Bordered to the east by the western end of Temple Bar and to the west by Bridge St, the city first built by the Danes and later fortified by the Normans stretched only as far south as the park north of St Patrick's Cathedral. Dublin's second great cathedral (after Christ Church) was actually outside the city walls, although you'd never know it to look at it now. Sadly, very little remains of Dublin's Viking era, but a walk in this area will give you a definite flavour of Dublin's past, from its two great Norman cathedrals to the historic Liberties area and Dublin Castle, for 800 years the stronghold of English power in Ireland.

This walk runs a loop of about 3.5km, and should take you no more than two hours to walk. Of course, it will take longer if you enter the various attractions and churches along the way.

Begin your walk at the corner of Parliament St and Essex Gate (1 on map), once a main entrance gate to the city. A bronze plaque on a pillar marks the spot where the gate (also known as Buttevant's Tower) once stood. The foundations of the gate have yet to be excavated, but you can see the original foundations of Isolde's Tower (2) through a grill in the pavement, in front of the pub of the same name.

Veering off to your right as you walk west down Essex Gate is the curved Upper Exchange St, which follows the contours of the old walls, and once called Blind Quay (because it was out of sight of the river). Back on Essex Gate, nearby is Dublin's Viking Adventure (3), a museum with a full-scale recreation of a part of the Viking city. It's near a marvellous panelled sculpture (4) by Dublin artist Grace Weir (1996) depicting a Viking ship navigating with the aid of the constellations. The western end of West Essex St – called at various times Stable Lane, Cadogan's Alley, Smock Alley and Orange St – was widened in the 1940s and so lost its medieval curve. At the south-east corner of West Essex St and Fishamble St is a house that is reckoned to be the oldest continuously inhabited home in Dublin, originally built in the early 17th century but 'remodelled' in 1720.

Fishamble St was one of the most important streets of Viking and medieval Dublin. It was originally laid down in the 10th century (at twice its present length) and served as the main thoroughfare from the port to the Viking High St, the main trading street. Its name is taken from the fish stalls (known as 'shambles') that once lined the pavements. At the southern end of Fishamble St is Handel's Hotel; the building immediately to its left once housed William Neal's Music Hall, where the famous composer first performed his *Messiah* in 1742.

It's impossible to ignore the huge buildings that line the western side of Fishamble St. The main offices of Dublin Corporation, they were originally built in the 1980s and immediately dubbed 'the bunkers' for their unwieldy appearance. Apart from aesthetic considerations, their construction generated a huge amount of protest as they were built on one of the most important Viking sites in the world. A lengthy excavation has unearthed a wealth of Viking artefacts, most of which are on display in Dvblinia (see later in this section).

Walk down to the quays and take a left along Wood Quay. Walk past the frontage of

Attention to detail: Dublin's decorative features range from lions and shamrocks to the Sunlight Chambers' frieze depicting the history of washing.

Gorgeous Georgian facades on Merrion Square

A palatial portal...

...and fine frontage on St Stephen's Green.

Dublin is packed with 18th-century style.

WALK 2: VIKING & MEDIEVAL DUBLIN

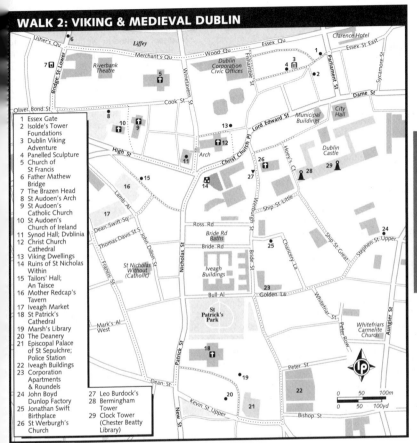

1 Essex Gate
2 Isolde's Tower Foundations
3 Dublin Viking Adventure
4 Panelled Sculpture
5 Church of St Francis
6 Father Mathew Bridge
7 The Brazen Head
8 St Audoen's Arch
9 St Audoen's Catholic Church
10 St Audoen's Church of Ireland
11 Synod Hall; Dvblinia
12 Christ Church Cathedral
13 Viking Dwellings
14 Ruins of St Nicholas Within
15 Tailors' Hall; An Taisce
16 Mother Redcap's Tavern
17 Iveagh Market
18 St Patrick's Cathedral
19 Marsh's Library
20 The Deanery
21 Episcopal Palace of St Sepulchre; Police Station
22 Iveagh Buildings
23 Corporation Apartments & Roundels
24 John Boyd Dunlop Factory
25 Jonathan Swift Birthplace
26 St Werburgh's Church
27 Leo Burdock's
28 Bermingham Tower
29 Clock Tower (Chester Beatty Library)

DUBLIN WALKS

the Dublin Corporation buildings, cross Winetavern St and proceed along Merchant's Quay. On your left is the Church of St Francis (5), which is also known as Adam & Eve's after a tavern through which worshippers gained access to a secret chapel during Penal times. The next bridge you'll come to is Father Mathew Bridge (6), built in 1818 on the spot of the fordable crossing that gave Dublin its Irish name, Baile Átha Cliath, or 'town of the hurdle ford'.

Take a left on to Bridge St. On your right is Ireland's oldest pub, The Brazen Head (7), which dates from 1198 (although the present

building dates from 1668). Take the next left into Cook St, where you will find the most significant remains of the medieval walls and an original gate, St Audoen's Arch (8), built in 1240. During the Middle Ages, Dublin was heavily protected by a double ring of walls and 32 towers and fortified gates; most of these were torn down and the stone used to build elsewhere. Climb through the arch up to the ramparts, site of the twin churches of St Audoen's, one a Catholic church (9), the other Church of Ireland (10). The latter, built in 1190, is the oldest parish church still in use in Dublin. Leave the little park and take a left on High St. On your left, the first corner is occupied by the former Synod Hall (11), now home to Dvblinia, a museum where medieval Dublin has been interactively recreated. Turn left and walk under the Synod Hall Bridge linking it to Christ Church Cathedral (12). Below the cathedral, on your left, is East John's Lane, and in the pavement you can see a pebble mosaic marking out the site of two Viking dwellings (13), a late consolation for those who had campaigned against the construction of the Civic Offices below. Continue along the lane and take a right into the cathedral grounds. The stone ruins just inside the grounds are all that is left of a priory once attached to the main cathedral.

A visit to Christ Church Cathedral is compulsory. It is one of the city's most important landmarks and, in medieval times, the most important church inside the city walls. Once you've finished, exit on to Christ Church Place and cross over onto Nicholas St, passing the ruins of St Nicholas Within (14), so-called because it was within the city walls. Take the first right on to Back Lane and proceed past Dublin's oldest surviving guild hall, Tailors' Hall (15), built between 1703 and 1707 (though 1770 is on the plaque) for the Tailors' Guild. It is now the headquarters of An Taisce, the National Trust for Ireland. Mother Redcap's Tavern (16) is opposite. Turn left down John Dillon St to Dean Swift Square and the imposing structure of the old Iveagh Market (17), established in 1907 by Lord Iveagh of the Guinness family. There are wonderfully expressive stone faces over the arches; round the corner, the face giving a broad wink is said to be modelled on Lord Iveagh himself. Currently closed, plans are afoot to re-open the market.

Continue down the street and take a left at the junction with Francis St. You are now in the heart of the Liberties area, so-called because medieval Dublin had a number of 'liberties' – areas outside the city jurisdiction where local courts were at liberty to administer the law. Today, Francis St is best known for its antique shops. At the bottom of the street, right will take you on to the Coombe, so called because it was once the 'coomb' or river valley of the Poddle. Turn left, how-

ever, on to Dean St, named after the deanery of St Patrick's Cathedral but previously known as Crosspoddle St because it used to cross the Poddle at this point. Take a left on to Patrick St and across the street you will see the imposing St Patrick's Cathedral (18). Also visible are the attractive red-brick houses apartments built by Lord Iveagh in the 19th century to house the company's workers. They have recently been restored to their former beauty. As you enter the grounds of St Patrick's, you will notice that the ground level drops about 2m – this was the original elevation of medieval Dublin.

Just beyond the bend is Marsh's Library (19) on the left. St Patrick's is inextricably linked with author, poet and satirist Jonathan Swift (see the boxed text 'Jonathan Swift' under St Patrick's Cathedral in the Things to See & Do chapter). The Deanery (20) where Swift once lived is on your right, even though the present building is a more recent replacement. On your way, you'll pass a medieval stone horse trough.

Continue along St Patrick's Close to Upper Kevin St. On your left along Kevin St is a police station (21) which was once the Episcopal Palace of St Sepulchre, seat of the Archbishops of Dublin from the end of the 12th century to the early 19th century. The Dublin Metropolitan Police took over the building in the 1830s.

Turn left into Bride St and then walk north past some more examples of Lord Iveagh's constructive philanthropy (22). When you reach Golden Lane (on your right), the north-eastern corner is taken up by a newer block of elegant public housing, though the links with the past are maintained through the beautifully sculpted roundels that depict scenes from *Gulliver's Travels* (23). To the east is Stephen St: at No 67 (now the offices of Dunnes Stores), John Boyd Dunlop founded the world's first pneumatic tyre factory in 1889 (24).

Take a left from Stephen St into Great Ship St, walk round the bend on to Little Ship St. Steps on the left at the end lead to 7 Hoey's Court (25), birthplace of Jonathan Swift (1687). At the end of Little Ship St is Werburgh St and the eponymous church (26) dedicated to the daughter of a Saxon king. From the church, take the next right into Castle St, passing (on your left) Dublin's most famous fish and chip shop, Leo Burdock's (27). Until the 20th century, this was the main westwards route out of the city. On your right is the enormous expanse of Dublin Castle. The striking powder-blue tower on the right is Bermingham Tower (28), built in the 13th century and used to detain state prisoners. It was badly damaged by a gunpowder blast in 1775 and rebuilt in an astonishing Strawberry Gothic style. Opposite the Bermingham Tower, the Old Barracks have been restored; the Clock Tower (29) now houses the Chester Beatty Library, one of Dublin's most fascinating collections of rare books and manuscripts.

WALK 3: DISTINGUISHED DUBLINERS

It's hard to believe that a small city like Dublin could have spawned no less than four Nobel laureates... and that's just for literature. But apart from George Bernard Shaw, William Butler Yeats, Samuel Beckett and Seamus Heaney (OK, not quite a Dubliner as he is from Derry, but an adopted one nonetheless), the city has produced far more than its fair share of famous citizens. From musicians to medical practitioners, poets to painters and writers to rebels, Dublin's honoured offspring and acclaimed adopted sons and daughters have all made their mark on the domestic and international stage.

This walk will allow you to discover a few of these distinguished Dubs, beginning on the Grand Canal and winding your way down through the south side to the city centre. This walk is about 3.5km and should take about two hours; you don't, of course, have to do it all in one go and can take plenty of breaks along the way. There are plenty of distractions (pubs, restaurants, shops, etc) to occupy your time. To get to the starting point, you can take bus No 14, 14A, 15A, 15B, 47, 47A, 47B or 83 from Trinity College to Portobello on the Grand Canal.

Start your walk on Richmond St South, right by the Grand Canal. On the north side of the canal, on your left if you're facing into the city centre, is Portobello College (1 on map), built in 1807 as Portobello House, one of the five original hotels that lined the banks of the canal between Dublin and the River Shannon. In the 20th century it served as a nursing home, and, since the mid-1980s, as a technical college. Between 1950 and 1957, this was the residence of Jack Butler Yeats (1871–1957), who though not quite as famous as his Nobel prize-winning brother William, is still reckoned to be the greatest artist Ireland has ever produced.

Turn left into Richmond Row; at the end of the street turn left into Lennox St (both streets are named after Charles Lennox, Duke of Richmond and Lord Lieutenant of Ireland between 1807–13). No 6 Lennox St was the birthplace of John McCann (1905–88), a playwright and twice Lord Mayor of Dublin. A few doors up at No 28 was the home of sculptor John Hughes (1865–1941), who had a pretty successful career in Ireland, England and France.

Take the next right on to Synge St, a very famous street. No 33 (2) was the birthplace of George Bernard Shaw, author of *Pygmalion* (which was subsequently hammed up and turned into the highly successful stage musical and film, *My Fair Lady*). In 1925 he won the Nobel Prize for Literature for his play *Saint Joan*. Today the house is a museum dedicated to the author. A little further north is a famous school – we'll get to it in a while.

Proceed west along Lennox St, take a left onto Kingsland Parade and then the first right into Walworth Rd. On your right, at No 4, is the Irish-Jewish Museum (3), which tells the (often tragic) story of the once prominent Jewish community in Dublin. Joyce fans will surely remember that Leopold Bloom, the hero of *Ulysses*, was Jewish, but Dublin has also had a couple of real-life famous citizens who were Jewish. The renowned stage and screen actor Barry Fitzgerald (1888–1969), however, was not one of them. He was born William Joseph Shields at No 1 Walworth Rd (4), and from here he went on to fame and (small) fortune as a principal lead with the Abbey Theatre before making an international name as the matchmaker in John Ford's *The Quiet Man*, also starring John Wayne and Maureen O'Hara. Fitzgerald also appeared in

DUBLIN WALKS

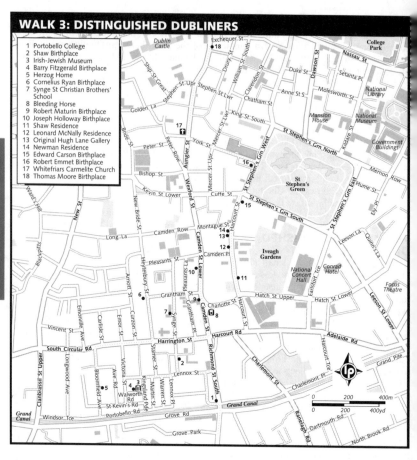

WALK 3: DISTINGUISHED DUBLINERS

1 Portobello College
2 Shaw Birthplace
3 Irish-Jewish Museum
4 Barry Fitzgerald Birthplace
5 Herzog Home
6 Cornelius Ryan Birthplace
7 Synge St Christian Brothers' School
8 Bleeding Horse
9 Robert Maturin Birthplace
10 Joseph Holloway Birthplace
11 Shaw Residence
12 Leonard McNally Residence
13 Original Hugh Lane Gallery
14 Newman Residence
15 Edward Carson Birthplace
16 Robert Emmet Birthplace
17 Whitefriars Carmelite Church
18 Thomas Moore Birthplace

DUBLIN WALKS

Going My Way and *How Green Was My Valley*, and while he was cast as the usual stereotype of the bumbling Irish fool who dispenses secret pearls of wisdom, his range was extraordinary and he is rightly considered one of the Irish greats.

Walk down to the canal and then walk farther westwards till you reach Bloomfield Ave. Turn right onto it. At No 33 (5), you will find the home of Ireland's first Chief Rabbi, Isaac Herzog. Hardly a famous Jewish Dubliner, but his son Chaim (1918–97), who was born in Belfast but brought up in the house, had a long and distinguished political career that culminated in his being elected President of Israel in 1983. During his tenure as Israeli Ambassador to the United Nations (1975–78), an English diplomat joked that Ireland was far too well represented in the General Assembly: apart from its own ambassador, it could call on the support of Herzog and of Jean Kirkpatrick, the American ambassador with Irish roots!

Walk north to the end of Bloomfield Ave and turn right onto the South Circular Rd. Take a left on to Heytesbury St and walk down to No 33 (6), the birthplace of Cornelius Ryan, author of *The Longest Day, The*

Last Battle and *A Bridge Too Far*, all of which have been made into highly successful films. Cross the street and take Grantham St as far as the first corner on the right, and you're back on Synge St. Immediately to your right is the long expanse of the Synge St Christian Brothers' School (7). The school has many distinguished alumni: apart from Herzog and Ryan, pupils of the school included TV host Gay Byrne, easily the most famous of all Irish TV celebrities. For over 30 years he was the host of the enormously popular *Late Late Show* (the longest-running chat show in the world), but he retired in 1999, only to be coaxed back in front of the cameras as the host of Ireland's version of *Who Wants to Be a Millionaire?* Former Irish president Cearbhall Ó'Dálaigh (pronounced 'carool o-dawly') was also a student here, as was the famous stage actor Cyril Cusack, English TV broadcaster Eamon Andrews and comedian and actor Noel Purcell.

Walk south back to Harrington St and take a left. Take the second left down Camden St. On your right is the Bleeding Horse (8), above which lived for a time a certain Captain Bligh of *Mutiny on the Bounty* fame. On the other side of Camden St are a couple of noteworthy addresses. No 57 (9) was the birthplace of Robert Maturin (1782–1824), whose most famous book was the Gothic horror novel *Melmoth the Wanderer.* Along with Joseph Sheridan Le Fanu *(The House by the Churchyard)* and the author of *Dracula*, Bram Stoker (see the Mountjoy Square to Stephen's Green walk earlier), they form an impressive trio of masters of the horror genre. His home is now a centre of the Simon Community, a charitable organisation that helps the homeless. Farther down, at No 71 (10), you will find the home of a certain Joseph Holloway (1861–1944), best known for his collection of theatrical memorabilia and 221 journals on life in Irish theatre. The journals are now in the possession of the National Library.

Walk back up and cross the street at the Bleeding Horse, and continue on down Charlotte St before taking a left on Harcourt St, a street replete with famous addresses. No 61 (11), now the Harcourt Hotel, was the last

residence of George Bernard Shaw before he moved permanently to England in 1876. On the opposite side of the street, farther down at No 22 (12), now part of the Russell Court Hotel, lived Leonard McNally (1752–1820), who was best known for his ill-fated defence of patriot Robert Emmet at his trial in 1803. It later emerged that he had betrayed Emmet to the authorities in the first place and had long been a British agent operating within Emmet's United Irishmen. A few doors down at No 17 (13) was the first gallery created by Hugh Lane – the gallery has since moved to a more permanent location on Parnell Square. No 6 (14) was residence from 1854 of John Henry Cardinal Newman, the first rector of the Catholic University of Ireland (later University College Dublin). Two doors down at No 4 (15) is the birthplace of Sir Edward Carson (1854–1935), the founder of Northern Unionism who also prosecuted Oscar Wilde during his trial for homosexuality in 1898.

Walk straight on to St Stephen's Green. Just after Glover's Alley, at No 124, is the birthplace of Robert Emmet (16). Then turn onto York St. A shadow of its former self, York St was once a proud residential street that was home to architect Richard Cassels (1690–1751), creator of Leinster House. His house has since been demolished, but other distinguished residents have included poet James Clarence Mangan (1803–49), who lived at No 6 and James Stephens (1880–1950), author of the popular Dublin novel *The Charwoman's Daughter*, who lived at No 30. Eamon de Valera secretly trained a unit of Irish Volunteers in No 41's basement.

Walk westwards to the end of York St. Facing you is the Whitefriars Carmelite Church (17) where, in one of the vaults, lie the remains of St Valentine (of 14 February fame). He wasn't born in Dublin and never visited Ireland, but his remains were donated to the church by Pope Gregory XVI in 1835.

You are now on Aungier St. Walk northwards until you get to No 12 (18). This final stop is the birthplace of composer and poet Thomas Moore (1779–1852), one of Ireland's most important writers of both lyric and song.

DUBLIN WALKS

Places to Stay

Finding a place to stay in Dublin will be one of the more important decisions you'll make while you're here, as it will play a part in dictating the kind of time you'll have. If you're only here for the weekend, you'll want to stay as close to the city centre as possible – at the heart of the action. If you're planning a longer visit, the choice becomes less important, but it'll matter nonetheless. If you're lodging in the suburbs, you'll have to plan your excursions carefully. Public transportation is slow, and, more importantly, virtually non-existent after midnight. That leaves you relying on taxis, which can be a nightmare to grab. Prices are cheaper in the suburbs, but you'll more than make up for it in the headache of public transport and expensive cab rides.

Like every other city in the world, the closer you stay to the centre, the more you'll pay, and in Dublin, that can be a lot. The city's renaissance as a tourist magnet has radically changed the accommodation map, with new hotels of varying quality springing up almost weekly. In the face of increased competition, many of Dublin's existing hotels, hostels and B&Bs have undergone serious makeovers, raising standards and improving services and amenities. The result is predictable. Sure, there's plenty more options for where to stay, but you'll pay for it. It is virtually impossible to get a really cheap room in Dublin anymore, and even the city's hostels, once the backbone of dirt-cheap accommodation, have substantially raised their prices. Consequently, Dublin is one of Europe's more expensive cities to sleep in. That said, you'll generally find cheaper accommodation on the city's north side, which is not as fancy or as tidy as the south side.

Accommodation prices vary according to season, reaching a peak during the main holiday periods or over public holidays. Prices quoted are those for the high season. You can usually get a bed in a hostel for €15 to €25. In a typical B&B the cost per person will be around €45 to €65. More expensive B&Bs or mid-range hotels cost around €57 to €82 per person. Dublin's top hotels cost upwards of €100 per person. Then there are the deluxe hotels, which can cost over €250 per person.

Another consequence of Dublin's popularity is that finding a bed is pretty tough in any price range, especially between April and September. If you can make a reservation, it will make life easier. The alternative is to go to one of the Dublin Tourism offices and ask them to book you a room. For €2.50 plus a 10% deposit on the cost of the first night, they'll find you somewhere to stay, and will do so efficiently and with a smile. Sometimes this may require a great deal of phoning around, so it can be money well spent. There are tourist offices in the city, at Dublin airport and in the ferry terminal at Dun Laoghaire (see Tourist Offices in the Facts for the Visitor chapter and Information under Dun Laoghaire in the Seaside Suburbs chapter).

The Backpackers Centre in Lower Gardiner St gives advice on the hostels run by Independent Holiday Hostels (IHH). See Useful Organisations in the Facts for the Visitor chapter for more information.

Places listed in this chapter are in central Dublin or the nearby suburbs. The suburbs of Dun Laoghaire and Howth are within easy commuting distance of the centre by car or Dublin Area Rapid Transit (DART); accommodation there is covered in the Seaside Suburbs chapter.

PLACES TO STAY – BUDGET
Camping
There is no convenient central camp site in Dublin. Do *not* try to camp in Phoenix Park; it is illegal and dangerous.

Shankill Caravan & Camping Park (☎ 282 0011, fax 282 0108, e shankill caravan@eircom.net, Shankill, County Dublin) Sites for 2 people €7.60-8.50. This camping ground with excellent views of the mountains and top-class facilities, is 16km south of the centre on the N11 Wexford Rd. Take bus No 46 or 46 from Eden Quay, or DART to Shankill to get here.

Camac Valley Tourist Caravan & Camping Park (☎ 464 0644, fax 464 0643, e camacmorriscastle@eircom.net, Naas Rd, Clondalkin, Dublin 22) Sites cost €5.10-5.80 per person. Only 35 minutes by bus No 69 or 69X from the city centre, this camping ground is spread across several fields, with an abundance of facilities, including a children's play room, a games room, tennis courts and even a pitch & putt course.

Hostels

Since there are no central camping grounds, travellers on any kind of budget should aim to stay in a hostel. They're cheaper than even the most flea-pit hotels and are also great centres for meeting other travellers and exchanging information. Whereas in times past there were only a handful in Dublin, the tourist boom has seen hostels open up all over the city, each competing fiercely for your custom. Consequently, the days of scabby bed sheets and dirty, dilapidated dormitories have gone and most of the city's hostels maintain a pretty high standard of hygiene and comfort. All but one are independently owned and run – the exception being the Dublin International Youth Hostel, run by An Óige, the national youth hostel association – and most offer various sleeping arrangements, ranging from a bed in a large dorm to a four-bed room and, in some cases, even doubles. Because this is a popular capital city, prices reflect this, and you won't get much change out of €15, even if you're bunked down with 11 other people.

Remember that hostels fill up quickly, particularly between April and September, so be sure to book in advance if you can.

North of the Liffey There are various well equipped hostels on the north side.

An Óige Dublin International Youth Hostel (☎ 830 1766, fax 830 1600, e dublin international@anoige.ie, 61 Mountjoy St) **Map 4** Dorm beds €12, private rooms €17. This 460-bed hostel is in a restored and con-

verted old building. Overseas visitors who are not members can stay at the hostel and may join by obtaining a guest card and paying €1.30 for a stamp on top of the nightly charge. If you buy six stamps (total €9.50) you become an HI member. To stay here, you must have, or hire, a sleeping sheet.

The hostel is in the run-down northern area of the city centre, and grilles on the side windows reflect the fact that this isn't the most salubrious part of town.

From Dublin Airport, bus No 41A drops you in Upper Dorset St, a few minutes' walk from the hostel. It's a longer but clearly signposted walk from the bus and train stations.

Marlborough Hostel (☎ 874 7629, fax 874 5172, e marlboro@internet-ireland .ie, 81-82 Marlborough St) **Map 4** Dorm beds/doubles from €11.50/12.70 per person. This hostel, next to the Pro-Cathedral, has a TV room, hot showers, lockers and a pleasant garden at the back. There's also a good information board in the lobby. Breakfast is included.

Abbey Court Hostel (☎ 878 0700, fax 878 0719, e info@abbey-court.com, 29 Bachelors Walk) **Map 4** Dorm beds/doubles from €15.50/23 per person, discounts in low season. All rooms in this convenient hostel are furnished handsomely and there are secure lockers throughout. Its excellent facilities include a dining hall, a conservatory and a barbecue area. It also has fabulous hot power showers, a welcome change from the drizzly lukewarm nonsense so common in other cheap accommodation. Breakfast is included. Not surprisingly, this is a popular option for travellers and reservations are advised.

Litton Lane Hostel (☎ 872 8389, fax 872 0039, e litton@indigo.ie, 2-4 Litton Lane) **Map 4** Dorm beds €15.25-17.50, doubles €28-32 per person. In a converted recording studio once used by Van Morrison and Sinead O'Connor, this new hostel is central, convenient and extremely comfortable. The public spaces are very well decorated and all of the rooms have been painted with murals representing some of the more famous musicians who recorded here. The musical theme is continued nearby, at the Hot Press

PLACES TO STAY

Irish Music Hall of Fame (see the Things to See & Do chapter).

Mount Eccles Court Budget Accommodation (☎ 873 0826, fax 878 3554, e info @eccleshostel.com, 42 North Great George's St) **Map 4** Dorm beds €12-23, doubles €16.50-30.50. In a renovated Georgian town-house on one of the north side's most beautiful streets, this pristine place is a great choice if you can get a room.

Isaac's Hostel & Hotel (☎ 836 3877, fax 855 6574, e hostel@isaacs.ie, 2-5 Frenchman's Lane) **Map 4** Dorm beds €10.10-20.50, singles & doubles in adjoining hotel €16.50-38.10 per person. Dorm lock-out 11am-3pm. Near the Busáras and Connolly station, this big IHH hostel is not far from the popular restaurants and pubs either side of the Liffey. In a converted 18th-century wine warehouse, the hostel has cooking facilities and a small Internet cafe, but is run along lines that make some old-fashioned An Óige hostels look laid back. Baggage in the basement locker room can only be retrieved exactly on the hour and half-hour. Trains also pass close to some of the rooms.

Jacob's Inn (☎ 855 5660, fax 855 5664, e jacobs@isaacs.ie, 21-28 Talbot Place) **Map 4** Dorm beds €12.70-24, doubles €22.30-35.50 per person. Isaac's new sister hostel is behind Busáras, and there's a restaurant and a self-catering kitchen on the premises. This is a clean, modern hostel with comfortable en-suite rooms and good amenities.

Globetrotter's Tourist Hostel (☎ 873 5893, fax 878 8787, e gtrotter@indigo.ie, 46-48 Lower Gardiner St) **Map 4** Dorm beds €19. With up to 12 people to some dorms there's bound to be a bit of disturbance, but this relaxed and welcoming IHH hostel is a clean, modern place with good security. Breakfast is included, and is served in a pleasant dining room overlooking a small garden.

Abraham House (☎ 855 0600, fax 855 0598, e stay@abraham-house.ie, 82-83 Lower Gardiner St) **Map 4** Dorm beds €12.70/20.30 in low/high season. Two large Georgian buildings have been joined to create this pleasant hostel in newly renovated

Gardiner St. Consequently, dorm rooms are large, airy and extremely well kept.

South of the Liffey Some well located options are scattered on the south side.

Ashfield House (☎ 679 7734, fax 679 0852, e ashfield@indigo.ie, 19-20 D'Olier St) **Map 5** Dorm beds €14.60-23 per person, doubles €18-38 per room. Ideally located just south of O'Connell Bridge, this relatively new hostel only has one dormitory, but its 25 other rooms include four-bed family rooms as well as doubles. A light continental breakfast is included.

Avalon House (☎ 475 0001, fax 475 0303, e info@avalon-house.ie, w www.avalon-house.ie, 55 Aungier St) **Map 5** Beds in 12-bed dorm €16.50, doubles/quads with bath €28/23 per person. This IHH hostel in a renovated old building is just west of St Stephen's Green. It's well equipped and some of the cleverly designed rooms have mezzanine levels, which are great for families. Prices include continental breakfast. Its location makes it extremely popular, but readers have complained that the staff can be a little rude. To get here, take bus No 16, 16A, 19 or 22 right to the door or No 11, 13 or 46A to nearby St Stephen's Green. From the Dun Laoghaire ferry terminal take bus No 46A to St Stephen's Green or the DART to Pearse station.

Barnacles Temple Bar House (☎ 671 6277, fax 671 6591, e tbh@barnacles.ie, 1 Cecilia St) **Map 6** Dorm beds/doubles €15.25/32 per person. The more expensive rooms in this place have en-suite bathrooms, and self-catering facilities are available. There's also a TV room with an open fireplace – very cosy in winter. The hostel has a discount deal with a nearby covered car park.

Brewery Hostel (☎ 453 8600, fax 453 8616, e breweryh@indigo.ie, 22-23 Thomas St) **Map 3** Dorm beds €12.70-20.50, doubles €19-32 per person. This small hostel, virtually next door to the Guinness Brewery, has five bedrooms and seven dorm rooms, all en suite. There is a private car park, barbecue facilities and a pleasant common room. Breakfast is included. Take bus No 68, 68A, 69A or 78A from Dame St to get here.

Cobblestones Budget Accommodation *(☎ 677 5614* e *cobblestones@ireland.com, 29 Eustace St)* **Map 6** Dorm beds €15.25-17.80, doubles €41-47. In the lively (and noisy) Temple Bar area, this hostel has no cooking facilities bar a microwave but breakfast is included and guests get discounts in the adjoining pizza parlour. During bank holidays and special events, prices go up.

Gogarty's Temple Bar Hostel & Apartments *(☎ 671 1822, fax 671 7637, 18-21 Anglesea St)* **Map 6** Dorm-beds/doubles from €16.50/22. This popular hostel in the heart of Temple Bar has basic, clean dorm rooms with comfortable wooden bunks. All rooms, including the dorms, are en suite. It's nearly always full, so be sure to book in advance.

Kinlay House *(☎ 679 6644, fax 679 7437,* e *kinlay-dublin@usitworld.com, 2-12 Lord Edward St)* **Map 6** Bus No 54A, 68A, 78A or 123. Beds in 4-bed dorm €16.50, in better room (some with en suite) €18.50-32. An institution among the city's hostels, IHH Kinlay House is central, but some rooms can suffer from traffic noise. It's big and well equipped, with cooking facilities and a cafe. Breakfast is included.

Student Accommodation
South of the Liffey From June to September you can stay in accommodation provided by the city's universities.

Trinity College *(☎ 608 1177, fax 671 1267,* e *reservations@tcd.ie, Accommodations Office, Trinity College)* **Map 5** Singles & doubles €44-57.50 per person. Although it's expensive, the college sometimes has wonderfully positioned accommodation on campus in the city. It is only available from mid June to the end of September, so be sure to book well in advance. Breakfast is included.

Mercer Court (Student Accommodation) *(☎ 478 2179, fax 478 0873,* e *reservations @mercercourt.ie, Lower Mercer St)* **Map 7** Doubles €38.10-49.50, 5-bed, self-catering apartment €750-876 per week. Owned and run by the Royal College of Surgeons, this is perhaps the best student-accommodation

option in the city: cheaper than Trinity but just as central, close to Grafton St and St Stephen's Green. The rooms are modern and up to hotel standard. They are available from late June to late September only.

Dublin City University *(☎ 704 5736, fax 700 5777,* e *campus.residences@dcu.ie, Larkfield Apartments, Campus Residences, Dublin City University, Glasnevin)* Singles & doubles €22-32 per person. It's only 15 minutes by bus No 11, 11A, 11B, 13, 13A, 19, 19A, 36 or 36A from Trinity College/Eden Quay in the city centre, and these rooms at DCU's Glasnevin campus are airy and spacious, with plenty of amenities at hand, including a kitchen and common rooms.

Bed & Breakfast (B&B)
If you're looking for budget accommodation, but want the kind of privacy you're unlikely to find in hostels, then a B&B is your best option. Traditionally the most popular kind of accommodation in Ireland, Dublin's B&Bs have undergone something of a renaissance recently, as demands for greater luxury and amenities have forced many owners to renovate, upgrade and – inevitably – raise their prices. Today you'll find two kinds of B&B: the townhouse, the more traditional kind with two or three rooms in someone's home; and the guesthouse, a kind of upmarket, specialist, more expensive B&B. Though still cheap in comparison to most of the city's hotels, it's unlikely that you'll find any kind of decent room for less than €25 or €40 per person in a townhouse or guesthouse respectively. What you're paying for is the kind of attentive service not usually found in hotels, as well as the more homely atmosphere.

Aside from budgetary considerations, staying in a B&B or guesthouse does have its advantages, most notably that they present an opportunity to meet Irish people in a relaxed and informal setting. Furthermore, the breakfast you'll get is usually extremely good, and is usually big enough to tide you over until at least mid-afternoon. Be warned, however, that the standard breakfast is a 'fry', which means fried eggs, bacon, sausages and toast, washed down with tea or coffee. If you prefer not to

PLACES TO STAY

exceed every international guideline on cholesterol intake, most B&Bs also offer the option of a continental breakfast, usually bread, cereal and fruit. All the room prices in this section include breakfast.

Dublin's B&B street is Gardiner St. Virtually every house is a B&B, though some are better than others.

Farther out, you can find a better price and quality combination north of the centre at Clontarf or in the seaside suburbs of Dun Laoghaire or Howth. The Ballsbridge area, just south-east of the centre, offers quality and convenience, but you pay more for the combination. Other suburbs to try are Sandymount (immediately east of Ballsbridge) and Drumcondra (north of the centre toward the airport). The staff at tourist offices can make bookings and will direct you to a suitable choice of accommodation.

Since most B&Bs are small (between two and four rooms), they can quickly fill up, and with Dublin's increased popularity as a tourist destination, that can happen pretty much year-round. Your best bet is to book as far in advance of your arrival as possible, otherwise you might find yourself making dozens of phone calls in an effort to find a bed for the night. There's bound to be someone with a spare room, but you may find yourself some distance from the centre. If you arrive when accommodation is tight and don't like the location offered, the best advice is to take it and then try to book something better for subsequent nights.

North of the Liffey There is a collection of places on Lower Gardiner St, near the bus and train stations, and another group on Upper Gardiner St, farther north near Mountjoy Square. Other B&Bs are in the streets around it. Thankfully, the street's reputation for late-night danger has receded in the face of urban rejuvenation, though we still advise a modicum of caution at night, particularly on Upper Gardiner St past Mountjoy Square.

Fatima House (☎ 874 5410, fax 878 1734, e hotels@indigo.ie, 17 Upper Gardiner St) **Map 4** Singles €23-38, doubles €24-37. One of the cheapest B&Bs on the street, its rooms are slightly shabby and its

comforts a little bare. But the owners are friendly and for the price you won't find much better.

Marian Guest House (☎ 874 4129, 21 Upper Gardiner St) **Map 4** Rooms from €25 per person, €3 supplement for single occupancy. This tiny guesthouse has only six rooms, so the staff are attentive, even if the rooms are fairly basic. On the plus side, the breakfast is excellent.

Clifden Guesthouse (☎ 874 6364, fax 874 6122, e bnb@indigo.ie, w www.clifdenhouse.com, 32 Gardiner Place) **Map 4** Singles €38-76, doubles €32-70 per person. It's expensive, but it's a beautifully refurbished Georgian house with gorgeous rooms and plenty of amenities. A nice touch is the free parking, even after you've checked out!

Harvey's Guesthouse (☎ 874 8384, fax 874 5510, w www.harveysguesthouse.com, 11 Upper Gardiner St) **Map 4** Singles/doubles/quads €45/89/152.50, less during the low season. Spread across two attached houses, this guesthouse, just north of Mountjoy Square, has comfortable, en-suite rooms with high ceilings and old-style wooden-frame beds. The service is very friendly.

Stella Maris (☎ 874 0835, e stella maris@ireland.com, 13 Upper Gardiner St) **Map 4** Singles/doubles €38/71. This pleasant little B&B has basic but comfortable en-suite rooms.

Carmel House (☎ 874 1639, fax 878 6903, 16 Upper Gardiner St) **Map 4** Singles €44-57, doubles €32-69 per person. Everything here is clean and pristine; the nine en-suite rooms are comfortable and relatively spacious.

Lyndon House (☎ 878 6950, fax 878 7420, e lyndonh@gofree.indigo.ie, 26 Gardiner Pl) **Map 4** Rooms from €90. This is a beautifully restored house, with comfortable, en-suite rooms and extremely friendly service.

Othello Guesthouse (☎ 855 4271/5442, fax 855 7460, 74 Lower Gardiner St) **Map 4** Singles/doubles from €45/84. All the bedrooms in this popular, tidy place are en suite.

Dergvale Hotel (☎ 874 4753, fax 874 8276, 4 Gardiner Place) **Map 4** Singles/

doubles €57/102. This hotel offers en-suite rooms. It describes itself as a luxury hotel, and it is, but only if you consider clean sheets and fresh towels luxurious.

Drumcondra About 30 minutes' walk (3km, five minutes by bus) east of Upper O'Connell St (along Dorset St), on the road to the airport, is the leafy suburb of Drumcondra, a popular area for B&Bs. Most of the houses here are late-Victorian or Edwardian, and are generally extremely well kept and comfortable. As they're on the airport road, they tend to be full virtually throughout the year, so advance booking is definitely recommended. Bus Nos 3, 11, 11A, 16 and 36A from Trinity College/O'Connell St all stop along the Drumcondra Rd.

St Andrew's Guesthouse (☎ 837 4684, fax 857 0446, @ andrew@dublinn.com, 1 Lambay Rd) Singles/doubles €51/90. This place has lovely en-suite rooms, with elegant period beds. Bus Nos 36 and 36A stop along Griffith Ave.

Griffith House (☎ 837 5030, fax 837 0343, @ griffhse@indigo.ie, 125 Griffith Ave) Doubles €63.50. This elegant house on a beautiful, tree-lined avenue has four bedrooms, three of them en suite. Each room is tastefully appointed, with large, comfortable beds and nice furniture. The house is strictly non-smoking.

Tinode House (☎ 837 2277, fax 837 4477, @ tinodehouse@eircom.net, 170 Upr Drumcondra Rd) Singles/doubles €63.50/70. This beautiful Edwardian house has four elegant bedrooms, all with bathrooms. The welcome is very friendly.

Willow House (☎/fax 837 5733, @ willow _house@hotmail.com, 130 Upr Drumcondra Rd) Singles/doubles €45/70. This is a pleasant place to stay, with six bedrooms (five en suite). The rooms are basic but very clean and neat.

Clontarf You'll find numerous B&Bs along Clontarf Rd, about 5km north-east of the centre, but this is a busy, noisy road and the views are as much of oil terminals as of the sea. Bus No 30 from Abbey St will get you here for €1.25.

Sea Breeze (☎ 833 2787, 312 Clontarf Rd) Singles/doubles €45/63.50. A tiny place, with only three bedrooms (all en suite), this is your basic Dublin suburban residence: comfortable, friendly and informal.

Bayview (☎/fax 833 9870, @ carmeldrain @eircom.net, 265 Clontarf Rd) Singles/doubles €45/63.50. Overlooking Dublin Bay, this is a cosy enough place; it's nothing fancy but neat and clean. There's no smoking allowed.

Slievenamon Manor (☎/fax 833 1025 or ☎ 086 241 6493, 302 Clontarf Rd) Singles/doubles €45/63.50. This B&B, in a beautiful Edwardian home, has three en-suite rooms.

Hedigan's (☎ 853 1663, fax 833 3337, @ hedigans@indigo.ie, 14 Hollybrook Park) Singles/doubles €57/102. Inside a late Victorian residence a short walk from the seaside, Hedigan's has large, comfortable rooms and a period drawing room. You won't beat this place for atmosphere, and for the price, it's worth it.

Ferryview (☎ 833 5893, fax 853 2141, @ ferryviewhouse@oceanfree.net, 96 Clontarf Rd) Singles/doubles €76/114. This place is friendly and welcoming. The rooms are beautifully kept, with the usual array of modern conveniences.

South of the Liffey You'll find a number of the city's better-quality B&Bs on the south side.

Ballsbridge Ballsbridge is Dublin's embassy quarter and the location of a number of its more upmarket hotels. It's only a ten-minute bus ride from the city centre; bus Nos 5, 7, 7A, 8, 18 and 45 all stop in the area.

Andorra B&B (☎ 668 9666, fax 667 5881, @ andorrabandb@eircom.net, 94 Merrion Rd) Singles/doubles €57/90. This is a beautiful, family-run B&B with four comfortable rooms (three en suite). The decor is strictly suburban Irish, but the real quality is in the attentive friendliness of the owners.

Glenogra House (☎ 668 3661, fax 668 3698, @ gelongra@indigo.ie, 64 Merrion Rd) Singles/doubles €89/102. Opposite the

PLACES TO STAY

Royal Dublin Showgrounds, this tasteful Edwardian residence has 12 bedrooms, decorated in a thoroughly modern style. They're all en suite, with hot, powerful showers and with the usual amenities. It is strictly non-smoking.

Ariel House (☎ *668 5512, fax 668 58 45,* e *reservations@ariel-house.com, 52 Lansdowne Rd)* **Map 2** Singles & doubles €100.50. With 28 rooms, all en suite, this is hardly your average B&B, but not many B&Bs are listed Victorian homes that have been given top rating by Bord Fáilte. Recently restored to its 19th-century elegance, every room is individually decorated in period furniture, which lends the place an air of genuine luxury. If you have the dosh, this place beats almost any hotel – although solo travellers will be put off by the fact that you pay for the room, not the bed.

PLACES TO STAY – MID-RANGE

There is a hazy line dividing B&Bs, guesthouses and the mid-range hotels. Places in this bracket usually cost from €57 to €83 per person per night. Some of the small, central hotels in this category are among the most enjoyable places to stay in Dublin.

The mid-range places are a big jump up from the cheaper B&Bs in facilities and price, but still cost a lot less than Dublin's expensive hotels. Another advantage is that breakfast is usually provided (it generally isn't in the top-notch hotels), with fruit, a choice of cereals, croissants, scones and other assorted delights to supplement the bacon and eggs.

North of the Liffey

Maple Hotel (☎ *874 0225, fax 874 5239, 75 Lower Gardiner St)* **Map 4** Singles/doubles €56/102. Run by the same family for over 35 years, this is more of a traditional Dublin hotel, and it shows. The decor is a little bland, but it's not the kind of place where you'll linger long in the lounge. On the plus side, the bedrooms, all en suite, are spotlessly clean and the service is friendly and attentive.

Caulfields Hotel (☎ *878 0643, fax 878 1650,* e *caulfieldshotel@tinet.ie, 18-19*

Gay- & Lesbian-Friendly B&Bs

Although most of the city's hotels wouldn't bat an eyelid if same-sex couples checked in, the same cannot be said of many of the city's B&Bs. There are, thankfully, a couple that actively pursue a gay clientele.

Frankies Guesthouse (☎/fax *478 3087* e *frankiesguesthouse@ireland.com, 8 Camden Place)* **Map 5** Singles/doubles from €44/77. This is a comfortable B&B with pleasant rooms equipped with TV and tea & coffee-making facilities.

Inn on the Liffey (☎ *677 0828, fax 872 4165,* e *innontheliffey@hotmail.com, 21 Upper Ormond Quay)* **Map 5** Singles/doubles/triples €57.50/82.50/121 Sun-Thurs, €63.50/95.50/140 Fri-Sat. This is a friendly, popular B&B on the north-side quays. The rooms are clean and very tidy. Guests have free access to the sauna (see Gay & Lesbian Dublin in the Entertainment chapter).

Dorset St) **Map 4** Singles/doubles €57.20/102, higher rates at weekends. The 20 rooms here are all very, very cosy. Some might say small, but for the price you won't get a city-centre location with anything much bigger. Full Irish breakfast is included. There's nightly traditional music in the bar downstairs.

Castle Hotel (☎ *874 6949, fax 872 7674,* e *hotels@indigo.ie, 3-4 Great Denmark St)* **Map 4** Singles/doubles/triples €63.50 /114.50/171.50. This 36-room hotel is just off Parnell Square, a few minutes walk from O'Connell St but on the edge of the better part of north Dublin. This is one of Dublin's oldest hotels, with Georgian features in every room. Unlike the newer hotels, this place has big windows, which allow for plenty of light.

The Townhouse (☎ *8/8 8808, fax 878 8787,* e *gtrotter@indigo.ie,* w *www.town houseofdublin.com, 47-48 Lower Gardiner St)* **Map 4** Singles/doubles €67/102. This is one of our favourite places to stay in Dublin. Each of the rooms is decorated differently: some in a contemporary style, such as No 328, called 'A Japanese Miscellany' with light wood floors and furniture. Others are more flamboyantly Victorian, such as the highly memorable 'Rip Van Winkle' honeymoon suite (No 208), which has a four-poster bed draped in red velvet – and a working fireplace. Breakfast is included. It shares a dining room with the Globetrotters Tourist Hotel next door. There is also a small Japanese garden, in tribute to Lafcadio Hearn (aka Koizumi Yakumo, 1850–1904), the Irish-born writer credited with opening up the inner workings of Japanese society to western minds, who lived in No 48 as a youth. No 47 was the childhood home of Dion Boucicault (1820–90), a playwright and actor.

Wynn's Hotel (☎ 874 5131, fax 874 1556, e info@qwynnshotel.ie, 35-36 Lower Abbey St) **Map 4** Singles/doubles €82.50/120, more at weekends. Just off O'Connell St and only a few steps away from the Abbey Theatre, this older hotel has 70 rooms, all en suite.

Hotel Saint George (☎ 874 5611, fax 874 5582, e hotels@indigo.ie, 7 Parnell Sq East) **Map 4** Singles/doubles €70/121. In a restored Georgian building, this hotel oozes elegance and class. The 36 rooms, all en suite, are surprisingly large, with simple but graceful furniture and large, comfortable beds. It's a little slice of Parisian style in Dublin.

Walton's Hotel (☎ 878 3131, fax 878 3090, e waltons@eircom.net, 2-5 North Frederick St) **Map 4** Singles/doubles €70/127. This relatively new place has proven very popular with the business community. Although in a restored Georgian building, the rooms are thoroughly modern, if a little small, as to maximise their number they have sacrificed space. The hotel has its own dining room.

Ormond Quay Hotel (☎ 872 1811, fax 872 1909, e ormondqh@indigo.ie, 7-11 Upper Ormond Quay) **Map 5** Singles/doubles €108/142, less midweek. Beside the river, this hotel has a plaque outside noting its role in the sirens episode of *Ulysses*. The 60 rooms are clean and neat, even if the decor is a little loud: some rooms have bright yellow wallpaper with bedspreads to match. This

hotel is openly gay-friendly (see also the boxed text 'Gay- & Lesbian-friendly B&Bs' earlier in this chapter).

Jurys Custom House Inn (☎ 607 5000, fax 829 0400, e customhouse_inn@jurys doyle.com, w www.doylehotels.ie, Custom House Quay) **Map 5** Singles & doubles €82.50. The newest of the Jurys hotels, this has clean but small rooms decorated in a standard, unimaginative manner. It's a mid-range chain, so you can't really expect more.

South of the Liffey

As soon as you cross the Liffey, prices go up. What passes for a top-range hotel on the north side can often be considered akin to mid-range on the south side.

Aston Hotel (☎ 677 9300, fax 677 9007, e stay@aston-hotel.com, 7-9 Aston Quay) **Map 6** Singles/doubles €89/178. The Aston, just off O'Connell Bridge, is a comfortable hotel with 27 rooms and all modern facilities, including cable TV and en-suite bathrooms.

Number 31 (☎ 676 5011, fax 676 29 29, e number31@iol.ie, 31 Leeson Close) **Map 5** Rooms €60-115. Architect Sam Stephenson's (of Central Bank fame) former home has been converted into this lovely guesthouse. There are 19 tastefully appointed rooms.

Grafton Guesthouse (☎ 679 2041, fax 677 9715, e graftonguesthouse@eircom.net, 26-27 South Great George's St) **Map 7** Singles/doubles €63.50/114.50. In a Gothic-style building just off Dame St, this guesthouse has beautifully appointed en-suite rooms, even if they're a little cramped.

Eliza Lodge (☎ 671 8044, fax 671 8362, e info@dublinlodge.ie, 23-24 Wellington Quay) **Map 6** Singles/doubles €82.50/165. It's priced like a hotel, looks like a hotel, but it's still a guesthouse. Its 18 bedrooms are fabulous: comfortable, spacious and – due to its position right over the Millennium Bridge – with great views of the Liffey. Expect air-conditioning, multichannel TVs and, in the fancier rooms, even Jacuzzis.

The Fitzwilliam (☎ 660 0448, fax 676 7488, 41 Upper Fitzwilliam St) **Map 5** Singles/doubles €70/121. This small hotel is

PLACES TO STAY

central but is nevertheless quiet at night. There are 12 rooms, all en suite.

Jurys Christ Church Inn (☎ *455 0000, fax 454 0012,* e *christchurch_inn@jurys doyle.com,* w *www.doylehotels.ie, Christchurch Pl)* **Map 5** Singles & doubles €82.50. This big hotel immediately opposite Christ Church Cathedral is, like its sister hotels at Custom House Quay and Pembroke Rd, big, basic and boring, but it's clean, tidy and cheap at the price. The location is excellent.

Latchford's (☎ *676 0784, fax 662 2764,* e *latchfords@eircom.net,* w *www.latchfords -accomm.com, 99-100 Lower Baggot St)* **Map 5** Singles/doubles €88/138.50, less for week-long stays. Latchford's offers serviced rooms with self-catering facilities in an impressive Georgian house. There's an excellent bistro too.

Merrion Square Manor (☎ *662 8551, fax 662 8556,* e *merrionmanor@eircom.net, 31 North Merrion Sq)* **Map 5** Singles/doubles €77/140. This is a real find, and for the price (breakfast included), there's nothing more central that quite as nice. The 18 bedrooms are exquisitely decorated in a kind of nouveau Georgian style, a perfect marriage of 18th-century elegance and 21st-century convenience. The sitting room is straight out of a Merchant-Ivory film.

Staunton's on the Green (☎ *478 2133, fax 478 2263,* e *hotels@indigo.ie, 83 St Stephen's Green)* **Map 5** Singles/doubles €95/178. Staunton's is in a Georgian house in an excellent position, and you're charged for it (breakfast included). The rooms, however, are very pleasant, with fine Georgian floor-to-ceiling windows and tasteful decor.

Bloom's Hotel (☎ *671 5622, fax 671 5997,* e *blooms@eircom.net, 6 Anglesea St)* **Map 6** Singles/doubles €114.50/155. Bloom's Hotel, behind the Bank of Ireland, has 86 rooms. It has taken advantage of its prime position in Temple Bar to substantially raise its rates in the last couple of years, without necessarily raising its standards. The rooms, though tidy and neat, are nothing special, but the staff are extremely courteous and friendly. Breakfast is included in the price.

Camden Deluxe Hotel (☎ *478 0808, fax 475 0713,* e *info@camden-deluxe.ie, 84-87 Lower Camden St)* **Map 5** Singles/doubles €102/152.50. Above the old Theatre Deluxe (a listed building), the 34 rooms in this hotel are fairly simple but clean and neat. Downstairs, the old theatre is now the Palace Nightclub which, depending on your interests, is either a good thing or a real pain in the neck.

Harcourt Hotel (☎ *478 3677, fax 475 2013,* e *reservations@harcourthotel.ie, 60 Harcourt St)* **Map 5** Singles/doubles €127 /204. George Bernard Shaw lived in this Georgian building from 1874 to 1876. Today it is a pretty fancy hotel with pleasant, tastefully furnished rooms (breakfast included). Downstairs is the George Bernard Shaw Restaurant and the Velvet Nightclub. Luckily, you won't hear a thing when you sleep.

Central Hotel (☎ *679 7302, fax 679 7303,* e *reservations@centralhotel.ie, 1-5 Exchequer St)* **Map 7** Singles/doubles €132/190. The rooms here are rather small but, being a short distance from Dublin Castle, this renovated hotel is well located.

Paramount Hotel (☎ *417 9900, fax 417 9904,* e *paramount@iol.ie, Parliament St & Essex Gate)* **Map 6** Singles/doubles €102/152.50. This is the newest addition to Temple Bar's already long list of accommodation, and in its range, it's by far the best of the lot. Behind its Victorian facade is a genuine recreation of a 1930s-style hotel, complete with stained wood floors, deep red leather couches and heavy velvet drapes. The 70 rooms are decorated along similar lines, with plenty of dark wood and subtle colours. Downstairs is the Turk's Head (see the Pubs & Bars section in the Entertainment chapter). If you've got a bit of money to spend and want to stay in Temple Bar, we recommend this one above the rest. Breakfast is included.

Russell Court Hotel (☎ *478 4991, fax 478 4066,* e *reservations@russellcourthotel.ie, 21-25 Harcourt St)* **Map 5** Singles/doubles €203/229. This 42-room hotel is in a magnificent Georgian building. Single travellers should avoid this place, as the price of a single room (breakfast included) is outrageous. Doubles are more reasonably priced.

Elsewhere in Dublin

Mount Herbert Hotel (☎ 668 4321, fax 660 7077, e info@mountherberthotel.ie, 7 Herbert Rd, Sandymount, Dublin 4) **Map 2** Singles/doubles €75/114.50. Farther down, Lansdowne Rd changes its name to Herbert Rd, where you'll find this 180-room hotel about 3km from the centre. All the rooms here have bathrooms and breakfast is included. It's close to Lansdowne Rd DART station.

Roxford Lodge Hotel (☎ 668 8572/660 8813, fax 668 8158, e roxfordlodge@eircom .net, 46 Northumberland Rd, Ballsbridge, Dublin 4) **Map 2** Singles/doubles €76/178. Within walking distance of the city centre, this elegant hotel has 20 bedrooms that are decorated to the highest standards. The real bonus, however, is that 15 rooms have Jacuzzis, something ordinarily found only in the city's top hotels. You won't need us to tell you to make sure to ask for one when you book. Breakfast is included.

PLACES TO STAY – TOP END

Unless otherwise indicated, breakfast is included in the prices quoted.

North of the Liffey (Map 4)

Gresham Hotel (☎ 874 6881, fax 878 7175, e gresham@indigo.ie, 20-22 Upper O'Connell St) Singles/doubles €222/246.50. The rooms at this long-established hotel are elegant, and the bar is a great place to go for a drink, even if you're not staying here. There have been some complaints, however, about the attitude of the staff, who have been accused of being insensitive to the needs of guests who don't look like they could buy the place. It is still, though, a classy place. Breakfast is not included.

Royal Dublin Hotel (☎ 873 3666, fax 873 3120, e enq@royaldublin.com, 40 Upper O'Connell St) Singles/doubles €127/178. Perhaps its proximity to the Gresham – it's directly across the street – and the fact that it lives somewhat in the shadow of the more famous hotel – makes this place a better option for those looking for a more relaxed ambience without sacrificing any of the high-class service.

Clarion Hotel (☎ 836 6404, fax 836 6522, e info@clarionhotelifsc.com, Custom House Quay) Singles & doubles €210. This hotel opened in 2001 in the Irish Financial Services Centre, right on Custom House Quay. Not surprisingly, it is geared almost exclusively to the business set. Consequently, you will be charged a rate per room rather than per person. The cafe serves a pretty good selection of international fare, and there's also the San Vitae Health Club for guests. Breakfast is not included in the price.

Chief O'Neill's Hotel (☎ 817 3838, fax 817 3839, e reservations@chiefoneills .com, Smithfield Village) Doubles/suites €165/375. Part of the Smithfield Village complex that is home to Ceol (the traditional music museum), near the Old Jameson Distillery, this hotel has smallish but elegant rooms replete with extremely modern, minimalist furnishings. There are three very nice suites.

South of the Liffey

Buswell's Hotel (☎ 676 4013, 661 3888, fax 676 2090, e buswells@quinn-hotels.com, 23-27 Molesworth St) **Map 5** Singles/doubles €127/216. This hotel close to the National Museum is a Dublin institution. It opened in the 1920s and has recently been completely restored to its former glory. The 69 bedrooms are beautifully furnished. You have to pay extra if you want breakfast.

Longfield's (☎ 676 1367, fax 676 1542, e lfields@indigo.ie, 9-10 Lower Fitzwilliam St) **Map 5** Singles/doubles €115/178. This 26-room hotel between Merrion and Fitzwilliam squares is a little slice of Georgian heaven. The decor is elegant and subtle, and all the rooms are tastefully appointed.

Mercer House (☎ 478 2179, fax 478 0328, e mcrcsi@iol.ie, Lower Mercer St) **Map 7** Singles/doubles €146/184. From the outside it doesn't look like much but once inside, this is a pretty nice hotel, with elegant, spacious rooms.

Brooks Hotel (☎ 670 4000, fax 670 4455, e reservations@brookshotel.ie, 59-62 Drury St) **Map 7** Singles/doubles from €165/222. Rooms here are comfortable and

PLACES TO STAY

modern, even if the neo-Georgian furnishings are a little overbearing. Breakfast costs extra.

Clarion Stephen's Hall Hotel (☎ 638 1111, fax 638 1122, ℮ stephens@premgroup.ie, 14-17 Lower Leeson St) **Map 5** Singles/doubles €197/250. This hotel near the south-eastern corner of St Stephen's Green has 37 rooms, all with bathroom. Recently bought by the Clarion group, it has raised its standards somewhat and its prices by a lot. What you're paying for, however, is the kind of personalised attention available in the world's best hotels. Breakfast is not included.

Georgian House (☎ 661 8832, fax 661 8834, ℮ hotel@georgianhouse.ie, 18-22 Lower Baggot St) **Map 5** Singles/doubles €140/242. This is a fine old Georgian building that has recently been restored to pristine condition. Its 47 rooms all have attached bathroom, the breakfast is excellent and the restaurant is noted for its seafood. There's also a car park.

Mont Clare Hotel (☎ 661 6799, fax 661 5663, ℮ montclares@ocallaghanhotels.ie, ⓦ www.ocallaghanhotels.ie, Clare St) **Map 5** Singles/doubles €190.50/254. The elegant, 74-room Mont Clare Hotel is just off Merrion Square. Not quite in the deluxe league, it is still a fabulous place, with excellent service and large, comfortable rooms that thankfully are not of the cram-them-in mentality that afflicts so many of Dublin's newer hotels.

Burlington Hotel (☎ 660 5222, fax 660 8496, ℮ burlington_hotel@jurysdoyle.com, ⓦ www.doylehotels.ie, Upper Leeson St) **Map 2** Singles/doubles from €203/235. Ireland's largest hotel, the modern Burlington is 2.5km south of the centre, over the Grand Canal. Once the standard bearer for modernity in Dublin, a new business centre and 506 really comfortable rooms ensure that it will continue to be one of the city's better hotels.

Sachs Hotel (☎ 668 0995, fax 668 6147, 19-29 Morehampton Rd) Singles/doubles €115/190. **Map 2** This small, elegant, expensive place in the residential area of Ballsbridge has plenty of modern amenities

but still retains its Georgian style. It only has 20 rooms, all en suite.

Airport Hotels

There are two hotels on the grounds of Dublin airport, both of which are subject to a 15% tax on top of the price.

Posthouse Dublin Airport (☎ 808 0500, fax 844 6002, ℮ posthousedublin@hotmail .com, Dublin Airport) Singles/doubles €229/257. As you might expect from an airport hotel, this place is high on comfort and low on imagination – but who wants the latter at an airport? There is a 24-hour shuttle to and from the terminal, and guests can use the health centre free of charge.

Great Southern Hotel Dublin Airport (☎ 844 6000, fax 844 6001, ℮ res@dub airport.gsh.ie, Dublin Airport) Singles/doubles €190.50/204. Only two minutes from the main terminal by courtesy coach (which runs round the clock), this is a typical airport hotel: expensive, comfortable and primarily for business travellers.

PLACES TO STAY – DELUXE

London has its Ritz and Savoy, Paris its Crillon and George V, and New York its Waldorf and Four Seasons. Every city worth its salt must have its prohibitively expensive, outrageously luxurious hotels, and Dublin is no different. The hotels listed below are truly in a class of their own, and cater to the kind of visitor who stays on the comfortable side of the maxim: 'If you need to ask how much it is, you probably can't afford it.' We quote the prices anyway. Again, unless otherwise indicated, breakfast is included in the price.

Berkeley Court (☎ 660 1711, fax 661 7238, ℮ berkeley_court@jurysdoyle.com, Lansdowne Rd) **Map 2** Singles/doubles from €254/286. South-east of the centre in a quiet and relaxed location in Ballsbridge, the rooms here are spacious. The penthouse suite is popular with visiting dignitaries.

Fitzwilliam Hotel (☎ 478 7000, fax 478 7878, ℮ enq@fitzwilliam-hotel.com, St Stephen's Green) **Map 7** Singles/doubles from €280/330. This is yet another of Dublin's new deluxe hotels. The service is impeccable

The Liffey is Dublin's greatest physical and psychological divide.

Temple Bar Music Centre

O'Connell St: the city's main thoroughfare and most imposing street

One of Dublin's oldest areas, nowadays Temple Bar seethes with pubgoers and shoppers.

RICHARD CUMMINS

RICHARD CUMMINS

Night-time Dublin's more retiring side: Father Mathew Bridge over the Liffey and an uncharacteristically quiet Grafton St and its luxury unquestionable. Conrad Gallagher's Michelin-starred restaurant, Peacock Alley (see the Places to Eat chapter) is on the premises.

Davenport Hotel *(☎ 661 6800, fax 661 5663, **e** davenportres@ocallaghanhotels.ie, **w** www.ocallaghanhotels.ie, Lower Merrion St)* **Map 5** Singles/doubles €320/381. There are 120 rooms housed in what was once Merrion Hall, built in 1863 for the Plymouth Brethren (a Puritan religious sect). This hotel has everything, from a gym to 24-hour room service. The rooms aren't bad either, decorated to the heights of elegance. Breakfast isn't included.

The Clarence *(☎ 670 9000, fax 670 7800, 6-8 Wellington Quay, **w** www.the clarence.ie)* **Map 6** Singles/double suites/penthouse from €267/572/1905. So much has been written about how fabulous this U2-owned hotel is that it is bound to disappoint, and it does. The service is excellent, the rooms are beautifully appointed (if a little compact), but we suspect that what you're really paying for is hype. Even the outrageously expensive penthouse, with amazing views over the Liffey, is a little too small to justify this kind of dough. Prices don't include breakfast.

Conrad International *(☎ 676 5555, fax 676 5424, **e** info@conrad-international.ie, Earlsfort Terrace)* **Map 5** Singles/doubles from €260/280. The Conrad is a popular business hotel run by the Hilton group. South of St Stephen's Green, it offers 'corporate rates' to both businesspeople and tourists.

Méridien Shelbourne *(☎ 676 6471, fax 661 6006, **e** shelbourneinfo@forte-hotels .com, 27 St Stephen's Green)* **Map 5** Singles/doubles from €267/362. This is indubitably the best address at which to meet in Dublin. Recently bought by the Forte-Méridien group, there was uproar at the suggestion that its name might change, such is the status of Dublin's most famous hotel. The rooms are a little cramped, but its afternoon tea (€10 a head) is something all Dublin visitors should experience.

The Merrion *(☎ 603 0600, fax 603 0700, **e** info@merrionhotel.ie, Upper Merrion St)* **Map 5** Singles/doubles/main-house doubles from €267/292/375. In time, the Merrion may come to rival the Méridian Shelbourne as the city's most famous hotel. Occupying four Georgian houses (one of which is the reputed birthplace of Arthur Wellesley, the duke of Wellington), this hotel is strictly for those who can afford the best. The rooms in the main house are nicer than the more sterile annexe at the back.

Westbury Hotel *(☎ 679 1122, fax 679 7078, **e** westbury_hotel@jurysdoyle.com, Grafton St)* **Map 7** Singles/doubles from €292/330. Along with the Clarence, this is *the* celebrity hotel, a grand, modern place close to St Stephen's Green in a small lane just off Grafton St, south Dublin's pedestrianised main shopping street. Rooms on the upper floors offer views of the Dublin Hills.

Stephen's Green Hotel *(☎ 607 3600, fax 661 5663, **e** stephensgreenres@ocallagh anhotels.ie, **w** www.ocallaghanhotels.ie, St Stephen's Green)* **Map 5** Singles/doubles €356/381. You can't miss this stunning glass-fronted hotel on the south-western corner of St Stephen's Green. Inside, the rooms do not disappoint: thoroughly contemporary, they all come equipped with modem lines and other electronic gadgetry such as satellite TV.

Westin *(☎ 604 0400, 865 6390, **w** www .westin.com, Westmoreland St)* **Map 6** Rooms from €280. Dublin's Westin hotel opened in spring 2001 directly opposite Trinity College, probably the best spot in town. Behind the Georgian facade is a modern hotel with traditional touches.

Morrison Hotel *(☎ 878 2999, fax 878 3185, Lower Ormond Quay)* **Map 5** Rooms from €190.50. Dublin's only designer hotel (the interiors are the work of Irish fashion guru John Rocha) is as fabulous as it is expensive. With a couple of top-quality restaurants, six stunning suites and virtually every convenience known to a city-centre hotel, this is the north side's number one choice for visiting superstars.

SELF-CATERING ACCOMMODATION

The self-catering option is becoming increasingly popular with many travellers, especially families with small children. Considering the relatively high price of the city's hotels, it often makes sound financial sense, as well as offering the possibility of a home away from home. In the city centre, all self-catering options consist of one- or two-bedroom apartments, which usually also include a sitting room, bathroom and a separate kitchen.

Gogarty's Temple Bar Hostel & Apartments *(☎ 671 1822, fax 671 7281,* **W** *www .olivergogartys.com, 18-21 Anglesea St)* **Map 6** 1-/2-bedroom apartments from €108/171.50 per night. Run by the same folk who own the hostel in Temple Bar (see Hostels earlier in the chapter), the one-bedroom apartments sleep two, while the two-bedroom ones sleep four. Cots are available for small children.

Litton Lane Apartments *(☎ 872 8389, fax 872 0039,* **e** *litton@indigo.ie, 2-4 Litton La)* **Map 4** 2-bedroom apartments €82.50 per night. Run by the Litton Lane Hostel (see Hostels earlier in the chapter), these apartments are in a secure complex right next door. Each apartment has basic, modern furniture, a separate kitchen and bathroom, and two bedrooms. Each accommodates up to four adults, but a couple of spare mat-

tresses will cater for more – though the price goes up accordingly. Off season, the rates drop substantially, and even in the summer, in the unlikely event that they're not taken by the end of the day, you can get them for cheaper.

LONG-TERM RENTALS

Finding long-term accommodation in Dublin is difficult for Dubliners, never mind visitors from abroad. Bord Fáilte runs a service called Ireland's Reservation (☎ 1800 668 668) that specialises in reserving accommodation. However, while it can find places for up to six months or even a year, it charges a non-refundable deposit of 10% of the total price.

There are several lettings agencies in Dublin. ***Matthews Letting & Management*** **(Map 6)** *(☎ 679 2434, fax 679 2453, 40 Dame St)* specialises in long and short-term lets of apartments and houses, furnished or unfurnished. ***Home Locators*** **(Map 7)** *(☎ 679 5233, fax 679 2715, 35 Dawson St)* has a wide selection of properties on its books. It charges a €6.50 registration fee and then helps you locate suitable accommodation.

A few British newspapers, notably the *Daily Telegraph*, carry advertisements for long-term rentals in Ireland.

Places to Eat

Not surprisingly, Ireland's largest city is also the nation's culinary capital. It's not that Dublin's restaurants have a monopoly on serving the country's finest food – though there's no shortage of quality cuisine – it's just that there's so many of them. From the lowliest greasy-spoon diner serving the kind

Dublin Alfresco

Sure, you can jostle your way through a busy lunchtime crowd to find that the only available seat is a narrow six-inch space between someone screeching into a mobile phone and a couple on the verge of breaking up and then getting back together.

But, on a sunny, warm day, why bother when you can stretch out on a patch of grass and eat away under the sun? Dublin's parks and gardens are perfect spots for a bit of alfresco dining, either at lunch or, in the long stretch of the summer day, at dinner.

St Stephen's Green, at the top of Grafton St, is the most obvious choice, and you won't be alone – the park is a Dubliner's favourite. Trinity College, at the street's other end, is another great option, especially if there's a summer cricket match going on at the sporting grounds. Iveagh Gardens, off Harcourt St, behind Newman House, are a wonderful and relatively unexplored garden paradise right in the middle of the city. North of the river, the Garden of Remembrance on Parnell Square is another pleasant option. Farther afield, we recommend Dartmouth Square, only 100m or so off Leeson St at the south side of the bridge over the Grand Canal. Herbert Park in Ballsbridge is a huge park with plenty of picnicking options. Phoenix Park, Europe's largest enclosed park, is another great spot, with ample room for a bit of idyllic privacy.

Finally, a nice promenade along the Liffey between Capel St and O'Connell bridges, complete with seating, gives you the option of having a riverside lunch, though the presence of traffic behind you might be slightly off-putting.

of deep-fried food that your heart will resent you for to the fanciest, Michelin-starred restaurants where eating is a veritable culinary experience, you can find it in Dublin. Food is now a well worn topic of conversation: What you ate, where you ate it and how much it cost is a Dublin favourite, with choice restaurants developing the kind of cool kudos formerly reserved for nightclubs.

Always eager to copy its big brother London, Dublin has wholeheartedly embraced virtually every cuisine known to humankind. From tacos to Thai, Middle Eastern to Mongolian, you name it and Dublin's got it – even if in some cases the more exotic restaurants have compromised their menus to suit a more traditional Irish palate. Consequently, most Chinese restaurants in town feature two menus, one in English and another in Chinese, with the more adventurous dishes safely tucked away on the latter.

You will also notice that Dublin is awash with all kinds of hip restaurants with fabulous decor, stylish menus and staff who might seem more at home parading down a catwalk. But decor, beauty and plenty of press do not necessarily a good restaurant make, and all too often you'll end up eating a meal that is far from memorable... until you get the bill. In comparison to Paris or New York, good food is expensive here and you'll pay for the privilege.

What we've included here is a mix of the best, from the choicest cheap eats to the top spots. In the city centre, there are a variety of budget options, from the traditional pub lunch – filling and inexpensive – to a takeaway pita wrap at a sandwich bar.

FOOD

Most people assume that the potato is the staple of every Irish meal, and while it is true that Dubs love their spuds, there is far more to Irish dining than the *prátai* (Irish for potato). Irish cooking has been thoroughly overhauled in the last decade or so, but what has emerged is not some precious, namby pamby 'new Irish cuisine' but a return to fundamental principles. Vegetables, for so long over-boiled and over-steamed as to defeat their nutritional purpose, are treated with care and respect rather than as colourful dressing for meat. Led by such culinary luminaries as Dorina Allen of Ballymaloe House in County Cork, the best Irish chefs now insist on using only the freshest seasonal vegetables, as well as exploring the vast potential of every home-grown veggie. Today, the list is exhaustive: aside from the ubiquitous potato, Irish cooking now uses liberal helpings of asparagus, beetroot, broad beans, broccoli, cabbage (no longer boiled to a noxious pulp), Brussels sprouts, carrots, cauliflower, courgettes (zucchini), celery, cucumber, garlic, leeks, lettuces, mushrooms, onions, parsnips, peas, peppers, spinach and all kinds of seaweed. There's never been a better time to be a vegetarian.

But the Irish adore their meat. Statistically, they don't eat nearly as much as their European neighbours, but flesh of some description or another is the centrepiece of virtually every Irish meal. The Irish climate produces some of the healthiest animals and tastiest meat in Europe. Although many of the best-quality cuts are reserved for export, there's still enough left over to ensure that on the whole, the meat served in Dublin's restaurants is of an excellent standard. In the best restaurants, meat is cut with care and cooked with great imagination; in the cheaper places the emphasis is more on ensuring that you'll have your fill.

Pork (in all its shapes and guises) is probably the most common; from the ubiquitous Irish breakfast composed of pork sausages, rashers and black and white puddings to the perennial favourite of bacon and cabbage, poor old porky has fed generations of Dubliners and will continue to do so for a long time to come. Lamb is another favourite, but it is best in spring, so beware some restaurants trying to flog spring lamb year-round. But the real treat is beef, and Ireland has justifiably earned a reputation for bovine brilliance. Unusually, the Irish prefer heifer meat, which they consider to have a more delicate flavour. Thankfully,

Irish Dishes

There are various traditional Irish dishes and several restaurants in Dublin where you can find them – Gallagher's Boxty House and Paddy's Place, for example. Irish dishes and specialities you might like to try include:

Bacon & Cabbage a stew consisting of its eponymous ingredients

Barm Brack a cake-like bread

Boxty rather like a filled pancake

Dublin Coddle a semi-thick stew made with sausages, bacon, onions and potatoes

Guinness Cake a popular fruitcake flavoured with Guinness

Irish Stew a quintessential Irish stew of mutton, potatoes and onions, flavoured with parsley and thyme and simmered slowly

Soda Bread Belfast is probably the best place in Ireland for bread, but soda bread in particular, white or brown, is found throughout the country.

the Irish beef industry escaped unscathed from the BSE crisis that engulfed Britain in the 1990s, so you can eat away in safety.

The food revolution has also seen a new attitude to fish and seafood, for so long treated as penance food thanks to the Catholic Church's edict that meat was banned on Fridays, which resulted in most Irish households having no option but to eat fish. Most people will be familiar with smoked salmon, truly an Irish delicacy, but in recent years many Dublin restaurants have taken care to put at least two cooked fish dishes on their menu, such is the demand for the less fattening kind of flesh. Apart from the deep-fried cod that is the staple of the traditional fish'n'chips, you will find trout (usually rainbow, but the inland Brown trout is tastier), monkfish, brill, hake, sole, salmon, plaice, whiting and newer, seasonal fish such as orange roughy, red snapper and turbot. And then there's shellfish, from the cockles and mussels of the popular Dublin song 'Molly Malone' to more delicate kinds such as scallops.

Irish bread has a wonderful reputation and is indeed very good, but there's a tendency to fall back on the infamous sliced white bread (*pan* in Irish). B&Bs in particular are often guilty of this. Irish scones are a delight, and tea and scones make a great snack at any time of day. Even some pubs can rise to tea and scones these days.

DRINKS

The staple Irish drink is tea, and the Irish drink more of it per capita than any other nation in the world. Over 10,000 tonnes of leaf are imported each year, which works out at an average of four cups of tea per day for every man, woman and child. Although you can opt for all kinds of herbal and fruit teas these days, simply asking for a cup of tea will result in you being served black tea, usually from Kenya, with additional strains from China, India and Rwanda. The Irish love their tea medium to strong, nothing like the watered-down versions outside the country. Walk into any household in Dublin and we'll guarantee that no sooner have you crossed the threshold you'll be offered a cup.

Coffee is tea's poor relation but in recent years Dublin has seen a radical change in its preparation. Gone are the days when the only coffee you'd get is of the instant kind: today virtually every kind of continental-style coffee is readily available, from the basic 'white coffee' (percolated coffee with milk) to the heights of caffeine creativity.

Yet in Dublin (as the rest of the country) the question 'do you want a drink?' refers almost exclusively to the alcoholic kind, usually a lager or a stout. Stout usually means Guinness, the world-famous black beer of Dublin, though other brands – Murphy's and Beamish – are available. If you don't develop a taste for stout (and you should at least try while you're in Dublin), a wide variety of lager beers are available, although the Irish don't brew a particularly nice lager. Harp is pretty bland, and you're usually better off opting for the usual imported varieties such as Budweiser, Foster's or Carlsberg, which are brewed in Dublin under licence. Smithwicks (the 'w' isn't pronounced) is the only locally brewed ale.

Simply asking for a Guinness or a Carlsberg will get you a pint (570mL, €3.20 to €3.70 in a pub). If you want a half-pint (€2 to €2.15) ask for a 'glass' or a 'half'.

Spirits, often referred to as 'shorts' in Dublin, are of the usual kind, but there's nothing mundane about Irish whiskey, reckoned by many connoisseurs to be the best in the world (with apologies to Scotland!). Top of the heap is the very expensive Midleton, but you'll find that most whiskey drinkers opt for Bushmills, Jameson, Paddy or Power's. Jameson has perhaps the smoothest taste, while Paddy has a harsher flavour. Spirits cost between €2.90 and €3.20; mixers range from baby bottles of tonic water for around €1.40 to soft drinks for €1.90.

PLACES TO EAT

For the sake of clarity, places to eat are divided into four areas: north of the Liffey; Temple Bar; the Grafton St area; and Merrion Row, Baggot St and beyond. Dining north of the river essentially involves fast food, cheap eats or chains, but there are a handful of restaurants that rate among the best in the city. Temple Bar is the area with the highest concentration of restaurants, even though many offer average fare at high prices. It's bounded by the river to the north, Westmoreland St to the east and Christ Church Cathedral to the west. The southern edge is formed by Dame St and Lord Edward St, but restaurants on both the northern and southern side of Dame St are listed in this section. Grafton St, from Trinity College to St Stephen's Green, is the heart of the city, and while there aren't many restaurants on the street itself, the area around it has a wide variety of places. Merrion Row, leading south-east from St Stephen's Green, and Baggot St have an eclectic selection of restaurants.

PLACES TO EAT – BUDGET

Despite the influx of trendy restaurants that seem to charge as much for decor and ambience as they do for food, it is still possible to eat well without denting your budget too much. Like most cities, Dublin has its fair share of fast-food outlets both local and international, but we don't include them here because we feel that you can do a hell of a lot better. In their stead, we recommend Dublin's rich selection of cafes and small restaurants catering for those on a tight budget, especially students.

North of the Liffey

Isaac's Hostel & Hotel *(☎ 836 3877, 2-5 Frenchman's Lane)* **Map 4** Mains €5-7. Open 9am-6pm Mon-Sat. Isaac's has a good, though small, cafeteria.

O'Brien's *(☎ 878 2124, 1 Lower Liffey St)* **Map 5** Sandwiches €3-5. Open 9.30am-5.30pm Mon-Sat. This popular chain sells sizeable sandwiches; it gets pretty busy between 1pm and 2pm as it caters to an office crowd.

Cobalt Café & Gallery *(☎ 873 0313, 16 North Great George's St)* **Map 4** Mains €4-6.50. This splendid little cafe is our favourite on the north side. On the ground floor of an elegant Georgian building, it is bright and airy with a big fireplace to warm you up in the cold weather. The food is as good as the surroundings, with big sandwiches stuffed with fresh produce.

Epicurean Food Hall *(Lower Liffey St)* **Map 4** Lunch €4-10. Open 9.30am-5.30pm Mon-Sat. This is a fabulous new food hall with a selection of takeaway counters offering French, Italian, Mexican, Japanese, Indian and Turkish dishes. There's a seating area in the middle of the hall.

Bewley's Oriental Café *(☎ 677 6761, 40 Mary St)* **Map 4** Breakfast €5. Open 7.30am-6pm Mon-Sat, 7.30am-7pm Thur. Bewley's is a Dublin institution, but its food certainly is not. This place is recommended more for its coffees, teas and ambience, than for its overcooked, underheated and overpriced fries.

Paddy's Place *(☎ 873 5130, Dublin Fruit Market, St Michan's St)* **Map 4** Breakfast €3.20, lunch €5.20. Open 7.30am-3pm Mon-Fri. The food at Paddy's Place is as staunchly Irish as the name. It's next to the Dublin Fruit Market, between Chancery St and Mary's Lane; you can have an early breakfast or a filling lunch-time Irish stew or Dublin coddle.

Winding Stair Bookshop & Café *(☎ 873 3292, 40 Lower Ormond Quay)* **Map 5** Lunch €5-10. Open 10.30am-6pm Mon-Sat. One of our favourite places in Dublin, this beautifully dusty old bookshop has a cafe spread across the second and third floors. It's perfect for reading while you eat and the vegetarian selections are pretty good.

Panem *(☎ 872 8510, 21 Lower Ormond Quay)* **Map 5** Mains €6-9. Open 9am-5pm Mon-Fri, 10am-5pm Sat. Pasta dishes and focaccia sandwiches are pretty good at this quayside cafe; on a nice day you can sit along the boardwalk and enjoy your lunch alfresco.

Temple Bar

Gruel *(☎ 670 7119, 68a Dame St)* **Map 6** Breakfast €3.75, lunch €4.75. Open 7.30am-7.30pm Mon-Fri, 10.30am-5.30pm Sat. This is *the* best sandwich place in the city centre, with a daily-changing menu of sublime sandwiches. Gruel uses the best produce and the cuts of meat are generous, succulent and delicious. You can eat in or take away, in which case we recommend that you take your sandwich across the street to Castle Gardens, in front of the Chester Beatty Library.

Bewley's Oriental Café *(☎ 677 6761, 11-12 Westmoreland St)* **Map 6** All-day breakfast €5. Open 7.30am-9pm Mon-Sat, 8.30am-9pm Sun. This is probably the most beautiful of all the Bewley's coffee houses, virtually untouched for over a century. Unfortunately, the food tastes like it too. Stick to a drink and a scone or cake.

Café Irie *(☎ 672 5090, 11 Upper Fownes St)* **Map 6** From €3. It isn't – as the name suggests – even vaguely Jamaican (even if some of the dreadlocked customers might wish it so), but at Café Irie the sandwiches, served on a variety of breads (the ciabatta is particularly nice) are excellent, filling and cheap.

Joy of Coffee *(☎ 679 3393, 25 East Essex St)* **Map 6** From €3. They don't do a whole lot of food besides sandwiches, but the coffee here is some of the best you'll find anywhere in town: hot, frothy and delicious.

Café Gertrude *(☎ 677 9043, 3-4 Bedford Row)* **Map 6** From €5.50. This cafe, offering sandwiches, salads and pizzas, is hidden down a side turning and is therefore likely to have tables when other, more obvious, places are full.

Irish Film Centre (☎ 677 6788, 6 Eustace St) **Map 6** Lunch €6-8. The cafe here is a lovely place for a lunch-time snack – mostly sandwiches and bar food – or a full evening meal, including plenty of vegetarian choices.

Queen of Tarts (☎ 670 7499, Cork Hill) **Map 6** From €2.50. As the name suggests, this is a great place for pastries, both savoury and sweet. It's tiny, with only a handful of tables, making the Victorian atmosphere all the more intimate.

Simon's Place (☎ 679 7821, George's St Arcade, South Great George's St) **Map 7** From €3.20. This is a great hangout, serving pretty big sandwiches and good coffee to a loyal clientele. Unless you're a depressed Goth you'll want to avoid the downstairs part – it's dark and dingy. On warm days you can sit outside and watch Dublin go by.

Guy Stuart (George's St Arcade, Drury St) **Map 7** From €2.50. 'Slow-food' exponents Jenny Guy and Lara Stuart opened this food stall in the George's St Arcade a couple of years ago to immediate success. The emphasis is on fresh Mediterranean produce, to be savoured slowly and with relish, either in a sandwich or in their range of delicious soups.

Leo Burdock's (☎ 454 0306, 2 Werburgh St) **Map 5** €4-8. Open 5.30pm-11pm Mon-Sat. OK, so we've relented and mentioned one fast-food joint, but this place round the corner from Dublin Castle and next to the Lord Edward Pub is a Dublin legend. For years it was commonly accepted that it served the best fish'n'chips in Ireland, but since the original owner's death the place has allowed its standards to slip as it has become a tourist mecca. Still, the fresh cod in batter with a single of chips is still pretty mouth-watering. You can eat them down the road in the park beside St Patrick's Cathedral or in the gardens of Dublin Castle.

Da Pino (☎ 671 9308, 38-40 Parliament St) **Map 6** Lunch €6.50. There are almost no cheap restaurants in Temple Bar; this is the exception. The lunch menu – offering a selection of delicious pizzas or a minute steak – is hard to beat.

Grafton St Area

Café Java (☎ 670 7239, 5 South Anne St) **Map 7** Lunch from €6.50. Café Java serves pretty good lunches.

Munchies (☎ 679 9296, 2 South William St) **Map 7** (☎ 670 9476, Castlegate, 19-22 Lord Edward St) **Map 5** €3-5.10. Now with two branches in the city centre, Munchies is cleaning up on the lunchtime sandwich trade. They claim to produce the best sandwiches in Ireland. They're not *that* good, but you won't be disappointed.

Nude (☎ 675 5577, 21 Suffolk St) **Map 7** Wraps from €3.75. This ultra-cool place has been a huge hit since it opened, serving really tasty hot and cold wraps with all kinds of Asian fillings. You can eat in or take away, but be sure to try one of their freshly squeezed fruit juices.

Harvey's Coffee House (☎ 677 1060, 14-15 Trinity St) **Map 6** Around €6.50. Closed evenings. In the morning, you can fill up on bagels, scones and toast at this lovely little cafe near the tourist office in St Andrew's Church. At lunchtime they do big open sandwiches.

Blazing Salads (☎ 671 9552, Top floor Powerscourt Townhouse Shopping Centre) **Map 7** Lunch around €6.50. This popular vegetarian restaurant serves a variety of salads for €1 each.

Lemon (☎ 672 9044, 66 South William St) **Map 7** Pancakes from €3.20. Finally, a proper pancake joint in Dublin. And not one of those thick, American-style pancakes either, but thin *crêpes*, which you can get with savoury or sweet fillings (the Almond, Nut & Honey Delight is really good) or plain, with just a bit of butter and lemon.

Chompys' (☎ 679 4552, 1st floor Powerscourt Townhouse Shopping Centre) **Map 7** From €3.75. This place boasts bagels, pancakes and sandwiches for less than €6.50.

Alpha (☎ 677 0213, 37 Wicklow St) **Map 7** From €5.10. Celebrating its 101st birthday in 2001, the city centre's most traditional restaurant has recently passed into Turkish ownership. Eager to maintain its proud tradition of serving solid lunches and dinners to the city's working community, the place has remained unchanged, even

PLACES TO EAT

though some have complained that the new cooks aren't as good as the old ones. Plans are afoot to open a second restaurant on the floor above, serving Turkish cuisine.

Kilkenny Kitchen (☎ *677 7066, 1st floor 6 Nassau St*) **Map 5** Lunch from €6.50. Right opposite Trinity College, on the 1st floor of the Kilkenny Shop, this place serves generally excellent cafeteria-style food, but at times the queues can be discouragingly long. There's a snack counter which, at peak times, may be faster.

Dáil Bía (☎ *670 6079, 46 Kildare St*) **Map 5** From €5. The name means 'parliament food' in Irish, and it's appropriate: this basement cafe opposite the Dáil has a bilingual menu and Irish-speaking staff, but you don't need to be an Irish speaker to enjoy its menu, which places a premium on health food.

Café Metro (☎ *679 4515, 43 South William St*) **Map 7** Sandwiches from €2.50, salads €6.50. This popular cafe on the corner of South William and Chatham Sts has the friendliest staff in town, which keeps the clientele very loyal. The toasted sandwiches are good, but the real treats are the salads: the chicken Caesar is a real winner.

Busyfeet & Coco Café (☎ *671 9514, 41 South William St*) **Map 7** Lunch from €6.50. This recently opened cafe is one of the only places in town to serve a really good *chai*, a marvellous alternative to the stronger Irish tea and a good caffeine-free choice.

Cornucopia (☎ *677 7583, 19 Wicklow St*) **Map 7** Mains around €5.50. Open to 8pm Mon-Fri, to 9pm Thur, lunchtime Sat. If you want to avoid the Irish cholesterol habit, Cornucopia is a popular wholefood cafe creating healthy goodies. There's even a hot vegetarian breakfast to make a change from muesli.

Gotham Café (☎ *679 5266, 8 South Anne St*) **Map 7** Pizza from €6.50. This trendy and popular cafe serves a really good selection of pizzas.

Merrion Row, Baggot St & Beyond (Map 5)

Fitzer's (☎ *667 1301, The National Gallery, Merrion Square*) Mains €7-10.50. The National Gallery Fitzer's is the best branch of the Dublin chain. It's rather hidden away –

you have to go through the gallery (admission is free) to find it – but the artistic interlude makes a pleasant introduction to this popular, if slightly pricier, restaurant. It offers hot dishes, as well as salads, cakes and wine. The chain's take-away service, called ***Perk*** (☎ *660 0644, 24 Upper Baggot St*) is not far away.

The Coffee Club (☎ *667 5522, 4 Haddington Rd*) Sandwiches €4-8. Open 7am-7pm Mon-Fri, 9am-4pm Sat-Sun. This is a very trendy, popular place with great sandwiches and, at weekends, a really good brunch. It gets overcrowded at weekends, though.

PLACES TO EAT – MID-RANGE

There is a surprising number of affordable restaurants in Dublin, largely on the south side, and with new ones opening all the time the competition is fairly stiff, keeping prices at similar levels across the board.

North of the Liffey (Map 4)

101 Talbot (☎ *874 5011, 100-102 Talbot St*) Mains from €6.30. Open 5pm-11pm Mon, 5pm-10pm Tues-Sat. Close to the river, 101 Talbot makes a brave attempt to bring good food north of the Liffey. The prices are reasonable and the food well prepared and moderately adventurous. The emphasis is on Mediterranean and Middle Eastern cuisine.

Bangkok Café (☎ *878 6618, 106 Parnell St*) Mains around €10.50. Close to the Gate Theatre, the Bangkok Café may look a little rough around the edges but inside you'll find good Thai cuisine.

Temple Bar

Bad Ass Café (☎ *671 2596, 9-11 Crown Alley*) **Map 6** Pizzas around €9. This popular, cheerful, warehouse-style cafe offers reasonable pizzas in a convivial atmosphere and has pulleys to whip orders to the kitchen at busy times. Sinéad O'Connor once worked here as a waitress.

Il Baccaro (☎ *671 4597, Meeting House Square*) **Map 6** Mains €6.50-10.50. At the south-eastern corner of Meeting House Square (known as Diceman's Corner after a

PLACES TO EAT

mime artist who used to perform on Grafton St) this Italian trattoria's rustic cuisine is very popular with Dublin's Italian community. No wonder, considering that it's run entirely by Italians who know what they're doing in the kitchen.

Nico's (☎ 677 3062, 53 Dame St) **Map 6** Mains €9.50-15.50. Open lunch and dinner Mon-Sat only. On the corner of Temple Lane, Nico's offers conservative Italian food with a strong Irish influence. It's popular, and there's an entertaining piano player.

Osteria Antica Ar Vicoletto (☎ 670 8662, 5 Crow St) **Map 6** Mains less than €19. For a truly excellent Italian meal at reasonable prices, this place is hard to beat. The warm Gorgonzola salad is sublime and the spaghetti carbonara is as authentic as it gets.

Tante Zoé's (☎ 679 4407, 1 Crow St) **Map 6** Set lunch €19. Open noon-4pm, 6pm-midnight daily. The Cajun and Creole menu at this popular restaurant is served up in a suitably relaxed environment.

Eamonn Doran's Imbibing Emporium (☎ 679 9773, 3a Crown Alley) **Map 6** Mains €6.50. This idiosyncratically named place serves great burgers and fish. It's really a club, but serves food till 8pm. There's a three-course early-bird special (€13; up to 7pm).

Elephant & Castle (☎ 679 3121, 18 Temple Bar) **Map 6** Mains around €9. Open to 11.30pm Sun-Thur, to midnight Fri & Sat. Omelettes are a speciality at the popular, bustling but overpriced Elephant & Castle. This doesn't deter the fairly big queues for Sunday brunch.

Gallagher's Boxty House (☎ 677 2762, 20-21 Temple Bar) **Map 6** Mains €8-11.50. A boxty resembles a stuffed pancake and tastes like a bland Indian masala dosa. Real Irish food is not something that's widely available in Dublin so it's worth trying this popular place.

Fans Cantonese Restaurant (☎ 679 4263/4273, 60 Dame St) **Map 6** Mains from €9. The menu is pretty standard – easy on the western palate with the more adventurous dishes reserved for their Chinese customers. Standard, but far from average.

Good World Restaurant (☎ 677 5373, 18 South Great George's St) **Map 7** Lunch €8.50-10.50. This restaurant has the best Chinese food in the area. It is popular with the Chinese community, who choose their dishes from a Chinese menu rather than the one presented to locals. Needless to say, the former has more exciting dishes than the latter.

Juice (☎ 475 7856, Castle House, 73 South Great George's St) **Map 7** Meals around €6.50, smoothies €3.20-4.50. A super-trendy vegetarian restaurant, Juice puts an imaginative, California-type spin on all kinds of dishes. The real treat is the selection of fruit smoothies.

Belgo (☎ 672 7555, 17-19 Sycamore St) **Map 6** Lunch €6.50, dinner €25. The popular Belgo chain has finally come to Dublin, and brought its various good-value specials along with it. Apart from *moules et frites*, they serve dishes such as wild-boar sausages and some really good seafood. But what is with a place that advertises dozens of beers to accompany its heavy-on-the-heart menu but doesn't serve soft drinks because *they're bad for you*?

Bruno's (☎ 670 6767, 30 East Essex St) **Map 6** Mains around €10.50. Italian restaurateur Bruno Berta recently opened this lovely Italian restaurant where you can get tasty pasta dishes cooked as his mamma would have liked.

Dish (☎ 671 1248, 2 Crow St) **Map 6** Set lunch €15.50. Dish is pretty pricey, but good, with a strong emphasis on organic produce and a constantly changing menu.

Pub Grub You can soak up some of that stout without straying far.

Stag's Head (☎ 679 3701, 1 Dame Court) **Map 6** Lunch €6.50. For a good pub lunch, we recommend the Stag's Head. Apart from being a popular drinking spot, this place turns out simple, well prepared, filling meals in elegant Victorian surroundings.

O'Neill's (☎ 679 3671, 2 Suffolk St) **Map 7** Lunch €8-9. The carvery lunch at this city-centre pub is rightfully renowned for its quality and size, attracting a loyal crowd daily.

The Brazen Head (☎ 679 5186, 20 Lower Bridge St) **Map 3** Lunch around €8. This place, with a variety of menus offering everything from sandwiches to a carvery, is always packed at lunch time.

Grafton St Area

Bewley's Oriental Café *(☎ 677 6761, 78 Grafton St)* **Map 7** Mains around €11.50. Open 7.15am-11.30pm Mon-Sat, 8.30am-10.30pm Sun. Apart from fast-food joints, Bewley's is the only place in which to eat on Grafton St proper. This is the flagship branch of the chain, and a recent renovation has converted it from an old-style cafe to a restaurant, with table service and fancier dishes than the other branches, though you can still get a lovely cup of coffee and a bun.

Avoca Handweavers *(☎ 677 4215, 11-13 Suffolk St)* **Map 7** Mains around €9. On this shop's top floor is an excellent cafe-restaurant serving wholesome Irish cuisine.

Cedar Tree *(☎ 677 2121, 11A St Andrew's St)* **Map 7** Mains €8.90-15.50. This Lebanese restaurant has a good selection of vegetarian dishes.

Aya *(☎ 677 1544, Clarendon St)* **Map 7** Mains €10.50-20. Attached to the swanky Brown Thomas department store, this relatively new Japanese restaurant is the best in the city centre. There's a revolving sushi bar where you can eat your fill for €25 Sunday to Tuesday between 6pm and 8pm (maximum 55 minutes) or go a la carte from the great menu. There's an early-bird special (up to 8pm) nightly for €16.50.

Café Mao *(☎ 670 4899, 2-3 Chatham Row)* **Map 7** From around €10.50. Café Mao serves up interesting and varied Asian dishes. This is a popular lunch-time spot.

Imperial Chinese Restaurant *(☎ 677 2580, 12A Wicklow St)* **Map 7** Dim sum from €3.20 per dish. Open lunch and dinner daily. This long-established place is a favourite with the Chinese community and is noted for its lunchtime dim sum. The Imperial serves brunch Chinese-style in what is known as *yum cha* (the Chinese for 'drink tea'), the traditional accompaniment to dim sum.

The Odessa *(☎ 670 7634, 13 Dame St)* **Map 7** Mains €13-20.50. The Odessa is a super-trendy restaurant where you can eat well in comfort and style. Sunday brunch is a favourite with the city's hip young things.

Judge Roy Bean's *(☎ 679 7539, 45-47 Nassau St)* **Map 7** Mains from €9. Open noon-midnight. For a taste of Mexico, head to Judge Roy Bean's on the corner of Grafton St for popular tacos and an equally popular bar.

Trocadero *(☎ 677 5545, 679 9772, 3 St Andrew's St)* **Map 7** Mains around €13. Open to midnight Mon-Sat, to 11.30pm Sun. The Troc offers no culinary surprises, which is one reason why it's so popular. Simple food, straightforward preparation, large portions and late opening hours are its selling points.

Rajdoot Tandoori *(☎ 679 4274/4280, 26-28 Clarendon St)* **Map 7** Mains from €10.50, set lunch €11.50, set dinner €23. Visitors to India may remember Rajdoot as a popular brand of Indian motorcycle. In Dublin, however, the name is a byword for Indian cuisine at its very best, particularly the more aromatic flavours of North India. There are plenty of excellent vegetarian options as well.

La Mère Zou *(☎ 661 6669, 22 North St Stephen's Green)* **Map 7** Set lunch €15.50, early-bird menu €18 served 6pm-7.30pm daily. Open lunch and dinner Mon-Fri, dinner only Sat & Sun. This Belgian-owned restaurant specialises in Provençale and Alsatian cooking.

Pub Grub You can eat well at several pubs close to Grafton St.

Davy Byrne's *(☎ 677 5217, 21 Duke St)* **Map 7** Mains around €7.60. Food served noon-9pm daily. Davy Byrne's has been famous for its food ever since Joyce's Leopold Bloom dropped in for a Gorgonzola cheese sandwich and a Burgundy in *Ulysses*. It's now a swish watering hole.

The Bailey *(☎ 670 4939, 2 Duke St)* **Map 7** Lunch €7.50-9. This place serves up a 'new cuisine' version of pub grub, with subtle pasta dishes more common than a ham-and-cheese toastie

Modern Green Bar *(☎ 478 0583, 31 Wexford St)* **Map 5** Mains around €7.50. Food served noon-8pm daily. Only a couple of minutes' walk from St Stephen's Green, this relatively new bar serves a really good mix of pub grub, including pasta, Irish stew, curry, salads and the ubiquitous sandwiches. The portions are huge and the food delicious.

Merrion Row, Baggot St & Beyond

There's an international line-up of restaurants mixing with the colourful Baggot St pubs.

The Ante Room (☎ 660 4716, 20 Lower Baggot St) **Map 5** Mains around €14. Underneath the Georgian House hotel, The Ante Room is a seafood specialist with traditional Irish music on most summer nights.

Langkawi (☎ 668 2760, 46 Upper Baggot St) **Map 2** Set lunch €14. Langkawi has reasonable, affordable Pacific Rim cuisine.

Ocean (☎ 668 8862, Charlotte Quay Dock, Ringsend, Dublin 2) **Map 2** Mains from €9. Fresh seafood is the mainstay at this trendy, minimalist eatery on the corner of Grand Canal Basin. We recommend the oysters followed by a crab salad.

PLACES TO EAT – TOP END
North of the Liffey (Map 4)

Chapter One (☎ 873 2266/2281) Mains from €13. Open lunch Mon-Fri & dinner Tues-Sat. The south side has all of Dublin's great restaurants... bar one. This fabulous spot in the basement of the Dublin Writers' Museum gives all the others a run for their money in its unerring pursuit of the best of classic French cuisine. The set lunch (€22) might not have the full range of choices, but it's an affordable way to sample some of the city's best cuisine.

Temple Bar (Map 6)

In Temple Bar the trick is to find a restaurant where the food justifies the expense.

The Tea Rooms (☎ 670 7766, The Clarence, 6-8 Wellington Quay) Mains €11.50-22, set lunch €22. This is one of the trendiest restaurants in Dublin, but for once the food matches the hype.

Eden (☎ 670 5372, Meeting House Square) Meals from around €25. Open noon-3pm & 6pm-10.30pm daily. Eden is the epitome of Temple Bar chic, with good, solid dishes served in minimalist surround-

ings. You can eat for less than €25 but it'll cost you more to eat well. It's very popular so book in advance.

The Mermaid Café (☎ 670 8236, 22 Dame St) Meals around €32. Open lunch and dinner Mon-Fri, dinner only Sat & Sun. This place has a reputation as one of the better seafood restaurants in the city. The food is light and delicious, the surroundings bright and airy.

Grafton St Area

La Stampa (☎ 677 8611, 35 Dawson St) **Map 7** Mains €11.50-20.50, set lunch €14.60. Open until late. This is Dublin's upmarket Italian restaurant, with a large, attractive Georgian dining area and bright modern paintings.

Cooke's Café (☎ 679 0536, 14 South William St) **Map 7** Mains around €14. The best way to describe the menu at this top spot is California-meets-Italy, frequented by the bold and beautiful – at least judging by the number of Mercedes limousines often parked outside.

Peacock Alley (☎ 478 7015, Fitzwilliam Hotel, 109 St Stephen's Green) **Map 7** Lunch around €25.40, dinner around €50.80. This Michelin-starred restaurant is owned by bad-boy super-chef Conrad Gallagher. His speciality is French provincial cuisine and getting himself into trouble with the law (he was recently accused of selling paintings belonging to the hotel without their permission).

Velure (☎ 670 5585, 47 South William St) **Map 7** Closed Sun evening and Mon. Three-course meal about €38 (without wine). Velure opened in June 1999 with a menu (and prices) fit to match those of the Clarence Hotel's Tea Rooms. If you plan on splashing out during your trip to Dublin, this is the place to do it. Reservations are advisable.

The Commons (☎ 475 2597, Newman House, 85-86 St Stephen's Green) **Map 5** Six-course 'tasting menu' €77. The food here is exquisite but pricey; it's as well to book ahead, especially at weekends.

Shanahan's on the Green (☎ 407 0939, 119 St Stephen's Green) **Map 5** Steak around

€32. Open Mon-Sat eves. Dublin's first top-quality American-style steakhouse has been rightfully lauded for its steaks (vegetarians won't have much luck here), but you'll pay dearly for the privilege of being served one.

Merrion Row, Baggot St & Beyond

Restaurant Patrick Guilbaud *(☎ 676 4192, The Merrion, 21 Upper Merrion St)* **Map 5** Gourmet dinner menu €102, set lunch €28. Open lunch & dinner Tues-Sat. With two Michelin stars on its resumé, this elegant restaurant is perhaps one of the best restaurants in Ireland, and head chef Guillaume Le Brun does his best to ensure that it stays that way. Needless to say, reservations are essential.

Thornton's *(☎ 454 9067, 1 Portobello Rd)* **Map 2** 6-course 'surprise' menu €75. Open Tues-Sat eves, lunchtime Fri only. Kevin Thornton is probably the only chef in Dublin able to challenge Guilbaud's top-dog slot (see above), and he does so with a mouth-watering interpretation of new French cuisine. The service is faultless, if a little formal.

Lobster Pot Restaurant *(☎ 668 0025, 9 Ballsbridge Terrace)* **Map 2** Mains from €11.50. This old-fashioned place, out from the centre, offers substantial dishes in an equally substantial atmosphere; seafood is the house speciality and prices are reasonably high.

Roly's Bistro *(☎ 668 2611, 7 Ballsbridge Terrace)* **Map 2** Roly's Bistro receives rave reviews for its adventurous food; advance booking is advisable.

Old Dublin *(☎ 454 2028, 90 Francis St)* **Map 3** Meals around €32. Long specialising in Russian and Scandinavian dishes, in recent times this place has added greater variety to its menu, including a whole section for vegetarians. For atmosphere as well as the food, this place is worth the splash.

Ayumi Ya *(☎ 283 1767, Newpark Centre, Newpark Ave, Blackrock)* Lunch around €25, dinner around €32. It's worth making the trip out to the south Dublin suburb of Blackrock if you want to eat Japanese food at its best. The dining room is quite small (reservations are advised) but it is the combination of superb cuisine and truly excellent service that separates this place from the rest. Its sister restaurant, Aya, is in the city centre (see earlier in the chapter), but it doesn't compare.

Entertainment

Dublin is undoubtedly one of Europe's most vibrant entertainment capitals, with a wide variety of options to satisfy (nearly) every desire. It has theatres, cinemas, nightclubs and concert halls; stadiums, racecourses and dog tracks; but the real centre of activity is still the pub, and in Dublin there are about 700 of them to suit every taste and trend. There's little doubt that Dublin now has something for everyone – a far cry from the days when the most you could hope for was a few drinks in an old-fashioned pub and a bit of a dance in one of the basement clubs on Lower Leeson St. Today a thriving nightlife, with bars, cafes and clubs packed virtually every night of the week, has made the city one of the most popular getaway destinations in Europe.

Where to play? The most obvious and most popular area is Temple Bar, which transforms itself nightly into a party district with few rivals in Europe. It is extremely popular with groups of English on a stag or hen weekend – although in 1998 many of Temple Bar's publicans announced that they would no longer cater for these often loud and raucous groups because they alienated local trade. But with one or two exceptions the best, most authentic bars and clubs are outside Temple Bar's narrow, cobbled streets, albeit not too far away. While much of the city's nightlife is concentrated on the south side, 'in' Dubliners have begun conquering the north side of the Liffey, where a number of very trendy bars have opened to great success. Although it's still a nascent scene, word is that the area immediately north of the river, from the Grattan Bridge in the west to Butt Bridge in the east, is *the* new place to see and be seen.

For entertainment information, pick up a copy of the weekly music review *Hot Press* (€2.50), the *Event Guide*, a bimonthly freebie available at many locations, including bars, cafes and hostels or the fortnightly magazine *In Dublin* (€2.50). Wednesday's *Irish Times* (€1.25) has a pull-out entertainment section called *The Ticket* that has comprehensive listings of clubs and gigs. The *Evening Herald* (€0.85), a city tabloid, also has a weekend pull-out on Thursday listing all events throughout the weekend. During the high season, Dublin Tourism publishes *Events of the Week*, a free leaflet listing all kinds of activities. A newer free monthly magazine, *The Slate*, also has a comprehensive list of what's going that is both informative and extremely funny.

PUBS & BARS

For information on the city's many and varied drinking establishments see the Pubs & Bars special section later in this chapter.

CLUBS

A few years ago, Dublin was awash with billboards that showed a sweaty, packed dance club with the words 'Open Your Windows, Tokyo, Dublin's Having a Party' across the top. Much of Dublin's success as a tourist destination comes from the fact that the city has developed a reputation as one of the party hotspots of Europe, despite the fact that nightclubs close earlier than in any other European capital!

Antiquated opening hours aside, Dublin's reputation is duly deserved. The small size of the city centre, coupled with the relative youth of Dublin's population, means that on virtually any given night you are bound to find crowds of clubbers looking for a place to dance. The Irish fondness for having a good time should not be underestimated either; it is a quality that has attracted foreigners to the capital in their thousands, all in search of the same.

Needless to say, nightclubs are big business in Dublin, and their close proximity to one another means that they are a competitive lot. Independent promoters are brought in by owners to define and refine the identity of each club, with the result that almost every night means something different. So you might find that one place does a drum-and-bass night on Sunday, followed by a

All Brawn and No Brain

You're out with friends, enjoying a Friday night. You saunter up to a bar, when all of a sudden a large man in black trousers, black bomber jacket and an earpiece sticks out a meaty paw and says nonchalantly, 'Not tonight, I'm afraid'. Those words are like a steel door quickly shutting you out, and there's nothing you can say or do that will open it up again. If you try to argue, you'll just harden his resolve not to let you in. If you argue too much, you might get a punch for your trouble.

This little scenario is played out thousands of times a week at many of Dublin's city-centre bars. The protagonists are bouncers, hired by the owner to provide security, but empowered to act as Dublin's fashion police. The problem is that most of them don't know the difference between fashion and fascism.

Initially, the dress code was designed to keep out two kinds of people. The first are Dublin's poorer working classes; the second are known as 'travellers', and are the Irish version of the European nomadic gypsies, who have been the victims of a virulent type of Irish racism for many decades. In years gone by, both were known for wearing sporting apparel, and despite the fact that sportswear is now at the height of fashion, the rules are simple: no tracksuits, no trainers. Not even a pair of €150 Nikes will do the trick; they just don't fit the bill.

But it isn't as simple as that. In some pubs, you need to fit a certain 'look', arbitrarily dictated by the doormen and constantly changing depending on who's trying to get in. In 2000, a documentary TV crew secretly filmed a group of young, well-dressed Irish men, which included two blacks, as they sought to gain entrance to 10 city centre pubs. With only one exception, the two black men were denied entry everywhere, while the whites were admitted without so much as a second glance. When confronted, the bouncers denied that they were being racist, and made up alternative reasons for not allowing them in.

As of July 2001, it has been illegal to exclude anyone from a public house because of how they appear. The problem remains, however, because bouncers don't have to tell you why they're not letting you in, or, if pressed, they just make something up. Thankfully, not all of the city's bouncers have become rude tyrants of their own little kingdom. Some are polite, friendly and courteous and judge potential entrants not by the clothes they wear but by their state of inebriation (it is illegal to serve alcohol to the visibly intoxicated) or their potential for troublemaking (alas a problem in Dublin). We only wish there were more of this breed of bouncer.

deep-house night on Monday, progressive house on Tuesday, techno on Wednesday and so on. The busiest nights are, invariably, Thursday to Saturday, but you can find something to suit your taste every other night of the week, as well as a crowd to share it with.

The seemingly endless list of 'what's on' is constantly changing, so check out the *In Dublin* listings and the *Event Guide* to keep abreast of the scene. Most clubs open just before pub-closing time (usually between 11.30pm and midnight) and close at 2.30am or 3am. Admission to most is between €5.10 and €7.60 on weekdays, rising to up to €12.70 at weekends. For discounts, look out for the thousands of fliers that are distributed around most of the city centre's pubs.

The PoD (Place of Dance; ☎ 478 0166, 35 Harcourt St) **Map 5** Dublin's most renowned nightclub, this futuristic, metal-gothic cathedral of dance attracts a large weekend crowd of twenty-somethings. To get past the notoriously difficult bouncers you'll really need to look the part. Sunday night is Odyssey, when the crowd goes mad to techno and house.

Red Box (☎ *478 0225, 35 Harcourt St*) **Map 5** Upstairs from the PoD, this is actually the coolest dance club in town. The floor is enormous and the crowds readily fill it up. Look out for the big-name international DJs who play here regularly.

The Kitchen (☎ *677 6635, The Clarence, 6-8 Wellington Quay*) **Map 6** In Temple Bar, this U2-owned place is surprisingly laid back, considering its widespread fame. The music is hard and fast on a pretty small and often claustrophobic dancefloor, while the back bar is usually patronised by celebrities and those eager to see and be seen. Tuesday night features the long-running Genius club, with some really smooth techno.

Switch (☎ *670 7655, 11 Eustace St*) **Map 6** Beneath a cheesy bar, this is one of our favourite nightclubs in town: It's small, sweaty and seriously hip, with a terrific selection of different dance beats mixed by excellent local DJs, helped along by international guests. Regular nights include a drum-and-bass extravaganza on Friday, techno on Saturday and the superb Central on Sunday night, featuring the city's best deep and funky house. On Monday night, the club hosts Freedom, a popular gay night.

Eamonn Doran's Imbibing Emporium (☎ *679 9773, 3a Crown Alley*) **Map 6** Open nightly. This is a large place with food, drink and music (mostly rock). On Monday night, however, it hosts Melting Pot, easily Dublin's best hip-hop night.

Rí Rá (☎ *677 4835, Dame Court*) **Map 7** Open nightly from 11.30pm. Rí Rá is one of the friendlier clubs in the city centre and is full almost every night of the week. Refreshingly, the bouncers here are friendly, funny and very fair. The musical emphasis is on funk, both old and new, with ne'er a house beat to be heard.

Parnell Mooney (☎ *873 1544, 71 Parnell St*) **Map 4** This late-night bar at the top of O'Connell St is only worth going to on a Wednesday, when it hosts the fabulous Firehouse Skank, Dublin's only hard reggae and dub night.

The Shelter (☎ *454 5533, Vicar Street,* *58-59 Thomas St*) **Map 4** A 300-capacity venue attached to the larger room has begun hosting a selection of clubs; the best of them is Velure on Saturday night, with a compelling mix of funky soul, Latin and percussive house that has generated a die-hard, loyal following. If you get in before midnight it's free.

Lillie's Bordello (☎ *679 9204, Adam Court, off Grafton St*) **Map 7** Lillie's is strictly for the well heeled – the favourite nightclub of local and visiting celebrities. As you might expect, the music is mostly safe and commercial.

Renard's (☎ *677 5876, South Frederick St*) **Map 5** Renard's is not quite as snooty as Lillie's, but it tries to be. The problem is, the big stars just aren't interested, so it has to settle for the little ones, as well as the wannabes.

Temple Bar Music Centre (☎ *670 9202, Curved St*) **Map 6** There's something going on nightly at the TBMC to suit every taste, from funk and disco to guitar-driven indie rock.

Break for the Border (☎ *478 0300, Lower Stephen St*) **Map 7** This huge, country-and-western style eatery reverts to a nightclub once the pubs close. It's good fun, if a little cheesy, and is renowned in Dublin as one of the biggest pick-up joints around.

The Vatican (☎ *478 4066, Russell Court Hotel, 21-25 Harcourt St*) **Map 5** Open Tues-Sat. This club offers precious little in terms of decor, but that doesn't seem to stop the droves of young people who flock to here. It's especially popular with British weekenders.

GAY & LESBIAN VENUES

Dublin's gay scene has never been more confident, more relaxed or more fun. Irish attitudes to homosexuality may still bear a conservative, traditional stamp in rural areas, but in Dublin nothing could be further from the truth. For a country with such a traditionally Catholic (hence anti-gay) reputation, laws that affect gays and lesbians are both progressive and respectfully liberal – despite the fact that homosexuality was only decriminalised in 1993 (among men, that is, as lesbianism was never illegal).

House – the predominant form of dance music heard in most of Dublin's clubs – had its roots in New York's 1970s gay culture, and that tradition is very much alive in Dublin today. Arguably, the city's best club nights are gay nights that – though not exclusive to gays and lesbians – advertise themselves openly as such. But the gay and lesbian scene is about much more than dancing. There are a handful of pubs in the city centre that cater predominantly to the city's growing gay community, while most others (at least the trendy, newer bars) don't mind what your sexual preferences are, so long as you're there to enjoy yourself and buy drink.

The fabulous annual Mardi Gras parade takes place over the last weekend in May, while the annual Alternative Miss Ireland pageant, now celebrating its eighth year, is another great event enjoyed by the bulk of Dublin's gay community. It usually takes place during the third weekend in March (call ☎ 873 4932 for details of both).

The *Gay Community News*, a free monthly give-away available in bars and cafes across the city, is a good newspaper that mixes serious issues affecting the gay community as well as more fun stuff such as club listings and bars. See also the Gay & Lesbian Travellers section in the Facts for the Visitor chapter.

Pubs

Gubu (☎ 874 0710, Capel St) **Map 5** This relatively new bar was fairly quiet when it first opened, so it changed tack and began advertising itself as a gay and lesbian bar: And it worked. Nicknamed 'gaybu', it is a stylish alternative to the increasingly dodgy Out on the Liffey. It opens at 4pm daily.

Out on the Liffey (☎ 872 2480, 27 Upper Ormond Quay) **Map 5** The north side's gay and lesbian stronghold for many years, this pub has developed a bit of a rough reputation, mostly due to party drugs. It is still a great bar, however, despite the presence of ever-watchful bouncers who are there to ensure that the place doesn't go too crazy. Saturday is men's night, while on Wednesday is the popular karaoke night, open to both men and women.

The George (☎ 478 2983, 89 South Great George's St) **Map 7** You can't miss the pink neon lettering of Temple Bar's only overtly gay bar, directly opposite The Globe. This huge place is full virtually every night, and on Sunday night there's the enormously popular gay bingo, which packs the place out.

Front Lounge (☎ 670 4112, 33-34 Parliament St) **Map 6** This sophisticated bar is popular with the cubs of the Celtic Tiger. The back section of the bar, known as the Back Lounge, has become a popular meeting place for the city's upwardly mobile gay and lesbian community.

Molloy's (☎ 677 3207, 13 High St) **Map 3** Near Christ Church, this bar has a lesbian-only night on Saturday called Stonewallz.

Clubs

There are plenty of clubs that run gay and lesbian nights. The scene is constantly changing, however, and while the nights mentioned below are pretty regular and steady, we recommend that you call ahead to confirm that they're still on.

Candy Club (☎ 677 6635, The Kitchen, The Clarence, 6-8 Wellington Quay) **Map 6** A regular Monday-night gay and lesbian club that is pretty relaxed.

Freedom (☎ 670 7655, Switch, 11 Eustace St) **Map 6** This Monday-night regular at one of Dublin's finest clubs sticks to a fun-but-safe formula of churning out house anthems and disco classics.

HAM (☎ 478 0166, The PoD, 35 Harcourt St) **Map 5** Friday night's HAM, aka Homo Action Movies, is one of Dublin's most enduring gay and lesbian nights – it's now all of five years old! The soundtrack is thumping house, uplifting and progressive.

Libida (☎ 817 3838, fax 817 3839, Chief O'Neill's Hotel, Smithfield Village) **Map 4** This excellent funk, big beat and Latin club has had several homes over the last few years. At the time of writing it was held in Chief O'Neill's hotel on Saturday night, but check the *Gay Community News* to see if it has moved.

[continued on p189]

TEMPLE
BAR
Estb. 1840

THE
EMPEROR
OF
MALTED LIQUORS
GUINNESS

Pubs & Bars

Title page: Dublin is probably the finest pub capital in the world. Pub culture runs deep: in the 17th century, one in five houses sold alcohol. (photographer: Richard Cummins)

Top: Pubs have a long tradition of live music, from rock bands to the more traditional jam sessions.

Middle: The Gravity Bar, atop the Guinness Storehouse, is a fine place to mull over any weighty matters.

Bottom: The Brazen Head, near Temple Bar, Dublin's busiest pub district.

DOUG McKINLAY

HANNAH LEVY

OLIVER STREWE

DOUG McKINLAY

PUBS & BARS

JANE SMITH

Since Irish life is so tied up with pub culture, a visit to one of the many pubs spread throughout the city is an absolute must. Despite the challenges of 'Europeanisation' – cafes, clubs and restaurants – the pub is still the hub of much of the social activity in the city. It is a meeting point for friends and strangers alike, the place where Dubliners are at their friendly and convivial best (and, it must be said, sometimes their drunken and incoherent worst!). Although there are about 700 pubs across the city (an average of one per 1119 population), many of those in the city centre are packed to the rafters most nights. This applies particularly to Temple Bar, which may officially be Dublin's 'cultural quarter' but once the sun goes down is more like Ibiza in the rain. In the summer months the cobbled streets are filled with thousands of Dubliners and foreigners, all out for a good time. A revealing statistic is that 15% of Dublin pubs have a turnover in excess of €1.25 million per year. And Dubliners are not yet satisfied. Even the relaxation of the licensing laws in 2000, which has seen pub hours extended later into the night (see the end of this section for details), is seen by many as being not nearly enough. To many Dubliners, the pub-opening laws, introduced during WWI to ensure that workers made it to the munitions factories on time, are antiquated relics that show little regard for people's free will. Meanwhile, the government continues to discuss further liberalisation, but change is surely destined to be slow and piecemeal.

Dublin's pub-going tradition has a long history. Even in medieval times the city had many drinking establishments, and in the late 17th century a survey revealed that one in every five houses in the city was involved in selling alcohol. A century later another survey counted 52 public houses along Thomas St in the Liberties alone. There may not be quite so many pubs today but Dublin still has a huge selection, so there's no possibility of not finding a Guinness should you develop a terrible thirst.

Apart from imbibing large quantities of alcohol, the Irish have also been responsible for some important developments in the field of drink production. They were pioneers in the development of distilling whiskey (distilled three times and spelt with an 'e', as opposed to the twice-distilled Scotch whisky). The Irish also adopted the dark British beer that had become known as porter due to its popularity with the porters at London's Covent Garden market. Promoted by the Guinness family, it soon gained an enduring stranglehold on the Irish taste for beer.

Yet you may be disappointed at the apparent disappearance of the traditional pub and the modernisation of the city's historic pubs, especially in Temple Bar, where this is most evident. Alas, it is becoming more and more difficult to find a pub whose decor has been untouched for 50 years and whose main feature isn't a 250-watt stereo system but a snug, a partitioned-off section where you can meet friends in privacy under low lighting. Some snugs have their own serving hatches, so drinks can be passed in discreetly should the drinkers not want to be seen ordering 'just the one'. In a rush to cash in on the tourist renaissance, tacky uberbars have sprung up around the city, serving bland beer (even in Dublin you can find a terrible pint of Guinness) in equally bland surroundings. But a few places have opened in recent years that can proudly hold their own as fine examples of modern Dublin pubs, offering a new home to the traditions that have made Dublin perhaps the best pub capital in the world.

Dublin pubs also have a long and proud tradition of live music, from rock bands to the more traditional *seisúns* – semi-improvised jam sessions that are at the heart of all Irish traditional music. See Walking Tours under Organised Tours in the Getting Around chapter for information on the highly recommended Literary and Musical Pub Crawls, which offer a fine introduction to some of Dublin's pubs on balmy summer nights. Be sure to check ahead as schedules can be wildly erratic. Extended opening hours mean that pubs now close at midnight from Monday to Wednesday (last drinks served at 11.30pm), 1am Thursday to Saturday (last drinks at 12.30am) and 11.30pm on Sunday (last drinks 11pm). However, many also avail themselves of late licenses, which means they can serve up until around 1.45am. Unless otherwise indicated, all pubs mentioned in this section are on the Dublin's Pubs & Bars map on the next page.

North of the Liffey

Traditional Slower to benefit from the Celtic Tiger's facelift, a number of the north side's traditional bars have been 'rediscovered' by south-siders looking for the genuine drinking experience.

The Oval (☎ 872 1259, 78 Middle Abbey St) This popular journalists' hangout is just off O'Connell St.

Flowing Tide (☎ 874 0842, 9 Lower Abbey St) Directly opposite the Abbey Theatre, this place attracts a great mix of theatregoers and north-side locals. It's loud, full of chat and a great place to drink.

Patrick Conway (☎ 873 2687, 70 Parnell St) Although slightly out of the way, this place, just across from the UGC Multiplex, is a true gem of a pub. It has been operating since 1745, and no doubt new fathers have been sipping celebratory pints here since the day the Rotunda Maternity Hospital opened across the road in 1757.

Joxer Daly's (☎ 860 1299, 103-104 Lower Dorset St) This Victorian-style pub is conveniently close to the Young Traveller and An Óige hostels. A word of warning, however; if you're in this area late at night, you should be particularly vigilant because the streets around here have been plagued by crime and a certain amount of violence due to heroin abuse.

Ryan's (☎ 677 6097, 28 Parkgate St) **Map 3** Near Phoenix Park, this is one of only a handful of city pubs that has retained its Victorian

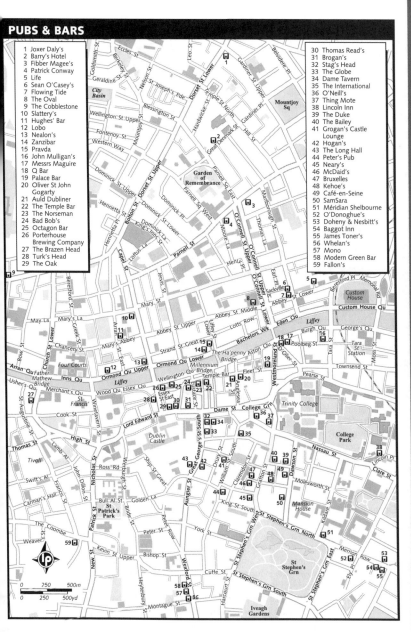

PUBS & BARS

1 Joxer Daly's
2 Barry's Hotel
3 Fibber Magee's
4 Patrick Conway
5 Life
6 Sean O'Casey's
7 Flowing Tide
8 The Oval
9 The Cobblestone
10 Slattery's
11 Hughes' Bar
12 Lobo
13 Nealon's
14 Zanzibar
15 Pravda
16 John Mulligan's
17 Messrs Maguire
18 Q Bar
19 Palace Bar
20 Oliver St John Gogarty
21 Auld Dubliner
22 The Temple Bar
23 The Norseman
24 Bad Bob's
25 Octagon Bar
26 Porterhouse Brewing Company
27 The Brazen Head
28 Turk's Head
29 The Oak

30 Thomas Read's
31 Brogan's
32 Stag's Head
33 The Globe
34 Dame Tavern
35 The International
36 O'Neill's
37 Thing Mote
38 Lincoln Inn
39 The Duke
40 The Bailey
41 Grogan's Castle Lounge
42 Hogan's
43 The Long Hall
44 Peter's Pub
45 Neary's
46 McDaid's
47 Bruxelles
48 Kehoe's
49 Café-en-Seine
50 SamSara
51 Méridian Shelbourne
52 O'Donoghue's
53 Doheny & Nesbitt's
54 Baggot Inn
55 James Toner's
56 Whelan's
57 Mono
58 Modern Green Bar
59 Fallon's

decor virtually intact, complete with ornate bar and snugs. An institution among Dublin's public houses, this is truly worth the trip. To get here, take bus No 23, 25 or 26 from the city centre.

JANE SMITH

Kavanagh's *(aka the Gravediggers'; 1 Prospect Square, Glasnevin, Dublin 9)* **Map 2** This pub, backing on to Glasnevin Cemetery, is where you can drink one of the best pints of Guinness in town, served in an atmosphere that appears not to have changed in 150 years. Here you'll find an older Dublin, unhurried and not so concerned with modernity. What you won't find, however, is a phone – far too contemporary for this wonderful spot. Bus No 13 from O'Connell St goes to Glasnevin.

Music Away from the tourist meccas of the south side, the city's north side is the best place to hear traditional music.

Slattery's *(☎ 872 7971, 129 Capel St)* On the corner of Mary's Lane, Slattery's is considered by many to be the home of Dublin pub rock.

Sean O'Casey's *(☎ 874 8675, 105 Marlborough St)* There's a weekly menu of live rock and Irish traditional sessions at this place.

Keating's *(☎ 873 1567, 10 Jervis St)* This is a modern bar with a nightly traditional seisún.

Fibber Magee's *(☎ 874 5253, Gate Hotel, Parnell St)* Fibber Magee's is a bit of a dive but has nightly music from DJs and live rock bands.

Barry's Hotel *(☎ 874 6943, 1 Great Denmark St)* The bar here is home to a time-honoured country music session.

Nealon's *(☎ 872 3247, Capel St)* There's live jazz on Sunday at this popular bar at the bottom of Capel St (near the river).

The Cobblestone *(☎ 872 1799, 77 North King St)* This is a splendid bar bordering Smithfield Square where traditional musicians usually play until after closing time. The quality of the music is excellent.

Hughes' Bar *(☎ 872 6540, 19 Chancery St)* By day, this pub is popular with barristers, solicitors and their clients from down the street in the Four Courts, all of whom probably need a pint – for different reasons! By night, however, once the last wigs have gone, this is where you'll hear some of the best traditional music in the city. The owner's son is an extraordinary fiddle player.

Other Pubs The north-side scene may not be quite the match of what's going on south of the Liffey, but there's a number of trendy hangouts that are drawing more and more crowds from across the river.

Pravda *(☎ 874 0076, 35 Lower Liffey St)* Pravda, near the Ha'penny Bridge, is Russian in name only. It's a big place, relaxed and easy-going. When it is full, however, the bouncers have been known to keep a careful eye on dress codes.

Zanzibar *(☎ 878 7212, 36 Lower Ormond Quay)* This enormous bar actually seems to pride itself on keeping you waiting before allowing you in. The African theme is slightly obnoxious, as are the attitudes of the staff, but if you can ignore them (which isn't hard to do) it can be a lot of fun.

Life *(☎ 878 1032, Irish Life Mall, Lower Abbey St)* This stylish bar near Busáras and Connolly Station may have lost some of the 'cool' appeal it had when it opened, but it's still a good place to spend a weekend night.

Lobo *(☎ 878 2999, Morrison Hotel, Upper Ormond Quay)* This is the north side's version of Temple Bar's Octagon Bar, only far more difficult to get into if you don't look the part. If you haven't spent a fortune on your outfit (or managed to fake it), forget it. If you do gain access, your prize is to spend an evening in the company of Dublin's well-to-do social climbers. We suggest you put this guide away before you attempt to get in here!

The Glimmer Man *(☎ 677 9781/4560, 14-15 Stoenybatter)* **Map 4** It's slightly out of the way, to the west of Smithfield, but this is a terrific bar. In warm weather, the beer garden out the back is a great place to enjoy a pint. Take bus No 38, 39 or 39A from Middle Abbey St or Essex Quay to get here.

Temple Bar

Traditional The refurbishment of Temple Bar has sadly left its cobbled streets virtually devoid of old-style, traditional pubs; with only a couple of exceptions, the pubs that have retained their old-world charm and nicotine-stained walls are outside the area's boundaries.

Palace Bar *(☎ 677 9290, 21 Fleet St)* With its mirrors and wooden niches, Palace Bar is often said to be the perfect example of an old Dublin pub. It's within Temple Bar and is popular with journalists from the nearby *Irish Times*.

John Mulligan's *(☎ 677 5582, 8 Poolbeg St)* Just off Fleet St, outside the eastern boundary of Temple Bar, John Mulligan's is another pub that has scarcely changed over the years. It featured as the local in the film *My Left Foot* and is also popular with journalists from the nearby newspaper offices. Mulligan's was established in 1782 and has long been reputed to have the best Guinness in Ireland, as well as a wonderfully varied collection of regulars.

Brogan's *(☎ 679 9570, 75 Dame St)* Only a couple of doors down from the Olympia Theatre, this is a wonderful old-style bar where conversation – not loud music – is king. The beer is also pretty good.

Stag's Head *(☎ 679 3701, 1 Dame Ct)* At the intersection of Dame Court and Dame Lane, just off Dame St, the Stag's Head was built in 1770 and remodelled in 1895, and is sufficiently picturesque to have featured in a postage-stamp series of Irish pubs.

The Long Hall *(☎ 475 1590, 51 South Great George's St)* Luxuriating in full Victorian splendour, this is one of the city's most beautiful and best-loved pubs. Check out the ornate carvings in the woodwork behind the bar and the elegant chandeliers. The bartenders are experts at their craft, an increasingly rare attribute in Dublin these days.

The Brazen Head *(☎ 679 5186, 20 Lower Bridge St)* West of Temple Bar, just south of the Liffey, is Dublin's oldest pub, though its history is uncertain. The pub's sign proclaims that it was founded in 1198, but the earliest reference to it dates back to 1613 and licensing laws did not come into effect until 1635. The present building dates from 1668, and the sunken level of the entrance courtyard clearly indicates how much street levels have altered since its construction. In the 1790s it was the headquarters of the United Irishmen, who apparently talked too much after a few drinks, leading to numerous arrests being made here. At that time Robert Emmet was a regular visitor. James Joyce mentioned it in *Ulysses* with a somewhat half-hearted recommendation for the food: 'You get a decent enough do in the Brazen Head'.

Music Some of Temple Bar's pubs advertise traditional Irish music: how good it is remains questionable, but it's certainly fun.

Oliver St John Gogarty *(☎ 671 1822, 58-59 Fleet St)* The traditional music sessions at this pub at the junction of Fleet and Anglesea Sts are extremely popular with tourists, most of whom don't mind that the music is less than authentic.

Dame Tavern *(☎ 679 3426, 18 Dame Court)* Directly opposite the Stag's Head, this is a hard-drinking bar, where the only nonalcoholic entertainment is the sport-spewing TV and the weekend bands that go through the catalogue of 1970s and '80s rock anthems with comfortable ease.

The Brazen Head (see Traditional under Temple Bar) has the occasional folk session.

Other Pubs There are bars to suit every taste in this area, from loud rock to minimalist joints that cater to the city's super-trendy.

The Norseman *(☎ 671 5135, 27-29 East Essex St)* This refurbished watering hole in the heart of Temple Bar is popular with an eclectic mix of people, from European tourists to businesspeople, as well as its traditional crowd, who are an interesting blend of theatre folk and left-wingers.

The Temple Bar *(☎ 677 3807, 48 Temple Bar)* When it was Flannery's, this was the area's original small-crowd boozer, but a massive refurbishment has seen it grow

JANE SMITH

JANE SMITH

bigger and more raucous; it even has a beer garden. At weekends the place is packed.

Auld Dubliner (☎ 677 0527, 17 Anglesea St) This bar is predominantly patronised by tourists, who come for its carefully manicured 'olde worlde' charm, still preserved after a couple of renovations. As a result, it's dubbed the 'Auld Foreigner'.

Bad Bob's (☎ 677 5482, 35 East Essex St) Open until late. Recently reopened after a two-year refurbishment, this huge place is Temple Bar's disco-bar *par excellence*: the music is loud and almost exclusively chart-orientated, and the crowd young enough to really enjoy it.

Octagon Bar (☎ 670 9000, The Clarence, 6-8 Wellington Quay). Temple Bar's trendiest watering hole is where you'll find many of Dublin's celebrities and their hangers-on. Drinks are marginally more expensive than elsewhere but judging by the clientele that have passed the bouncer's strict entry test this is hardly a concern.

Turk's Head (☎ 679 9701, 27-30 Parliament St) This is one of the oddest – and so most interesting – bars in Temple Bar. Decorated in two completely different styles – one really gaudy, the other a recreation of LA circa 1930 – it attracts a huge crowd nightly. It's very, very popular with the tourists.

Porterhouse Brewing Company (☎ 679 8847, 16-18 Parliament St) This microbrewery and pub has dared challenge the legendary supremacy of Guinness. Those who tell you that its Wrassler XXXX is the best stout in the city wouldn't be far wrong.

Thomas Read's (☎ 670 7220, 1 Parliament St) The clientele at this spacious, airy bar spread across two levels seems to favour a selection of wine and coffee over beer. During the day, it's a great place to relax and read a newspaper. For a more traditional setting, its annexe, The Oak, is still a great place for a pint.

The Globe (☎ 671 1220, 11 South Great George's St) The Globe is one of the first of a new breed of trendy pubs to open in the city. Still immensely popular, it is one of the few 'cool' pubs in town not to give a fig what you look like. Consequently, it is truly hip.

Hogan's (☎ 677 5904, 35 South Great George's St) Once an old-style, traditional bar, Hogan's is now a gigantic boozer spread across two floors. A popular hangout for young professionals, it gets very full at weekends with folks eager to take advantage of its late licence.

Messrs Maguire (☎ 670 5777, 1-2 Burgh Quay) This is a gigantic uber-bar spread across three levels connected by a truly imperious staircase. At weekends, there are literally thousands of people crammed into it.

Q Bar (☎ 677 7835, O'Connell House, D'Olier St) Owned by the same folk who own Messrs Maguire (virtually next door), this is another huge place, only the style is much more modern, with plenty of chrome and velvet. There are DJs nightly, but to get in you'll have to run the gauntlet of bouncers, who can be selective.

Grafton St Area

Traditional Amidst the designer shops and trendy eateries of the Grafton St area are a few top-notch pubs where Victorian elegance and traditional style pulls in the punters.

Kehoe's (☎ 677 8312, 9 South Anne St) This is one of the most atmospheric pubs in the city centre and a favourite with all kinds of Dubliners. It has a beautiful Victorian bar, a wonderful snug and plenty of other little nooks and crannies. Upstairs, drinks are served in what was once the publican's living room – and looks it!

McDaid's (☎ 679 4395, 3 Harry St) McDaid's was Brendan Behan's (see the boxed text 'Deep Thinker, Heavy Drinker' in the Facts about Dublin chapter) 'local', but is little more than a tourist trap these days. It's better during the day, when you can really appreciate the Gothic decor.

In Search of the Best Guinness

In Irish pubs, talk is just as important as the beer and the talk will often turn to the perfect Guinness. But just what is the perfect pint? Proximity to the St James's Gate Brewery is one requirement, for although a Guinness in the Ivory Coast can still be a fine thing, it's frequently asserted that Guinness at its best can only be found in Ireland.

Long-time drinkers have a million and one ideas of what the perfect pint is, but a good test of quality is the following. When you're about halfway through the pint, look at the sides of the glass; if there are rings of white foam around the inside edge (the thicker the better), then you can be sure the pint is a pretty good one.

Personnel is also important. The apprenticed bartender is sadly a dying breed, but a few who have served a full apprenticeship in the trade still remain, and it is not just their skill in pouring the pint, but their diligence in ensuring that the glasses and pipes are kept clean that will make the difference.

The pouring of the pint is, of course, vital. The glass should be tilted at a 45-degree angle under the tap, which is pulled forward and the black liquid pours against the back of the glass. When it is about three-quarters full it is set to one side to 'settle', which means that the heavier black liquid settles underneath the lighter, creamy top. Once the pint's white head has fully formed – which should take about two minutes – the glass is once more stuck under the tap, but this time the tap is pushed back so that only black liquid (without any froth) fills the rest of the pint. The glass is once more allowed to settle before serving.

Last, and most importantly, is your palate. Guinness is an acquired taste, it's true, but once you've got used to its slightly bitter taste (English ale drinkers will have no problems at all), you'll find that your ability to discern a good pint from a bad one is much better than you think.

So where will you find the best pint? Below we have set out a short itinerary that will take you the pubs that are commonly believed to serve the best pint. We have taken care to include only those pubs where atmosphere – that intangible but all-important factor – makes for greater enjoyment, a real Guinness experience. All the pubs mentioned below are included in this section.

Begin at the source, it is said, and the source is the *Guinness Storehouse* **(Map 3)**. Not surprisingly, the brewery that makes the stuff also serves the nicest pint, cold and delicious. From the elevated Gravity Bar you can survey the lay of the land that you will be travelling through. When you're done, take a right outside the storehouse entrance and walk around to Thomas St via Echlin St. Take a left on Thomas St and walk westwards for a couple of hundred metres

Neary's (☎ 677 8596, 1 Chatham St) Neary's is a showy Victorian-era pub with a particularly fine frontage and is popular with actors from the nearby Gaiety Theatre. The upstairs bar is one of the only spots in the city centre where you stand a chance of a seat on a Friday or Saturday night.

Grogan's Castle Lounge (☎ 677 9320, 15 South William St) This place is known simply as Grogan's (after the original owner), and it is a city-centre institution. It has long been a favourite haunt of Dublin's writers and painters as well as others from the Bohemian, alternative set, most of whom seem to be waiting for the 'inevitable' moment when they are finally recognised as geniuses. A peculiar quirk of the pub is that drinks are marginally cheaper in the area with a stone floor than in the carpeted lounge, even though they are served by exactly the same bar!

In Search of the Best Guinness

and take a right down Steeven's Lane. Cross the river over Frank Sherwin Bridge and take a left up to Parkgate St. On your right is **Ryan's (Map 3)**, one of the city's finest Victorian pubs and a splendid stop for a pint (or two).

Your next destination is back down the Liffey towards town, so you can opt to take a taxi or catch bus No 25, 25A or 26 at Islandbridge (just outside the pub to your left) and get off at Father Mathew Bridge. Recross the river and walk about 50m up Bridge St to **The Brazen Head** on your right. Dublin's oldest pub serves a really great pint pulled expertly by the long-standing bartenders.

If you're really participating in this mini-crawl you'll most likely be feeling the effects of your activities by now, so your next destination won't seem nearly as far away. Walk up the hill (southwards) to Christ Church Cathedral and take a left on High St. Take a right down Werburgh St, stopping for food at **Leo Burdock's chipper (Map 5)** – believe us, you'll need it for later on. Continue southwards along the street and take a left on to Upper Stephen's St. Continue until you reach Aungier St and take a left. About 100m or so down the street (which turns into South Great George's St) you'll reach the fourth of our chosen pubs, **The Long Hall**, another Victorian gem that is well worth the stop.

Next, walk northwards to Dame St, take a right, and walk until you reach Anglesea St on your left. You are now in the heart of Temple Bar. Walk northwards on Anglesea St and take a left on to Fleet St. On your left you'll find (if you can see by this stage) the **Palace Bar**, a well worn and favoured hangout for the city's literary types. If anyone knows a good pint of Guinness, it's Dublin's journalists and aspiring novelists!

Take a left from the Palace Bar and cross Westmoreland St and D'Olier St, always on Fleet St. At the **Screen Cinema (Map 5)**, take a left down Hawkins St and the first right onto Poolbeg St. Here you'll find the inimitable **John Mulligan's**, where the Guinness is a thirst-quencher, a favourite conversational topic, a tonic and – to many of the regulars – a way of life.

You now have a choice as to the final leg of our crawl. You can either make your way south-westwards, back via Aungier St, turning right onto Kevin St and going as far as the Coombe where you'll find **Fallon's**, one of the city's great 'locals', or you could head northwards across the Liffey to Glasnevin and **Kavanagh's**, also known as the Gravediggers' because it is frequented by the gravediggers of the adjacent Prospect Cemetery. Even if you could walk at this stage you wouldn't want to; the best way of getting here is by bus No 13 from O'Connell St.

JANE SMITH

Music You won't find traditional music round here, but good, old-fashioned rock, as well as a little jazz.

The International (☎ 677 9250, 23 Wicklow St) The International has live jazz and blues most nights.

Bruxelles (☎ 677 5362, 7-8 Harry St) This place has weekly live rock music, perhaps the only connection the now-trendy pub has to its heavy-metal past.

Mono (☎ 478 0391, 30 Wexford St) This large pub is spread over two floors and the decor is all futuristic neon lights and metal, befitting the techno and house acts that provide the musical entertainment.

*Whelan's (☎ 475 8555, 26 Wexford St, **W** www.whelanslive.com)* This is one of the premier venues for live music in Dublin, of the singer-songwriter kind at least. Their Web site lists all upcoming gigs. The attached bar is old-fashioned and quite pleasant.

Other Pubs Dublin's trendiest area is naturally where you'll find many of the city's trendiest pubs.

The Bailey (☎ 670 4939, 2 Duke St) This is one of two pubs on Duke St made famous by James Joyce in *Ulysses* (the other is Davy Byrne's). Neither pub bears any resemblance to its Joycean predecessor, but it is The Bailey that has come out best. Wall light boxes, comfortable, minimalist seating and a continental lunch menu ensure that this place is popular with business folk and older trendies.

The Duke (☎ 679 9553, 9 Duke St) The Duke is a fairly bland-looking bar (thanks to a bad refurbishment) but the crowd is less pretentious and more relaxed than in any of the other bars along Duke St.

O'Neill's (☎ 679 3671, 2 Suffolk St) This is a fine old pub near Trinity College, and it has long been a student haunt.

Thing Mote (☎ 677 8030, 15 Suffolk St) Just off Grafton St, this grungy little bar is very popular with students. At night it is almost too popular, but during the day it is a nice *thing mote* (the Anglo-Saxon for 'meeting place').

Café-en-Seine (☎ 677 4369, 40 Dawson St) This was Dublin's 'in' bar when it opened in 1995, but has slipped in the face of stiff competition. So the owners decided to overhaul the place, and by the time you read this it will have reopened with a new look and the same old crowd.

SamSara (☎ 671 7723, 35-36 Dawson St) A very new addition to the pub scene, this place is absolutely huge and themed to look like a huge Middle Eastern tea house. The terminally trendy immediately flocked to it and stayed, air kissing and comparing designer gear with the best of them.

Modern Green Bar (☎ 478 0583, 31 Wexford St) This is one of our favourite new bars in town. The decor is fairly simple, but it is highlighted by a series of beautiful digital photos tracing the flow of the Liffey from source to mouth. What people come here for, however, is the combination of great music (there are DJs nightly) and a convivial, friendly atmosphere that attracts both students and professionals alike. The all-day menu is also excellent (see the Places to Eat chapter).

JANE SMITH

Peter's Pub (☎ 677 8588, 1 Johnston Place) This is a quiet, pleasant bar at the top of South William St that is great for early evening drinks.

Horseshoe Bar (Méridian Shelbourne; ☎ 676 6471, St Stephen's Green) A joke in Dublin is that the major political decisions of the day aren't made in the Dáil but in the Méridian Shelbourne's Horseshoe Bar. Politicians of every hue rub shoulders with journalists and businessfolk in a fairly relaxed atmosphere – the perfect ambience for Irish politicking!

Merrion Row, Baggot St & Beyond

Traditional Away from the city centre there are a number of fine pubs worthy of the trek.

James Toner's (☎ 676 3090, 139 Lower Baggot St) Toner's, with its stone floor, is almost a country pub in the heart of the city. The shelves and drawers are reminders that it once doubled as a grocery shop, not that its be-suited business crowd would ever have shopped here...

Doheny & Nesbitt's (☎ 676 2945, 5 Lower Baggot St) This pub is equipped with antique snugs and is a favourite place for high-powered gossip among politicians and journalists; Leinster House is only a short stroll away.

Hartigan's (☎ 676 2280, 100 Lower Leeson St) **Map 5** This is about as spartan a bar as you'll find in the city, and is the daytime home to some serious drinkers, who appreciate the quiet, no-frills surroundings. In the evening it's popular with students from the medical faculty of University College Dublin (UCD).

Lincoln Inn (☎ 676 2978, 19 Lincoln Place) What is it about medical students and dingy bars? If UCD students love Hartigan's (see above), then their Trinity equivalents flock to this pokey little hole at the back of the college. Perhaps doctors-to-be like slumming it before they hit pay dirt. Don't be put off by the complete lack of decor: this is a wonderful little place with an ambience created entirely by its clientele.

Fallon's (☎ 454 2801, 129 The Coombe) Just west of the city centre in the heart of medieval Dublin, this is a fabulously old-fashioned bar that has been serving a great pint of Guinness to a most discerning clientele since the end of the 17th century. Prize fighter Dan Donnelly, the only boxer ever to be knighted, was head bartender here for a while in 1818.

Music The best traditional music can be heard outside the city centre, but there are also a couple of places worth checking out for rock music.

O'Donoghue's (☎ 661 4303, 15 Merrion Row) This is the most renowned traditional music bar in all Dublin, where the world-famous folk group The Dubliners started out in the 1960s. On summer evenings a young, international crowd spills out into the courtyard beside the pub.

Baggot Inn (☎ 676 1430, 142-143 Lower Baggot St) This is a popular pub for live rock music.

Comhaltas Ceoltóiri Éireann (☎ 280 0295, 35 Belgrave Square Monkstown) **Map 2** Serious aficionados of traditional music should make the trip here. The name, pronounced 'keol-tas quail-tori Erin', means 'Fraternity of Traditional Musicians of Ireland', and it is here that you'll find the best Irish music and dancing in all of Dublin, featuring some of the country's top players. Take bus No 7, 7A or 8 from Trinity College, or DART to Seapoint. From Monkstown village (where the bus will drop you), follow the blue signs. It's a five-minute walk from Seapoint DART station.

Other Pubs Listed below are pubs worth making a journey for.

Odeon (☎ 478 2088, Old Harcourt St Station, 57 Harcourt St) **Map 5** At the top of Harcourt street, this is a gigantic place with a 50m-long bar and ample space for the hundreds of punters who flock there to show off their designer gear.

Thomas House (☎ 671 6987, 86 East Thomas St) **Map 3** This place is a real dive, and so is very popular with the alternative crowd, who love its total absence of decor and its great music, played by DJs nightly.

The Clock (☎ 677 5563, 110 Thomas St) **Map 3** For decades this bar has been a favourite haunt of students (and teachers) of the nearby National College of Art & Design, who mix easily with the more conservative (and older) locals.

The Ginger Man (☎ 676 6388, 40 Fenian St) **Map 5** Although we were refused entry due to our 'inappropriate' attire (trainers), once we managed to get in we found it to be a lovely bar with a nice atmosphere. It's very popular, so it can get very crowded.

JANE SMITH

[continued from p176]

Hilton Edwards *(☎ 677 0014, Spy Bar, Powerscourt Townhouse Shopping Centre, South William St)* **Map 7** This is one the hardest places to get into unless you're dripping with glamour, but Sunday night's Hilton Edwards club (named after the gay co-founder of the Gate Theatre) requests only that you're gay and reasonably well dressed. It's cool, chic and, at the time of writing, the hottest ticket in town.

Saunas
Dublin also has a number of saunas where it's not just the water that gets steamy.

The Vortex *(☎ 878 0898, 1 Great Strand St, Dublin 1)* **Map 5** Admission €10.20 before 6pm, €12.70 after 6pm. Open 1pm-5am Sun-Thurs, non-stop 1pm Fri-5am Mon. This huge place is the most luxurious of Dublin's saunas, with excellent facilities.

The Boilerhouse *(☎ 677 3130, 12 Crane La)* **Map 5** Admission €12.70. Open 1pm-5am Sun-Thurs, 24hrs Fri-Sat. This is a popular late-night destination for people looking to sweat it out after partying in the George, just around the corner. It's big and very clean, and is reputed to be the best-run of Dublin's saunas.

The Dock *(☎ 872 4172, 21 Upper Ormond Quay)* **Map 5** Admission €8.90 before 7pm, €11.45 after 7pm. Open 1pm-5am Sun-Thurs, non-stop 1pm Fri-5am Mon. A few doors down from Out on the Liffey, this intimate little sauna is strictly for more adventurous types.

COMEDY
The Irish have a reputation for being funny. Whether you agree or not, you can find out for sure at a number of comedy clubs within the city centre. We must warn you, however, that the quality of comedians appearing on Dublin stages can be questionable at best.

Laughter Lounge *(☎ 1800 266 339, Eden Quay)* **Map 4** Dublin's best venue for comedy has a relatively good reputation for putting on quality acts.

Ha'Penny Bridge Inn *(☎ 677 0616, 42 Wellington Quay)* **Map 6** From Tuesday to Thursday you can hear some fairly funny comedians (as well as some truly awful ones) do their stuff in the upstairs room of this Temple Bar pub. Tuesday night's Battle of the Axe, an improvisation night that features a lot of 'crowd participation' (read 'trading insults'), is the best of them.

The International *(☎ 677 9250, 23 Wicklow St)* **Map 7** There are comedy nights in the basement room of this bar on Monday, Wednesday and Thursday.

MUSIC
In recent years Dublin has become a major stop on the touring schedules of international rock bands, while the Irish scene is also as vibrant as ever. Bookings can be made either at the concert venue or through **HMV** *(☎ 679 5334, 24-hour credit-card bookings; ☎ 456 9569, 65 Grafton St)* **(Map 7)**. There's another branch of HMV *(☎ 873 2899)* **(Map 4)** at 18 Henry St. **Ticketmaster** *(☎ 1890 925 100)* also sells tickets for many Dublin gigs, both large and small. Dublin's top venues are listed in this section.

Point Depot *(☎ 836 3633, East Link Bridge, North Wall Quay)* **Map 2** This is the premier indoor venue for all rock and pop acts playing in Dublin. Originally constructed as a rail terminus in 1878, it has a capacity of around 6000.

Slane Castle *(☎ 041-982 4207, Slane, County Meath)* 46 kilometres north-west of Dublin, Slane Castle is home to the yearly Slane Festival, a one-day extravaganza featuring top names in international pop and rock. The Rolling Stones, Bob Dylan, Bruce Springsteen and REM have all played here over the years to crowds in excess of 60,000; in 2001, U2 played their only Irish performances of the year here.

Lansdowne Rd Stadium *(☎ 668 9300, Ballsbridge)* **Map 2** This mecca for rugby and soccer enthusiasts is also used for the occasional big rock performance.

Croke Park Stadium *(☎ 855 8176, Clonliffe Rd)* **Map 2** This 65,000-capacity stadium north of town hosts the odd big rock concert.

Vicar Street *(☎ 454 5533, W www .vicarstreet.com, 58-59 Thomas St)* **Map 3** Smaller performances take place at this new all-seater near Christ Church Cathedral. The venue has a capacity of 750 and offers a varied program of performers, with a strong emphasis on folk and jazz.

Red Box (☎ *478 0166, Harcourt St*) **Map 5** In the old Harcourt St Station, this is the best venue for dance gigs, with top European dance bands and DJs strutting their stuff to crowds of groovy movers.

Temple Bar Music Centre (☎ *670 0533, Curved St*) **Map 6** This centre hosts all kinds of gigs, from traditional Irish music to drum-and-bass.

Whelan's (☎ *478 0766, 26 Wexford St,* W *www.whelanslive.com*) **Map 5** Whelan's hosts mostly rock and folk gigs.

Olympia Theatre (☎ *677 7744, 72 Dame St*) **Map 6** This pleasantly tatty place features everything from disco to country on their Friday night session, Midnight at the Olympia, from midnight to 2am.

Folk

Traditional Irish music is still alive and well in Dublin, and it thrives in many drinking establishments around the city (see the Pubs & Bars special section earlier in this chapter). Some of the music venues listed also play a mixture of rock, jazz and folk (see also earlier in this section). There are even tours focusing on this part of Irish culture; see Walking Tours in the Getting Around chapter.

Classical Concerts

Classical music is constantly fighting an uphill battle in Dublin, plagued by inadequate funding, poor management and questionable repertoires; all of which contribute to its limited appeal. Count John McCormack may have been one of the great tenors of the 20th century, but he's the only Irish singer to come near the top of the list, and he's been dead for nearly 75 years! Irish orchestras have neither the talent nor the funds to match their European counterparts, and the top Irish classical musicians usually do a short stint in a local orchestra before going overseas to join more reputable ensembles. Still, there are a number of companies that perform admirably in such difficult circumstances, and Dublin's classical music scene

is often enhanced by visiting performers and orchestras.

Dublin has a number of venues that host classical concerts and opera. Bookings can be made at the venues or through Ticketmaster and HMV (see earlier in this section).

National Concert Hall (☎ *475 1572,* W *www.nch.ie, Earlsfort Terrace*) **Map 5** Ireland's premier orchestral hall hosts a variety of concerts throughout the year, including a series of lunchtime concerts (€5.10) from 1.05pm to 2pm on Tuesday, June to September.

Bank of Ireland Arts Centre (☎ *671 1488,* W *www.bankofireland.ie, Foster Place*) **Map 6** The arts centre hosts a regular Wednesday-lunchtime recital at 1.15pm (free) as well as an irregular evening program of concerts.

Gaiety Theatre (☎ *677 1717,* W *www .gaietytheatre.net, South King St*) **Map 7** This popular Dublin theatre hosts, among other things, a program of classical concerts and opera.

Hugh Lane Municipal Gallery of Modern Art (☎ *874 1903, 22 North Parnell Square*) **Map 4** From September to June, the art gallery hosts up to 30 concerts of contemporary classical music. The concerts are at noon on Sunday.

Royal Dublin Showground Concert Hall (☎ *668 0866, Ballsbridge, Dublin 4*) **Map 2** The huge hall of the RDS hosts a rich lineup of classical music and opera throughout the year.

There are also programs of lunchtime concerts in some churches.

St Stephen's Church (☎ *288 0663, Upper Mount St*) **Map 5** The acoustics in this church are superb; it hosts concerts on an ad-hoc basis.

St Anne's Church (☎ *676 7727, Dawson St*) **Map 7** Admission free. St Anne's lunchtime organ recitals are well worth attending. They take place at 1.15pm on Thursday, in July and August. For details, call between 10.30am and 4pm on weekdays.

CINEMAS

Many of Dublin's city-centre cinemas, which were mostly spread out across the north side of the Liffey, have been forced out of business by large suburban multiplex cinemas. Nevertheless, a number of older cinemas remain, with commercial features shown on the north side and independent movies more popular on the south side. Admission generally costs €4.45 for all afternoon shows, rising to €7 for evening shows.

UGC Multiplex (☎ *872 8400, Parnell Centre, Parnell St)* **Map 4** This seven-screen cinema has replaced many smaller cinemas.

Savoy (☎ *01874 6000, Upper O'Connell St)* **Map 4** The Savoy is a four-screen first-run cinema, and has late-night shows at the weekend.

Irish Film Centre (☎ *679 5744, 6 Eustace St)* **Map 6** The Irish Film Centre has a couple of screens and shows classics and new independent films. The complex also has a bar, a cafe and a bookshop.

Screen (☎ *671 4988, 2 Townsend St)* **Map 5** Screen shows fairly good art-house films on its three screens.

THEATRE
Dublin's theatre scene is small but busy. Theatre bookings can usually be made by quoting a credit-card number over the phone; you can collect your tickets just before the performance. Most plays begin between 8pm and 8.30pm.

Abbey Theatre & Peacock Theatre (Map 4)
Opened in 1904, the Abbey Theatre (☎ *878 7222,* W *www.abbeytheatre.ie, Lower Abbey St)* is just north of the Liffey. The Irish National Theatre, founded by WB Yeats and Lady Gregory among others, soon made a name not only for playwrights such as JM Synge and Sean O'Casey but also for Irish acting ability and theatrical presentation. The theatre became renowned as much for the uproars it provoked as for artistic appreciation. The use of the word 'shift' (petticoat) at the 1907 premiere of Synge's *The Playboy of the Western World* brought a storm of protest from theatregoers and O'Casey's *The Plough and the Stars* prompted a similar reaction in 1926. On the latter occasion WB Yeats himself came on stage after the performance to remonstrate with the audience!

Sadly, however, the days of furious debate over controversial plays have long since gone, and while the Abbey is still the best venue in Dublin to see classic Irish plays performed by the cream of Ireland's acting talent, it no longer challenges audiences as it used to. Tickets cost €23.50 (cheaper on Monday). Newer, more experimental work is staged in the Abbey's second, smaller room, the Peacock Theatre (☎ *878 7222; €10-15.25),* at the same venue.

Perhaps the Abbey's dimmed lustre is to do with the building, which was opened in 1966 after the original theatre burnt down in 1951. It is a dull, uninspiring place that does not do justice to its famous name. Thankfully, plans are afoot to either completely refurbish the building or – more likely – to move it completely down to the Grand Canal Docks on the river's south side. The proposed move has generated furious debate, however, as purists object to removing the Abbey from the north side. By the time you read this a decision will undoubtedly have been reached as to the theatre's future.

Gate Theatre (Map 4)
The Gate Theatre (☎ *874 4045, East Parnell Sq)* was opened in 1929 by Micheál MacLiammóir and Hilton Edwards. The former continued to act at the theatre until 1975, when he finally retired at the age of 76 after his 1384th performance of the one-man show *The Importance of Being Oscar* (Oscar being Oscar Wilde, of course). The Gate Theatre stage saw Orson Welles' first professional appearance and also featured James Mason early in his career. The building dates from 1784 to 1786 when it was built as part of the Rotunda Hospital complex. Today, the theatre stages some of the best plays to be seen in Dublin, with a repertory of American and European plays as well as the work of Irish dramatists. Tickets usually cost around €19, depending on what's on.

Other Theatres
Olympia Theatre (☎ *677 7744,* W *www.olympia.ie, 72 Dame St)* **Map 6** This theatre specialises in light plays and, at Christmas time, panto.

Gaiety Theatre (☎ *677 1717,* W *www .gaietytheatre.net, South King St)* **Map 7** Opened in 1871, the Gaiety Theatre is used for modern plays and TV shows as well as musical comedies and revues.

Tivoli Theatre (☎ *454 4472, 135-136 Francis St)* **Map 3** Experimental and less-commercial performances take place at the Tivoli.

Andrew's Lane Theatre (☎ *679 5720, 9-17 St Andrew's Lane)* **Map 7** This is a well established fringe theatre.

Project Arts Centre (☎ *1850 26 00 27,* W *www.project.ie, 39 East Essex St)* **Map 6** The Project Arts Centre puts on excellent productions of experimental plays by up-and-coming Irish and foreign writers.

Players' Theatre (☎ *677 2941 ext 1239, eastern end of Trinity College Campus)* **Map 5** The Trinity College Players' Theatre hosts student productions throughout the academic year as well as the most prestigious plays from the Dublin Theatre Festival in October.

The International (☎ *677 9250, 23 Wicklow St)* **Map 7** This is one of several pubs that host theatrical performances.

Lambert Puppet Theatre and Museum (☎ *280 0974, Clifton Lane, Monkstown)* Puppet performances are staged at this theatre every Saturday and daily at Christmas and Easter.

The Ark (☎ *670 7788, 11a Eustace St)* **Map 6** This children's centre has a 150-seater venue that stages shows for kids aged between three and 13.

Eblana Theatre (☎ *679 8404, Busáras)* **Map 4** Irish work is the mainstay of this small theatre on the north side of the city.

Focus Theatre (☎ *676 3071, 6 Pembroke Place)* **Map 5** This small theatre puts on some interesting interpretations of classic plays as well as contemporary work.

Draoicht Theatre (☎ *885 2622, Blanchardstown Shopping Centre)* This is a brand new, 250-seater theatre that stages interesting new work by emerging Irish and international writers. Take bus No 39 or 39A from Middle Abbey St to get here.

Pavilion Theatre (☎ *231 2929, Pavilion Complex, Dun Laoghaire)* This small theatre mostly stages experimental works.

BUSKERS

Dublin has a good deal of free entertainment in the form of buskers – donations are always gratefully accepted. The best work on busy Grafton St, where they are occasionally hassled by shopkeepers (for blocking access to their establishments) and by the police, but are mainly left alone. At the Trinity College end of Grafton St you'll usually trip over pavement artists, most of whom are students at the various art colleges, busily chalking their pictures around the statue of Molly Malone. Farther along the street you are likely to come across crooning folk singers, raucous rock bands, classical string quartets and oddities such as the poet who breaks into verse only when paid cash in advance.

SPECTATOR SPORTS

Dublin offers plenty of sporting opportunities for the spectator. If you're more interested in taking part in sports, see Activities in the Things to See & Do chapter.

Hurling & Gaelic Football

According to legend, hurling, that most Irish of sports, began with Sétanta, the five-year-old hurling genius and nephew of King Conor of Ulaid (Ulster) who later became known as Cuchulainn. Hurling has elements of hockey and lacrosse; players can hit the ball along the ground or through the air or even carry it on the end of their hurley or *camán*. Dublin itself is not, however, a great power in hurling. The best teams are more likely to be from Kilkenny or Cork.

Ireland's most popular sport, Gaelic football, is a high-speed, aggressive activity too. It features a round ball that can be kicked along the ground as in soccer or passed between players as in rugby. Australian-rules football has many similarities with Gaelic football, as evidenced by the Compromise Rules series between Ireland and Australia that has taken place since 1998, with the Irish team featuring players who have become major stars in Australia. (Ireland was originally the superior side, but the Australians have since taken their revenge.)

The All-Ireland Hurling Final takes place

JANE SMITH

The traditional Gaelic sport of hurling resembles hockey and lacrosse.

on the second Sunday in September and attracts a crowd of more than 80,000 spectators. The All-Ireland Football Final takes place on the third Sunday in September. Both sports are played at Dublin's *Croke Park* **(Map 2)**. For information call ☎ 836 3222.

Football & Rugby

The truly Gaelic sports, hurling and Gaelic football, have their greatest following in rural Ireland and it's probably true to say that football (soccer) and rugby are more popular in Dublin itself. Support for British teams is huge here; in fact, the most popular football teams in Ireland are probably Manchester United, Liverpool and Glasgow Celtic! Although popular interest in the Republic of Ireland national team is no longer at the frenzied level it was from 1986 to 1996, when, under the management of Jack Charlton (who played for England when they won the World Cup in 1966), it was considered one of the more difficult sides to beat in Europe, the current team still attracts full houses to every game. For details of international matches, contact the Football Association of Ireland (☎ 676 6864, **e** info@ fai.ie, **W** www.fai.ie) at 80 Merrion Square South.

Ireland is also a power in world rugby and great attention is paid to the annual Six Nations Championship, which pits Ireland against England, Wales, Scotland, France and Italy. Even more passion is likely to be roused when the national team plays Australia. International soccer and rugby matches take place at *Lansdowne Rd Stadium* **(Map 2)** in Ballsbridge. For information call ☎ 668 4601 or check the Irish Rugby Football Union Web site (**W** www.irfu.ie).

Horse & Greyhound Racing

The Irish love of horse racing is strongly evident at *Leopardstown* (☎ 289 3607, **e** *info @leopardstown.com*, **W** *www.leopardstown .com, Foxrock*), home of the prestigious Hennessey Gold Cup in February. On race days buses run to the course from Eden Quay.

There are several other racecourses within an hour's drive. The Irish Grand National is held on Easter Monday at *Fairyhouse* (☎ 825 6167, **W** indigo.ie/~fairyhse, Ratoath), 25km north of Dublin in County Meath.

The Curragh (☎ 045-441 205, **W** www .curragh.com, County Kildare), 50km to the west of Dublin, hosts five classic flat races between May and September. The popular April Steeplechase Festival is held 40km south-west of the city at *Punchestown* (☎ 045-897 704, **W** www.punchestown.com, Naas, County Kildare).

Greyhound racing takes place at *Harold's Cross Park* (☎ 497 1081, 151 Harold's Cross Rd) **(Map 2)** near Rathmines, a short hop from the city centre on the No 16 bus, and the more comfortable *Shelbourne Stadium* (☎ 668 3502, Shelbourne Park) **(Map 2)** in Ringsend, only 10 minutes from the centre on the No 3 bus. Races are held two or three times a week from February to early December; call to check days and starting times (they usually begin at about 7.30pm).

Golf

The popularity of Ireland's fastest-growing sport is due in part to the success of Irish golfers such as Darren Clarke, Padraig Harrington and Paul McGinley. They can be seen driving, chipping and putting against the best players in Europe in the Smurfit European Open, which takes place in late July/early August at the *K Club* (☎ 676 6650, **W** www .kclub.ie, Straffan, County Kildare), which was designed by Arnold Palmer.

Other Sports

Polo matches can be viewed for free in Phoenix Park on Wednesday, Saturday and Sunday. Car and motorcycle races are held at Mondello Park, although they have also been held in Phoenix Park. Ireland is not a major player in the cricket world but there is an Irish national team, who can be seen playing on the green at College Park in Trinity College.

Shopping

If it's made in Ireland, you can probably buy it in Dublin. Popular buys include fine Irish knitwear, such as the renowned Aran sweaters; jewellery with a Celtic influence, including Claddagh rings with two hands clasping a heart; books on Irish topics; crystal from Waterford, Galway, Tyrone and Tipperary; Irish coats of arms; china from Belleek; and Royal Tara chinaware or linen from Donegal.

Dublin's new-found economic wealth has resulted in an increase in the number of top fashion outlets, previously the preserve of the select few. Today you can find every major label on display in the shops along and around Grafton St, and it is no longer unusual to overhear the city's trendsetters discuss where the best deals on Diesel gear are or where to find a nice Prada shirt.

There are all sorts of weird and wonderful small shops in Temple Bar, including a number of interesting record shops, an equally varied collection of small bookshops, some of Dublin's most eclectic clothes shops and a variety of other unusual outlets.

See Taxes & Refunds under Money in the Facts for the Visitor chapter for information on claiming back sales tax (called value-added tax or VAT).

SHOPPING CENTRES & DEPARTMENT STORES

St Stephen's Green Shopping Centre (☎ 478 0888, St Stephen's Green; open 9am-6pm Mon-Wed, Fri & Sat, 9am-7pm Thurs, noon-6pm Sun) **Map 7** In the heart of the city, this flash shopping centre (see also under South of the Liffey in the Things to See & Do chapter), with its white wrought-iron balconies, overlooks the north-western corner of St Stephen's Green at the top of Grafton St. Inside you'll find a diverse mixture of chain stores and individual shops (including a Levi's shop and a Benetton outlet), plus an outlet of the Dunne's Stores department store, which also has a supermarket in the basement.

Powerscourt Townhouse Shopping Centre (☎ 679 4144, 59 South William St; open same hours as St Stephen's) **Map 7** The wonderful Powerscourt Townhouse Shopping Centre between South William St and Clarendon St, just to the west of Grafton St, is a big, modern centre in a fine old 1774 building. The main arcade underwent a substantial renovation in 1998, and is worth visiting just for the architecture. Among its top-class outlets are an antique market and several high-fashion stores.

Royal Hibernian Way Centre (☎ 679 5919, Dawson St; open same hours as St Stephen's) **Map 7** This is also a relatively exclusive shopping centre with a collection of small shops on the site of the old Royal Hibernian Hotel.

ILAC Centre (☎ 704 1460, Henry St; open same hours as St Stephen's) **Map 4** The ILAC Centre, off Henry St close to O'Connell St, is a little dilapidated but still has some interesting outlets with goods at affordable prices.

Irish Life Centre (☎ 704 1451, entrances on Lower Abbey St & Talbot St; open same hours as St Stephen's) **Map 4** This shopping centre just off O'Connell St has seen better days, but it still has a couple of retail outlets worth checking out for their low prices.

Westbury Mall (☎ 679 1589, Grafton St; open same hours as St Stephen's) **Map 7** This centre is small, very trendy... and quite expensive to boot. Hardly surprising considering this exclusive little spot is just off Grafton St and next to the Westbury Hotel, one of Dublin's poshest.

Jervis Shopping Centre (☎ 878 1323, Jervis St; open same hours as St Stephen's) **Map 6** Just north of Capel St Bridge, this is an ultramodern centre with dozens of outlets.

Arnott's (☎ 805 0400, 12 Henry St; open same hours as St Stephen's) **Map 4** Occupying a huge block with entrances on Henry St, Liffey St and Abbey St, this formerly mediocre department store has been completely overhauled and is now probably

Dublin's best. It stocks virtually everything you could possibly want to buy, from garden furniture to high fashion, and everything is relatively affordable.

Penney's (☎ 888 0500, 47 Mary St; open same hours as St Stephen's) **Map 4** This is a branch of the cheapest department store in Ireland.

Brown Thomas (☎ 605 6666, 92 Grafton St; open same hours as St Stephen's) **Map 7** This is Dublin's most expensive department store, suitably stocked to cater to the city's more moneyed shoppers. You'll find every top label represented here.

Marks & Spencer (☎ 679 7855, 15-20 Grafton St) **Map 7** *(☎ 872 8833, 24-29 Mary St)* **Map 3** With a branch on either side of the Liffey, each open same hours as St Stephen's Shopping Centre, this British chain caters to the mid-range shopper, with affordable good-quality clothing.

Clery & Co (☎ 878 6000, O'Connell St; open same hours as St Stephen's) **Map 4** This graceful shop on O'Connell St is a Dublin classic. Recently restored to its elegant best, it caters to the Dublin shopper's conservative side.

MARKETS

Dublin has some very colourful markets.

Moore St Market (Moore St) **Map 4** Open Mon-Sat. This open-air market has suffered in recent years due to lack of interest, but the influx of immigrants has given the street a new lease of life. Here you can buy almost anything, from flowers, fruit, vegetables and fish to cheap cigarettes, tobacco and chocolate. Moore St runs from Henry St to Parnell St, parallel to O'Connell St in north Dublin. In 2001, the Moore St Indoor Market opened just off the street; here you'll find a genuine Chinese tea-and-noodle shop, an excellent reggae music store and other outlets.

George's St Arcade (between South Great George's St & Drury St) **Map 7** Open 10am-6pm Mon-Sat. This is the best of Dublin's markets, and it has the advantage of being sheltered within an elegant Victorian Gothic complex. It has a mixture of shops selling everything from olives to drums, jewellery to dresses.

Dublin Corporation Fruit and Vegetable Market (St Michan's St; open Mon-Fri) **Map 4** This giant arcaded market runs along both sides of St Michan's St, between Chancery St and Mary's Lane near the Four Courts. It caters mostly to the wholesale trade, who buy large stocks of fruit and vegetables here.

Meeting House Square Market (Meeting House Square, open 9am-2pm Sat & Sun) **Map 6** An open-air market takes place every weekend in this Temple Bar Square, and you can buy all kinds of organic food and other delectable titbits.

Camden St Market (Camden St) **Map 5** Open 8am-6pm Mon-Sat. One of Dublin's traditional street markets, the stalls along Camden St sell fruit and vegetables of varying quality.

Temple Bar Square Market (Temple Bar Square) **Map 6** This Saturday market sells only books.

IRISH CRAFTS & SOUVENIRS

There is a common misconception about Irish crafts. The 'traditional' crafts, which include everything from hawthorn walking sticks to anything with a shamrock on it, are not all necessarily traditional. Much of it is mass-produced, factory-made junk that is strictly for tourists, hence its presence at the airport and in tacky shops all over town. However, in the last decade or so the crafts market has benefited from a new generation of artisans who have introduced modern concepts and ideas to traditional work, with great success.

The Kilkenny Shop (☎ 677 7066, 6 Nassau St) **Map 5** This shop has a wonderful selection of finely made Irish crafts, featuring clothing, glassware, pottery, jewellery, crystal and silver from some of Ireland's best designers.

House of Ireland (☎ 671 4543, 38 Nassau St) **Map 7** This is another all-purpose shop with all types of Irish crafts.

Trinity College Library Shop (☎ 608 2320, East Pavilion, Library Colonnades, Trinity College) **Map 5** This bookshop has a wide variety of books and other Irish souvenirs, but, of course, it's best known for reproductions from the Book of Kells.

The Tower Craft Design Centre (☎ 677 5655, Pearse St) **Map 5** Housed in a 19th-century warehouse that was Dublin's first iron-structured building, the design centre has studios for local craftspeople. They produce jewellery in both contemporary and Celtic-inspired designs, Irish pewter, ceramics, silk and other fabrics, pottery, rugs and wall hangings, cards, leather bags and various other handcrafted items. It's immediately opposite the Waterways Visitors' Centre, off Lower Grand Canal St.

Irish Celtic Craftshop (☎ 667 9912, 10-12 Lord Edward St) **Map 5** This shop near Christ Church Cathedral specialises in well made, nontacky Irish crafts.

Whichcraft (☎ 670 9371, 5 Castle Gate, Lord Edward St) **Map 5** Whichcraft sells wonderful Irish traditional crafts with a contemporary feel, both old and new, at reasonable prices.

The Crafts Council Gallery (☎ 679 7368, Powerscourt Townhouse Shopping Centre) **Map 7** This is just one of the craft shops in the Powerscourt Townhouse Shopping Centre. The fine selection of glassware, pottery and jewellery is quite expensive.

CLOTHING

Clothing, particularly woollen sweaters, is probably the most authentically Irish buy. The Irish also make some high-quality outdoor-activity gear, perhaps because they have plenty of wet weather to motivate them. Also worth checking out are the fashion outlets and Dublin's excellent selection of second-hand shops. As a rule of thumb, the shops on or around Grafton St are usually more expensive and have a greater selection of high fashion.

Knitwear

Irish knitwear is justly famous, though the demand for those superb heavy Aran sweaters is so great that even the most genuine-looking is unlikely to have been knitted on the islands.

Dublin Woollen Company (☎ 677 5014, 41 Lower Ormond Quay) **Map 5** Near the Ha'penny Bridge, this is one of the major wool outlets in Dublin. It has a large collection of sweaters, cardigans, scarves, rugs, shawls and other woollen goods and runs a tax-free shopping scheme.

The Sweater Shop (☎ 671 3270, 9 Wicklow St) **Map 7** Traditional and exciting contemporary designs in knitwear can be found at this shop just off Grafton St and near Trinity College.

Second-Hand Clothing

There's lots of rummage potential around Temple Bar and Grafton St.

Celtic Gifts (☎ 679 7087, 2 Crown Alley) **Map 6** This is one of Temple Bar's most popular second-hand shops, with a vast array of all kinds of gear, from three-piece suits to funky shirts and more.

Eager Beaver (☎ 677 3342, 17 Crown Alley) **Map 6** Need a black suit for a wedding, a cricket jumper or a Victorian shirt, but don't want to spend a fortune? This is your place; spread across two floors, it's a clothing hunter's paradise.

Flip (☎ 671 4299, 4 Upper Fownes St) **Map 6** Flip specialises in 'vintage' US clothing. The prices are higher than in other second-hand stores, but that's because the clothing is genuine.

Harlequin (☎ 671 0202, 13 Castle Market) **Map 7** This is a wonderful shop with a great selection of second-hand jeans, shirts and – upstairs – suits.

Jenny Vander (☎ 677 0406, George's St Arcade) **Map 7** Jenny Vander's selection of second-hand clothes is pretty wild. You can get your tarot cards read here too.

Big Whiskey (☎ 677 9299, George's St Arcade) **Map 7** This shop has plenty of vintage clothes for both men and women.

Fashion Outlets

There are quite a few high- and low-fashion outlets around the city that are worth a look.

Extrovert (☎ 873 5100, 21 Henry St) **Map 4** Extrovert, on the north side of the Liffey, specialises in youthful fashions imported from the USA, which tend to be really cheap.

No Name Depot (☎ 873 0953, 38 Henry St) **Map 4** Just off O'Connell St, this cheap shop caters almost exclusively to those aged between 16 and 24.

Schuh (☎ 873 0621, 10 O'Connell St) **Map 4** This is the best shoe shop in town, with a vast selection of trendy, designer shoes as well as more conservative footwear.

Hobo (☎ 670 4869, 6-9 Trinity St) **Map 7** This is an Irish designer shop that sells clothes best described as 'clubber's clobber' – perfectly suited to the vast market of young people who are eager to look the part on the dance floor. The clothes are well made and quite snazzy.

Urban Outfitters (☎ 670 6202, 4 Cecilia St) **Map 6** With a blaring techno soundtrack, the only Irish branch of this large American chain sells ridiculously cool clothes to the most discerning of young buyers. Besides the clothing, the shop sells all kinds of interesting gadgets, accessories and furniture, and, on the second floor, you'll find a hypertrendy record shop (hence the techno).

Aspecto (☎ 671 9302, 6 South Anne St) **Map 7** Just off Grafton St, this is one of the best shops for trendy designer gear. On the ground floor they have shoes and on the second floor is clothing.

Richard Alan (☎ 677 5149, 58 Grafton St) **Map 7** This is one of Grafton St's better designer shops for women's clothing.

Costume (☎ 679 4188, 10 Castle Market) **Map 7** This shop, opposite the Drury St entrance to the George's St Arcade, specialises in well made designer clothes for women by mostly Irish designers. It's expensive, but the clothes are beautiful.

Alias Tom (☎ 671 7200, Duke House, Duke La) **Map 7** On the corner of Lemon St and Duke Lane, Alias Tom has the latest designer wear for men, stocking most of Europe's top labels (and a couple of Irish ones as well). The prices are steep though.

Powerscourt Townhouse Shopping Centre (☎ 679 4144, 59 South William St) **Map 7** You'll find everything from custom-made shoes to exotic wedding dresses and wonderful one-off pieces of jewellery in this attractive shopping centre.

CAMPING & BACKPACKING EQUIPMENT

Plenty of places sell good-quality camping, walking and backpacking equipment.

Great Outdoors (☎ 679 4293, 20 Chatham St) **Map 7** This is the best of Dublin's camping equipment shops, with an enormous selection of all kinds of gear for all kinds of activities, from gentle hill walking to surfing to hardcore mountaineering.

A number of outlets, including *surplus specialists*, are to be found north of the river along Talbot St off Marlborough St, and Mary's Lane off Capel St.

RECORDS & MUSICAL INSTRUMENTS

Music plays an important role in Ireland, whether it's traditional Irish music or the contemporary style that has given Ireland a position on the cutting edge of modern rock.

Virgin Megastore (☎ 677 7361, 14 Aston Quay) **Map 6** This is Dublin's biggest record store. If you can play it in a CD player, they've probably got it.

Claddagh Records (☎ 677 0262, 2 Cecilia St) **Map 6** Nearby in Temple Bar, but far more intimate in size, is this knowledgeably staffed shop, which specialises in traditional music.

Comet Records (☎ 671 8592, 5 Cope St) **Map 6** Comet Records specialises in independent label releases – metal, indie, ska and techno.

Borderline Records (☎ 679 9097, 17 Temple Bar) **Map 6** Indie music and hardcore sounds from thrash metal to techno make up the selection at this Temple Bar shop.

Road Records (☎ 671 7340, 16 Fade St) **Map 7** At Road Records you'll find all the latest in indie music.

Big Brother Records (☎ 672 9355, 16 Fade St) **Map 7** In the basement of Road Records, vinyl junkies and indie fans get a kick out of Big Brother's selection, a good mix of hip-hop, deep house, jazzy beats and drum-and-bass, as well as jazz and soul.

The Golden Disc Group (☎ 677 1025, Grafton Arcade) **Map 7** This is a small, Irish-owned chain that has been eclipsed in recent years by the arrival of the music superstores such as HMV, Tower and Virgin. There are five other outlets throughout the city centre.

HMV (☎ 679 5334, 65 Grafton St) **Map 7** This is the best of the megastores, with a massive selection of all kinds of music across three floors. The staff are knowledgeable and always on hand to answer a query.

Waltons (☎ *874 7805, 2 North Frederick S)* **Map 4** (☎ *475 0661, 69-70 South Great George's St)* **Map 7** Waltons has traditional Irish records and music as well as *bodhráns* and other traditional musical instruments.

ANTIQUES

For more antiquarian purchases try the antique market at the Powerscourt Townhouse Shopping Centre or head for Francis St in the Liberties area, Dublin's best antique shopping street.

Johnston Antiques (☎ *473 2384, 69-70 Francis St)* **Map 3** Johnston Antiques is a great place for jewellery, fashion antiques and other curios.

Antiques and Collectibles Fair (☎ *475 7255, Newman House, 85-86 St Stephen's Green)* **Map 5** Open 11am-6pm every second Sun. Bring your discerning eye and a credit card with plenty of credit to this antiques fair, which specialises in merchandise of the highest quality.

Check the *Irish Times* on Sunday for information on antiques sales and auctions.

BOOKSHOPS

Most of the bookshops in Dublin offer an extensive choice of books on Ireland and subjects of Irish interest, as well as Irish literature and more. A number of bookshops cater for special interests too.

Eason's – Hanna's Bookshop (☎ *677 1255, 27-29 Nassau St)* **Map 7** This excellent shop is directly opposite Trinity College.

Hodges Figgis (☎ *677 4754, 57 Dawson St)* **Map 7** Round the corner from Fred Hanna's, Dublin's best bookshop carries the city's widest range of titles. There's a pleasant cafe on the second floor.

Waterstone's (☎ *679 1415, 7 Dawson St)* **Map 7** (☎ *878 1311, Jervis St Shopping Centre)* **Map 4** Waterstone's is the city's second-largest bookshop, with a full stock of titles.

Hughes & Hughes (☎ *478 3060, St Stephen's Green Shopping Centre)* **Map 5** This shop is pretty good for bestsellers, mag-

azines and the like, although you'll have to go elsewhere for more academic tomes. There's a branch at Dublin Airport, too.

International Books (☎ *679 9375, 18 South Frederick St)* **Map 5** Try this place for a large range of phrasebooks and an extensive language section.

The Dublin Bookshop (☎ *677 5568, 24 Grafton St)* **Map 7** There's a particularly good selection of books of Irish interest here.

Eason's (☎ *873 3811, 40 Upper O'Connell St)* **Map 4** North of the Liffey near the GPO, Eason's has a wide range of books and one of the biggest selections of magazines in Ireland.

Winding Stair Bookshop & Café (☎ *873 3292, 40 Lower Ormond Quay)* **Map 5** This shop has new and second-hand books.

Forbidden Planet (☎ *671 0688, 5-6 Crampton Quay)* **Map 6** This is a wonderful science-fiction and comic-book specialist.

Sub-City (☎ *677 1902, 2 Exchequer St)* **Map 7** Sub-City has a good selection of sci-fi and comics.

Sinn Féin Bookshop (☎ *872 7096, 44 West Parnell Square)* **Map 4** In the same building as the Sinn Féin Irish headquarters, this bookshop is predictably stocked with all kinds of pro-republican material. To dismiss it, however, would be a mistake, as many of the most brilliant Irish minds ever to put pen to paper had strong republican tendencies.

An Siopa Leabhar (☎ *478 3814, 6 Harcourt St)* **Map 5** Just off St Stephen's Green, this shop has books in Irish (the name simply means 'bookshop' in Irish).

Dúchas Bookshop (☎ *671 0309, Sun Alliance House, Molesworth St)* **Map 7** Try this place for official publications and maps.

Dublin Writers' Museum (☎ *872 2077, 18 North Parnell Square)* **Map 4** The museum has an excellent bookshop.

Irish Museum of Modern Art (IMMA; ☎ *612 9900, Military Rd)* **Map 3** The bookshop at the IMMA has a good range of books.

National Gallery (☎ *661 5133, Merrion Square)* **Map 5** The gallery has a bookshop offering a good range of art books.

Trinity College Library Shop (☎ *608 2320, East Pavilion, Library Colonnades, Trinity College)* **Map 5** The bookshop at

SHOPPING

Trinity College has a wide selection of Irish-interest books, including, of course, various titles on the Book of Kells.

Greene's Bookshop (☎ 873 3149, 16 Clare St) **Map 5** This dusty old bookshop is a fabulous place to browse, as it has a sprawling collection of new and second-hand books.

Cathach Books (☎ 671 8676, 10 Duke St) **Map 7** This specialist bookshop near Grafton St stocks Irish-interest books only, including as near complete a collection of signed first editions as you're ever likely to find.

JEWELLERY & CRYSTAL

As well as those listed below, there are also several jewellery shops in the Powerscourt Townhouse Shopping Centre.

Weir & Son's (☎ 677 9678, 96 Grafton St) **Map 7** This is the best-known jewellery shop in Dublin, with a huge selection of watches and crystal and an impressive collection of gold and silver trinkets.

Appleby's (☎ 679 9572, 5-6 Johnson's Court) **Map 7** This little shop is renowned for the high quality of its jewellery.

Sleaters (☎ 677 7532, 9 Johnson's Court) **Map 7** This place sells Irish and Celtic-style jewellery.

John Brereton (☎ 677 5350, Chatham St) **Map 7** (☎ 878 7651, 29 Lower O'Connell St; ☎ 872 6759, 108 Capel St) **Map 4** This jeweller, with several outlets throughout the city, has some affordable jewellery.

Brown Thomas Department Store (☎ 605 6666, 92 Grafton St) **Map 7** Brown Thomas is one of a number of places stocking an extensive range of world-famous Waterford crystal. Although Waterford is the best-known Irish crystal, there are other companies that cut good-quality crystal glass, such as Tyrone and Tipperary.

DESIGNER GOODS & ODDITIES

Knobs & Knockers (☎ 671 0288, 19 Nassau St) **Map 5** If you've admired those wonderful brass door knockers on Dublin's fine Georgian doors, this place has plenty.

Condom Power (☎ 677 8963, 57 Dame St) **Map 6** This basement sex shop belies Dublin's squeaky-clean image.

Art

Dublin has a large number of galleries that exhibit and sell the works of contemporary Irish artists. For a list of these galleries and where to find them, see the Other Galleries section in the Things to See & Do chapter.

Seaside Suburbs

There are a number of seaside suburbs around the curve of Dublin Bay that make worthwhile trips from the city centre. Dun Laoghaire to the south and Howth to the north are historic ports. The former has pleasant beach walks and a vibrant town centre with a fascinating museum, while the latter is one of the most beautiful spots in all of County Dublin. Accessible on the DART rail service, both are interesting alternatives to staying in the city.

South of Dublin

DUN LAOGHAIRE

Dun Laoghaire (dun **lear**-y), 13km south-east of central Dublin, is Dublin's busiest port, with ferry connections to Britain. For most of the 19th century it was a popular seaside resort, attracting droves of Dubliners to its shores. Decline set in during the latter half of the 20th century, but in the last few years the town has been in the midst of an enormous program of urban renewal, all thanks to the benefits of a prosperous economy. The most obvious development is the new Pavilion Complex, near the central DART station, which has shops, cafes and a theatre. A new shopping centre, Bloomfield's Shopping Mall, has also opened in the town.

Following his visit to Ireland, King George IV left for England from this port in 1821, and to commemorate his visit the port was then known as Kingstown, a name it kept until 1922, after Irish independence, when it was changed back to Dun Laoghaire.

There are numerous B&Bs in Dun Laoghaire and they are a bit cheaper than those in central Dublin. The fast, frequent DART rail connections also make it a convenient base.

Sadly, the town has developed a bit of a reputation for roughness, with gangs of indolent and bored youths looking for trouble. There have been a couple of publicised attacks on foreigners, including that in 2000 of a 12-year-old German girl who was badly beaten up. Although these attacks are the exception and not the rule, we advise that you exercise caution, particularly at night.

History

There was a coastal settlement on the site of Dun Laoghaire more than a thousand years ago but it was little more than a small fishing village until 1767, when the first pier was built. Dun Laoghaire grew rapidly after that time. The Sandycove Martello tower (see the boxed text 'Martello Towers' in this section) was erected in the early 19th century out of fear of an invasion from Napoleonic France.

Construction of a harbour was proposed in 1815 to provide refuge for ships unable to reach the safety of Dublin Harbour in bad weather. The original plan was for a single pier, but engineer John Rennie proposed two massive piers enclosing a 100-hectare artificial harbour. Work began in 1817 and by 1823 the workforce comprised a thousand men. Despite huge expenditure the harbour wasn't actually completed until 1842. Carlisle Pier was only added in 1859 and parts of the West Pier stonework have never been finished. The total cost approached IR£1 million, an astronomical figure in those days.

The commencement of shipping services to and from Liverpool and Holyhead, and the completion in 1834 of a train line from Dublin, the first anywhere in Ireland, made this a state-of-the-art transport centre.

From Dun Laoghaire to Holyhead is a distance of just over 100km and a ferry service has operated across the Irish Sea on this route since the mid-19th century. The first mail steamers took nearly six hours to make the crossing but by 1860 the time was less than four hours, and on one occasion in 1887 the paddle steamer *Ireland* made the crossing in less than three hours. In 1918 RMS *Leinster* was torpedoed by a German U-boat 25km from Dun Laoghaire and more than 500 lives were lost.

Car ferries to Dun Laoghaire were introduced in the early 1960s.

Orientation

Dun Laoghaire is fairly small with one main street, George's St (Upper and Lower), which runs parallel to the coast. The most prominent landmark is the new ferry terminal, which is next to the central DART station by the sea. The huge harbour is sheltered by the East and West Piers. Sandycove, with the James Joyce Museum and the Forty Foot Pool, is about 1km south-east of central Dun Laoghaire.

Information

The Dun Laoghaire & Rathdown Tourist Office (☎ 205 4855) is at 8 Royal Marine Rd,

about 100m from the ferry terminal. Just inside the terminal is an office of Dublin Tourism (☎ 1800 668 668).

At the top of Royal Marine Rd is George's St. Here you'll find a branch of **Eason's** *(☎ 280 5528, 5 Lower George's St)*, a newsagent and bookshop chain. Nearby is **Crowley's Pharmacy** *(☎ 280 7352, 6 Lower George's St, open 9am-10pm daily)*. The Star Laundry (☎ 280 5074) is at 47 Upper George's St. They also do dry cleaning; four items will cost €12.70.

There is a branch of the Bank of Ireland at 101 Upper George's St, which has an ATM.

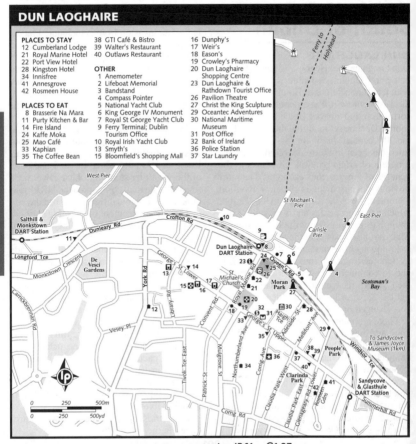

DUN LAOGHAIRE

PLACES TO STAY
12 Cumberland Lodge
21 Royal Marine Hotel
22 Port View Hotel
28 Kingston Hotel
34 Innisfree
41 Annesgrove
42 Rosmeen House

PLACES TO EAT
 8 Brasserie Na Mara
11 Purty Kitchen & Bar
14 Fire Island
24 Kaffe Moka
25 Mao Café
33 Kaphian
35 The Coffee Bean

38 GTI Café & Bistro
39 Walter's Restaurant
40 Outlaws Restaurant

OTHER
 1 Anemometer
 2 Lifeboat Memorial
 3 Bandstand
 4 Compass Pointer
 5 National Yacht Club
 6 King George IV Monument
 7 Royal St George Yacht Club
 9 Ferry Terminal; Dublin
   Tourism Office
10 Royal Irish Yacht Club
13 Smyth's
15 Bloomfield's Shopping Mall

16 Dunphy's
17 Weir's
18 Eason's
19 Crowley's Pharmacy
20 Dun Laoghaire
   Shopping Centre
23 Dun Laoghaire &
   Rathdown Tourist Office
26 Pavilion Theatre
27 Christ the King Sculpture
29 Oceantec Adventures
30 National Maritime
   Museum
31 Post Office
32 Bank of Ireland
36 Police Station
37 Star Laundry

SEASIDE SUBURBS

It is open 10am to 4pm Monday to Wednesday and Friday (to 5pm on Thursday). The post office, next door at No 102, is open 9am to 6pm Monday to Friday and 9am to 5.30pm on Saturday.

Dial ☎ 999 or ☎ 666 5000 for the police station, at 34–35 Corrig Ave.

The Harbour

The 1290m East and 1548m West Piers, each ending in a lighthouse built in the 1850s, are popular for walking (especially the East Pier), bird-watching and fishing (particularly from the end of the West Pier). You can also ride a bicycle out along the piers (bottom level only).

The **East Pier** has an 1890s bandstand and a memorial to Captain Boyd and the crew of a Dun Laoghaire lifeboat, who were drowned in a rescue attempt. Near the end of the pier is an anemometer (1852), one of the first of these wind-speed measuring devices to be installed anywhere in the world. The East Pier ends with a lighthouse and The East-Pier Battery, from which VIPs arriving by sea may receive a gun salute.

The harbour has long been a popular yachting centre and the **Royal Irish Yacht Club building** (☎ 280 9452, Dun Laoghaire Harbour; not open to the public), dating from around 1850, was Ireland's first purpose-built yacht club. The Royal St George Yacht Club building dates from 1863 and that of the National Yacht Club from 1876.

St Michael's Pier was added in 1969 and is now the only operating pier for ferries. The older Carlisle Pier, features a fine Victorian terminal, which has been temporarily boarded up while possible plans to convert it into a museum are discussed. On the West-Pier side of the harbour are two anchored lightships whose jobs are now done by automatic buoys.

National Maritime Museum

The National Maritime Museum (☎ 280 0969, Haigh Terrace; closed for repairs) is in the former Mariners' Church, built in 1837 'for the benefit of sailors in men-of-war, merchant ships, fishing boats and yachts'. The beautiful window in the chancel is a replica of the 'Five Sisters' window at York Minster in England. Exhibits include a French ship's longboat, used to land troops from a larger vessel, captured at Bantry in 1796 from Wolfe Tone's abortive French-backed invasion.

The huge clockwork-driven Great Baily Light Optic came from the Baily Lighthouse on Howth Peninsula (see Howth later in this chapter). Its herringbone-patterned lens reflected light across the bay from 1902 until 1972, when it was replaced with an electrically driven lens. The museum also has a model of the *Great Eastern* (1858), an early steam-powered vessel built by the English engineer Isambard Kingdom Brunel. Although it proved a commercial failure as a passenger ship, it successfully laid the first transatlantic telegraph cable. There are also various items from the German submarine *U19*, which landed Sir Roger Casement in Kerry in 1916 (see the Sandycove section). These were donated 50 years after the event by the U-boat's captain, Raimund Weisbach.

The museum closed in 2001 for 'serious repairs' and at the time of writing there was no definite date for its reopening.

Around the Town

Nothing remains of the *dún* or fort that gave Dun Laoghaire its name because it was destroyed during the construction of the train line. The train line from Dun Laoghaire to Dalkey was built along the route of an earlier line known as The Metals, which was used to bring stone for the harbour construction from the quarries at Dalkey Hill. By means of a pulley system, the laden trucks trundling down to the harbour pulled the empty ones back up to the quarry.

On the waterfront is a curious **monument** commemorating George IV's visit in 1821 consisting of an obelisk balanced on four stone balls. On the other side of Queen's Road, a little farther down, is the **Christ the King sculpture**, created in Paris in 1926 by Andrew O'Connor as a memorial to the dead of WWI. It was bought in 1949 but kept in storage until 1978 because the local church authorities expressed reservations

SEASIDE SUBURBS

about its 'appropriateness' as it somewhat contorts Christ's features.

Sandycove

One kilometre south-east of Dun Laoghaire is Sandycove, with a pretty little beach and a Martello tower (see the boxed text 'Martello Towers'). The tower is home to a James Joyce museum.

Sir Roger Casement, who attempted to organise a German-backed Irish opposition force during WWI, was born here in 1864. He was captured after being landed in County Kerry from a German U-boat and was executed by the British as a traitor in 1916.

James Joyce Museum The Martello tower at Sandycove is where the action begins in James Joyce's epic novel *Ulysses*. The tower now houses a James Joyce museum (☎ *280 9265/8571, Sandycove, County Dublin; adult/student/child €5.10/ 3.80/2.55; open 10am-1pm, 2pm-5pm Mon-Sat, 2pm-6pm Sun April-Oct, by prior arrangement only Nov-Mar)*, which has documents, letters, photographs, various editions of Joyce's work and two death masks of the author on display. The museum was opened in 1962 by Sylvia Beach, the Paris-based publisher who first dared to put *Ulysses* into print.

In 1904 Oliver St John Gogarty, upon whom the 'stately, plump' Buck Mulligan in *Ulysses* is based, rented the tower from the army for the princely sum of IR£8 per year. Joyce stayed there for a few days, though not for as long as he had planned. An incident involving an excess of alcohol and a loaded gun convinced Joyce that this was perhaps not the safest place, so he promptly left (although his decision was further influenced by his belief that Gogarty was somewhat of a snob).

There are fine views from the tower. To the south-east you can see Dalkey Island with its signal tower and Killiney Hill with its obelisk. Howth Head is visible on the northern side of Dublin Bay. Next to the tower is the house of architect Michael Scott, who owned the tower from 1950 until it was turned into a museum. There's an-

Martello Towers

Thirty-four Martello towers were built around the coast of Ireland between 1804 and 1815 to counter a feared invasion by Napoleon's forces. A typical Martello tower stands about 12m high with 2.5m-thick walls. Originally, the entrance to the tower led straight into what is now the 'upstairs'. These towers were copied from one at Cape Mortella in Corsica. Among other sites near Dun Laoghaire, towers can be found at Sandycove, Dalkey Island, Killiney and Bray to the south, and Howth and Ireland's Eye (the island off Howth) to the north.

other Martello tower not far to the south, on Dalkey Island, overlooking Bullock Harbour.

You can get to the tower by a 30-minute walk along the seafront from the harbour at Dun Laoghaire, a 15-minute walk from the Sandycove & Glasthule DART station or a five-minute walk from West Sandycove Ave, which is served by bus No 8.

Forty Foot Pool Just below the Martello tower is the Forty Foot Pool, an open-air, sea-water bathing pool that probably took its name from the army's 40th Foot Regiment, which was stationed at the tower until it was disbanded in 1904. At the close of the first chapter of *Ulysses,* Buck Mulligan heads to the Forty Foot Pool for a morning swim.

A morning wake-up here is still a Dun Laoghaire tradition, winter or summer, though a winter dip isn't much braver than a summer one because the water temperature is only about 5°C lower than that in summer. Basically, it's bloody cold any time of year.

When it was suggested that in these enlightened times a public stretch of water like this should be open to both sexes, the 'forty foot gentlemen' put up strong opposition. A compromise eventually saved the day; it was agreed that a 'togs must be worn' ruling would apply after 9am. Prior to that hour, however, nudity prevails and the swimmers are still predominantly 'forty foot gentlemen'.

Activities

A series of walks in the area make up the signposted Dun Laoghaire Way. The *Heritage Map of Dun Laoghaire*, available from the tourist office and from bookshops, includes a map and notes on the seven separate walks.

Dinghy sailing courses are offered by the **Irish National Sailing School** (☎ *280 6654, 115 Lower George's St*) and by the **Irish Sailing Association** (☎ *280 0239, 3 Park Rd*).

Scuba divers head for the waters around Dalkey Island. **Oceantec Adventures** (☎ *280 1083, fax 284 3885, 10-11 Marine Terrace*) is a dive shop in Dun Laoghaire. It hires out diving equipment at €38 per day (€30.50 for a half day); a one-hour local dive with a dive master costs €44.50.

Places to Stay

Staying in Dun Laoghaire is a popular (and often cheaper) alternative to staying in Dublin. Although the suburb is quite a distance from the centre, the DART makes it easy to get to and from town.

Rosmeen House (☎ *280 7613, 13 Rosmeen Gardens*) Singles €38, doubles €63.50. This is the best of the B&Bs on Rosmeen Rd, a lovely Spanish villa with elegant bedrooms that are supremely comfortable.

Annesgrove (☎ *280 9801, 28 Rosmeen Gardens*) Singles €32, doubles €72. This is a pleasant and large suburban residence with well appointed bedrooms that come with the usual B&B perks, including tea- and coffee-making facilities as well as TV.

Innisfree (☎ *280 5598, fax 280 3093, e djsmyth@clubi.ie, 31 Northumberland Ave*) Singles with/without bath €35.50/ 28.50, doubles with/without bath €49.50/ 44.50. Only a couple of minutes' walk from George's St, there is nothing spectacular about this B&B, but it is clean and neat, the bedrooms are tidy (if a little small) and the owners are gracious hosts.

Cumberland Lodge (☎ *280 9665, fax 284 3227, e cumberlandlodge@tinet.ie, 54 York Rd*) Singles €35-45, doubles €45-57.50. The four rooms in this fabulous Georgian house are all en suite, and each is spacious and very comfortable.

Other B&Bs can be found on nearby Mellifont and Corrig Aves.

Hotels Dun Laoghaire also has a number of pleasant hotels.

Port View Hotel (☎ *280 1663, fax 280 0447, e portview@clubi.ie, Royal Marine Rd*) Singles/doubles with en suite €58/115. This small 20-room hotel is pleasantly located. It's a little gloomy inside, so be sure to ask for a room with a sea view.

Kingston Hotel (☎ *280 1810, fax 280 1237, e reserv@kingstonhotel.ie, Adelaide St*) Singles €82, doubles €115. A (long-overdue) refurbishment has restored this fine hotel to its rightful position as one of Dun Laoghaire's best; gone are the antiquated notions of pre-WWII tourism and in are all the comforts of an upper-range contemporary hotel. The rooms are absolutely gorgeous and, for the money, better value than the town's top dog, the Royal Marine Hotel.

Royal Marine Hotel (☎ *280 1911, fax 280 1089, e ryan@indigo.ie, Royal Marine Rd*) Rooms €229. Built in 1865, this is easily the best hotel in town. Sea-facing rooms have incredible views of much of Dublin Bay, while the general facilities are top class. It's very expensive, though: for the price, there's better (only not in Dun Laoghaire).

Places to Eat

There's no shortage of places to eat in Dun Laoghaire; you'll find everything from the ubiquitous fast-food joints and small cafes to charming restaurants with menus to suit all price ranges.

Cafes You can take your pick from a good selection of local cafes.

Kaphian (☎ *280 8337, 21 Upper George's St*) Breakfast €3.70-6.40, lunch around €7. Kaphian is a new cafe with good sandwiches and nice coffee.

The Coffee Bean (☎ *236 0853, 7 Anglesea Bldgs, Upper George's St*) From €2.90. This place is popular at lunchtime, with a good selection of takeaway sandwiches.

Kaffe Moka (☎ *284 6544, Pavilion Complex*) From €2.50. This is a branch of the popular chain. The coffee here is delicious,

SEASIDE SUBURBS

and you can get virtually any caffeine concoction you can think of.

GTI Café & Bistro *(☎ 284 6607, 59 Upper George's St)* Sandwiches €5.10-6.40. The town is all the better for this new cafe. The sandwiches – Italian *panini*, Mexican wraps and American sandwiches – are extremely good.

Restaurants George's St is particularly well stocked with restaurants, but there are many more in the surrounding area to choose from.

Walter's Restaurant *(☎ 280 7442, 68 Upper George's St)* Main courses €6.50-9. This trendy new eatery has a pretty basic but good menu of pastas, salads and pizza. There's a large beer garden out back.

Outlaws Restaurant *(☎ 284 2817, 62 Upper George's St)* Main courses €11-18.50. Open from 5.30pm. Outlaws Restaurant has steak, burgers (including veggie burgers) and other 'Wild West' fare.

Fire Island *(☎ 280 5318, 107 Lower George's St)* Main courses €14-20.50. Open from 5.30pm Tues-Sat. Owner/chef Tim Rooney was trained at the renowned cooking school at Ballymaloe House in County Cork, and it shows. The adventurous 'new-Irish' cuisine is delicious.

Mao Café *(☎ 214 8090, Pavilion Complex)* Main courses around €10.50. This is a branch of the popular restaurant in Dublin's city centre. The menu is 'Asian fusion', with European spins on Chinese and Thai dishes.

Brasserie Na Mara *(☎ 280 6787, Royal Marine Rd)* Main courses €25.50. Near the harbour and next to the DART station, Brasserie Na Mara is the best restaurant in Dun Laoghaire, with an award-winning menu that puts an emphasis on seafood.

There are also a couple of excellent restaurants in Sandycove.

Bistro Vino *(☎ 280 6097, 56 Glasthule Rd, Sandycove)* Main courses around €17. Dinner only. This little restaurant is near the seafront, up a steep flight of stairs. It's a favourite with locals, who flock here for the early-bird menu (€15.50), available between 5pm and 7pm daily.

Caviston's Seafood Restaurant *(☎ 280 9120, e caviston@indigo.ie, 59 Glasthule Rd, Sandycove)* Main courses €10.50-20.50. Open lunch only Tues-Sat; three sittings: noon-1.30pm, 1.30pm-3pm & 3pm-5pm. Reservations advised. Renowned throughout Dublin for the quality of its produce, this restaurant serves up mouth-watering platters of fishy delights.

Entertainment

Weir's *(☎ 230 4654, 88 Lower George's St)* Despite a change in management, look and name (it used to go by the name of Cooney's), this town-centre pub is still one of the most popular in Dun Laoghaire.

Dunphy's *(☎ 280 1668, 41 Lower George's St)* This is one of the more traditional pubs in Dun Laoghaire, appealing to a mix of older drinkers and young swingers.

Smyth's *(☎ 280 1139, 128 Lower George's St)* Smyth's has a nautical interior. It is a quiet bar popular with an older crowd.

Purty Kitchen & Bar *(☎ 284 3576, 2 Old Dunleary Rd)* This place often has traditional Irish music or rock on Friday and Sunday. The rest of the week it's just a bar, frequented by the town's younger crowd.

Getting There & Away

See the Getting There & Away chapter for details of the ferry services between Dun Laoghaire and Holyhead in the UK.

Bus Nos 7, 7A and 8 from next to Trinity College cost €1.50 one way to Dun Laoghaire. The trip can take anywhere from 25 minutes to one hour depending on the traffic. The DART rail service takes you from Dublin to Dun Laoghaire in 15 to 20 minutes and also costs €1.50 one way.

DALKEY

Dalkey, just over 1km south-east of Sandycove, is smaller and prettier than Dun Laoghaire. In medieval times it was Dublin's most important port town (though you'd hardly notice that now) and as such, the town had the grand total of seven castles! Overlooking Bullock Harbour are the remains of an eighth structure, **Bulloch Castle**, built by the monks of St Mary's Abbey around 1150 but not included as one of the seven as it was in a different parish. A restoration of the castle is currently underway, but it will be some time before it is open to the public.

Of Dalkey's seven castles, only two remain. The roofless **Archibold's Castle** *(Castle St; closed to public)* is not in use, save for Christmas time, when a nativity crib is open to visitors *(free)*. The other castle is the 15th-century Goat Castle, which along with the remains of the 11th-century **St Begnet's Church and graveyard** is now the **Dalkey Castle and Heritage Centre** *(☎ 285 8366, Castle St; adult/student/child €3.80/3.20/ 2.55; open 9.30am-5pm Mon-Fri, 11am-5pm at weekends, May-Oct, closed weekdays Nov-Apr)*. Models, displays and exhibitions form an interesting history of Dalkey and an insight into the area during medieval times. It's worth paying close attention to the different panels, written by writer Hugh Leonard.

Dalkey has several holy wells, including **St Begnet's Holy Well** *(Dalkey Island; admission free)*, next to the ruins of another church dedicated to St Begnet on the nine-hectare Dalkey Island, a few hundred metres offshore from Coliemore Harbour. Reputed to cure rheumatism, the well is a popular destination for tourists and the faithful alike. To get there, you can rent a boat with a small outboard engine in Coliemore Harbour. To get one, simply show up (you can't book them in advance); they cost around €25 per hour.

The waters around the island are popular with local scuba divers. A number of rocky swimming pools are also along the coast at Dalkey.

Dalkey Quarry, now a popular site for rock climbers, once provided most of the stone for the gigantic piers at Dun Laoghaire Harbour.

Places to Eat
The Queen's *(☎ 285 4569, 12 Castle St)* Lunch from €6.35. This is an institution in Dalkey, a large friendly pub that does a delicious pub lunch, offering both meat and fish.

Kish *(☎ 285 0377, Coliemore Rd)* Lunch €25. Closed Mon. This is a new place that has already earned rave reviews for its inventive take on Irish cuisine. It is halfway between the town and the harbour.

Munkberry's *(☎ 284 7185, Castle St)* Main courses from €10.20. Open dinner only Tues-Sat, all day Sun, closed Mon. This is an established restaurant in the centre of town, serving up an Irish take on Mediterranean cuisine. It has a large selection of vegetarian dishes.

Getting There & Away
Dalkey is on the DART suburban line. Alternatively you can catch bus No 8 from Burgh Quay in the city centre. Both cost €1.50, but you're better off using the DART as the bus usually gets caught in traffic.

BRAY
The arrival of the railway in the 1850s turned Bray, 19km south of Dublin, into another popular and easily accessible seaside destination for Dubliners. Its central position between the city and the Wicklow Mountains is a draw, but it's not a very attractive seaside town, with a long seafront parade of tacky fast-food places and tackier amusement arcades. The young James Joyce lived here from 1888 to 1891.

Like Sandycove, Bray has a **Martello tower** *(not open to the public)*, which is now a private residence owned by none other than U2's Bono. From Bray Head there are fine views southwards to the Great Sugar Loaf Mountain, a prominent peak in the Wicklow Mountains. There's an 8km **cliff walk** around Bray Head to the pleasant coastal resort of Greystones further south.

National Sealife *(☎ 286 6939, W www .sealife.com, Strand Rd; adult/child €7/5)* is on the seafront in Bray. The old and pitiful National Aquarium was taken over by a British company a couple of years ago and is now a much more pleasant place to visit, with a fairly big selection of different aquariums stocked with 70 different sea and freshwater species, ranging from seahorses to sharks.

Kilruddery House & Gardens *(☎ 286 3405, Kilruddery; €5.70 house & gardens, €3.80 gardens only; open 1pm-5pm May, June & September)*, about 3km south of Bray on the Greystones Rd, includes one of the oldest gardens in Ireland.

SEASIDE SUBURBS

Places to Eat

The Tree of Idleness (☎ *286 3498, The Seafront*) Main courses from €12.70. This restaurant with delicious Greek-Cypriot food is one attraction for which it's worth making the foray from Dublin. The suckling pig, filled with apple and apricot stuffing, is one of its most popular dishes.

The Porter House (☎ *286 0668, Strand Rd*) This pub claims to have Ireland's largest selection of beers from around the world.

Getting There & Away

Bray is on the DART suburban line from Dublin, or you can catch bus No 45 (from Hawkins St) or No 84 (from Burgh Quay). Both the DART and the buses cost €1.50 one way; the DART has the advantage that it can't get stuck in traffic.

North of Dublin

HOWTH PENINSULA

The bulbous Howth Peninsula delineates the northern end of Dublin Bay. Howth town, 15km north-east of central Dublin, is a popular destination for an excursion and has also developed as a residential suburb. There's a pleasant little port replete with boats of all shapes and sizes; looming above it is the Hill of Howth, wonderful for walking and with some splendid views of Dublin city and the bay. A night in Howth makes an agreeable seaside escape and, like Dun Laoghaire to the south, it's a short commute to Dublin.

Howth is easily reached by DART train or by simply following the Clontarf Rd around the northern bay shoreline. En route you pass Clontarf, site of the pivotal clash between Irish and Viking forces at the Battle of Clontarf in 1014 (see History in the Facts about Dublin chapter). Farther along is North Bull Island, a wildlife sanctuary where many migratory birds pause in winter.

History

Howth has Viking origins and its name (it rhymes with both) comes from the Viking word *hoved* or head. Howth Harbour, dating from 1807 to 1809, was Dublin's main har-

The Bloody Stream

On August 10, 1177, the Norman baron, Sir John de Courcy, sailed into the harbour in an attempt to take the headland from the Vikings. Unable to leave his ship due to bad weather, he entrusted command of his troops to a certain Sir Almeric Tristram, who claimed to be a descendant of Sir Tristram, a knight of King Arthur's Round (and mythical) Table. The two forces clashed at Evora Bridge, which crossed a small stream just west of today's harbour. The battle was so fierce and the casualties so many that the stream turned red with blood, and subsequently became known as the 'bloody stream'. Now underground, the stream runs directly beneath the DART station.

bour for packet boats from England. Howth Rd was built to ensure the rapid transfer of incoming mail and dispatches into Dublin. The replacement of sailing packets with steam packets in 1818 reduced the transit time from Holyhead to seven hours. But by 1813 the harbour was already silting up and in 1833 Howth was superseded by Dun Laoghaire.

Howth's most famous arrival was King George IV, who visited Ireland in 1821 and is chiefly remembered for staggering drunk off the boat. He left his footprint at the point where he stepped ashore on West Pier.

In 1914 Robert Erskine Childers' yacht *Asgard* brought a cargo of 900 rifles into the port to arm the nationalists. During the Civil War, Childers, who was on the IRA side, was court-martialled and executed by firing squad for the illegal possession of a revolver (given to him by Michael Collins). The *Asgard* is now on display at Kilmainham Gaol in Dublin.

Howth's popularity as a seaside escape from Dublin made the Howth electric trams famous. They were withdrawn in the late 1950s, and all that remains of them is an exhibit in the National Transport Museum.

Howth

This is a pretty little town built on steep streets running down to the waterfront. Al-

Whether you're looking to browse through books...

...sample spirits...

...or chomp cheese, there's plenty of scope to indulge yourself.

Dublin has some colourful markets, such as that on Moore St, which specialises in flowers, fruit and veg though the harbour's role as a shipping port has long gone, Howth is now a major fishing centre and yachting harbour.

St Mary's Abbey *(Abbey St; admission free)* stands in ruins near the town centre. It was originally founded in 1042, supposedly by the Viking king Sitric, who also founded the original church on the site of Christ Church Cathedral in Dublin. St Mary's Abbey was amalgamated with the monastery on Ireland's Eye (see the section later in this chapter) in 1235. Some parts of the ruins date from that time but most are from the 15th and 16th centuries. The tomb of Christopher St Lawrence (Lord Howth) in the south-eastern corner dates from around 1470. You can walk around the grounds but to enter the abbey you need to obtain the key from the caretaker; see the instructions on the gate.

There's an ATM (but no bank) directly across the street from the DART station.

Howth Castle & Demesne Howth Castle's demesne was acquired by the Norman noble Sir Almeric Tristram in 1177 and has remained in the family ever since, though the unbroken chain of male succession finally came to an end in 1909. The family name was changed to St Lawrence when Sir Almeric won a battle at the behest (so he believed) of St Lawrence.

Originally built in 1564, Howth Castle *(not open to the public)* itself, which also belongs to the family, has been much restored and rebuilt over the years, most recently in 1910 by the British architect Sir Edwin Lutyens. Today it is occupied by four different families, who have divided the castle into residences.

You can visit the **castle gardens** *(admission free)*, noted for their rhododendrons, which bloom in May and June, for their azaleas and for a long, 10m-high beech hedge planted in 1710.

Also in the grounds are the ruins of the 16th-century **Corr Castle** and an ancient *dolmen* (a Neolithic grave memorial, built of vertical stones topped by a table stone) known as Aideen's Grave. It's said that Aideen died of a broken heart after her husband was killed at the Battle of Gavra near

Tara in 184 AD, though the dolmen is actually much older than that.

The castle is a short walk from the centre of Howth and there's the very popular **Deer Park Golf Course** *(☎ 832 2624, Howth Castle; €13-25)* in the demesne.

National Transport Museum

The somewhat ramshackle National Transport Museum *(☎ 848 0831, Howth Castle; adult/student €2.55/1.90; open 10am-5.30pm Mon-Fri Easter-Sept, 2pm-5pm weekends Oct-Easter)* has a range of exhibits, including double-decker buses, a bakery van, fire engines and trams, including a Hill of Howth electric tram that operated from 1901 to 1959. To reach the museum go through the castle gates and turn right just before the castle.

Around the Peninsula

The 171m-high **summit**, about 5km up the hill to the south-east of town, offers views across Dublin Bay to the Wicklow Mountains. From the summit you can walk to the top of the Ben of Howth, which has a cairn said to mark a 2000-year-old Celtic royal grave. The 1814 **Baily Lighthouse** *(Baily, Howth Head; closed to public)* at the south-eastern corner is on the site of an old stone fort or 'baily' and can be reached from the town by a dramatic 3km clifftop walk. There was an earlier hilltop beacon here by 1670.

Ireland's Eye

About 1.5km offshore from Howth is Ireland's Eye, a rocky sea-bird sanctuary with the ruins of a 6th-century monastery. A Martello tower (see the boxed text 'Martello Towers' earlier in this chapter) is at the north-western end of the island, where boats from Howth land, while at the eastern end a spectacular rock face plummets into the sea. In addition to the sea birds wheeling overhead, you can see young birds on the ground during the nesting season. Seals can also be spotted around the island.

Doyle & Sons *(☎ 831 4200)* take boats out to the island from the East Pier of Howth Harbour during the summer, usually on weekend afternoons. The cost is €7.60/5.10

SEASIDE SUBURBS

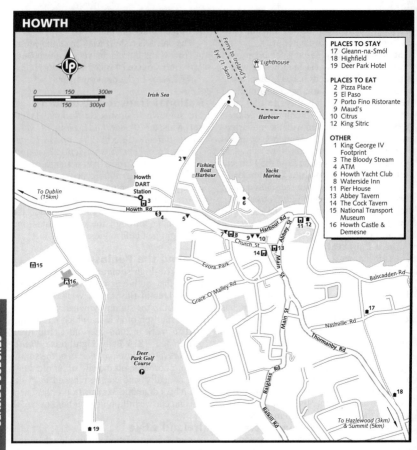

HOWTH

PLACES TO STAY
17 Gleann-na-Smól
18 Highfield
19 Deer Park Hotel

PLACES TO EAT
2 Pizza Place
5 El Paso
7 Porto Fino Ristorante
9 Maud's
10 Citrus
12 King Sitric

OTHER
1 King George IV
   Footprint
3 The Bloody Stream
4 ATM
6 Howth Yacht Club
8 Waterside Inn
11 Pier House
13 Abbey Tavern
14 The Cock Tavern
15 National Transport
   Museum
16 Howth Castle &
   Demesne

Lighthouse

Ferry to Ireland's Eye (1.5km)

Irish Sea

Harbour

Fishing Boat Harbour

Yacht Marina

Howth DART Station

To Dublin (15km)

Howth Rd

Harbour Rd

Abbey St

Church St

Main St

Evora Park

Balscadden Rd

Grace O'Malley Rd

Deer Park Golf Course

Nashville Rd

Thormanby Rd

Balglass Rd

Balkill Rd

To Hazlewood (3km) & Summit (5km)

SEASIDE SUBURBS

return. Don't wear shorts if you're planning to visit the monastery ruins because they're surrounded by a thicket of stinging nettles. And bring your rubbish back with you – far too many island visitors don't.

North of Ireland's Eye is **Lambay Island**, a larger, more remote sea-bird sanctuary.

Places to Stay

All of the B&Bs listed here are on Howth Hill, above the town. You can walk, but they are all served by bus No 31A from the port. Tickets are €0.70.

Gleann-na-Smól (☎ 832 2936, fax 832 0516, e rickards@indigo.ie, Nashville Rd) Singles/doubles €38.50/53.50. This modern, two-storey house has four en suite bedrooms.

Hazelwood (☎/fax 839 1391, 2 Thormanby Woods, Thormanby Rd) €28 per person. This large, white bungalow has fabulous views of Ireland's Eye and the harbour. The rooms are quite nice, with colourful bedspreads. All are en suite.

Highfield (☎ 832 3936, Thormanby Rd) €32 per person. This is a fine Victorian house set back from the road. The rooms are beautifully decorated, with a mix of antiques and modern comforts.

King Sitric (☎ *832 5235, fax 839 2442,* e *info@kingsitric.ie, Harbour Rd)* Singles/ doubles from €83/121. Howth's most famous restaurant (see Places to Eat below) has added eight marvellous rooms to its premises right on the port. Each is named after a lighthouse, and each is extremely well decorated, providing maximum comfort. All of the rooms have wonderful views of the port.

Deer Park Hotel (☎ *832 2624, fax 839 2405,* e *sales@deerpark.iol.ie, Howth Castle)* Singles/doubles €102/153. Deer Park Hotel is by the golf course in the grounds of Howth Castle. The rooms are elegant and comfortable (as you would expect from a top-class hotel), but the hotel is a little too modern to give a genuine sense of the place's ambience.

Places to Eat

Howth has fine seafood that self-caterers can buy fresh from the trawlers at the string of *seafood shops* along West Pier.

Maud's (☎ *839 5450, Harbour Rd)* Sandwiches €5.10. Apart from some pretty good sandwiches, Maud's is known for its gorgeous ice creams.

El Paso (☎ *832 3334, 10 Harbour Rd)* Main courses €8.90. This harbour-front restaurant serves up Tex-Mex cuisine in the evening Monday to Saturday and from 2pm on Sunday.

Porto Fino Ristorante (☎ *839 3054, Harbour Rd)* Main courses from €10.10. This place serves really delicious Italian food.

Citrus (☎ *832 0200, Harbour Rd)* Main courses around €12.70. This is a fancy new place that serves up imaginatively done continental-style cuisine. For a harbourfront place, it has a surprising emphasis on meat dishes.

The Bloody Stream (☎ *839 0203, Howth Rd)* Seafood platter €14.60-17.50. Located directly below the DART station, this fine pub has a wonderful restaurant where you can eat two kinds of seafood platter, both delicious. In fine weather you can eat *al fresco*.

King Sitric (☎ *832 5235, Harbour Rd)* Main courses €28, 5-course set dinner €44.

Open noon-11.30pm Mon-Sat. This place, near East Pier, is rightfully praised for its fine seafood. Try the excellent crab, which is always fresh. The wine list is superb and has won a number of domestic and international awards.

Alternatively, Howth's many pubs provide economic dining options (see Entertainment later in this section).

Entertainment

Howth's pubs are noted for their jazz performances. The annual Howth Jazz Festival (☎ *873 3199)* is the port's lively celebration of jazz music; the town's pubs are literally thronged.

The Cock Tavern (☎ *832 3237, 18 Church St)* This friendly pub just above the harbour is popular with Howth's younger crowds.

Waterside Inn (☎ *832 5568, Harbour Rd)* Not a bad spot, but there's more life elsewhere.

Pier House (☎ *832 4510, 4 East Pier)* Directly overlooking the harbour, you can sit out the front of this pub and watch life go by in the port.

Abbey Tavern (☎ *839 0307, Main St)* Open evenings only. Opposite St Mary's Abbey, this tavern occasionally has traditional Irish entertainment in the evenings.

Getting There & Away

The easiest and quickest way to get to Howth from Dublin is on the DART train, which whisks you there in just over 20 minutes for a fare of €1.50. For the same fare, bus Nos 31 and 31A from Lower Abbey St in the city centre run as far as the Summit, 5km to the south-east of Howth.

MALAHIDE

Though Malahide has been virtually swallowed up by Dublin's northwards expansion, it remains a pretty place with a small marina, a cluster of B&Bs, several coffee shops and a choice of ethnic restaurants. The well tended, 101 hectare Malahide Demesne (castle grounds) incorporates Malahide Castle, the town's principal attraction, as well as Talbot Botanic Gardens and the extensive Fry Model Railway.

SEASIDE SUBURBS

Malahide Castle

Despite the vicissitudes of Irish history, the Talbot family managed to keep Malahide Castle (☎ 846 2184, Malahide, County Dublin; family/adult/student/child €14/5.10/3.80/2.55, €22.25/8.90/6.70/3.80 including the Fry Model Railway; open 10am-5pm Mon-Sat, 11am-6pm Sun & holidays Apr-Oct, 10am-5pm weekdays, 2pm-5pm Sat, Sun & holidays Nov-Mar) under its control from 1185 to 1976, apart from when Cromwell was in power (1649–60). It's now owned by Dublin County Council. The castle is the usual hotchpotch of additions and renovations. The oldest part is a three-storey, 12th-century tower house. The façade is flanked by circular towers, tacked on in 1765.

The castle is packed with furniture and paintings. Highlights include a 16th-century oak room with decorative carvings and the medieval Great Hall with family portraits, a minstrel's gallery and a painting of the Battle of the Boyne (see under The Protestant Ascendancy in the History section of the Facts about Dublin chapter). Puck, the Talbot family ghost, is said to have last appeared in the castle in 1975.

The **parkland** (☎ 846 2184, Malahide Castle; admission free; open 10am-9pm, to 5pm Nov-Mar) around the castle is a good place for a picnic.

Fry Model Railway

Ireland's biggest model railway (☎ 846 3779, Malahide Castle Demesne; family/adult/student/child €14/5.10/3.80/2.55, €22.25/8.90/6.70/3.80 including Malahide Castle; open 10am-5pm Mon-Sat, 2pm-6pm Sun & holidays Apr-Oct, 10am-5pm Sat, 2pm-5pm Sun & holidays Nov-Mar) at 240 sq metres, this model authentically displays much of Ireland's rail- and public-transport system, including the DART line and Irish-Sea ferry services, in O-gauge (32mm track width). A separate room features model trains and other memorabilia. Unfortunately, the operators suffer from the over-seriousness of some grown men with complicated toys; rather than let you simply look and admire, they

herd you into the control room in groups for demonstrations.

Places to Stay & Eat

There are a few B&B options in Malahide.

Sonas (☎ 845 1953, fax 845 7032, ⓔ jmoodley@indigo.ie, 39 The Old Golf Links) Rooms €32 per person. Near the sea, this modern and luxurious house is an excellent choice. The rooms are extremely comfortable and neat.

Seabreeze (☎ 845 0271, ⓔ seabreeze_irl@hotmail.com, Coast Rd) Rooms €32 per person. This modern house is directly across from the beach, and the rooms are quite nice, with large, comfortable beds and pleasant furnishings.

Grand Hotel (☎ 845 000, fax 816 8025, ⓔ booking@thegrand.ie, Coast Rd) Singles/doubles from €120/178. Malahide's only top-grade hotel, the Grand is a sprawling white building overlooking the tennis club. The rooms are elegant, pretty big and extremely comfortable.

Apart from a selection of **cafes** and **fast-food** outlets, there are a couple of restaurants worth checking out.

Siam Thai (☎ 845 4698, Gas Lane) Main courses around €10.20. This place offers some of Dublin's best Pacific-Rim cuisine, although the emphasis is on Thai dishes such as Ghung Phad Phong Garee (tiger prawns, spring onions, mushrooms and basil). The food is delicious.

Cruzzo (☎ 845 0599, The Marina) Main courses from €7.60. What exactly is 'global cuisine'? Pretty much anything the chef wants to make, from pasta dishes to curries and all things in between. This large new restaurant overlooking the marina has all of that and more.

Getting There & Away

Malahide is 13km north of Dublin. Bus No 42 (€1.50) from Talbot St takes about 45 minutes. The DART now stops in Malahide (€1.70), but be sure to get on the right train (it's marked at the front of the train) as the line splits at Howth Junction.

SEASIDE SUBURBS

Excursions

Ireland is so small that almost anywhere is within day-trip distance of Dublin – it's no problem to zip up to Belfast for the day, for example. Bus Éireann has day tours from Dublin as far as Kilkenny, Waterford and even Lough Erne in Northern Ireland. The places described in this chapter, however, are all easy and popular day trips from the capital, by car or public transport, and feature on many day-tour itineraries. For details on tour operators, see Organised Tours in the Getting Around chapter.

A trio of attractions immediately south of Dublin must surely earn top honours in their respective categories. Just outside the County Wicklow town of Enniskerry are the exquisite Italianate gardens of Powerscourt House. Further south, the medieval monastic site of Glendalough nestles in a wonderful forested valley. Completing the threesome is the Wicklow Way, a superb eight- to 10-day walk through what is known as 'the garden of Ireland', a superb landscape of meadows, forests, dramatic cliffs and mountains. This is perhaps the most popular long walk in Ireland (shorter sections can also be tackled). For more information on the Wicklow Way see Lonely Planet's *Walking in Ireland*.

About 20km west of the city centre, near Maynooth in County Kildare, is Castletown, with a fine stately home from the days of the Anglo-Irish Ascendancy, plus two unusual follies. In Tully, just outside Kildare Town, is the National Stud, a centre for the breeding of race horses. Next door are the Japanese Gardens, considered by experts to be among the finest in Europe.

The Boyne Valley makes an excellent day excursion from Dublin. Apart from sites associated with the 1690 Battle of the Boyne (see The Protestant Ascendancy in the History section of the Facts about Dublin chapter), the valley has a number of prehistoric remains, including magnificent Newgrange, Europe's largest Neolithic passage grave (a burial place with a passageway leading to one or more chambers). North of Newgrange are

another fine monastic site at Mellifont and some of Ireland's most magnificent high crosses (crosses carved in stone, combining engraved Celtic swirls with scenes from the Gospels) at Monasterboice. The town of Drogheda makes a good base for touring the Boyne Valley and has some interesting points of its own.

In the upper valleys of the River Boyne and its tributaries are the ancient site of Tara, the ruins of Trim Castle and various medieval ruins at Kells, the original home of the Book of Kells (see The Book of Kells in the Things to See & Do chapter).

POWERSCOURT ESTATE

About 1km from the picturesque village of Enniskerry and about 22km south of Dublin is **Powerscourt House** (☎ 204 6000, Ⓦ *www .powerscourt.ie, Enniskerry; adult/student/ child €7.60/6.35/3.80 house & gardens, €2.55/1.90/1.30 house only, €5.10/4.45/ 2.55 garden only; open 9.30am-5.30pm Feb-Oct, to 4.30pm Nov-Jan)*, built in 1731. The house was designed by Richard Cassels (who was also the architect of Russborough House and the obelisk at Castletown House, both described later in this chapter). Much of the house accidentally burnt down in 1974, just after a major renovation had been completed. Plans to restore the house have been abandoned, though the main hall has an exhibition with a film on the history of the site from 1200 to the present day. The only other parts of the house presently open to the public are the ballroom and the garden room, which are also used for private functions. But it's the magnificent 20-hectare **garden** that attracts the crowds. The owners now live in one wing of the house.

The terraced gardens descending the hill in front of the house are backed by the peak of the 506m-high Great Sugar Loaf Mountain on the horizon. The Japanese call this 'borrowed scenery'. Powerscourt also has its own small Japanese garden, as well as curiosities such as a pets' cemetery.

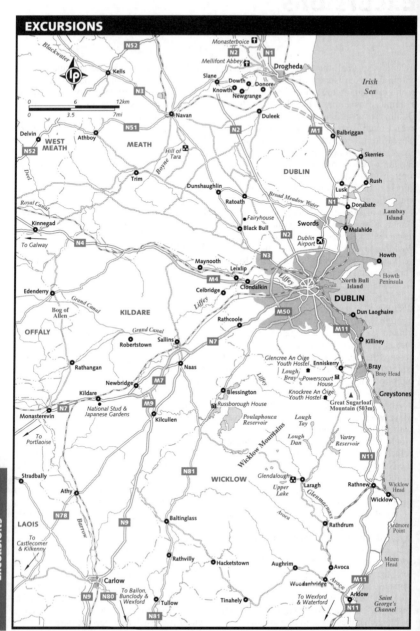

EXCURSIONS

Free guided tours are available. There is a teashop, a garden centre and an outlet of the popular Avoca Handweavers shop, which has a range of fine Irish clothing. The nearest place to stay is Glendalough.

Powerscourt Waterfall

A 5km walk to a separate part of the estate takes you to this 130m waterfall *(☎ 204 6000, Powerscourt Estate, Enniskerry; adult/student/child €3.20/2.55/1.90; open 9.30am-7pm, or to dusk in winter)*. It's the highest waterfall in Britain and Ireland. It's most impressive after heavy rain. You can also get to the falls by road, following the signs from the estate. In 2000, a playground was opened nearby, complete with a space net and a sand castle machine.

Places to Eat

Poppies Country Cooking (☎ 282 8869, The Square) Lunches less than €11.45. This place, on the main square, is the best place to eat in Enniskerry. It offers solid lunches (including several vegetarian options) and great buns and cakes, all in a rustic atmosphere.

Getting There & Away

Enniskerry is 3km west of the N11, the main road from Dublin to Wicklow, Arklow and Wexford. A Bus Éireann *(☎ 836 6111)* express bus from the Busáras in Dublin drops you at the turnoff for Enniskerry. Dublin bus No 44 goes to Enniskerry from Hawkins St in Dublin, or you can take the DART train to Bray and get bus No 85 from the station.

Bus Éireann *(☎ 836 6111)* runs a tour to Powerscourt on Tuesday from June to mid-September. It departs from Busáras in Dublin at 10am and returns at 5pm. The tour costs adult/student/child €25.50/23/12.70 (admission to Powerscourt is included). Mary Gibbons Tours *(☎ 283 9973)* does full-day tours of Wicklow (Powerscourt admission included), leaving from the Dublin Tourism office at 10.45am and returning between 5pm and 5.30pm on Thursday, Saturday and Sunday (€28). See the Getting Around chapter for details of other tours.

GLENDALOUGH

Pronounced 'glendalock', and meaning 'glen of the two lakes', this is a magical place – an ancient monastic settlement beside a pair of dark lakes, overshadowed by the sheer sides of a deep valley. Its setting in the Wicklow Mountains is one of Ireland's most picturesque, and the **monastery** is one of the country's most important historical sites. It's 54km south of Dublin – close enough to attract big crowds in summer.

Things to See & Do

The monastery, founded by St Kevin (see the boxed text 'St Kevin') in the 6th century, grew to be one of the most important in Ireland, surviving Viking raids in the 9th and 10th centuries and an English incursion in 1398 before final suppression in the 16th century.

The site is entered through Ireland's only surviving monastic gateway. The ruins include a round tower, the cathedral, a fine high

---

St Kevin

St Kevin was born in around 498 AD into the royal house of Leinster. His name is derived from Ceomghan (or Coemhghein), meaning the 'fair one' or 'well featured'. As a child he studied under the charge of three holy men – Éanna, Eoghan and Lochan. While under their tutelage he went to Glendalough where, it is said, he lived in a tree. He left and later returned to spend his days as a hermit in the cave that became known as St Kevin's Bed. He couldn't completely escape the world, however; knowledge of his piety spread and many people came to Glendalough to share his isolated existence. They were not always welcome and he is reputed to have pushed one of his followers (who disturbed his isolation) over a cliff edge into one of the lakes.

His monastic settlement eventually spread from the Upper Lake to the site of the remains we see today. St Kevin became abbot of the monastery in 570 and is said to have died in 617 or 618, which would have made him about 120 years old.

cross and the curious **St Kevin's Church**. The latter is sometimes referred to as St Kevin's Kitchen because of its chimney-like tower.

Just under 1km beyond the monastic site is **Upper Lake**, with a cave known as St Kevin's Bed, to which the saint is said to have retreated. There are other reminders of St Kevin dotted around the lake.

The on-site **Glendalough Visitor Centre** (☎ 0404-45325/45352, Glendalough, Bray; adults/seniors/students & children €2.55/ 1.90/1.25; open 9am-5.15pm June-Aug, 9.30am-5.15pm Sept–mid-Oct and mid-Mar–end May, 9.30am-4.15pm mid-Oct– mid-Mar) has some interesting displays, including a model of the monastery in its prime. A high-quality 20-minute audiovisual display is shown regularly.

Places to Stay & Eat

An Óige Glendalough Hostel (☎ 0404-45342, fax 45690, e glendaloughyh@ ireland.com, The Lodge, Glendalough) Dorm beds €15.90. This recently renovated hostel is near the round tower, set amid the deeply wooded glacial area that makes up the Glendalough Valley. Thankfully, though, the accommodation here is far more luxurious than that experienced by the 6th-century monks who once lived in the area!

Tudor Lodge (☎ 0404-45297, fax 45554, e tudorlodgeireland@eircom.net, Laragh) Singles/doubles €38/57. About 1km from the monastic ruins in the village of Laragh, this comfortable B&B has four well appointed rooms.

Glendalough Hotel (☎ 0404-45135, fax 45142, e info@glendaloughhotel.ie, Glendalough) Singles/doubles €95/153. This hotel is next to the monastic ruins. Its 44 rooms have been thoroughly upgraded in the last couple of years to afford maximum comfort and not a small amount of luxury – which is adequately reflected in the prices. Breakfast is included.

Wicklow Heather Restaurant (☎ 0404-45157, Laragh) Set lunch €13.35. Next to the post office, this is about the best bet for a substantial meal in Laragh, although in summer several other places are open for tea, coffee, sandwiches and cakes.

The Monastic Life, 2002-Style

From about the 6th century AD, Glendalough was renowned for its monastic settlement, where monks retired to contemplate in the quiet solitude of the valley. In an effort to offer a modern-day version of their experiences, a new *Heritage Retreat Centre* (☎ 0404-45140) was opened in 2001. It consists of five *cillíns* or hermitages designed to provide one-person self-catering accommodation consisting of a bed, bathroom, small kitchen area and an open fire supplemented by a storage heating facility. Mobile phones, laptops, TVs and other electronic distractions are not quite forbidden, but the absence of electricity will make them redundant. And how much the price of this tranquil solitude? A snip at €32 per night.

Getting There & Away

St Kevin's Bus Service (☎ 281 8119) departs from Dublin to Glendalough at 11.30am from outside the Royal College of Surgeons on West St Stephen's Green. Glendalough departures are at 4.15pm (5.30pm on Sunday). Tickets cost €7.60/12.70 one way/return.

Bus Éireann has a daily tour to Glendalough and Wicklow from April to October (Wednesday, Friday and Sunday only between January and March). The tour departs from Busáras at 10.30am and returns at 5.45pm (4.30pm in winter), and costs adult/ child €25.50/12.70 (€20.50/10.25 in winter). You can also pick up the tour at the Dublin Tourism office at the ferryport in Dun Laoghaire at 11am. The Mary Gibbons tour to Powerscourt (see Powerscourt Estate earlier in this chapter) also includes a visit to Glendalough. Check the Getting Around chapter for details of other tours.

WICKLOW WAY

Running for 132km from County Dublin through County Wicklow to County Carlow, this is the oldest and one of the most popular of Ireland's long-distance scenic walks. It's well documented in leaflets, which can be picked up at the beginning of the walk or from a Dublin Tourism office. For more detail on the Wicklow Way and other walks in the Dublin area and the rest of Ireland, see Lonely Planet's *Walking in Ireland*. Much of the trail traverses country above 500m in altitude, so be prepared for rapid changes in the weather. If you don't feel up to tackling the whole eight- to 10-day walk, the three-day section from Knockree (near Enniskerry) to Glendalough is the most attractive and has easy transport connections at both ends. At the Dublin end the walk starts at Marlay Park in Rathfarnham.

Places to Stay
There are hostels along the route, as well as numerous B&Bs.

Glencree An Óige Hostel *(☎ 01-286 4037, e mailbox@anoige.ie, Stone House, Glencree)* Dorms €9.50. In a lovely old stone house, this hostel is clean and neat, if a little bare. It is closed between 10am and 5pm daily.

Knockree An Óige Hostel *(☎ 01-286 4036, e mailbox@anoige.ie, Lacken House, Knockree)* Dorms €9.50. This 58-bed hostel is situated in an old farmhouse with commanding views of Glencree and the surrounding mountains. Accommodations can only be booked through the head office in Dublin (see Hostels in the Places to Stay chapter).

Greenane An Óige Hostel *(no phone or fax, e mailbox@anoige.ie, Glenmalure, Greenane)* Dorms €9.50. Open daily June-Aug; Sat only for the rest of the year. Once owned by Maud Gonne (WB Yeats' greatest inspiration) and the setting for JM Synge's play *Shadow of the Glen,* this small mountain hut has been converted into a 16-bed hostel. It has virtually no facilities save running water and beds, and is as close to monastic spartan living as you're likely to get.

RUSSBOROUGH HOUSE
Five kilometres south of Blessington, Russborough House *(☎ 045-865239, Blessington; adult/student/child €5.10/3.85/2.55; open 10.30am-5.30pm May-Sept, 10.30am-5.30pm Sun & bank holidays Apr & Oct)* was designed by the architect Richard Castle and built between 1740 and 1751. The house is a magnificent example of Palladian architecture, with a facade that extends more than 200m between two semicircular loggias. Inside, the style is exuberantly Baroque, especially in the ornate plasterwork created by the LaFranchini brothers, who also worked on Castletown House (see later in this chapter). In 1952 the house was bought by Sir Alfred Beit, the co-founder (with Cecil Rhodes) of the De Beers Mining Co in South Africa. He brought with him one of Europe's finest private art collections, with work by Goya, Gainsborough, Rubens and Vermeer.

In 1974, a chunk of the collection was stolen by Rose Dugdale for the IRA, but all of the paintings were subsequently recovered undamaged. No such luck in 1986, however, when Martin Cahill, the notorious 'General' of Dublin's criminal underworld (and the subject of a film, *The General*, by director John Boorman; see Cinema under Arts in the Facts about Dublin chapter) successfully burgled the house for his own profit. The bulk of this heist was never found, while some of the works that were had been permanently ruined. Keen to avoid being robbed a third time, the Beit family donated the majority of the remaining collection to the National Gallery in 1988. Alas, Russborough's misfortunes were not yet finished, and in June 2001 two thieves drove a jeep through the front door and made off with a couple more paintings.

Getting There & Away
Blessington is 35km south-west of Dublin. It is served by bus No 65 from Eden Quay in the city from 6am to 11.15pm (€3, 10 daily).

KILDARE TOWN
This is a charming, picturesque town, with a pleasant triangular square lined with pubs on each side. To the south of the town is a huge tract of flatlands known as the Curragh, the heartland of Ireland's multi-million euro horse breeding and racing industry. The stud farms in the area are – along with those in Kentucky – the most powerful and successful in the world, largely due to a 1969 law that made stud fees in Ireland tax free. Consequently, the bigger trainers can afford to pay top prices for the best stallions in the

EXCURSIONS

knowledge that they will recoup their investment many times over. With the exception of the National Stud, none of the studs are open to the public, but if you're up early in the morning you'll catch sight of dozens of healthy-looking, expensive horses being put through their paces.

The tourist office (☎ 045-522696) at Market House, in the middle of the square, opens 10am to 1pm and 2pm to 5.30pm Monday to Saturday, and Monday to Friday only in May.

Things to See & Do
The town is dominated by the imposing presence of the Church of Ireland **St Brigid's Cathedral** *(☎ 045-521352, Market Square; admission free, open 10am-1pm & 2pm-5pm Mon-Sat, 2pm-5pm Sun May-Oct)*, named after one of Ireland's most important saints, who founded a monastery here in AD 490. Inside there are the remains of an ancient fire temple, where a perpetual fire was kept burning until the dissolution of the monasteries in 1537. The cathedral has a fine stained-glass window, facing west, which depicts the three main saints of Ireland: Patrick, Brigid and Columba. In the graveyard is a **round tower** *(adult/student €1.25/0.65; open 10am-1pm, 2pm-5pm Mon-Sat & 2pm-5pm Sun Apr-Sept)*, which, at 32.9m, is the second highest in the country. The views of the surrounding countryside are terrific.

National Stud & Japanese Gardens
In the small village of Tully, three kilometres south of Kildare, is the National Stud *(☎ 045-521251, W www.irish-national-stud.ie, Tully; adult/student & senior/child €7.60/5.70/3.80, includes Japanese Gardens; open 9.30am-6pm daily mid-Feb–mid-Nov)*, the only government-sponsored horse stud farm in Ireland. Founded in 1900 by Colonel William Hall-Walker (of the Johnnie Walker distilling family) and handed over to the state in 1943, it is the home of some of Ireland's top breeding stallions. Its most famous tenant is 19-year-old Indian Ridge, who covers 75 mares a season for €44,500 each. Not surprisingly, he's insured for €13 million. There is also a museum with the impressively large

skeleton of champion racehorse Arkle, winner of many races in the 1960s. It isn't necessary to be a racing aficionado to appreciate a visit here; the setting is beautiful and in fine weather makes for a great afternoon walk.

Next door are the Japanese Gardens *(☎ 045-521617, Tully; adult/student & senior/child €7.60/5.70/3.80, includes National Stud; open 9.30am-6pm Feb-Nov)*, founded by Colonel Hall-Walker in 1906 and laid out by master gardener Tasso Eida and his son Minoru. In 1912 Tasso died while returning to Japan, and nothing more was heard of the family until the 1950s, when Minoru's son Brian Eida turned up to admire his father's and grandfather's work as a tourist! The gardens chart the symbolic journey from birth to death through a series of landmarks, including a Tunnel of Ignorance, a Hill of Ambition and bridges signifying engagement and marriage. Although not entirely oriental in style (they include western trees such as Scots pine), these are considered to be among the finest Japanese gardens in Europe.

Places to Stay & Eat
Curragh Lodge Hotel *(☎ 045-522144, fax 521247, Dublin Street)* Rooms €45-63.50 per person, breakfast included. About a two-minute walk south of Market Square on the main Dublin road (N7), this charming hotel has elegant, comfortable rooms.

Silken Thomas *(☎ 045-522252, Market Square)* Meals around €11.50. This popular pub, partly converted from a cinema, in the town square has reasonable food in an old-world atmosphere.

Getting There & Away
Bus Éireann serves Kildare from Dublin (€10.80 return, one hour). There are 14 buses daily Monday to Friday, 13 on Saturday and eight on Sunday. One service a day stops at the National Stud and Japanese Gardens; it departs Busáras at 9am and picks up from the gardens at 3.45pm. On Sunday, there are two services, departing Dublin at 10am and noon, picking up at 3pm and 5.30pm. The Arrow train (☎ 836 3333) runs every 35 minutes from Heuston station (€10.20/10.80 single/return, 30 minutes).

CASTLETOWN HOUSE

Castletown House (☎ 628 8252, Celbridge; adult/child & student €3.80/1.60; open 10am-6pm weekdays, from 1pm weekends June-Sept, 10am-5pm weekdays, 1pm-5pm Sun Oct, 2pm-5pm Sun only Nov-Dec, 1pm-5pm Sun only Apr-May) near Maynooth, built between 1722 and 1732 for William Conolly, speaker of the Irish House of Commons and at that time Ireland's richest man, is another fine example of an imposing Anglo-Irish home. In 1979 the Castletown Federation took it over and it is now cared for by Dúchas, who touched the property up with a €6.25 million restoration. The design of the house was begun by Alessandro Galilei and finished by Edward Lovett Pearce, architect of the Bank of Ireland. The adjacent village of Celbridge, with its tree-lined avenue leading directly to the house, was built as an adjunct to the house. Descendants of Conolly continued to live at Castletown House until 1965. Lady Louisa Conolly commissioned the stucco work and the unusual print room, but she also had a passion for building follies. A curious tower known to locals as the **Obelisk**, designed by Richard Cassels, can be seen to the north from the Long Gallery at the back of the house. Immediately to the east of Castletown's grounds, on private property that never belonged to the house, is the even more curious conical **Wonderful Barn** (☎ 624 5448, Leixlip; admission free). The barn opens erratic hours at the weekend, so be sure to phone ahead to find out.

Getting There & Away

Castletown is 21km west of Dublin on the N4. Bus Nos 67 and 67A leave D'Olier St in Dublin about every hour for Celbridge and take a little over an hour to get there; the fare is €2.25/3.80 single/return. The bus stops at the gates of Castletown House.

SWORDS

The village of Swords is 16km north of Dublin. The Archbishop of Dublin built a fortified **palace** (Swords, County Dublin; admission free; open 9am-dusk) here in the 12th century, though the castellated walls date from the 15th century and numerous other modifications were made over the centuries. The windows to the right of the main entrance date from around 1250.

Swords also had an ancient monastery but today only its 23m-high round tower remains and even that was rebuilt several times between 1400 and 1700. It stands in grounds owned by the Church of Ireland. The body of Brian Ború was kept overnight in the monastery after his death in 1014 at the Battle of Clontarf, when his forces defeated the Vikings (see The Vikings Are Coming! under History in the Facts about Dublin chapter).

Getting There & Away

Bus Nos 33 and 33B leave Dublin's Eden Quay every 30 minutes or so and take less than an hour. The fare is €1.50 one way.

NEWBRIDGE HOUSE

North-east of Swords at Donabate is Newbridge House (☎ 843 6534, Donabate, County Dublin; family/adult/student/child €14/5/3.80/2.50; open 10am-1pm, 2pm-5pm Mon-Sat, to 6pm Sun & holidays Apr-Sep, 2pm-5pm Sat, Sun & holidays Oct-Mar). This historic Georgian mansion has fine plasterwork, a private museum, an impressive kitchen and a large traditional **farm** (see the boxed text 'Kids' Stuff') with cows, pigs and chickens. In the stables is an astonishingly elaborate coach, built for the Lord Chancellor in 1790. It was painted black for Queen Victoria's funeral and it wasn't until 1982 that the paint was scraped off to reveal the glittering masterpiece beneath. The coach's size is almost as impressive as its decoration: the back wheels alone stand 1.65m high.

You can wander around the 144 hectares of grounds, Newbridge Demesne (€3.80; open 10am-9pm Apr-Sept, to 5pm the rest of the year), surrounding the house.

Getting There & Away

Donabate is 19km north of Dublin. Bus No 33B runs every 30 minutes (€2.20, one hour) from Eden Quay to Donabate village. You can also get there on the Suburban Rail service (€1.75, 30 minutes, hourly) from either Connolly or Pearse station in the city centre.

EXCURSIONS

LUSK

On the way to Skerries you'll spot the dominating turrets of Lusk church, now a **heritage centre** (☎ *833 1618, Lusk, County Dublin; adult/child €1.25/€0.50; open 10am-5pm Fri mid-June–mid-Sept only*) where a 9th-century round tower stands beside and joined to a medieval tower.

On the medieval tower's various floors are displays of medieval and later stone effigies from various churches in north County Dublin. The much less impressive 19th-century nave houses Willie Monks' dusty, somewhat forlorn collection of household and other items.

Bus No 33 from Eden Quay goes to Lusk (€3.45, one hour, every 40 minutes).

SKERRIES

The sleepy seaside resort of Skerries is 30km north of Dublin. St Patrick is said to have made his arrival in Ireland here at Red Island, which is now joined to the mainland.

There's a good cliff walk south from Skerries to the bay of Loughshinny. At low tide you can walk to Shenick's, a small island off Skerries. Colt and St Patrick's are two other small islands, the latter with an old church ruin.

Farther offshore is Rockabill island with its lighthouse. The 7th-century oratory and holy well of **St Moibhi** and the ruins of **Baldongan Castle** are all near the town and are open to visits at any time.

Kids' Stuff

There are a couple of fine attractions to entertain the younger members of your party if you feel like venturing out of the city. And they may well appeal to bigger kids too. See the boxed text 'Dublin for Children' in the Facts for the Visitor chapter for more information on juvenile things to see and do in and around Dublin.

Fort Lucan Adventureland

This adventureland (☎ 628 0166, off Strawberry Beds Rd, Westmanstown, Lucan, north-west County Dublin; €5.70, adults & under-2s free; 10am-6pm daily Easter-Sept, 1.30pm-6pm daily 17 Mar-Easter) is essentially an assault course for children, complete with 40ft slides, giant trampolines, mazes and suspension bridges. You can catch the No 25 bus from Middle Abbey St to get there. Even in summer, however, the weather can dictate its opening hours, so be sure to call before setting off.

Fry Model Railway

Covering 240 sq metres of ground in a purpose-built house, is the world's largest display of model narrow-gauge trains, trams, boats and vehicles (see Fry Model Railway under Malahide in the Seaside Suburbs chapter for details). Children can also while away the time in the excellent playground in the grounds of the estate.

Newbridge Demesne Traditional Farm

In the grounds of Newbridge House, the courtyard and grounds of Newbridge Demesne Traditional Farm (☎ 843 6064, Donabate, County Dublin; family €2.50; 10am-5pm Tues-Fri, 11am-6pm Sat, 2pm-6pm Sun Apr-Oct, 2-5pm Sat & Sun Nov-Mar) have been converted to accommodate an imitation self-sufficient 18th-century farm. Alongside more familiar domestic animals and birds there are also rare breeds like the Kerry cow, Connemara pony and Jacob sheep; children will like the exotic chickens with punk hairdos too. In restoring the courtyard buildings and deciding what to grow and rear, Dublin County Council Parks Department has been able to draw on the records of the Cobbe family who used to own the house and still live there occasionally.

If you are visiting Newbridge House (see Newbridge House in this chapter), admission to the farm is included in the ticket price.

EXCURSIONS

Skerries Watermill & Windmills Heritage Centre

This fully restored **industrial mill** (☎ *849 5208, Skerries, County Dublin; family/adult/ student €9.50/3.80/2.90; open 10.30am-6pm daily Apr-Sept, to 4.30pm daily other months, closed 20 Dec-1 Jan)* comprises a watermill, five- and four-sail windmills, wetlands and a mill pond. Constructed in the 16th century for the Priory of Canons Regular of St Augustine, there has been a bakery on the site since 1840. It's an interesting place, and will even give you the chance to try your own hand at grinding (which is far harder than you might think!). It is a five-minute walk from the Skerries train station, and is well signposted.

Getting There & Away

Bus No 33 (€3.45, one hour, hourly) departs from Eden Quay for Skerries. Trains from Connolly station (€1.75) are less frequent but take around 30 minutes.

DROGHEDA

Drogheda, on the River Boyne about 5km inland, was captured by the Danes in 911 and later fortified by the Normans under the command of Hugh de Lacy. By the 14th century it was one of Ireland's four major towns; parts of the medieval walls and early monastic buildings lie scattered around the town.

In 1649 Drogheda was the scene of Cromwell's most notorious Irish slaughter. He met with stiff resistance and when his forces eventually overran the town the defenders were shown no mercy. Nearly 3000 people were massacred, including innocent civilians and children. When 100 of the town's inhabitants hid in the steeple of St Peter's Church, Cromwell's men simply burnt the church down. Many of the women and children who survived the barbarity were shipped off to the West Indies and sold into slavery. Drogheda was also on the losing side at the Battle of the Boyne in 1690, but quickly surrendered the day after James II was defeated.

It took many years for the town to recover from these events. The massive train viaduct and the string of quayside buildings hint at the town's brief Victorian-era industrial boom, when it was a centre for brewing and the manufacture of cotton and linen.

Orientation & Information

Drogheda's attractions are all in or near the centre of town. The town straddles the River Boyne, with the main shopping area on the northern bank along West and Laurence Sts. The tourist office (☎ 041-983 7070, W www .drogheda-tourism.com), near the junction of West and George's Sts, only opens 10am to 6pm Monday to Saturday, June to mid-September. The main post office and most of the banks are on West St.

Things to See & Do

Dominating the centre of town is the 1791 **St Peter's Roman Catholic Church** (☎ *041-983 8239, West St; admission free)* In an ornate glass case on the left side of the church is the head of St Oliver Plunkett (1629–81), who was executed by the perfidious English after being wrongly accused of taking part in the 1678 Popish Plot (a supposed Catholic conspiracy to murder Charles II and massacre Protestants).

At the corner of West and Shop Sts is the **Tholsel**, an imposing 18th-century granite building that was once the town hall. Today it is a bank.

Straddling Laurence St, the eastwards extension of West St, is **St Laurence Gate**, the finest surviving portion of the city walls. The only other remaining city gate is the 13th-century **Butter Gate**, north-west of the Millmount Museum.

On top of the hill is the 14th-century **Magdalene Tower** *(not open to the public)*. Originally part of a Dominican friary founded in 1224, it played a dramatic role in fierce fighting during the 1922 Civil War. Anti-Treaty soldiers occupied the tower and fired on pro-Treaty forces from this vantage point until it was bombarded by the pro-Treaty troops. But for the finest views over the town you must go to Millmount, across the river. The **Millmount Museum & Tower** *(☎ 041-983 3097, Millmount; adult/student €3.20/2.50 for museum, €2.50/1.90 for tower, €4.45/2.55 for both; open 10am-6pm Mon-Sat, 2.30pm-5pm Sun year-round)* has

EXCURSIONS

interesting displays on the town and its history; curiously, however, there is very little on Cromwell's 1649 atrocities. The adjacent round tower has no exhibits (though it is planned to show the town's sword and mace in the future) but there are some fabulous views of the town and surrounding countryside from the top. To get here, you can drive up to the hilltop or climb the steps from St Mary's Bridge, to the north-west of the bus terminal and to the north-east of the train station.

Places to Stay & Eat
The Green Door (☎/fax 041-983 4422, e greendoorhostel@hotmail.com, 47 John St) Dorm beds/triples €12.70/16.50 per person. This relatively new hostel only 150m from the bus station has pleasant dorms and family rooms with handcrafted wooden bunks.

There are also quite a few **B&Bs** in and around the town. Check with the tourist office for details.

Jalapeno's (☎ 041-983 8342, West St) From €3.80. This pleasant cafe on West St serves really good sandwiches and brews an excellent cup of coffee.

Getting There & Away
Drogheda is 48km north of Dublin, on the main N1 route to Belfast. Buses depart hourly from the Busáras in Dublin and take about an hour (€5.70 one way). In Drogheda the Bus Éireann station (☎ 041-983 5023) is on the corner of New St and Donore Rd, south of the river.

Trains leave Dublin's Connolly Station about every two hours and take around 30 minutes. Drogheda's train station is south of the river and east of the centre, off the Dublin road.

Drogheda is the central jumping-off point for a visit to the Boyne Valley sites.

BOYNE VALLEY
Many historic markers along the Boyne Valley are sites of the Battle of the Boyne, the epic struggle between the forces of Catholic James II and Protestant William of Orange. The defeat of the Catholic forces was to have long-running and tragic consequences for Ireland. In spite of their significance, the sites are of limited interest unless you're a student of Irish history, though the fertile valley has other worthwhile attractions.

Brú na Bóinne
The prehistoric passage tombs of the Boyne Valley are collectively known as Brú na Bóinne or Boyne Palace. At first it was surmised that they were the grave sites of the kings of Tara (who ruled in the first few centuries AD), but it's now known that they predate that period of Irish history by many centuries. At that time this fertile valley sheltered some of Ireland's earliest farming communities. As well as the site at Newgrange, there are two lesser, but still impressive, sites at Dowth and Knowth.

These ancient passage tombs were the largest constructions in Ireland until Norman castles were erected, and the country between the three major tombs is littered with countless other ancient mounds and standing stones. Over the centuries the tombs have been plundered by everybody from Vikings to Victorian treasure hunters and the mounds have decayed and been covered by grass and trees.

You can access the site and its tombs only through the **Brú na Bóinne Visitor Centre** (☎ 041-988 0300, w www.heritageireland.ie, Donore; adult/senior/student €2.55/1.90/1.25 including guided tour; open 9am-7pm daily June–mid-Sept, 9am-5.45pm daily mid-Sept–end Sept, 9.30am-5.30pm daily Oct & Mar-Apr, to 5pm Nov-Feb), on the southern side of the River Boyne, 2km west of Donore. Architecturally, the building is quite stunning, but its construction in the mid-1990s generated a storm of controversy that has not yet fully abated. Inside, however, you will find an extraordinary exhibition devoted to the passage tombs and the history of the pre-Celts, illustrated through audiovisual displays, dioramas and interactive exhibits. The centre can only be visited by guided tour.

Newgrange The finest Celtic passage tomb in Europe is a huge flattened mound just north of the River Boyne about 13km west of Drogheda. It's believed to date from 3200 BC, making it older than Stonehenge or the Egyptian pyramids. The **site** *(family/adult/ senior/student €12.75/5.10/3.80/2.55 for centre & Newgrange, €22.30/8.90/6.40/4.20 for centre, Newgrange & Knowth)* was restored in the 1970s and you can walk down a narrow passage to the tomb chamber, about a third of the way across the colossal mound. At dawn on five mornings surrounding the winter solstice (19 to 23 December) the rising sun's rays shine directly down the long passage and illuminate the tomb chamber for about 15 minutes. It's truly one of the most spectacular sights in all of Ireland but most visitors will have to settle for a simulated version; there is a 10-year waiting list for the 20 or so places offered on each of the five days.

The grass-covered mound is about 80m in diameter and 13m high. It's faced by a pebbled wall, which in turn is encircled by huge horizontal stones, many finely decorated with curious designs. Farther out from the mound is a circle of standing stones, many of which have been broken off or removed. From the entrance, with its extravagantly incised entrance stone, the passage leads 19m into the mound to the cross-shaped central chamber. This has huge standing stones and dished stones in which burnt bones of the bodies buried here were originally found. Above the chamber massive stones form a ceiling.

Knowth The third major **burial mound** *(family/adult/student/child €9.55/3.80/2.55/ 1.60 for centre & Knowth, €22.30/8.90/ 6.40/4.20 for centre, Knowth & Newgrange)* is between Newgrange and Slane. Modern excavations began at Knowth in 1962 and a 35m-long passage to the central chamber was soon cleared. This passage is much longer than the one at Newgrange. In 1968 an extraordinary discovery was made when a second passage was unearthed. There are 18 smaller passage graves around the main mound. The site is famous for its artwork, which includes ornate kerbstones. The last tour starts about 45 minutes before closing time.

Dowth The **circular mound** *(closed to the public)* at Dowth, between Newgrange and Drogheda, is several hundred years younger than the one at Newgrange. It's smaller – at about 63m in diameter – but slightly higher, at 14m. An 8m-long passage leads into a cross-shaped central chamber similar to Newgrange's. Dowth was excavated by archaeologists from the Royal Irish Academy in 1847 and for a time it even had a teahouse on top. Unfortunately the site is not able to be visited in the foreseeable future because it's still being excavated.

Getting There & Away Knowth, Dowth and Newgrange are all well signposted from Drogheda and Slane. The easiest way to visit is with your own transportation. The only public transportation is from Drogheda, with Bus Éireann running a service from 10.15am to 4pm (€1.45, 20 minutes, six daily) that drops passengers off at the main gate. Alternatively, Bus Éireann runs tours to Newgrange and the Boyne Valley from Busáras in Dublin. These depart at 10am and return at 5.45pm daily except Friday, May to September and Thursday and Saturday only in April (adult/student/child €25.50/22.90/12.70); and 10am to 4.15pm Thursday and Saturday only, October to December (adult/student/child €20.35/17.80/10.20). The best tour, however, is run by Mary Gibbons Tours, which comes complete with expert guide who seemingly knows more about the place than anyone. They depart from the Dublin Tourism office at 10.45am on Monday to Wednesday and Friday, returning at 5.30pm or 6pm. It costs €28.

DONORE & DULEEK

In 1429 Henry VI offered a £10 grant to anybody who would build a castle within the area known as the Pale, which essentially meant the counties of Dublin, Kildare, Meath and Louth. To ensure that there was no cheating, minimum dimensions were stipulated. The result is here at Donore: a **miniature castle** *(closed to the public)* barely big enough to claim the £10.

Duleek claims to have had Ireland's first stone church, founded by St Patrick; the

EXCURSIONS

town's name itself comes from *An Damh Liag*, meaning 'stone church'. Duleek's 12th century **abbey ruins** contain a number of excellent effigies and tombstones. Outside the ruins is a 10th- or 11th-century high cross.

There are buses to Donore and Duleek from Drogheda.

MELLIFONT ABBEY

Mellifont Abbey *(☎ 041-982 6459, [W] www .heritageireland.ie, Tullyallen; adult/student €1.90/0.75; open 9.30am-6.30pm daily mid-June–mid-Sept, 10am-5pm daily May–mid-June & mid-Sept–Oct)* is on the R168, and can be easily reached by bus from Drogheda. It was Ireland's original Cistercian monastery and in its prime was the most magnificent and important centre of this monastic sect. The abbey was founded in 1142 by the Archbishop of Armagh, who, dismayed by corruption in the local order, brought in a troupe of monks from France. They were deliberately placed in this remote location, far from any distracting influences. The French and Irish monks failed to get on and the visitors soon returned to the continent but, within 10 years, nine more Cistercian monasteries followed and Mellifont eventually became the mother house for 21 lesser monasteries.

Only fragments of the settlement remain but the plan of the monastery can be easily traced. The buildings are clustered around an open garth (courtyard surrounded by a cloister). Other buildings include a cross-shaped church, a chapter house, an east range that once had the monks' dormitories above it, and a south range that had the refectory or dining area, the kitchen and the warming room. The most recognisable building is the lavabo, the monks' octagonal washing house. Near the car park is a small but interesting architectural museum.

MONASTERBOICE

About 6km north of Drogheda is Monasterboice *(off N1; admission free; open from sunrise-sunset daily)*, with an intriguing little enclosure containing a cemetery, two ancient though unimportant church ruins, a fine though topless round tower and two of the best high crosses in Ireland. Monasterboice is signposted from Mellifont.

The **high crosses**, depicting biblical scenes, are superb examples of Celtic art with an important didactic use for an often illiterate populace. Like Greek statuary, they may once have been brightly painted, though there is no trace of colour now. Muiredach's Cross is the older, dating from the early 10th century, and is also in better condition. The newer West Cross stands 6.5m high, making it one of the highest high crosses, but it's much more worn, with only a dozen or so of its 50 panels still legible.

The original monastic settlement is said to have been founded by St Buithe, a follower of St Patrick, in the 5th century. Over the centuries his name evolved into Boyne, hence the river's name. Though a little-known saint, he is said to have ascended directly to heaven on a ladder lowered from above. Buses run to the site every 20 minutes or so (€1.80, 15 minutes) from Drogheda between 6.15am and 9.45pm.

SLANE

At the junction of the N2 and N51, 15km west of Drogheda, Slane is perched on a hillside overlooking the River Boyne. It's a picturesque town with a curious quartet of identical houses facing each other at the junction. A local tale relates that they were built for four sisters who had developed an intense mutual dislike and kept watch on each other from their doorways.

It's said that St Patrick announced the arrival of Christianity from the top of Slane Hill. The ruins of a 16th-century church occupy the site of St Patrick's original church. On the Slane Castle estate is St Eric's Hermitage, a ruined Gothic church (closed for restoration at the time of writing) on the site where the saint is said to have spent his last days some time between 512 and 535 AD. Slane Castle is now a concert venue (see the Entertainment chapter for details).

Getting There & Away

There are buses to Slane from Dublin (€7.40, 45 minutes, five daily) and three Monday to Saturday from Drogheda (€3, 30 minutes).

ray is a popular seaside retreat.

Sculpture onboard a ferry deck, Dun Laoghaire

Looking over Dublin Bay from Howth

Balscadden Bay near Howth

Killiney calm

TONY WHEELER

High Cross, Monasterboice

RICHARD CUMMINS

Life's a beech in the formal gardens of the Powerscourt Estate.

RICHARD CUMMINS

Hoar frost settles over the valley of the Glendalough National Park.

EOIN CLARKE

The Yellow Steeple of St Mary's Abbey (1368), Trim

RICHARD CUMMINS

Powerscourt's tranquil ground

KELLS

Almost every visitor to Ireland visits the Book of Kells exhibition in Dublin's Trinity College (see The Book of Kells in the Things to See & Do chapter), but fewer pause to see the town where it came from.

Little remains of the ancient monastic site, but there are some fine high crosses, a 1000-year-old round tower, the equally ancient St Columba's Oratory and an interesting exhibition in the gallery of the church.

St Columba established a monastic settlement here in the 6th century, and in 807 AD it was augmented by monks from a sister monastery on the remote Scottish island of Iona, retreating from a Viking onslaught. They probably brought the Book of Kells with them. Kells proved little safer, for Viking raids soon spread to Ireland, and the town was plundered on several occasions.

Things to See & Do

The mainly 18th–19th century **St Columba's Church** *(Kells; admission free; open 10am-5pm weekdays, 10am-1pm Sat Apr-Sept)* stands in the grounds of the old monastic settlement. In the church's gallery is an exhibit about the settlement and its famous book. In the churchyard the 30m-high round tower lacks its original roof but is known to date back to at least 1076, because a murder was recorded to have taken place there in that year. Best preserved of the several high crosses in the churchyard is the 9th-century **South Cross** or **Cross of SS Patrick & Columba**. A medieval **church tower** stands beside the modern church and has a number of interesting tombstones set into its walls.

Round the corner from the church is **St Columba's Oratory** *(opening erratic, if it's locked, get keys from the brown house near the stop sign at the bottom of the hill)*, a squat, thick-walled survivor from the old monastic settlement. The original entrance door to this 1000-year-old building was more than 2m above ground level in order to make entry difficult for raiders. Inside, a ladder leads to a low attic room under the roofline.

The **Market High Cross** was placed in Cross St by Jonathan Swift, and in 1798 the British garrison executed rebels by hanging them from the crosspiece.

Getting There & Away

Kells is 63km north-west of Dublin on the N3. Bus Éireann runs seven buses Monday to Saturday and five on Sunday from Dublin (€8.50, one hour).

HILL OF TARA

Tara *(Navan, County Meath; admission free; open all times)*, 12km south of Navan on the N3 road, was already a place of legend 1000 years ago, when it was held to be the palace and fort of Ireland's original high kings, priest-kings who ruled the many over-kings and kings but had no law-making powers. Only mounds and depressions in the grass mark where an Iron Age hill fort and surrounding ringforts once stood. The rather romantic names attached to the various features have no obvious basis in fact. Behind St Patrick's Church, the **Rath of the Synods** has four concentric ditches and banks. South of this is the large **Royal Enclosure**, which was once a hill fort and contains a passage tomb, similar to the tombs of Newgrange (see Newgrange in the Boyne Valley section of this chapter). It has been dubbed the Mound of the Hostages. The **Royal Seat**, an ancient ringfort, and **Cormac's House** are also within the Royal Enclosure. The **Stone of Destiny** in Cormac's House is claimed to be the inauguration stone of the kings of Tara. Another hill fort stands south of the Royal Enclosure. To the north of the site is the **Banquet Hall**, which was probably the entranceway to the Hill of Tara. To the north-west of this feature are three smaller circular enclosures.

In 1843 Daniel O'Connell held one of his 'monster meetings' protesting against the 1801 Act of Union here (see History in the Facts about Dublin chapter).

There's an **interpretative centre** *(☎ 046-25903, Navan, County Meath; adult/student & child €1.90/0.75; open 9.30am-6.30pm mid-June–mid-Sept, 10am-5pm May–mid-June & mid-Sept–Oct)* in a church on the site. Inside, there's an audiovisual presentation called 'Tara: Meeting Place of Heroes'; 40-

EXCURSIONS

minute guided tours of the site are available on request.

Getting There & Away

Buses linking Dublin and Navan pass within 1km of the site. There are five daily Monday to Saturday and four on Sunday (€7.40, 45 minutes); ask the driver to drop you off at the Tara Cross.

TRIM

A pleasant little town on the River Boyne, Trim has several interesting ruins including those of Ireland's largest Anglo-Norman castle, a sprawling construction with a huge keep. The original Trim Castle was completed in the late 12th century, but was destroyed a year later. Its successors had a dramatic history. The town surrendered to Cromwell's forces in 1649, but not before the town walls, parts of the castle walls and the Yellow Steeple were severely damaged.

According to locals, Elizabeth I considered Trim as a possible site for Trinity College. *Truim* means 'ford of the elder trees'; there was an ancient ford over the river here.

The tourist office (☎ 046-37111) in Mill St sells a handy *Trim Tourist Trail* walking-tour booklet.

Things to See & Do

The ruins of **Trim Castle** (☎ 046-38619, Trim, County Meath; adult/student €3.20/1.25; open 10am-6pm daily mid-June–mid-Sept only) are reached both by a riverside path and through the Town Gate. King John visited Trim in 1210, giving the castle its alternative name of King John's Castle. Geoffrey de Greneville, who was responsible for the second stage of the keep's construction between 1220 and 1225, was a keen crusader and later became a monk at the Dominican Abbey just outside the town's northern wall. Although still in ruins, the castle has been restored in recent years and now houses a **heritage centre**, where you can learn of the town's medieval history. Guided tours of the castle are available upon request.

The open grassy area at the heart of the castle is dominated by de Greneville's mas-

sive stone keep. Outside the central keep are the remains of an earlier wall and moat. The main outer wall, still standing, dates from around 1250. The finest stretch of the outer wall is from the Dublin Gate to the River Boyne. The outer wall has five towers and a number of sally gates from which sorties could 'sally' out to meet the enemy.

Across the river from the castle are the ruins of the Augustinian **St Mary's Abbey**, originally built in the 12th century but rebuilt after a fire in 1368. Part of the abbey cloister was converted into a manor house known as Talbot Castle in 1415 and the Talbot coat of arms is on the northern wall. The building was later used as a school, whose pupils included Arthur Wellesley (later the Duke of Wellington), Jonathan Swift and his friend Stella Johnson.

North of the abbey building is the **Yellow Steeple**, dating from the restoration of 1368 but damaged in the 1649 Cromwell takeover.

East of town is an interesting group of ruins around **St Patrick's Cathedral** in Newtown Cemetery. The 13th-century **Chapel of the Victorines** encloses the 16th-century tomb effigies of Sir Lucas Dillon and his wife, Lady Jane Bathe, known locally as 'the jealous man and woman'. The other buildings here are the remains of the **Cathedral of SS Peter & Paul**, which was founded in 1206 by Simon Rochfort, and **Newtown Abbey**.

Over the river from these ruins is the **Crutched Friary**, built as a hospital after the crusades by the Knights of St John of Jerusalem. There are ruins of the keep and traces of a watchtower and other buildings. The bridge beside the friary is thought to be the second-oldest bridge in Ireland, and Marcy Regan's Pub, beside the bridge, claims to be Ireland's second-oldest pub.

Getting There & Away

Trim is about 45km north-west of Dublin. Buses depart from the Busáras in Dublin six times daily Monday to Saturday and four times on Sunday; the journey takes just over an hour and costs €6.75 one way.

Glossary

AIB – Allied Irish Banks
An lár – city centre; appears on buses
An Óige – literally The Youth, Ireland's Youth Hostel Association
An Taisce – National Trust for Ireland
An tUachtaran (pronounced 'an ukta-rawn') – Irish president

Baile Átha Cliath – 'Town of the Hurdle Ford'; the Irish name for Dublin
ball of malt – Dublin slang for a glass of (Irish) whiskey
Black and Tans – British soldiers recruited to fight during the War of Independence, noted for their brutality
bodhrán (pronounced 'bore-run') – hand-held goatskin drum
Bord Fáilte – literally 'Welcome Board'; Ireland's national tourist authority

céad míle fáilte (pronounced 'kade meala fawlcha') – the traditional Irish greeting, meaning '100,000 welcomes'
ceilidh (pronounced 'kaylee') – traditional communal dance
ceol (pronounced 'kee-ole') – music
chancer – Dublin slang word for a person who doesn't really know what they're talking about
chiseller – Dublin slang word for young boy or girl

Dáil Éireann – House of Representatives, or lower house, of the Irish parliament; usually shortened to Dáil (pronounced 'doyle')
DART – Dublin Area Rapid Transit train line
demesne – castle grounds
dolmen – Neolithic grave memorial, built of vertical stones and topped by a table stone
Dubh Linn – Black Pool; the origin of Dublin's name

Dúchas – National Heritage Service; administers state-owned properties such as parks, museums and gardens
dún – fort

Fianna Fáil (pronounced 'fianna foyle') – literally 'Warriors of Ireland'; political party
Fine Gael (pronounced 'fina gael') – literally 'Gaelic Nation'; political party
fir – men (singular *fear*); sign on men's toilets

Gaeltacht area – area where Irish is the predominant language
Garda Síochána – Irish Police Force, also known as the Gardaí
garth – courtyard surrounded by a cloister
Georgian – name given to the predominant architectural style of the 18th century, after the four King Georges of England

high cross – Celtic ringed cross, decorated with geometrical motifs and, later, scenes from the Bible

Iarnród Éireann – Irish Rail

mná – women (singular *m'naw*); sign on women's toilets

ná caitear tobac – no smoking

Oireachtas (pronounced 'orawk-tas') – Parliament
oifig an phoist (pronounced 'offig awn fwist') – post office

passage tomb – Neolithic subterranean burial place with a passageway leading to one or more chambers
pint of plain – pint of Guinness
prátai – potato
Progressive Democrats – minor political party that split from Fianna Fáil in 1986

sean nos – old-style tunes often sung in Irish

Senead Éireann (pronounced 'shanad erin') – Senate, or upper house, of the Irish parliament; usually shortened to Senead

seisún – session, or impromptu Irish music gig

Sinn Féin (pronounced 'shin fain') – literally 'We Ourselves'; Republican political party

Sláinte (pronounced 'slawncha') – literally 'health', it is the traditional Irish 'cheers' when toasting

snug – a partitioned-off section of a pub

Taoiseach (pronounced 'teashok') – Irish prime minister

teachta Dála (pronounced 'tchawkta dawla') – members of the lower house of parliament, commonly referred to as TDs

tricolour – Ireland's flag, divided into green, white and orange

LONELY PLANET

You already know that Lonely Planet produces more than this one guidebook, but you might not be aware of the other products we have on this region. Here is a selection of titles that you may want to check out as well:

Dublin Condensed
ISBN 1 74059 269 7
US$11.99 • £5.99

Dublin City Map
ISBN 1 86450 176 6
US$5.99 • £3.99

Ireland
ISBN 1 86450 379 3
US$19.99 • £12.99

Walking in Ireland
ISBN 0 86442 602 X
US$17.95 • £11.99

World Food Ireland
ISBN 1 86450 093 X
US$11.99 • £6.99

Europe on a Shoestring
ISBN 1 86450 150 2
US$24.99 • UK£14.99

Read This First: Europe
ISBN 1 86450 136 7
US$14.99 • UK£8.99

Western Europe
ISBN 1 86450 163 4
US$27.99 • UK£15.99

Europe Phrasebook
ISBN 1 86450 224 X
US$8.99 • UK£4.99

Available wherever books are sold

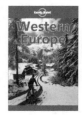

LONELY PLANET

ON THE ROAD

Travel Guides explore cities, regions and countries, and supply information on transport, restaurants and accommodation, covering all budgets. They come with reliable, easy-to-use maps, practical advice, cultural and historical facts and a rundown on attractions both on and off the beaten track. There are over 200 titles in this classic series, covering nearly every country in the world.

 Lonely Planet Upgrades extend the shelf life of existing travel guides by detailing any changes that may affect travel in a region since a book has been published. Upgrades can be downloaded for free from **www.lonelyplanet.com/upgrades**

For travellers with more time than money, **Shoestring** guides offer dependable, first-hand information with hundreds of detailed maps, plus insider tips for stretching money as far as possible. Covering entire continents in most cases, the six-volume shoestring guides are known around the world as 'backpackers bibles'.

For the discerning short-term visitor, **Condensed** guides highlight the best a destination has to offer in a full-colour, pocket-sized format designed for quick access. They include everything from top sights and walking tours to opinionated reviews of where to eat, stay, shop and have fun.

CitySync lets travellers use their Palm™ or Visor™ hand-held computers to guide them through a city with handy tips on transport, history, cultural life, major sights, and shopping and entertainment options. It can also quickly search and sort hundreds of reviews of hotels, restaurants and attractions, and pinpoint their location on scrollable street maps. CitySync can be downloaded from **www.citysync.com**

MAPS & ATLASES

Lonely Planet's **City Maps** feature downtown and metropolitan maps, as well as transit routes and walking tours. The maps come complete with an index of streets, a listing of sights and a plastic coat for extra durability.

Road Atlases are an essential navigation tool for serious travellers. Cross-referenced with the guidebooks, they also feature distance and climate charts and a complete site index.

LONELY PLANET

ESSENTIALS

Read This First books help new travellers to hit the road with confidence. These invaluable predeparture guides give step-by-step advice on preparing for a trip, budgeting, arranging a visa, planning an itinerary and staying safe while still getting off the beaten track.

Healthy Travel pocket guides offer a regional rundown on disease hot spots and practical advice on predeparture health measures, staying well on the road and what to do in emergencies. The guides come with a user-friendly design and helpful diagrams and tables.

Lonely Planet's **Phrasebooks** cover the essential words and phrases travellers need when they're strangers in a strange land. They come in a pocket-sized format with colour tabs for quick reference, extensive vocabulary lists, easy-to-follow pronunciation keys and two-way dictionaries.

Miffed by blurry photos of the Taj Mahal? Tired of the classic 'top of the head cut off' shot? **Travel Photography: A Guide to Taking Better Pictures** will help you turn ordinary holiday snaps into striking images and give you the know-how to capture every scene, from frenetic festivals to peaceful beach sunrises.

Lonely Planet's **Travel Journal** is a lightweight but sturdy travel diary for jotting down all those on-the-road observations and significant travel moments. It comes with a handy time-zone wheel, a world map and useful travel information.

Lonely Planet's eKno is an all-in-one communication service developed especially for travellers. It offers low-cost international calls and free email and voicemail so that you can keep in touch while on the road. Check it out on **www.ekno.lonelyplanet.com**

FOOD & RESTAURANT GUIDES

Lonely Planet's **Out to Eat** guides recommend the brightest and best places to eat and drink in top international cities. These gourmet companions are arranged by neighbourhood, packed with dependable maps, garnished with scene-setting photos and served with quirky features.

For people who live to eat, drink and travel, **World Food** guides explore the culinary culture of each country. Entertaining and adventurous, each guide is packed with detail on staples and specialities, regional cuisine and local markets, as well as sumptuous recipes, comprehensive culinary dictionaries and lavish photos good enough to eat.

LONELY PLANET

OUTDOOR GUIDES

For those who believe the best way to see the world is on foot, Lonely Planet's **Walking Guides** detail everything from family strolls to difficult treks, with 'when to go and how to do it' advice supplemented by reliable maps and essential travel information.

Cycling Guides map a destination's best bike tours, long and short, in day-by-day detail. They contain all the information a cyclist needs, including advice on bike maintenance, places to eat and stay, innovative maps with detailed cues to the rides, and elevation charts.

The **Watching Wildlife** series is perfect for travellers who want authoritative information but don't want to tote a heavy field guide. Packed with advice on where, when and how to view a region's wildlife, each title features photos of over 300 species and contains engaging comments on the local flora and fauna.

With underwater colour photos throughout, **Pisces Books** explore the world's best diving and snorkelling areas. Each book contains listings of diving services and dive resorts, detailed information on depth, visibility and difficulty of dives, and a roundup of the marine life you're likely to see through your mask.

OFF THE ROAD

Journeys, the travel literature series written by renowned travel authors, capture the spirit of a place or illuminate a culture with a journalist's attention to detail and a novelist's flair for words. These are tales to soak up while you're actually on the road or dip into as an at-home armchair indulgence.

The range of lavishly illustrated **Pictorial** books is just the ticket for both travellers and dreamers. Off-beat tales and vivid photographs bring the adventure of travel to your doorstep long before the journey begins and long after it is over.

Lonely Planet **Videos** encourage the same independent, tough-minded approach as the guidebooks. Currently airing throughout the world, this award-winning series features innovative footage and an original soundtrack.

Yes, we know, work is tough, so do a little bit of deskside dreaming with the spiral-bound Lonely Planet **Diary** or a Lonely Planet **Wall Calendar**, filled with great photos from around the world.

TRAVELLERS NETWORK

Lonely Planet Online. Lonely Planet's award-winning Web site has insider information on hundreds of destinations, from Amsterdam to Zimbabwe, complete with interactive maps and relevant links. The site also offers the latest travel news, recent reports from travellers on the road, guidebook upgrades, a travel links site, an online book-buying option and a lively traveller's bulletin board. It can be viewed at **www.lonelyplanet.com** or AOL keyword: lp.

Planet Talk is a quarterly print newsletter, full of gossip, advice, anecdotes and author articles. It provides an antidote to the being-at-home blues and lets you plan and dream for the next trip. Contact the nearest Lonely Planet office for your free copy.

Comet, the free Lonely Planet newsletter, comes via email once a month. It's loaded with travel news, advice, dispatches from authors, travel competitions and letters from readers. To subscribe, click on the Comet subscription link on the front page of the Web site.

Lonely Planet Guides by Region

Lonely Planet is known worldwide for publishing practical, reliable and no-nonsense travel information in our guides and on our Web site. The Lonely Planet list covers just about every accessible part of the world. Currently there are 16 series: Travel guides, Shoestring guides, Condensed guides, Phrasebooks, Read This First, Healthy Travel, Walking guides, Cycling guides, Watching Wildlife guides, Pisces Diving & Snorkeling guides, City Maps, Road Atlases, Out to Eat, World Food, Journeys travel literature and Pictorials.

AFRICA Africa on a shoestring • Botswana • Cairo • Cairo City Map • Cape Town • Cape Town City Map • East Africa • Egypt • Egyptian Arabic phrasebook • Ethiopia, Eritrea & Djibouti • Ethiopian Amharic phrasebook • The Gambia & Senegal • Healthy Travel Africa • Kenya • Malawi • Morocco • Moroccan Arabic phrasebook • Mozambique • Namibia • Read This First: Africa • South Africa, Lesotho & Swaziland • Southern Africa • Southern Africa Road Atlas • Swahili phrasebook • Tanzania, Zanzibar & Pemba • Trekking in East Africa • Tunisia • Watching Wildlife East Africa • Watching Wildlife Southern Africa • West Africa • World Food Morocco • Zambia • Zimbabwe, Botswana & Namibia
Travel Literature: Mali Blues: Traveling to an African Beat • The Rainbird: A Central African Journey • Songs to an African Sunset: A Zimbabwean Story

AUSTRALIA & THE PACIFIC Aboriginal Australia & the Torres Strait Islands •Auckland • Australia • Australian phrasebook • Australia Road Atlas • Cycling Australia • Cycling New Zealand • Fiji • Fijian phrasebook • Healthy Travel Australia, NZ & the Pacific • Islands of Australia's Great Barrier Reef • Melbourne • Melbourne City Map • Micronesia • New Caledonia • New South Wales • New Zealand • Northern Territory • Outback Australia • Out to Eat – Melbourne • Out to Eat – Sydney • Papua New Guinea • Pidgin phrasebook • Queensland • Rarotonga & the Cook Islands • Samoa • Solomon Islands • South Australia • South Pacific • South Pacific phrasebook • Sydney • Sydney City Map • Sydney Condensed • Tahiti & French Polynesia • Tasmania • Tonga • Tramping in New Zealand • Vanuatu • Victoria • Walking in Australia • Watching Wildlife Australia • Western Australia
Travel Literature: Islands in the Clouds: Travels in the Highlands of New Guinea • Kiwi Tracks: A New Zealand Journey • Sean & David's Long Drive

CENTRAL AMERICA & THE CARIBBEAN Bahamas, Turks & Caicos • Baja California • Belize, Guatemala & Yucatán • Bermuda • Central America on a shoestring • Costa Rica • Costa Rica Spanish phrasebook • Cuba • Cycling Cuba • Dominican Republic & Haiti • Eastern Caribbean • Guatemala • Havana • Healthy Travel Central & South America • Jamaica • Mexico • Mexico City • Panama • Puerto Rico • Read This First: Central & South America • Virgin Islands • World Food Caribbean • World Food Mexico • Yucatán
Travel Literature: Green Dreams: Travels in Central America

EUROPE Amsterdam • Amsterdam City Map • Amsterdam Condensed • Andalucía • Athens • Austria • Baltic States phrasebook • Barcelona • Barcelona City Map • Belgium & Luxembourg • Berlin • Berlin City Map • Britain • British phrasebook • Brussels, Bruges & Antwerp • Brussels City Map • Budapest • Budapest City Map • Canary Islands • Catalunya & the Costa Brava • Central Europe • Central Europe phrasebook • Copenhagen • Corfu & the Ionians • Corsica • Crete • Crete Condensed • Croatia • Cycling Britain • Cycling France • Cyprus • Czech & Slovak Republics • Czech phrasebook • Denmark • Dublin • Dublin City Map • Dublin Condensed • Eastern Europe • Eastern Europe phrasebook • Edinburgh • Edinburgh City Map • England • Estonia, Latvia & Lithuania • Europe on a shoestring • Europe phrasebook • Finland • Florence • Florence City Map • France • Frankfurt City Map • Frankfurt Condensed • French phrasebook • Georgia, Armenia & Azerbaijan • Germany • German phrasebook • Greece • Greek Islands • Greek phrasebook • Hungary • Iceland, Greenland & the Faroe Islands • Ireland • Italian phrasebook • Italy • Kraków • Lisbon • The Loire • London • London City Map • London Condensed • Madrid • Madrid City Map • Malta • Mediterranean Europe • Milan, Turin & Genoa • Moscow • Munich • Netherlands • Normandy • Norway • Out to Eat – London • Out to Eat – Paris • Paris • Paris City Map • Paris Condensed • Poland • Polish phrasebook • Portugal • Portuguese phrasebook • Prague • Prague City Map • Provence & the Côte d'Azur • Read This First: Europe • Rhodes & the Dodecanese • Romania & Moldova • Rome • Rome City Map • Rome Condensed • Russia, Ukraine & Belarus • Russian phrasebook • Scandinavian & Baltic Europe • Scandinavian phrasebook • Scotland • Sicily • Slovenia • South-West France • Spain • Spanish phrasebook • Stockholm • St Petersburg • St Petersburg City Map • Sweden • Switzerland • Tuscany • Ukrainian phrasebook • Venice • Vienna • Wales • Walking in Britain • Walking in France • Walking in Ireland • Walking in Italy • Walking in Scotland • Walking in Spain • Walking in Switzerland • Western Europe • World Food France • World Food Greece • World Food Ireland • World Food Italy • World Food Spain **Travel Literature:** After Yugoslavia • Love and War in the Apennines • The Olive Grove: Travels in Greece • On the Shores of the Mediterranean • Round Ireland in Low Gear • A Small Place in Italy

Lonely Planet Mail Order

Lonely Planet products are distributed worldwide. They are also available by mail order from Lonely Planet, so if you have difficulty finding a title please write to us. North and South American residents should write to 150 Linden St, Oakland, CA 94607, USA; European and African residents should write to 10a Spring Place, London NW5 3BH, UK; and residents of other countries to Locked Bag 1, Footscray, Victoria 3011, Australia.

INDIAN SUBCONTINENT & THE INDIAN OCEAN Bangladesh • Bengali phrasebook • Bhutan • Delhi • Goa • Healthy Travel Asia & India • Hindi & Urdu phrasebook • India • India & Bangladesh City Map • Indian Himalaya • Karakoram Highway • Kathmandu City Map • Kerala • Madagascar • Maldives • Mauritius, Réunion & Seychelles • Mumbai (Bombay) • Nepal • Nepali phrasebook • North India • Pakistan • Rajasthan • Read This First: Asia & India • South India • Sri Lanka • Sri Lanka phrasebook • Tibet • Tibetan phrasebook • Trekking in the Indian Himalaya • Trekking in the Karakoram & Hindukush • Trekking in the Nepal Himalaya • World Food India **Travel Literature:** The Age of Kali: Indian Travels and Encounters • Hello Goodnight: A Life of Goa • In Rajasthan • Maverick in Madagascar • A Season in Heaven: True Tales from the Road to Kathmandu • Shopping for Buddhas • A Short Walk in the Hindu Kush • Slowly Down the Ganges

MIDDLE EAST & CENTRAL ASIA Bahrain, Kuwait & Qatar • Central Asia • Central Asia phrasebook • Dubai • Farsi (Persian) phrasebook • Hebrew phrasebook • Iran • Israel & the Palestinian Territories • Istanbul • Istanbul City Map • Istanbul to Cairo • Istanbul to Kathmandu • Jerusalem • Jerusalem City Map • Jordan • Lebanon • Middle East • Oman & the United Arab Emirates • Syria • Turkey • Turkish phrasebook • World Food Turkey • Yemen **Travel Literature:** Black on Black: Iran Revisited • Breaking Ranks: Turbulent Travels in the Promised Land • The Gates of Damascus • Kingdom of the Film Stars: Journey into Jordan

NORTH AMERICA Alaska • Boston • Boston City Map • Boston Condensed • British Columbia • California & Nevada • California Condensed • Canada • Chicago • Chicago City Map • Chicago Condensed • Florida • Georgia & the Carolinas • Great Lakes • Hawaii • Hiking in Alaska • Hiking in the USA • Honolulu & Oahu City Map • Las Vegas • Los Angeles • Los Angeles City Map • Louisiana & the Deep South • Miami • Miami City Map • Montreal • New England • New Orleans • New Orleans City Map • New York City • New York City Map • New York City Condensed • New York, New Jersey & Pennsylvania • Oahu • Out to Eat – San Francisco • Pacific Northwest • Rocky Mountains • San Diego & Tijuana • San Francisco • San Francisco City Map • Seattle • Seattle City Map • Southwest • Texas • Toronto • USA • USA phrasebook • Vancouver • Vancouver City Map • Virginia & the Capital Region • Washington, DC • Washington, DC City Map • World Food New Orleans **Travel Literature:** Caught Inside: A Surfer's Year on the California Coast • Drive Thru America

NORTH-EAST ASIA Beijing • Beijing City Map • Cantonese phrasebook • China • Hiking in Japan • Hong Kong & Macau • Hong Kong City Map • Hong Kong Condensed • Japan • Japanese phrasebook • Korea • Korean phrasebook • Kyoto • Mandarin phrasebook • Mongolia • Mongolian phrasebook • Seoul • Shanghai • South-West China • Taiwan • Tokyo • Tokyo Condensed • World Food Hong Kong • World Food Japan **Travel Literature:** In Xanadu: A Quest • Lost Japan

SOUTH AMERICA Argentina, Uruguay & Paraguay • Bolivia • Brazil • Brazilian phrasebook • Buenos Aires • Buenos Aires City Map • Chile & Easter Island • Colombia • Ecuador & the Galapagos Islands • Healthy Travel Central & South America • Latin American Spanish phrasebook • Peru • Quechua phrasebook • Read This First: Central & South America • Rio de Janeiro • Rio de Janeiro City Map • Santiago de Chile • South America on a shoestring • Trekking in the Patagonian Andes • Venezuela **Travel Literature**: Full Circle: A South American Journey

SOUTH-EAST ASIA Bali & Lombok • Bangkok • Bangkok City Map • Burmese phrasebook • Cambodia • Cycling Vietnam, Laos & Cambodia • East Timor phrasebook • Hanoi • Healthy Travel Asia & India • Hill Tribes phrasebook • Ho Chi Minh City (Saigon) • Indonesia • Indonesian phrasebook • Indonesia's Eastern Islands • Java • Lao phrasebook • Laos • Malay phrasebook • Malaysia, Singapore & Brunei • Myanmar (Burma) • Philippines • Pilipino (Tagalog) phrasebook • Read This First: Asia & India • Singapore • Singapore City Map • South-East Asia on a shoestring • South-East Asia phrasebook • Thailand • Thailand's Islands & Beaches • Thailand, Vietnam, Laos & Cambodia Road Atlas • Thai phrasebook • Vietnam • Vietnamese phrasebook • World Food Indonesia • World Food Thailand • World Food Vietnam

ALSO AVAILABLE: Antarctica • The Arctic • The Blue Man: Tales of Travel, Love and Coffee • Brief Encounters: Stories of Love, Sex & Travel • Buddhist Stupas in Asia: The Shape of Perfection • Chasing Rickshaws • The Last Grain Race • Lonely Planet ... On the Edge: Adventurous Escapades from Around the World • Lonely Planet Unpacked • Lonely Planet Unpacked Again • Not the Only Planet: Science Fiction Travel Stories • Ports of Call: A Journey by Sea • Sacred India • Travel Photography: A Guide to Taking Better Pictures • Travel with Children • Tuvalu: Portrait of an Island Nation

Index

Text

Places to Stay

Bold indicates maps.

Places to Eat

Boxed Text

MAP 1

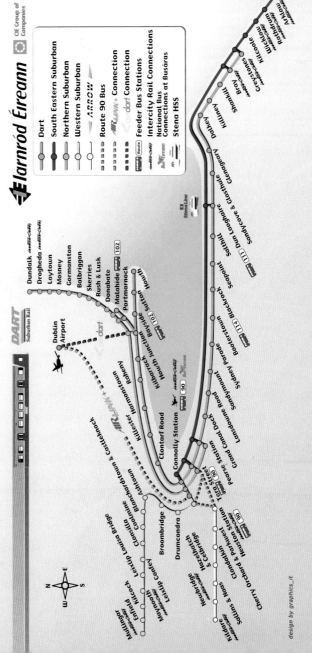

MAP 2

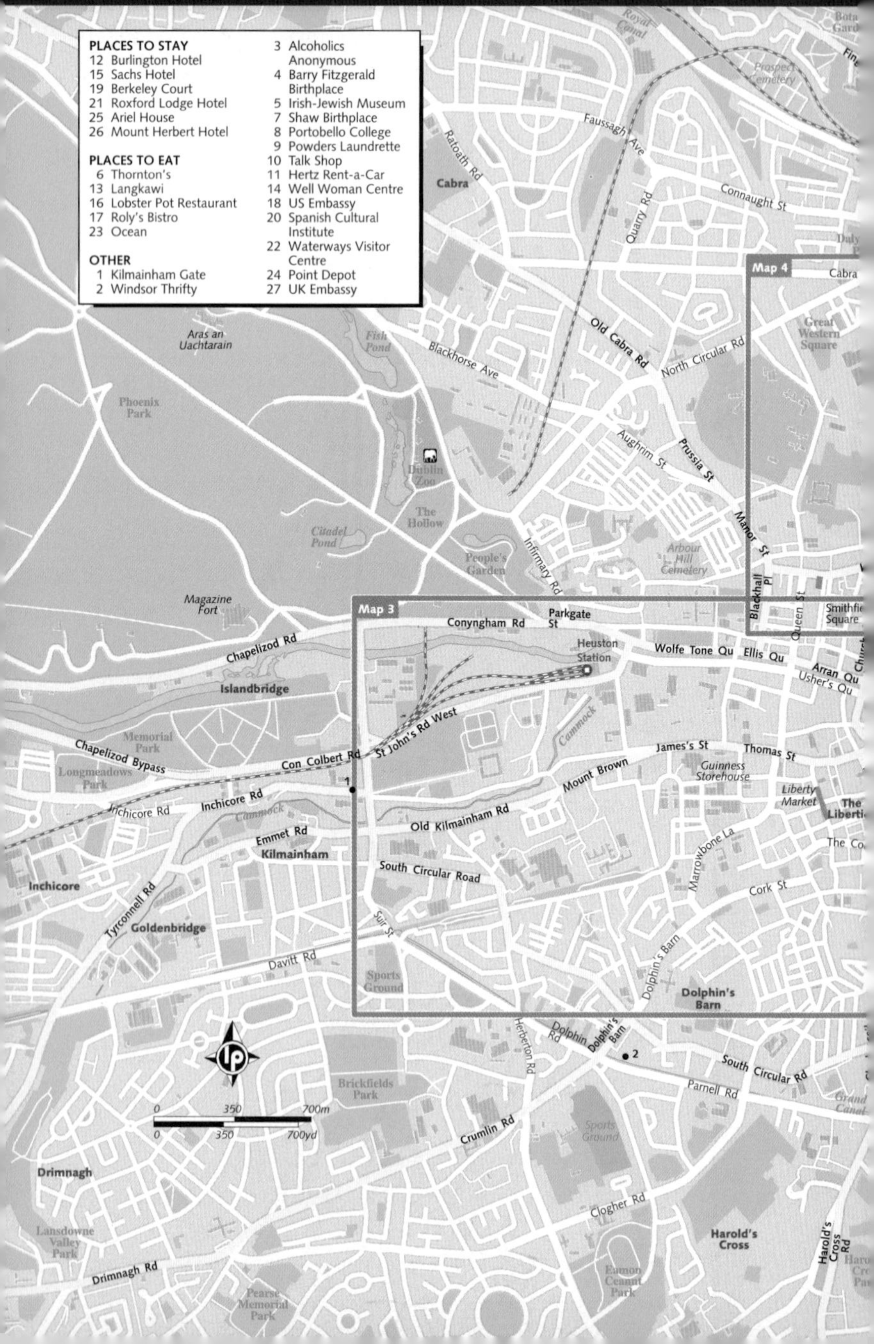

PLACES TO STAY
12 Burlington Hotel
15 Sachs Hotel
19 Berkeley Court
21 Roxford Lodge Hotel
25 Ariel House
26 Mount Herbert Hotel

PLACES TO EAT
6 Thornton's
13 Langkawi
16 Lobster Pot Restaurant
17 Roly's Bistro
23 Ocean

OTHER
1 Kilmainham Gate
2 Windsor Thrifty
3 Alcoholics Anonymous
4 Barry Fitzgerald Birthplace
5 Irish-Jewish Museum
7 Shaw Birthplace
8 Portobello College
9 Powders Laundrette
10 Talk Shop
11 Hertz Rent-a-Car
14 Well Woman Centre
18 US Embassy
20 Spanish Cultural Institute
22 Waterways Visitor Centre
24 Point Depot
27 UK Embassy

Royal Canal
Bota Gard
Fine
Prospect Cemetery
Faussagh Ave
Connaught St
Ratoath Rd
Quarry Rd
Cabra
Old Cabra Rd
North Circular Rd
Daly
Cabra
Map 4
Great Western Square
Aras an Uachtarain
Fish Pond
Blackhorse Ave
Aughrim St
Prussia St
Blackhall Pl
Manor St
Phoenix Park
Dublin Zoo
The Hollow
Infirmary Rd
Arbour Hill Cemetery
Queen St
Smithfield Square
Citadel Pond
People's Garden
Arran Qu
Usher's Qu
Church
Magazine Fort
Map 3
Conyngham Rd
Parkgate St
Heuston Station
Wolfe Tone Qu
Ellis Qu
Chapelizod Rd
Islandbridge
Con Colbert Rd
St John's Rd West
Cammock
James's St
Thomas St
Guinness Storehouse
Liberty Market
The Liberti
Chapelizod Bypass
Memorial Park
Longmeadows Park
Inchicore Rd
Mount Brown
Old Kilmainham Rd
Marrowbone La
The Co
Inchicore Rd
Cammock
Emmet Rd
Kilmainham
South Circular Road
Cork St
Inchicore
Tyrconnell Rd
Goldenbridge
Davitt Rd
Suir St
Sports Ground
Dolphin's Barn
Dolphin's Barn
Drimnagh
Brickfields Park
Heberton Rd
Dolphin's Barn Rd
Dolphin's Barn
South Circular Rd
Parnell Rd
Grand Canal
Crumlin Rd
Sports Ground
Lansdowne Valley Park
Drimnagh Rd
Pearse Memorial Park
Clogher Rd
Eamon Ceannt Park
Harold's Cross
Harold's Cross Rd
Har

0   350   700m
0   350   700yd

MAP 2

Kavanagh's (500m)

Botanic Rd

Botanic Ave

Drumcondra Rd

Drumcondra

Whitworth Rd

Phibsborough

Clonliffe Rd

Casino at Marino (500m)

Clontarf Golf Course

Clontarf & North Bull Island (5km)

Marino

Malahide Rd

Philipsburgh Ave

Fairview Strand

Fairview Rd

North Strand Rd

Fairview Park

Fairview Park

Dublin Harbour

Berkeley St

Dorset St Lower

North Circular Rd

Mountjoy Square

Summerhill Pde

Diamond

Portland Row

Aite Byrne Rd

East Wall Rd

East Wall

Western Way

Dorset St Upper

Parnell St

Parnell Sq West

Parnell Sq East

Hill St

Gardiner St Lower

Seville Pl

East Wall Rd

Alexandra Quay

Bolton St

O'Connell Upper

Capel St

Jervis St

Mary St

Henry St

Talbot St

Busáras

Connolly Station

Sheriff St Upper

North Wall

Alexandra Basin

North Quay Extension

Abbey St Upper

Ormond Qu Lower

Ormond Qu Upper

Bachelors Wk

Wellington Qu

Aston Qu

Westmoreland St

Temple Bar

Dame St

College Grn

Tara St

Townsend St

Pearse St

Custom House Qu

City Qu

Hanover St East

Macken St

North Wall Qu

Map 5

24

Dublin Harbour

Tara Street Station

Map 6

Nassau St

Clare St

Fenian St

Hogan Pl

Grand Canal Docks

Charlotte Quay

Ringsend Rd

Ringsend

Ringsend Park

Patrick's Park

Auugier St

Great Georges St South

Grafton St

Dawson St

Kildare St

Merrion Square

Pearse Station

23 ▾

22

Shelbourne Greyhound Stadium

Irishtown

Map 7

Kevin St Upper

Wexford St

Camden St

St Stephen's Green South

St Stephen's Green

Leeson St Lower

Merrion Row

Fitzwilliam Square

Mount St Lower

Mount St Upper

Baggot St Lower

Annesley Bridge Rd

Grand Canal St

Grand Canal

Bath Ave

Landsdowne Road Stadium

Sandymount Rd

Iveagh Gardens

Hatch St Upper

Baggot St Upper

Haddington Rd

Northumberland Rd

21

20

25

26 ▪ Sandymount

Richmond St

Adelaide Rd

10

Charlemont St

Wilton Tce

Mespil Rd

Pembroke Rd

13 ▾

14

19 ▪

18 ▾

17 ▾

16 ▾

Ballsbridge

7

9

8

5

4 ▪

6 ▾

Grove Rd

Charlemont

Grand Pde

Dartmouth Square

11

Sussex Rd

Leeson St Upper

12

Waterloo Rd

Pembroke Rd

Clyde Rd

Merrion Rd

Shelbourne Rd

Sandymount Ave

Mountpleasant Ave Lower

Mountpleasant Square

Ranelagh

Ranelagh Rd

The Appian Way

15

Morehampton Rd

Herbert Park

Royal Dublin Society Showground

27

Grosvenor Square

Rathmines Rd Lower

Earl St North

Amiens St

Donnybrook

Marlborough Rd

Herbert Park

Comhaltas Ceoltóirí Éireann (6km)

Netherlands Embassy (500m) & Andorra B&B Glenogra House

MAP 3

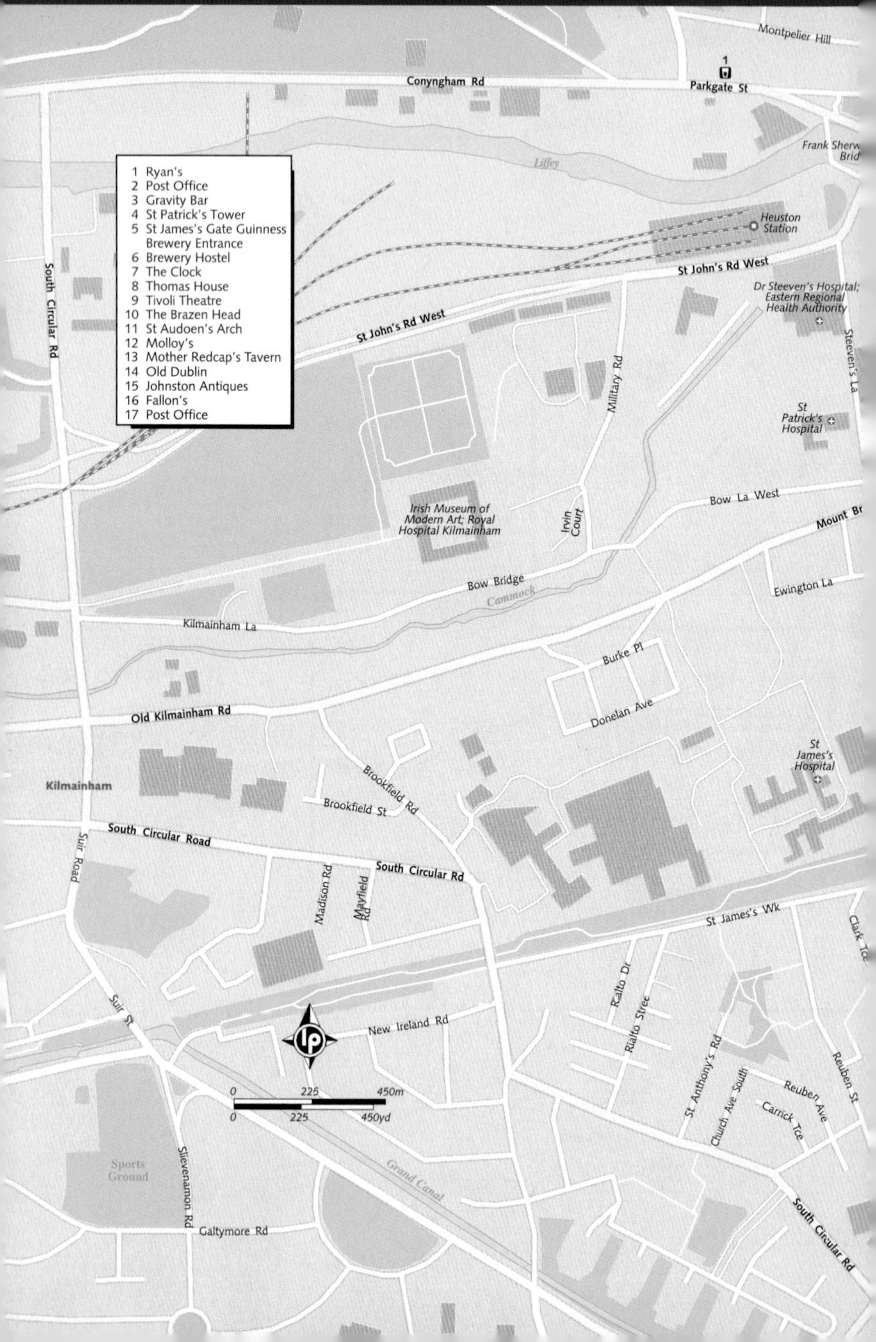

Montpelier Hill

Conyngham Rd

1
Parkgate St

Frank Sherw
Brid

Liffey

1 Ryan's
2 Post Office
3 Gravity Bar
4 St Patrick's Tower
5 St James's Gate Guinness
   Brewery Entrance
6 Brewery Hostel
7 The Clock
8 Thomas House
9 Tivoli Theatre
10 The Brazen Head
11 St Audoen's Arch
12 Molloy's
13 Mother Redcap's Tavern
14 Old Dublin
15 Johnston Antiques
16 Fallon's
17 Post Office

Heuston
Station

St John's Rd West

Dr Steeven's Hospital;
Eastern Regional
Health Authority

Steeven's La

St John's Rd West

Military Rd

St
Patrick's
Hospital

Bow La West

Mount Br

Irish Museum of
Modern Art; Royal
Hospital Kilmainham

Irvin
Court

Ewington La

Bow Bridge

Cammock

Kilmainham La

Burke Pl

Donelan Ave

St
James's
Hospital

Old Kilmainham Rd

Brookfield Rd

Kilmainham

Brookfield St

Suir Road

South Circular Road

South Circular Rd

St James's Wk

Clair Tce

Madison Rd

Mayfield

Rialto Dr

Rialto Stree

St Anthony's Rd

Reuben Av

Reuben St

Suir St

New Ireland Rd

Church Ave South

Carrick Tce

0   225   450m
0   225   450yd

South Circular Rd

Sports
Ground

Slievenamon Rd

Galtymore Rd

Grand Canal

MAP 3

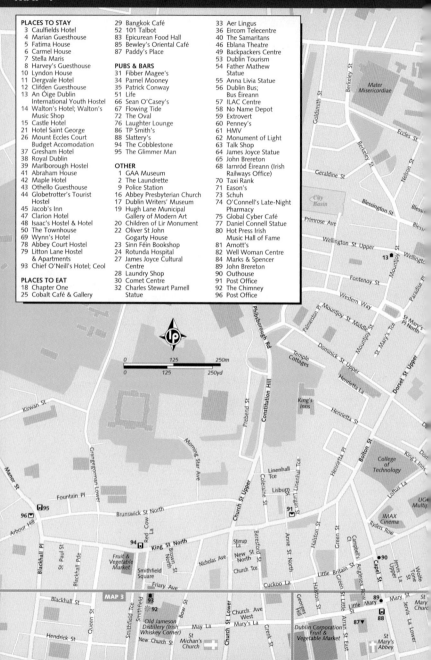

MAP 4

PLACES TO STAY
3 Caulfields Hotel
4 Marian Guesthouse
5 Fatima House
6 Carmel House
7 Stella Maris
8 Harvey's Guesthouse
10 Lyndon House
11 Dergvale Hotel
12 Clifden Guesthouse
13 An Óige Dublin
   International Youth Hostel
14 Walton's Hotel; Walton's
   Music Shop
15 Castle Hotel
21 Hotel Saint George
26 Mount Eccles Court
   Budget Accomodation
37 Gresham Hotel
38 Royal Dublin
39 Marlborough Hostel
41 Abraham House
42 Maple Hotel
43 Othello Guesthouse
44 Globetrotter's Tourist
   Hostel
45 Jacob's Inn
47 Clarion Hotel
48 Isaac's Hostel & Hotel
50 The Townhouse
69 Wynn's Hotel
78 Abbey Court Hostel
79 Litton Lane Hostel
   & Apartments
93 Chief O'Neill's Hotel; Ceol

PLACES TO EAT
18 Chapter One
25 Cobalt Café & Gallery
29 Bangkok Café
52 101 Talbot
83 Epicurean Food Hall
85 Bewley's Oriental Café
87 Paddy's Place

PUBS & BARS
31 Fibber Magee's
34 Parnel Mooney
35 Patrick Conway
51 Life
66 Sean O'Casey's
67 Flowing Tide
72 The Oval
76 Laughter Lounge
86 TP Smith's
88 Slattery's
94 The Cobblestone
95 The Glimmer Man

OTHER
1 GAA Museum
2 The Laundrette
9 Police Station
16 Abbey Presbyterian Church
17 Dublin Writers' Museum
19 Hugh Lane Municipal
   Gallery of Modern Art
20 Children of Lir Monument
22 Oliver St John
   Gogarty House
23 Sinn Féin Bookshop
24 Rotunda Hospital
27 James Joyce Cultural
   Centre
28 Laundry Shop
30 Comet Centre
32 Charles Stewart Parnell
   Statue
33 Aer Lingus
36 Eircom Telecentre
40 The Samaritans
46 Eblana Theatre
49 Backpackers Centre
53 Dublin Tourism
54 Father Mathew
   Statue
55 Anna Livia Statue
56 Dublin Bus;
   Bus Éireann
57 ILAC Centre
58 No Name Depot
59 Extrovert
60 Penney's
61 HMV
62 Monument of Light
63 Talk Shop
64 James Joyce Statue
65 John Brereton
68 Iarnród Éireann (Irish
   Railways Office)
70 Taxi Rank
71 Eason's
73 Schuh
74 O'Connell's Late-Night
   Pharmacy
75 Global Cyber Café
77 Daniel Connell Statue
80 Hot Press Irish
   Music Hall of Fame
81 Arnott's
82 Well Woman Centre
84 Marks & Spencer
89 John Brereton
90 Outhouse
91 Post Office
92 The Chimney
96 Post Office

MAP 4

Croke Park Stadium
Royal Canal
Innisfallen Pde
Portland Pl
1
Killarney Pde
Derynane Pde
Valentia Pde
Synnott Row
North Circular Rd
Belvidere Rd
Sherrarde St Lower
Rutsel St
Synnott Pl
Dorset La
North Circular Rd
Leo St
Dorset St Upper
Richmond St North
2 Dorset St Lower
Eccles Pl
Leopold & Molly Bloom's House
3
Sherrarde St Upper
Belvidere Pl
Fitzgibbon La
Fitzgibbon St
9
Emmet St
Joseph's Pde
Kelly's Row
4
5
6
7
8 Gardiner St Upper
Belvidere Ct
Charles St Great
Charles La Great
Sumner St North
Rutland Pl North
Richmond St North
St George's Church
Temple St North
Anthony's Ct
Nerney's Ct
Mountjoy Sq North
Mountjoy Square
Mountjoy Sq East
Charles St Great
Rutland St Upper
Sumner St North
Matt Talbot Ct pig Lane
Hardwicke St
Belvedere House
Grenville Pl
11 **10** Gardiner Pl
12
Mountjoy Sq West
Mountjoy Sq South
Mountjoy Pl
Hutton's La
Summerhill Pl
Buckingham St
Frederick St North
Bath La
Grenville St
Summerhill Pde
Rutland St Lower
Bella St
Frederick La
Great Denmark St
14
15
Great Georges
Hill St
Temple La North
Gardiner St Upper
SUMMERHILL
Summerhill Pl
16
19 **17**
18
21
Rutland Pl West
26
25 St North **27**
28
29 Gardiner La
Gardiner St Lower
Gloucester Pl
Sean MacDermot St Lower
Railway St
Beaver St
Parnell Sq North
Garden of Remembrance
Parnell Sq East
22
20
Cumberland St North
Diamond
Gloucester Pl Lower
Foley St
30
Parnell St
Britain Pl
Marlborough
Sean MacDermot St Upper
Gate Theatre
31
32
23 Parnell Sq West
24
Granby Row
Cathal Brugha St
Champions Avenue
Corporation St
Malbot La
Foley St
36
33 **34**
35
37 O'Connell St Upper
Thomas Lane
39
41
42
43
Amiens St
Moore La
Moore St
38
Savoy Cinema
40
St Mary's Pro-Cathedral
44
45
Police Station
Talbot Pl
Parnell St
Moore St
54
53
Cathedral St
Talbot St
Moland Pl
Frenchman's La
Store Street
46 Busáras
Moore Street
57
Henry Pl
55
52
50
49
48
Sampson's La
56
63
64 Earl St North
Beresford La
Amiens St
60
59 **58**
62
Earl Pl
Memorial Rd
International Financial Services Centre
Henry St
61
General Post Offfice (GPO)
65
51
North Earl St Lowe
Beresford Pl
47
85 **84**
Mary St
Prince's St North
Sackville Pl
Irish Life
66
67
Abbey Theatre; Peacock Theatre
Abbey St Old
Custom House
O'Connell St Lower
71
Abbey St Lowe
Liberty Hall
Tara St
Custom House Qu
MAP 5
72
70 **69** **68**
75
Eden Qu
86
Jervis St Shopping Centre
Abbey St Upper
Abbey St Middle
73
74 Harbour Ct
80
76
George's Qu
82
83
Lotts Row
79
78
77
O'Connell Bridge
Liffey

MAP 5

Little Mary St
St Michael's St
Fish Market
Dublin Corporation Fruit & Vegetable Market
Jervis La Lower
St Mary's Abbey
Abbey St Middle
Abbey St Upper
Harbour Ct
Eden Qu
MAP 4
Burgh Qu
17
Charles St West
Ormond Sq
Strand St Little
Bachelors Wk
Liffey
Screen Cinema
Chancery Pl
Ormond Qu Upper
Ormond Qu Lower
Millennium Bridge
Grattan Bridge
Smith Row
Aston Qu
Bedford La
Westmoreland St
D'Olier St
16
Pearce St Police Station
13 14
15
11 12
7
6
8
9
10
4 5
2 3
1
Wood Qu
Fishamble St
Essex Qu
Exchange St Lower
Essex St West
Parliament St
Crane St
Sycamore Street
Temple Bar
Meeting House Square
Temple Bar Square
Cope St
Central Bank
Bank of Ireland
College St
College Green
College St
Dining Hall
Chapel
Trinity College
Exam Hall
Front Square
Botany Bay
Graduates' Memorial Building
Rubrics
New Square
Library Square
Dublin Corporation Civic Offices
Christ Church Cathedral
44
43
42
Lord Edward St
41
45
Wellington Qu
Dame St
Dame La
City Hall
St Andrew's Church
Suffolk St
Nassau St
Fellows' Square
Provost's Garden
Old Library
Berkeley Library
Arts & Social Science Buildings
Museu
Winetavern St
Nicholas St
Dvblinia
Christ Church
48
Ruins of St Nicholas
St Werburgh's Church
46
47
Dublin Castle
Great George's St South
Dame Court
George's St Arc
Castle Market
Fade St
Johnson's Ct
Grafton St
St Anne's Church
37
38
36
35
34
32
Bride Road Baths
Iveagh Buildings
Iveagh Trust
49
Coporation Apartments & Roundels
40
39
Batie St
Hary St
Grafton Street
Anne's La
Dawson St
Mansion House
31
30
Schoolhouse La
Kildare St
Na Mu
St Patrick's Park
Wood St
Aungier St
Diggers La
Bow La East
Johnson's Place
Glover's Al
St Stephen's Grn North
77
50
78
79
Hugo Cem
St Patrick's Cathedral
St Patrick's Cl
Marsh's Library
The Deanery
Police Station
Kevin St Upper
New St
51
Wexford St
Cuffe La
Proud's La
Unitarian Church
68
St Stephen's Grn West
St Stephen's Green
76
75
Children's Playground
80 81
Cuffe St
67
66
65
Kennedy Gallery
52
53
54
55
64
63
62
69
St Stephen's Grn South
70
71
74
Newman House
Newman University Church
Iveagh House (Department of Foreign Affairs)
72
73
St Stephen's Grn East
RH Galla Gal
115
Camden St Lower
57
Harcourt St
Iveagh Gardens
National Concert Hall
Legal Aid Board
114
113
Earlsfort Tce
Leeson St Lower
61
60
Charlotte St
Hatch St Upper
Hatch St Lower
Synge St Christian Brothers' School
Camden St
58
59

0 150 300m
0 150 300yd

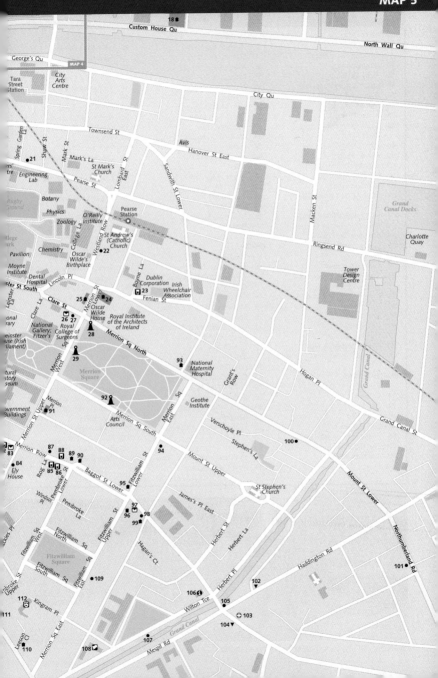

MAP 5

North Wall Qu

Custom House Qu

18

George's Qu

MAP 4

Tara Street Station

City Arts Centre

City Qu

Townsend St

Spring Garden La

Mark St

Mark's La

21

Avis

Hanover St East

Macken St

St Mark's La

Engineering Lab

Pearse St

St Mark's Church

Lombard St East

Sandwith St Lower

Grand Canal Docks

Botany

Rugby Ground

Physics

O'Reilly Institute

Pearse Station

Ringsend Rd

Charlotte Quay

Zoology

College La

Westland Row

St Andrew's (Catholic) Church

College Park

Chemistry

Oscar Wilde's Birthplace

22

Tower Design Centre

Pavilion

Moyne Institute

Dental Hospital

Lincoln Pl

Boyne La

Dublin Corporation

23

Irish Wheelchair Association

Leinster St South

Clare La

Clare St

25

Merrion Row

24

Fenian St

ional rary

National Gallery; Fitzer's

26 27

Royal College of Surgeons

Oscar Wilde House

Royal Institute of the Architects of Ireland

leinster use (Irish liament)

28

Merrion Sq North

tural story seum

Merrion West

29

Merrion Square

93

National Maternity Hospital

Grant's Row

Hogan Pl

Grand Canal

overnment Buildings

Merrion Pl

91

92

Merrion St Upper

Merrion Sq

Merrion Sq East

Arts Council

Merrion Sq South

Geothe Institute

Verschoyle Pl

Grand Canal St

83

Merrion Row

87

88

Stephen's La

100

84

Ely House

85

Baggot St Lower

89

90

Fitzwilliam Lower

94

Mount St Upper

Roig La

Pembroke La

Tower St

86

95

Fitzwilliam St Lower

James's Pl East

St Stephen's Church

Mount St Lower

Windsor pl

97

96

98

99

Hagan's Ct

Herbert St

Herbert La

Northumberland Rd

Fitzwilliam West

Fitzwilliam North

Fitzwilliam Sq

Fitzwilliam Upper

Herbert Pl

Haddington Rd

Fitzwilliam Square

Fitzwilliam Sq East

109

101

Fitzwilliam Sq South

mbroke Upper

112

Kingram Pl

106

102

111

Leeson Cl

110

108

107

Mespil Rd

Wilton Tce

105

104

103

Grand Canal

MAP 5

PLACES TO STAY
3 Inn on the Liffey
5 Ormond Quay Hotel
10 Morrisson Hotel
16 Ashfield House
18 Jurys Custom House Inn
24 Davenport Hotel
25 Mont Clare Hotel
31 Buswell's Hotel
43 Kinlay House; Refectory
   Restaurant
48 Jurys Christ Church Inn
50 Avalon House
56 Camden Deluxe Hotel
57 Frankies Guesthouse
61 Harcourt Hotel
63 Russell Court Hotel; The
   Vatican
67 St Stephen's Green Hotel
71 Staunton's on the Green
79 Méridien Shelbourne
89 Georgian House;
   Ante Room
90 Georgian House
91 The Merrion; Restaurant
   Patrick Gilbaud
93 Merrion Square Manor
95 Longfield's
96 The Fitzwilliam
99 Latchford's
110 Number 31
113 Clarion Stephen's Hall
114 Conrad International

PLACES TO EAT
9 Panem
14 O'Brien's
33 Dali Bía
45 Munchies
47 Leo Burdock's
68 Shanahan's on the Green
70 The Commons
102 The Coffee Club
104 Perk

PUBS & BARS
1 Hughes' Bar
2 Out on the Liffey
6 Nealon's
7 Gubu
11 Zanzibar
13 Pravda
17 John Mulligan's
23 The Ginger Man
39 The Long Hall
53 Modern Green Bar
54 Mono
58 Bleeding Horse Pub
59 Odeon
62 Copper Face Jack's
82 O'Donoghue's
85 The Baggot Inn
86 James Toner's
88 Doheny & Nesbitt's
115 Hartigan's

OTHER
4 The Dock
8 The Vortex
12 Winding Stair Bookshop &
   Café
15 Cyclelogical
19 Markevicz Leisure Centre
20 Spar
21 Drugs Advisory & Treatment
   Centre (Trinity Court)
22 Dan Dooley Car &
   Van Hire
26 Post Office
27 Greene's Bookshop
28 Oscar Wilde Statue
29 Rutland Fountain
30 Bram Stoker's House
32 Renard's
34 Kilkenny Shop; Kilkenny
   Kitchen
35 Eason's – Hanna's Bookshop
36 Northern Irish Tourist Board
37 Knobs & Knockers

38 International Bookshop
40 John Boyd Dunlop
   Factory
41 Whichcraft
42 Irish Celtic Craft Shop
44 Viking Dwellings
46 Chester Beatty Library
49 Swift Birthplace
51 National Map Centre
52 MacDonald's Cycles
55 Whelan's
60 PoD; Red Box
64 Original Hugh Lane Gallery;
   Newman House
65 Edward Carson Birthplace
66 An Siopa Leabhar
69 English Language
   Institute
72 Canadian Embassy
73 Countess Markievicz Bust
74 James Joyce Bust
75 Three Fates Statue
76 WB Yeats Sculpture
77 Rubicon Gallery
78 Taylor Galleries
80 Famine Victims Memorial
81 Wolfe Tone Monument
83 Post Office
84 Dúchas
87 Irish Ferries
92 Michael Collins Statue
94 No 29 Lower Fitzwilliam St
97 Post Office
98 Film Bank
100 British Council
101 Spanish Cultural Institute
103 Baggot St Hospital
105 Murrays Europcar
106 Bord Fáilte
107 P Kavanagh Bench
108 Australian Embassy
109 Italian Cultural Institute
111 Rape Crisis Centre
112 Focus Theatre

Even the details are imposing on James Gandon's Custom House (1781-91)

TONY WHEELER

DENNIS JOHNSON

RICHARD MILLS

RICHARD CUMMINS

Dublin's watermarks: top and bottom, Liffey bridge views, and centre, looking across to an industrious area of Dublin Bay

MAP 6

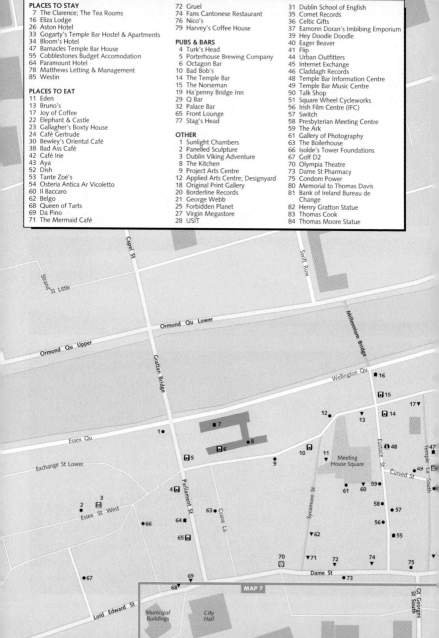

PLACES TO STAY
7 The Clarence; The Tea Rooms
16 Eliza Lodge
26 Aston Hotel
33 Gogarty's Temple Bar Hostel & Apartments
34 Bloom's Hotel
47 Barnacles Temple Bar House
55 Cobblestones Budget Accomodation
64 Paramount Hotel
78 Matthews Letting & Management
85 Westin

PLACES TO EAT
11 Eden
13 Bruno's
17 Joy of Coffee
22 Elephant & Castle
23 Gallagher's Boxty House
24 Café Gertrude
30 Bewley's Oriental Café
38 Bad Ass Café
42 Café Irie
43 Aya
52 Dish
53 Tante Zoé's
54 Osteria Antica Ar Vicoletto
60 Il Baccaro
62 Belgo
68 Queen of Tarts
69 Da Pino
71 The Mermaid Café

72 Gruel
74 Fans Cantonese Restaurant
76 Nico's
79 Harvey's Coffee House

PUBS & BARS
4 Turk's Head
5 Porterhouse Brewing Company
6 Octagon Bar
10 Bad Bob's
14 The Temple Bar
15 The Norseman
19 Ha'penny Bridge Inn
29 Q Bar
32 Palace Bar
65 Front Lounge
77 Stag's Head

OTHER
1 Sunlight Chambers
2 Panelled Sculpture
3 Dublin Viking Adventure
8 The Kitchen
9 Project Arts Centre
12 Applied Arts Centre; Designyard
18 Original Print Gallery
20 Borderline Records
21 George Webb
25 Forbidden Planet
27 Virgin Megastore
28 USIT

31 Dublin School of English
35 Comet Records
36 Celtic Gifts
37 Eamonn Doran's Imbibing Emporium
39 Hey Doodle Doodle
40 Eager Beaver
41 Flip
44 Urban Outfitters
45 Internet Exchange
46 Claddagh Records
48 Temple Bar Information Centre
49 Temple Bar Music Centre
50 Talk Shop
51 Square Wheel Cycleworks
56 Irish Film Centre (IFC)
57 Switch
58 Presbyterian Meeting Centre
59 The Ark
61 Gallery of Photography
63 The Boilerhouse
66 Isolde's Tower Foundations
67 Golf D2
70 Olympia Theatre
73 Dame St Pharmacy
75 Condom Power
80 Memorial to Thomas Davis
81 Bank of Ireland Bureau de Change
82 Henry Gratton Statue
83 Thomas Cook
84 Thomas Moore Statue

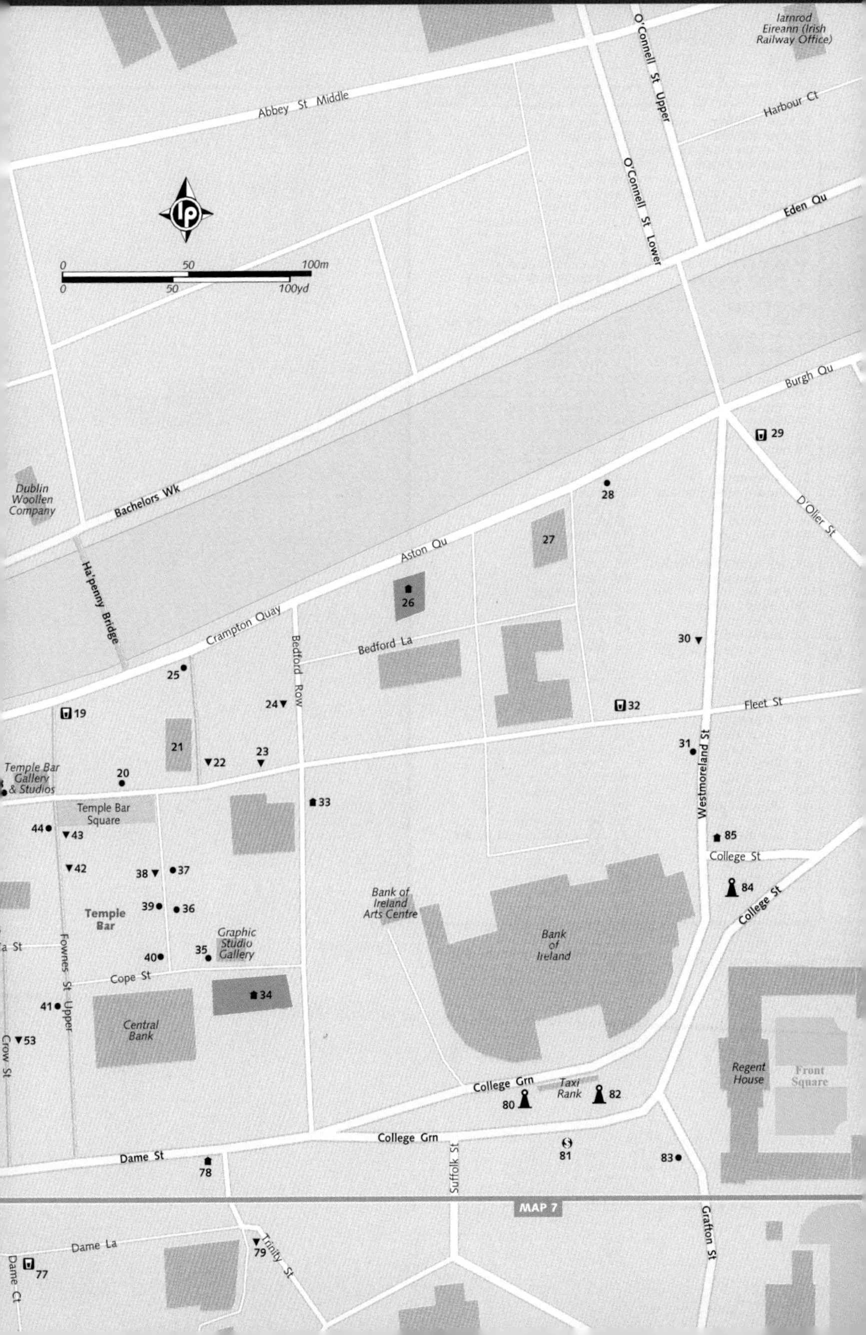

MAP 6

Iarnrod
Eireann (Irish
Railway Office)

Harbour Ct

O'Connell St Upper

Abbey St Middle

O'Connell St Lower

Eden Qu

Burgh Qu

0   50   100m
0   50   100yd

🚇 29

D'Olier St

Dublin
Woollen
Company

Bachelors Wk

28

Aston Qu

27

■ 26

Ha'penny Bridge

Crampton Quay

Bedford La

30 ▼

Bedford Row

25 ●

24 ▼

23 ▼

Fleet St

🚇 32

31 ●

Westmoreland St

🚇 19

21 ■

▼ 22

Temple Bar
Gallery
& Studios

20 ●

■ 33

85 ■

College St

Temple Bar
Square

84

44 ●

▼ 43

College St

▼ 42

38 ▼   ● 37

Fownes St Upper

Temple
Bar

39 ●   ● 36

Bank of
Ireland
Arts Centre

Bank
of
Ireland

La St

40 ●

35 ●

Graphic
Studio
Gallery

Cope St

41 ●

▼ 53

Central
Bank

■ 34

Crow St

Regent
House

Front
Square

College Grn

Taxi
Rank

80   82

Dame St

■ 78

College Grn

Suffolk St

81

83 ●

Grafton St

MAP 7

Dame La

▼ 79

Trinity St

Dame Ct

🚇 77

MAP 7

PLACES TO STAY
33 Central Hotel
68 Westbury Hotel; Westbury
   Shopping Arcade
71 Brooks Hotel
73 Grafton Guesthouse
87 Home Locators
94 Fitzwilliam Hotel;
   Peacock Alley
97 Mercer Hotel
98 Mercer Court (Student
   Accommodation)

PLACES TO EAT
2 Juice
5 The Odessa
7 Trocadero
10 Nude
16 Judge Roy Bean's
26 Imperial Chinese
   Restaurant
27 Alpha
28 Cornucopia
29 Lemon
31 Cedar Tree
32 Munchies
35 Good World Restaurant
37 Simon's Place
40 Guy Stuart
44 Cooke's Café
46 Aya
49 Bewley's Oriental Café
63 Gotham Café
65 Café Java
69 Rajdoot Tandoori
70 Velure
77 Café Metro
78 Busy Feet & Coco Café
81 Café Mao
88 La Stampa
90 La Mère Zou

PUBS & BARS
1 The George
3 The Globe
9 O'Neill's
14 Thing Mote
30 The International
43 Grogan's Castle Lounge
45 Spy Bar
52 Davy Byrne's
53 The Bailey
54 The Duke
62 Kehoe's
75 Hogan's
79 Break for the Border

80 Peter's Pub
84 Neary's

OTHER
4 Rí Rá
6 Hobo
8 Post Office
11 Dublin Tourism; Internet
   Exchange
12 Automobile Association
13 Avoca Handweavers
15 Statue of Molly Malone
17 AmEx
18 House of Ireland
19 Eason's – Hanna's Bookshop
20 Central Cyber Café
21 Lillie's Bordello
22 Weir & Son's
23 The Golden Disc Group
24 Brown Thomas Department Store
25 The Sweater Shop
34 Sub-City
36 Walton's
38 Jenny Vander
39 Big Whiskey
41 Costume
42 Harlequin
48 Appleby's
50 Dublin Bookshop
51 Marks & Spencer
55 Cathach Books
56 Iberia
57 Hodges Figgis
58 Waterstone's
59 Dúchas Bookshop
60 Alias Tom
61 Kerlin Gallery
64 Aspecto
66 Central Bank
67 Eager Beaver
72 Road Records & Big Brother
   Records
74 Foko
76 All-American Laundrette
   Company
82 John Brereton
85 Great Outdoors
85 HMV
86 Royal Irish Academy
89 Academy of English Studies
91 Aer Lingus
92 Rubicon Gallery
93 Fusilier's Arch
95 Richard Alan
96 Gaiety Theatre

MAP 7

Trinity St

6

Suffolk St

9

8

10 ▼

11 Andrew's Church

MAP 6

Grafton St

Provost's House

1937 Reading Room

Old Library

Trinity College

Fellows' Square

rew's Theatre allery

7 ▼

12

Suffolk St

13

14

15

Nassau St

16 ▼

17 18

19

Provost's Garden

Douglas Hyde Gallery

Arts & Social Science Buildings

31 ▼

30

Wicklow St

28 ▼

32 ▼

29

26 ▼

25

20

21

Grafton St

27 ▼

22

23

Grafton Arcade

24

46 ▼

51

57

58

Dawson St

56

45

Powerscourt Townhouse Shopping Centre

in c m

Coppinger Row

Johnson's Ct

47

48

Duke St

53

52

54

55

50

49 ▼

Westbury Mall

68

67

Harry St

66

60

Royal Hibernian Way

59

Molesworth St

Clarendon St

69 ▼

Balfe St

65 64 63

Anne St South

62

St Anne's Church

81

82

85

Chatham St

83

84

Anne's La

61

86

87

Schoolhouse La

96

King St South

95

Grafton St

St Stephen's Green Shopping Centre

Mansion House

Schoolhouse La

93

92

88 ▼

89

94

91

St Stephen's Grn West

St Stephen's Green

St Stephen's Grn North

90 ▼

Dawson St

MAP LEGEND

BOUNDARIES

............International
............Provincial, State
............Regional, Suburb

HYDROGRAPHY

............Coastline
............River, Creek
............Lake
............Canal

............Building
............Hotel

⊚ **DUBLIN**	Large City
Carlow	City
● Wicklow	Town or Village

●	Point of Interest
⌂	Place to Stay
⌂	Camp Site
▼	Place to Eat
⊡	Pub or Bar
✈	Airport
	Ancient or City Wall

ROUTES & TRANSPORT

............Freeway
............Highway
............Major Road
............Minor Road
............Unsealed Road
............City Freeway
............City Highway
............City Road
............City Street, Lane

............Pedestrian Mall
............Tunnel
............Train Route & Station
............Metro & Station
............Tramway & Tram Stop
............Cable Car or Chairlift
............Walking Track
............Walking Tour
............Ferry Route & Terminal

AREA FEATURES

............Park, Gardens
............Cemetery
............Market
............Pedestrian

MAP SYMBOLS

▣	Archaeological Site	🏛	Museum
◐	Bank		National Park
🏖	Beach	�P	Parking
🚌 🚏	Bus Stop, Station	➕	Police Station
🏰	Castle or Fort	✉	Post Office
⌂	Cave	▣	Ruins
✚	Church or Cathedral	✪	Shopping Centre
🎬	Cinema	🏛	Stately Home
🏛	Embassy		Swimming Pool
✛	Hospital		Taxi
💻	Internet Cafe	☎	Telephone
🗼	Lighthouse		Theatre
☀	Lookout	⊕	Toilet
⚐	Monument	❶	Tourist Information
▲	Mountain or Hill		Zoo

Note: not all symbols displayed above appear in this book

LONELY PLANET OFFICES

Australia
Locked Bag 1, Footscray, Victoria 3011
☎ 03 8379 8000 fax 03 8379 8111
email: talk2us@lonelyplanet.com.au

USA
150 Linden St, Oakland, CA 94607
☎ 510 893 8555 TOLL FREE: 800 275 8555
fax 510 893 8572
email: info@lonelyplanet.com

UK
10a Spring Place, London NW5 3BH
☎ 020 7428 4800 fax 020 7428 4828
email: go@lonelyplanet.co.uk

France
1 rue du Dahomey, 75011 Paris
☎ 01 55 25 33 00 fax 01 55 25 33 01
email: bip@lonelyplanet.fr
www.lonelyplanet.fr

World Wide Web: www.lonelyplanet.com *or* AOL keyword: lp
Lonely Planet Images: lpi@lonelyplanet.com.au